# A FOREST *of* HISTORY

# A FOREST *of* HISTORY

## THE MAYA AFTER THE EMERGENCE OF DIVINE KINGSHIP

EDITED BY

Travis W. Stanton AND M. Kathryn Brown

UNIVERSITY PRESS OF COLORADO
*Louisville*

Published by University Press of Colorado
245 Century Circle, Suite 202
Louisville, Colorado 80027

 The University Press of Colorado is a proud member of
the Association of University Presses.

The University Press of Colorado is a cooperative publishing enterprise supported, in part, by Adams State University, Colorado State University, Fort Lewis College, Metropolitan State University of Denver, Regis University, University of Colorado, University of Northern Colorado, University of Wyoming, Utah State University, and Western Colorado University.

∞ This paper meets the requirements of the ANSI/NISO Z39.48–1992 (Permanence of Paper)

ISBN: 978-1-64642-045-2 (hardcover)
ISBN: 978-1-64642-235-7 (paperback)
ISBN: 978-1-64642-046-9 (ebook)
https://doi.org/10.5876/9781646420469

Library of Congress Cataloging-in-Publication Data

Names: Stanton, Travis W., 1971– editor. | Brown, M. Kathryn, 1965– editor.
Title: A forest of history : the Maya after the emergence of divine kingship / Travis W. Stanton, M. Kathryn Brown.
Description: Louisville, Colorado : University Press of Colorado, [2020] | Includes bibliographical references and index.
Identifiers: LCCN 2020001812 (print) | LCCN 2020001813 (ebook) | ISBN 9781646420452 (cloth) | ISBN 9781646422357 (paperback) | ISBN 9781646420469 (ebook)
Subjects: LCSH: Schele, Linda. Forest of kings. | Mayas—Kings and rulers. | Mayas—History. | Mayas—Antiquities. | Indians of Central America—Antiquities. | Tikal Site (Guatemala)—Antiquities. | Caracol Site (Belize)—Antiquities. | Calakmul Site (Mexico)
Classification: LCC F1435.3.K55 F67 2020 (print) | LCC F1435.3.K55 (ebook) | DDC 972.81—dc23
LC record available at https://lccn.loc.gov/2020001812
LC ebook record available at https://lccn.loc.gov/2020001813

The University Press of Colorado gratefully acknowledges the generous support of the University of Texas at San Antonio toward the publication of this book.

Cover photograph, "A Lady from Tikal bows to a Ruler from the Ik site," © Justin Kerr. K2573

# Contents

glyph, upper, Codex Dresden lower, Codex Madrid; (f) fragmentary panel with possible *witz* mask with crossed bands.　160

10.2. Postclassic portrayals of anthropomorphic witz heads: (a) witz head, Codex Dresden, p. 66b; (b) witz head, Codex Dresden, p. 34c; (c) witz head, Codex Dresden, p. 41a; (d) witz head, Codex Madrid, p. 11c; (e) witz head on corner of Structure 16, Tulúm; (f) witz head, Upper Temple of the Jaguars, Chichén Itzá; (g) witz head, Mercado, Chichén Itzá; (h) witz head merged with split turtle carapace with emerging Maize God, Lower Temple of the Jaguars, Chichén Itzá.　161

10.3. Portrayals of plumed serpents and flowers on Flower Mountain facades appearing in Late Classic Chenes architecture: (a) bicephalic plumed serpent with clouds and central blossom on back, El Tabasceño (see figure 3c); (b) bicephalic plumed serpent with clouds and blossoms on back, Hochob; (c) Flower Mountain facade, El Tabasceño; (d) plumed serpent with floral as zoomorphic breath of witz facade, Hochob.　162

10.4. Classic and Early Postclassic portrayals of War Serpents: (a) Feline War Serpent with bifurcated tongue, detail of Early Classic Thin Orange vessel; (b) Early Classic War Serpent, detail of Early Classic censer attributed to Xico; (c) Early Classic bundle figure wearing War Serpent platelet headdress, Becán; (d) Late Classic Tlaloc figure wearing War Serpent platelet headdress, Cacaxtla (after photograph courtesy of Andrew Turner); (e) goggled figure wearing War Serpent headdress,

*Tables*

*Foreword*

JEREMY A. SABLOFF

I am delighted to write a foreword to this volume that celebrates the publication of *A Forest of Kings* by the late Linda Schele and David Freidel over a quarter of a century ago. I have known David since he was an undergraduate at Harvard University in the late 1960s, invited him to undertake his doctoral fieldwork in Mexico with the late Bill Rathje and me, and was a member of his doctoral committee at Harvard. I have been exceedingly fortunate to have worked with a number of gifted graduate students during the course of my career, and David was clearly one of this outstanding group.

Although some of David's archaeological colleagues dismissed *Forest of Kings* as "speculation," David, though at a relatively early stage in his career, was undaunted and set out to empirically test many of the ideas in the book. In thinking about the quarter of a century since the publication of *Forest of Kings*, I am deeply impressed by all the David has accomplished and by the tremendous advances in Maya archaeology and epigraphy that Schele and Freidel, among many others, helped stimulate and that have led to stronger understandings of the ancient Maya. Coupled with all the recent archaeological attention to the nonelite world beyond Maya kings and queens that the methodology of settlement patterns studies has brought to the field, scholars now have a much richer and broader understanding of the pre-Columbian Maya than ever before.

DOI: 10.5876/9781646420469.c000

*Forest of Kings* was published at a time when Maya studies were in the midst of significant change. The traditional model of Maya society (see Sabloff 1990, 2015), which had been principally promulgated by Sylvanus Morley and J. Eric Thompson and their Carnegie Institution of Washington colleagues, had been successfully challenged by Clyde Kluckhohn (1940) and Walter Taylor (1948) in principle and then empirically by Gordon Willey (1956), R. F. Carr and J. E. Hazard (1961), and the archaeologists of the Tikal Project, and E. W. Andrews IV and the Dzibilchaltún research project, among others, through the use of a settlement pattern methodology (Ashmore 1981; see also Sabloff and Ashmore 2001; Sabloff 2004). With the new advances in the decipherment of Maya writing and the publication of works such as Linda Schele and Mary Miller's *Blood of Kings* (1986)—with its combination of art historical, epigraphic, and archaeological materials—the final nails were being placed in the coffin of the traditional model. All these new trends were just beginning to be synthesized at the time of publication of Schele and Freidel's *Forest of Kings*, which in retrospect marked a key point in this intellectual transition. The current model of ancient Maya society has been refined continuously in the past quarter century since that point through both new data acquisition and empirical testing of the model. The chapters in this volume exhibit such ongoing refinements in many important ways.

In the brief remarks that follow, I will focus on just one of such refinements—the topic of Classic Maya polities and territories—because despite the great strides just mentioned, we still do not fully understand the nature of Classic Maya politics (also see Baron 2016a: 17; Sabloff 1983).

Why do I hold such concerns about the current, but ever-changing, model of ancient Maya politics? Let me be more specific. With the richness of new data from field research in recent years, it is now clear that the peer-polity model of the 1980s (see Freidel 1986; Renfrew and Cherry 1986; and specifically Sabloff 1986) was too simple. On the other hand, the more recent "super state" model (Martin and Grube 1995) also is not widely accepted (also see Culbert 1991). Even a basic question such as "What is a Maya polity in economic and political terms during Classic times?" is not fully clear. Thus, I am very encouraged by the chapters in this book, as they point the way to possible new directions in better understanding the ancient Maya political world.

However, scholars still have a way to go. For example in the conflicts between Calakmul and Tikal and their allies, we appear to have defeats in battles leading to "control" by one city over another. But what does such "control" entail on the ground? From an examination of archaeological, iconographic, and epigraphic data, it does not appear that one city was occupied by another city's "conquering" army during Classic times. Until recently, the question of how the losing city was controlled after the defeat of its ruler was an open one.

The research at Caracol discussed in chapter 3, by Arlen F. Chase and Diane Z. Chase, makes important new strides in answering this key question. Looking at the wars between Caracol and Tikal and between Caracol and Naranjo, the Chases provide new insights into postwarfare political relations between major polities.

The scholars make a strong argument for the presence of two Caracol lords at Tikal after defeating Tikal in battle, positing that they acted a "stranger-kings" at Tikal and were buried in a prominent place there (see Joyce Marcus, chapter 4 in this volume). They further argue for the direct territorial control of Tikal via the city of Naranjo, which Caracol also had defeated. Moreover, they note a significant population increase at Caracol at the time, possibly due to an influx of people from the defeated sites.

Nevertheless, despite these key findings and new hypotheses, the nature of this hypothesized territorial control and how it was administered remains to be inferred. Chapter 8, by Wendy Ashmore, and chapter 9, by Travis W. Stanton and colleagues, among others, also provide useful new understanding of polities and territories in Classic times, while Annabeth Headrick and Marilyn A. Masson and colleagues, in chapters 11 and 12, respectively, do so for later periods.

The question of Classic Maya polities is just one of the areas that is reexamined in refreshing new ways in this volume, just as *Forest of Kings* challenged traditional ways of thinking in such a stimulating manner. Yet, a robust understanding of the Classic Maya world (let along the Preclassic and Postclassic) is still very much a work in progress. This volume nicely illustrates both the progress the field has made in the past quarter century and the myriad exciting questions that still remain and that animate the field.

A FOREST *of* HISTORY

# 1

This volume is part of a two-part reflection on the impact that *A Forest of Kings*, written by Linda Schele and David Freidel (1990), has had on the field of Maya archaeology since its publication. Stemming from a Society for American Archaeology double-symposium held in San Francisco in 2015 to mark the twenty-fifth anniversary of this momentous publication, this volume focuses on Maya archaeology, iconography, and history from the Classic period onward. We believe that the title of this chapter, "See the forest for the trees," aptly describes the vision that Schele and Freidel shared with scholars and the public through their significant publication. *A Forest of Kings* was more than a retelling of ancient Maya history through the use of a conjunctive approach, but rather, for the first time, a holistic and discerning attempt to explain how Maya history was constructed in both the past and present. As Arthur Demarest notes in chapter 2 of this volume, they truly saw the forest, and not just the trees. Schele and Freidel realized that the ancient Maya history that they constructed in *A Forest of Kings* would by reshaped by future scholars with new discoveries and shifts in theoretical approaches. Through their contribution, they opened the door, or rather a portal, to another world of Maya scholarship. As the chapters in this volume demonstrate, the journey of "time travel in the jungle" first embarked on by Schele and Freidel has continued in their wake. The contributors to this tribute volume were asked to reflect on the legacy of *A Forest of Kings* in

*See the Forest for the Trees*

*An Introduction to the Volume*

TRAVIS W. STANTON AND
M. KATHRYN BROWN

DOI: 10.5876/9781646420469.c001

3

shaping the study of ancient Maya societies and where we stand today regarding some of the key questions posed by Schele and Freidel's work. The result is a rich collection of papers that situate current research in historical context. In this brief chapter, we contextualize and introduce the following chapters to provide a roadmap to this book. Longer treatments of the overall impact of *A Forest of Kings* are undertaken by Guernsey and Reese-Taylor (n.d.) in the companion volume and Demarest in chapter 2 of this volume.

As discussed by Guernsey and Reese-Taylor (n.d.) and Demarest (chapter 2, this volume), *A Forest of Kings* was a watershed publication in many regards. From the postmodern style of writing to the ambitious historical narrative woven throughout the text, Schele and Freidel's work made an impact on both scholars of the Maya and the public. Written at a critical time when many of the old models created by the first generation of Maya archaeologists were finally being laid to rest (see Jeremy Sabloff, foreword to this volume) and advances in epigraphy were providing a way to historicize the Maya, the publication of *A Forest of Kings* can be seen as a key piece of scholarship that ushered in a paradigm shift for the field. As Demarest makes abundantly clear in chapter 2, however, *A Forest of Kings* was highly controversial, and not only because it marked the shift to a conjunctive approach that combined epigraphy and archaeology. Many of the more theoretical concepts proposed Schele and Freidel, such as termination rituals, were not received well, even by more junior scholars. Demarest's contribution provides a highly personal reflection on some of the more transformative and revisionist ideas laid out in *A Forest of Kings* that are widely accepted by the field today, demonstrating its lasting legacy on how scholars conceptualize ancient Maya societies. In the second half of his chapter he frames some of these ideas in terms of his own work at the site of Cancuén and discusses the implications for the timing of the Classic Maya collapse across the southern lowlands.

In chapter 3, Arlen Chase and Diane Chase take up the topic of Maya warfare, a major theme of Classic period Maya inscriptions and one of the primary threads holding together the chapters in *A Forest of Kings*. In the late 1980s, epigraphers were just beginning to build a more holistic sense of the broader sociopolitical landscape of Classic Maya society. At this time, increased understanding of the conflicts, marriage alliances, and other forms of interaction that elites commemorated in durable forms of writing was resulting in the crystallization of real regional histories, at least for parts of the Maya lowlands. This work would eventually reach an apex of sorts that is best typified by the superstate model proposed by Simon Martin and Nikolai Grube (1995, 2000) not long after the publication of *A Forest of Kings*. Focusing on the importance of warfare in the inscriptions, Chase and Chase revisit the topic of the nature of Maya warfare and its implications for understanding the relationship between the sites of Caracol and Tikal, squarely situated in chapter 5 of *A Forest of Kings*. Using the conjunctive approach espoused by Schele and Freidel, they argue that the concept of "stranger-kings" can be useful in understanding burial patterns at Tikal that suggest lords from Caracol were interred at this important Maya city. Embarking on the historical journey set out by Schele and Freidel in *A Forest of Kings*, Chase and Chase's contribution exemplifies an example of reshaping Maya history through new data and interpretations.

Using examples from several sites throughout the Maya lowlands, Joyce Marcus also discusses the idea of "stranger-kings" in her treatment of usurpation during the Classic period in chapter 4. *A Forest of Kings* began to open up the elite history of the Classic Maya to wider academic and public audiences when it was published, and this history highlighted the political machinations that occurred in both intersite and intrasite contexts. Using two examples each from Tikal and Copán, Marcus explores the idea of usurpation, especially in light of "Teotihuacan influence."

Continuing along the themes of Late Classic wars and hegemonies found in chapter 5 of *A Forest of Kings*, Olivia Navarro-Farr and her colleagues discuss the relationship between the realm of the Kaanul lords and the site of El Perú–Waka', where at the beginning of the third millennium David Freidel began testing many of the hypotheses first laid out in *A Forest of Kings* a decade earlier. Work at El Perú–Waka' has added to a growing body of epigraphic, iconographic, and archaeological evidence that indicates Kaanul's hegemonic success, during the latter part of the Classic period at least, was due in large part to the role played by particular women of Kaanul ancestry. Presenting the role of these women at El Perú–Waka' as active agents in the building and maintenance of intersite alliances rather than solely in terms of their relationships to male peers or seniors, Navarro-Farr and her colleagues continue in the tradition of multivocality that Schele and Freidel so embraced in *A Forest of Kings*. Through this contribution, the authors move the narrative forward from a discussion dominated by generally androcentric language, to one that is more gender inclusive.

Work at El Perú–Waka' is again the focus of chapter 6, where Michelle Rich and Keith Eppich address agency and alliance building among the elite of El Perú–Waka' itself. Chapter 7 (Bird-Jaguar and the Caholob) of *A Forest of Kings* focuses more on the internal sociopolitical dynamics of the site of Yaxchilán and its local allies along the Usumacinta River than the contribution to this volume by Rich and Eppich, which emphasizes a more regional gaze. Taking this internal focus as a starting point, Rich and Eppich discuss the similarities of two Early-to-Late Classic transition tombs, only one of which is considered to be the resting place of a member of the royal family, as evidence of alliance building and maintenance among the elite of El Perú–Waka. Having the kind of power that Classic Maya rulers wielded required negotiating the support of other important members of the community. Much like the intrapolity alliances commemorated on the Late Classic Yaxchilán region monuments that depict secondary elites performing activities with the ruler, the similarities of the tombs, Rich and Eppich contend, is a material manifestation of the garnering of nonroyal support for the El Perú–Waka' dynasty. This chapter emphasizes the valuable role that the material focus of archaeology plays in the construction of Maya history.

The question of intrapolity political dynamics along the Usumacinta is revisited by Charles Golden and Andrew Scherer in chapter 7. Taking the Late Classic history of the Yaxchilán polity (chapter 7 of *A Forest of Kings*) as the focus of study, Golden and Scherer discuss the symbiotic social relationships between the ruler and subordinate elite that characterized the upper levels of the social hierarchy during the Classic period. Using the concept of personhood, the authors argue that *sajal* were crafted, or in their terms "cultivated," as particular kinds of humans, humans who through performance could "constitute, activate, and perpetually maintain and redefine the limits of the kingdom and the bounds of its moral community" in concert with the person of the ruler.

Moving to the southeastern limits of the Maya world, Wendy Ashmore revisits chapter 8 of *A Forest of Kings* and the rivalry between Copán and Quiriguá. In 1990 interdisciplinary work at Copán was in full swing and many data were available, from epigraphic texts and iconography to artifacts and architecture. As Ashmore details, Schele and Freidel used these data to craft a well-grounded narrative of rulers in the southeastern fringes of the Classic period Maya world using their conjunctive approach that was so aptly applied to the such a detailed, copious, and diverse data set. This truly pioneering research at Copán, however, continued past the publication of *A Forest of Kings*. Ashmore reconsiders the early work by Schele and Freidel in light of significant discoveries over the following years.

Moving to the northern Maya lowlands in chapter 9, Travis Stanton and his colleagues revisit the theme of struggles for sociopolitical dominance among the later Classic period polities of Chichén Itzá, Cobá, and the Puuc kingdoms, the focus of chapter 9 of *A Forest of Kings*. Freidel had begun work at the site of Yaxuná in 1986 in part to test the idea that these polities vied for control of the northern lowlands at the close of the Classic period. Focusing heavily on data from Yaxuná and Chichén Itzá, Schele and Freidel had proposed an alliance between the Puuc region and Cobá against the expanding hegemony of Chichén Itzá. Using new data from Yaxuná, Stanton and his colleagues propose an alternative chronology for understanding interpolity interactions during the latter part of the Classic.

Continuing on the theme of Chichén Itzá, Karl Taube analyzes the iconography of war and the afterlife at this important northern lowland center in chapter 10. Warfare is a consistent theme throughout *A Forest of Kings*, though in chapter 9 of Schele and Freidel's volume it is discussed in the explicit framework of empire building. Situating militarism at Chichén Itzá in a broader spatial-temporal perspective that includes Teotihuacan and the Contact period Aztec, Taube illustrates that much of the copious amount of iconography dedicated to warriors and organized violence relates to broader concepts of an otherworld paradise where the souls of heroic warriors reside.

In chapter 11, Annabeth Headrick rounds out the discussion of Chichén Itzá in a rather personal account of the treatment of empire and governance, among other topics such as captive taking and trade, in *A Forest of Kings*. The question of Central Mexican iconography, with its more anonymous depictions of human figures, at Chichén Itzá has raised questions about the nature of political organization at the site since the beginning of professional archaeology in Yucatán (e.g., Tozzer 1957). Schele and Freidel furthered these debates by proposing the controversial concept of *multepal* for the site in *A Forest of Kings*. In her contribution, Headrick broadly reviews concepts such as multepal, situating the narrative surrounding Chichén Itzá in chapter 9 of *A Forest of Kings* as but a snapshot of an extended discussion of these issues that continues to the present day.

While the time depth represented in the narratives woven throughout *A Forest of Kings* was extensive, one period that did not receive systematic treatment was the Late Postclassic. In chapter 12, Marilyn Masson and her colleagues discuss data from the most important Late Postclassic urban center from this period, the city of Mayapán. Framing their discussion in terms of termination rituals, a controversial proposal at the time *A Forest of Kings* was published (see Demarest, chapter 2 in this volume), Masson and her colleagues analyze a series of broken censers dating to the some 50 to 150 years prior to the collapse of the city. The authors argue that the termination deposit from the Itzmal Ch'en group indicates violence and/or abandonment of this public architecture well before the "storied collapse due to the Xiu-Cocom war of

Katun 8 Ahau in the mid-fifteenth century AD." This chapter illustrates the important contribution of archaeological data to a more nuanced understanding of Maya history.

Moving into the Colonial period, in chapter 13 Stanley Guenter discusses the significance of the date of Katun 8 Ahau, characterized by several of the books of Chilam Balam as a moment of collapse, abandonment, migration, and political change. Inspired by the broad temporal and spatial reach to interpreting data used in *A Forest of Kings*, in chapter 13 Guenter provides an analysis of the hieroglyphic inscription of Copán Stela 11, a monument of the last ruler of this site, Yax Pasaj Chan Yopaat. He suggests that the text on the stela may allude to the destruction of an actual building, perhaps the Temple of the Sun at Teotihuacan, and the associations with calamity that the 8 Ahau date had during the Colonial period may have much deeper origins.

Finally, Freidel provides a cogent summary chapter of this book interlaced with ample personal narratives of academic contexts surrounding the writing of *A Forest of Kings* in chapter 14. As discussed by Reese-Taylor and Guernsey (n.d. in the companion volume), personal narratives were an integral and novel part of *A Forest of Kings*, and Schele and Freidel made the book about their own interactions with the ancient Maya through their materials remains as well as about those material remains themselves. As they note: "The first time you cross the boundary into that world, you may not have an intellectual definition for what is happening to you, but you will sense a change" (Schele and Freidel 1990:38). More than a quarter century after this groundbreaking work, Maya archaeologists still reflect on this change, and embrace it.

**2**

First, the reader should be forewarned that this perspective on the core contributions of *A Forest of Kings* and their most recent implications will deliberately follow the conjunctive perspectives and almost postmodern style of that work. Perhaps that is risky since at the time of its debut that very style was considered by many academics to be too literary, if not "unscholarly." It is appropriate here because I first wish to first present some retrospective commentary on the initial and later reactions to new ways of viewing the ancient Maya that were presented and disseminated by Schele and Freidel in their 1990 volume and related articles. I begin then with some honest personal remembrances of the debut of these ideas and their subsequent path toward academic acceptance.

*"Terminal" Termination Rituals and the Felling of* A Forest of Kings

*Past Struggles and Recent Triumphs of the Core Concepts of a Seminal Work*

Arthur A. Demarest

## A FRANK RETROSPECTIVE COMMENT ON THE SKEPTICAL RECEPTION DEBUT OF *A FOREST OF KINGS*

It is sometimes difficult for younger scholars to imagine that major concepts in the field, accepted by all today, were initially considered by most to be radical and dubious, or simply not credible. Often revisionist viewpoints face such a rocky start. Then the second phase of evaluation by colleagues of such new insights is often that those ideas or hypotheses may have a basis, but their importance and applicability are greatly exaggerated. In many cases, over time, if the new proposals pass multiple

DOI: 10.5876/9781646420469.c002

testing and more examples are found, they achieve final acceptance by many. That acceptance, however, is often initially in the form of "We already knew about that" followed by citations of some elements of those new integrative concepts in previous comments or parts of articles. Of course, that assertion is almost always true, because new general perspectives always arise by pulling together elements and evidence in the field into a broader structure or paradigm. While such comments may be obnoxious in not giving appropriate credit, they do signal that the hypothesis or viewpoint has been widely accepted. In the end, such ideas, if sound, become a shared part of our knowledge, more or less taken for granted, and few remember the protracted process toward that acceptance.

Over the years, I've frequently seen this sequence in academic critique to bold insights by archaeologists, epigraphers, iconographers, and ethnohistorians—most frequently applied critically to the work of scholars with more theoretical leanings. In the case of David Freidel, however, that pattern and that same sequence of responses have characterized much of his academic career. Sometimes his breakthroughs were received with sarcasm, perhaps exacerbated by Freidel's enthusiasm and eloquent "evangelizing" for concepts that he had embraced. Most of that criticism was in the most common form of academic communication: snotty verbal comments or envious gossip! Back in the period of the debut of *A Forest of Kings* volume you would often hear statements such as "David's gone off the deep end again" or later, more specifically, "David sees termination rituals in every pile of mud on a staircase!" Those two, of many examples, were a common response to Freidel's advocacy of new interpretations.

Of course, it was already assumed by some back then that Linda Schele had long ago completely "gone off the deep end." But Freidel, as an actual digging archaeologist, "one of us." was a more attractive target. Yet I have found repeatedly that his insights were correct, and the "evangelizing" was, of course, due to his own intense intellectual engagement and excitement over new ideas. When viewed retrospectively, that degree of enthusiasm and "preaching" has proven to have been both effective and necessary. Otherwise general concepts (the "Forests," not just trees) would have taken a decade or longer to be absorbed into our field.

## A "HYPERCONJUNTIVE" APPROACH AND STYLE

The presentation of the key ideas in *A Forest of Kings* was also in what I hereby formally dub as a "Hyperconjunctive" approach. This is evident not just in interpretations, but in "its paradigm" and even in the style of presentation.

When scholars describe a "Conjunctive Approach" they often really mean something like "multidisciplinary," for example, combining archaeological, epigraphic, and ecological evidence and interpretations. *A Forest of Kings* incorporated not only archaeology, iconography, epigraphy, ethnohistory, and ethnography, but also contemporary examples *and* their own personal experiences and those of shaman informants, as well as the possible significance of those personal experiences.

This style was so incorporative and ecumenical that it was bewildering to many colleagues. The book used a "multivocalic" mix of viewpoints that actually had been common in the humanities since the entrance of postmodern thought, but was not used in archaeology. If that kaleidoscopic effect were not bad enough from a traditional scholastic perspective, the volume was explicitly also addressed to the nonacademic public and "aficionados," regarded then by some (and sometimes still) as the "unwashed." Thus, some judged the volume a priori as an "unscholarly" popular work, not to be taken seriously. Perhaps they failed to study carefully their ninety pages of fine-print erudite end notes, almost equal to the word count of the entire main text.

For those and other reasons, it took years for the importance of some of its ideas (whether in text or end notes) to gain acceptance. Now, however, for some of us, the concepts promoted in *A Forest of Kings* increased in importance over time and even currently have led to an exciting breakthrough to yet another set of exciting breakthroughs, as described below.

## ANIMATE VERSUS INANIMATE DISTINCTIONS AND THEIR IMPORTANCE

With careful reading, one can see the broad underlying major themes, and their correlates, that define the book. It incorporated understandings that were previously minor elements in some work on ancient to contemporary Maya societies. Two of the most central themes, even "embodied" in the title, are the connecting threads throughout the work and also in many articles by Freidel and/or Schele in the same period. Those were

1. the central role of Divine Kingship in almost every aspect of ancient Maya civilization, fossilized in their architecture, site configurations, iconography, written texts, and identifiable rituals; and
2. the absence of a clear distinction by the Maya between what we would call "inanimate things" and "animate beings," especially in ideological perceptions and rituals.

If you look through the publications on the Maya in that period, these elements had been previously commented on in some places, primarily in the work of David Stuart and some other epigraphers and in the writings of Freidel and Schele themselves. Yet in *A Forest of Kings*, those elements were linked to a general reevaluation of the nature of ancient Maya kingdoms and the beliefs that had created and sustained them and that had generated their built environments, much of their material culture, and the treatment of those contexts and "things." Most had previously underestimated, or not noted at all, the centrality and ubiquity of these themes in Maya culture and practice.

Of course, the sacred or divine nature of the kings had been discussed and in some publications was compared to Southeast Asian or African kingdoms. Yet we had not realized how truly central it was to the rise, history, and fall of southern lowland Maya civilization and how universally it was incorporated into all aspects of ancient Maya civilization. Stuart and others had discussed the textual presentations showing the Maya perspective on "inanimate." Their equivalent of "souls" and active spiritual power was possessed by everything from a pot, to a house, sculpture, architecture, hills, springs, caves, an entire site's very design and placement, trees, and, of course, *forests*. The nature of Maya rituals was tailored to the specific forms of spiritual power possessed by different types of objects and contexts, powers that shifted over time in their relation to humans, and over the "life" of those physical elements of the Maya cosmos. The centrality of divine kingship, together with this understanding of the Maya view of the "inanimate" formed the central themes of *A Forest of Kings*—literally from its very title to its annotations and end notes.

## TERMINATION RITUALS AND "RUDE EVANGELIZING"

A third more specific theme in the book and their contemporaneous articles is a correlate that follows directly from those two central themes, especially from the implications of the Maya lack of distinction, in ideological terms, between the inanimate and the animate. If those "things" had a spiritual essence, then like humans they would need to be treated with respect as animate entities including sending them "into the beyond" with clear ritualized endings, burials, funerals, to set their "souls" safely to rest. That is the essence of a termination ritual. Of course, "everybody knew" about the ritual killing of objects placed in burials to accompany the deceased to the next world. The carefully partial defacement of monuments also had been frequently noted, as well as dedicatory caches and treatment of "sacred" substances such as jade or stingray spines.

None of us, however, had any idea of the almost universal nature of these practices of termination in architecture and all manner of contexts. In his applications and reinterpretations based on such contexts, Freidel was particularly effective—and perhaps most irritating! He drew upon evidence from every period and context, whether from his own projects *or those of others*, to identify and interpret termination rituals. In some cases these identifications were badly received, since he was reinterpreting the very excavations, field data, and published interpretations from decades of work by others. It seems insulting for someone to reinterpret your very unit profiles and artifact distributions to challenge your specific published presentation of *your* site contexts, or even worse, *your* palace. *Your* midden deposits, wall fall debris, or postcollapse occupations were suddenly being converted into the remains of single rituals. In some cases, the populations and nature *of your* site's final phase or phases were greatly reduced, and some chronological periods could be radically shortened or even eliminated. There were some angry (but fun) exchanges at meetings over Freidel's presented papers on this topic.

Worse still, Freidel then "infected" many of his students and colleagues, especially younger colleagues, with this "termination ritual disease"; see, for example, the 15 chapters of *The Sowing and The Dawning* volume, and articles and sections of monographs by his Cerros collaborators such as Robin Robertson, James Garber, Debra Walker, Michelle Rich, and others. They began to look for these types of deposits in their own investigations and in the reports of others. Those of us with more resilient egos began to revise some of their own previous interpretations of the contexts excavated by our projects.

To return to a rather late confession, I personally never doubted Freidel's views on the nature, the importance, and presence of such rituals at Maya sites—but I accepted that mostly for *other people's* sites. However, I had no idea of the ubiquity and broader implications of such deposits for the work and interpretations of all of us. Indeed, many contexts from the decades of Vanderbilt projects in Petén had been initially misinterpreted as ninth-century occupation deposits, wall fall, or garbage contemporary with the architecture. Because of that, termination rituals were missed in important contexts at Dos Pilas, Punta de Chimino, Aguateca, Arroyo de Piedra, Tamarindito, and even from some minor centers. (Note how I cleverly shifted to the third person to distance myself from the two previous embarrassing sentences.)

## IMPORTANT RECENT IMPLICATIONS: "NINTH-CENTURY" CANCUÉN AND ITS TERMINATION "ENIGMA"

A very recent example of such initial misinterpretations at the port city of Cancuén then led to a series of corrections that reflect an important general pattern. The details and interpretation of those revisions of Cancuén history are just now being presented in delivered papers and *in press* publications and are briefly described here. When correlated with evidence from similar discoveries or reinterpretations at other sites, these corrected identifications of circa AD 800 Cancuén termination rituals change our understanding of the final years and the collapse of the Classic period kingdoms of the southern lowlands.

At the rich port capital of Cancuén itself, and at the sites of some of its economic network partners, we had clear evidence of a ninth-century occupation, with both domestic and palace middens and construction activity. In addition to late eighth-century Chablekal Fine Gray, there were significant deposits of Altar Fine Orange in some areas indicating a reduced, but significant, ninth-century occupation. Evidence of this occupation was also visible in a deposit from alleged "elite feasting with non-elite artisans" in front of the range structure above the large jade workshop. Also in the initial ninth century there was a truly massive construction operation moving tons of earth and stone and placing that fill over the previous palace, presumably to form the base for a new ninth-century royal palace of the last king, Kan Maax. We believed that this final palace reconstruction had never been completed. Together all of that evidence represented an usually large amount of ninth-century activity.

The first blow to "ninth-century Cancuén" came from Ronald Bishop and his Instrumental Neutron Activation Analysis (INAA) ceramic composition results. Our Fine Orange ceramics, which really were truly identical in appearance to typical Altar Fine Orange, were proven definitively to instead be Late Classic (AD 600 to 800) Campamento Fine Orange from Veracruz. That identification was later confirmed by Chris Pool, who analyzes this ceramic in his Veracruz projects. The implications of this revision for sweeping economic change on the eve of collapse became a central feature of our 2008–2017 publications and papers on ancient Maya economy and on the collapse controversy.

However, this ceramic revision left us with an awkward problem: it totally eradicated our entire ninth-century chronology and occupation. What then could be the meaning of those late "feasting" deposits, the palace massive construction fill, and so on, that had been interpreted as early ninth-century activity? Going back to the drawing board, we had to review all aspects of our late occupations unit by unit, lot by lot, structure by structure, year by year, and review and reinterpret all late Cancuén deposits. That review of the evidence and comparisons to other sites led to a clear conclusion: at some point between AD 800 and 810, in a matter of days, *all* of Cancuén was ritually terminated including royal or noble objects, all royal and noble architectural contexts, its palace, and its royal ballcourt. The "elite/nonelite feasting" deposits were termination rituals at that one final moment of Cancuén's history. The massive platform construction fill and burial of the main entrances and other most sacred or royal sectors of the royal palace were not to create a platform in preparation for continued dynastic occupation. Rather, they were a spectacular "killing" of the entire royal palace similar to versions of such deposits recently identified at many other coeval sites. The many three-meter-high stucco sculptures, most of them portraits of the rulers and nobles surrounded by symbols of divinity, were toppled from the facades of the royal palace, as well as various other noble palaces, and then were buried. The beautiful sculptured monuments were respectfully killed by carefully chipping away just a part of the faces and then carefully placed face down and buried.

Finally, the sacred lords and nobles, inseparably linked to those sacred settings and objects, were also ritually terminated. Perhaps the most sacred contexts in the royal epicenter were the two beautifully constructed, plastered, and red-painted cisterns fed by the two springs of the site epicenter. The royalty and nobles were "respectfully" executed and deposited together with rich offerings into these sacred cisterns, thirty-one in one the south pool and over twenty-five (and still counting) in the north cistern. Obviously, this watery interment also effectively "killed" those cisterns and their springs.

The last king, Kan Maax, fully identified by his name and titles on his mother-of-pearl necklace, and his queen were buried in splendid regalia, not in a tomb, but only in the upper 60–80 cm of the mud fill of the termination deposit of earth, rocks, and debris that had been placed over the entire eastern entrance to the royal palace and its outer audience chambers. In his burial were beautiful mother-of-pearl and coral artifacts, imported fine vessels, a massive obsidian cache, and an exquisite large headdress. Clearly, to his executors Kan Maax was still a divine lord, and the divinity of "Holy Lords" and their dangerous spiritual power could transcend death. Thus, he was killed and was buried, albeit hastily, with great respect and sacred offerings.

The realization of the sitewide termination ritual of Cancuén was not just an interesting new ideological feature of the site's archaeology. It altered the whole history of the site and revealed the nature of the relationship of this kingdom with its non–Classic Maya trading partner sites on this southeastern frontier of the Maya lowlands. Many of the contexts destroyed were settings created specifically for shared rituals and visits by these piedmont, transversal, and highland leaders. All of the Cancuén evidence including ceramics, imports, INAA, common highland wares, jade and obsidian sources, architecture styles, and a Cancuén presence in the other southern partner sites have together demonstrated that between 760 and 800/810 Cancuén was the leading center of a southern network, an asymmetrical exchange relationship linking Cancuén with all of these non–Classic Maya piedmont and highland partners (e.g., Raxruha Viejo, Sesakkar, La Linterna, and La Caoba). The apogee of all of those centers began at about AD 760 and then all dramatically collapsed together between AD 800 and 810. The unequal nature of these partnerships, greatly favoring commodity-deficient Cancuén, was largely based on an adoration of the divine rulers of Cancuén and on pilgrimages and shared rituals at Cancuén itself in special architectural contexts of highland form or of fused lowland/highland form.

However, in divine kingships the king is responsible for all prosperity, but also responsible for any failure, be it ecological, political, military, or economic. Responsibility for late eight-century economic failure fell squarely upon the shoulders of its last divine king, Kan Maax. In this case, his betrayal of divine duties was seen in the rapid decline of Cancuén's economic network between 790 and 810 and the loss of its benefits to all of the populace in the highland/lowland exchange network. The judgment of the disillusioned piedmont peoples was the same as with the end of divine kingships everywhere: it was a violation of the lord's contracts with their people. Therefore, as with many divine kingships in Africa and Southeast Asia, in those circumstances "the king must die."

The major themes integrated in *A Forest of Kings* volume and coeval publications were dramatically manifest in the violent ending of Cancuén: the centrality of divine kingship, the ideological equity between the animate and inanimate, and the combination of those beliefs in practice in the form of ritual termination of the divine rulers and their associated powerful objects and contexts.

### THE FOREST FALLS: SWEEPING RITUALIZED TERMINATIONS OF KINGDOMS ACROSS THE SOUTHERN LOWLANDS

In just the last several years, the overarching themes of *A Forest of Kings* volume have become ever more critical to Maya lowland archaeology. While the Cancuén's violent, ritualized, termination may have been particularly spectacular, recent work at many other sites and intersite comparisons has found almost the same phenomenon across the southern lowlands (but *not* the northern lowlands). In the AD 760–830 period we see across the southern lowlands a balkanization of power reflected in new offices, more minor sites with emblem glyphs, and administrative palaces. That specialization was often accompanied by a mix of rapid changes, meteoric apogees and declines, destructive wars, internal migrations, and, finally, the ritual termination of dynasties and their associated material manifestations. We now know that at most, but not all, major kingdoms and most minor centers this crisis ended in dynastic collapse between 760 and 830; a few dated broadly a decade or two later.

The rejection of the divine kingship system at those centers was clearly marked with great termination rituals including the "killing" of royal architecture. Evidence of this has been found at most sites where there has been careful recent examination or reexamination of "garbage" deposits over public or elite architecture, of building destruction and burning, and of the blockage of palace entrances or the filling of royal or noble rooms with earth, rocks sherds, and other debris.

In a recent symposium and subsequent edited volume and other articles, as well as detailed chapters in site reports, just such ritualized terminations of dynasties have been convincingly identified and described at many sites, including at Aguateca, Altar de Sacrificios, Arroyo de Piedra, Blue Creek, Cancuén, Caracol, Chan Chich, Colha, Copán, Dos Hombres, Dos Pilas, El Perú–Waka, Hershey, Ixtonton, Minanhá, Nakum, Palenque, Piedras Negras, Punta de Chimino, Raxruja Viejo, Río Azul, Sesakkar, Tamarindito, Tikal, Xunantunich, Yaxchilán, and many small centers in the Petexbatún, in the Cancuén region, the Mirador Basin, Central Petén, and northeastern Belize. In many cases the presence of termination deposits, even large ones, had not been originally identified by the excavators. At some sites continuing occupation is found, but at a much reduced level of complexity, with substantial population reduction and without evidence of dynastic rule.

In general, across the southern lowlands after these termination rituals the evidence of dynastic rule by holy lords disappears. Exceptions include centers such Ceibal, Caracol, and others where the ninth-century constructions and monuments are fewer and with hiatus periods and in quite different forms. These centers also dwindle away during the ninth century.

In terms of the "surviving" dynastic centers, recent investigations or "reexaminations" have shown that in the late eighth or early ninth century that crisis impacted those sites as well. The best example of this is the current work by Inomata's project at Ceibal. Reexamination of the monographs on other sites and zones and refinement of details of previous chronology revealed that the 760–800/810 Petexbatún collapse also hit Ceibal, and it was only after that disjunction that Watul Chatel and his heir presided over a revitalization, but only for several decades. Some exceptions, such as Toniná and Naachtún, were centers much reduced in wealth, power, and population with little (e.g., Toniná) or no (e.g., Naachtún) evidence of dynastic power and with general depopulation of much of their regions, respectively the Ocosingo Valley and the Mirador Basin.

It is impossible to overestimate the importance of these most recent applications of themes from *A Forest of Kings* that are combined in the identifications of these terminal rituals. While termination rituals are seen through Mesoamerican history, the chronological correlation and shared form of these extreme examples of that practice at the very end of the Classic period has direct implications for interpretations of the end of most of the southern kingdoms. This pattern makes it clear that, at least in the *southern* lowlands, there was truly a "collapse" (or if you prefer, "a disaster") and one that can be specifically defined as the disintegration of a political system and its integrated ideology, that is, Classic Maya Divine Kingship. The recurring fashionable position that "there was no collapse" or "it was more of a transition" is refuted for the southern lowlands by this recent comparative evidence.

Of course, most elements of the cultural tradition continued and there were exceptions at some sites, but the above pattern fits any accepted, not hyperbolized, definition of "collapse": an unusually disjunctive and relatively rapid end of a political system or its reduction to a significantly lower level of political complexity. In the southern lowland case, beyond that minimal definition of collapse, there also was great general population reduction across Petén, shifting of trade routes and florescence of coastal centers, endemic warfare, epicenter destructions, and more. Specific features and the broader cultural traditions continued, but it was, in fact, a usually definitive collapse with minimal recovery in most parts of the south.

Causes or "causality" of this phenomenon involved a complex process having many chronologically layered factors. Now, however, the specific nature of the endings of kingdoms is revealed in all of these "terminal" termination rituals. The evidence from these rituals clearly tells us *what* collapsed: specifically the Maya form of a divine kingship system. With that understanding, it is now far easier to go back and examine earlier Maya culture-history to seek to elucidate the process leading to collapse and its implications for the nature of southern lowland Classic Maya civilization.

## JUST ONE UNDERSTATED CONTRIBUTION
## OF *A FOREST OF KINGS*

Thus, in the last five years working backward from this dramatic ending many archaeologists have been utilizing and evolving the concepts from *A Forest of Kings* and the related Freidel and Schele publications to try to resolve the century-old debate on the end of this civilization. In retrospect, the book and Freidel's subsequent presentations and "evangelizing" on the centrality of its concepts—initially perceived skeptically as "hyperbolizing"—were, in fact, *very understated*. Its themes have been repeatedly proven to be transformative contributions to the subsequent decades of research and to the current, and future, history of Maya archaeology.

# 3

## The Materialization of Classic Period Maya Warfare

### Caracol Stranger-Kings at Tikal

Arlen F. Chase and
Diane Z. Chase

The publication of *A Forest of Kings* by Linda Schele and Davidv Freidel in 1990 reignited a nascent academic interest not only in Maya history and historical figures, but also in the nature and impact of Maya warfare. Schele and Freidel were among the first scholars to combine readings of the Maya hieroglyphic records from the monuments at a series of sites into a coherent history, reflecting events that had transpired during a period of time that many other scholars considered to be unwritten history.

> Theirs was a civilized world: a world of big government, big business, big problems, and big decisions by the people in power. The problems they faced sound familiar to us today: war, drought, famine, trade, food production, the legitimate transition of political power. It was a world which mirrors our own as we wrestle with the present in search of a future. (Schele and Freidel 1990:17–18)

In essence, *A Forest of Kings* constituted the first cohesive work to present the ancient Maya in contemporary-world terms.

A key component of the focus in their landmark book was Maya warfare and its role in changing and shaping Maya society. They wrote about conflict as central to ancient Maya society and as being well represented in hieroglyphic texts. They also presented a case for the Maya as practicing "sacred war" (Schele and Freidel 1990:144) in which the "Maya lords fought

DOI: 10.5876/9781646420469.c003

their own battles" (65) using techniques involving "traditional hand-to-hand combat of proud nobles" (145) that often ended in the sacrifice of a king (65). In their model (see also Freidel 1986), early warfare was practiced predominantly for religious rather than economic reasons; there was "raiding for captives," accompanied by "captive sacrifice" and "decapitation" as forms of "sacrificial gifts to give to the gods." In accord with its ritual aspects, warfare was also correlated with the astronomical passage of Venus (Schele and Freidel 1990:147; see also Aldana 2005), and the "dry season" was noted as being "the time for wars" (Schele and Freidel 1990:62). The authors noted that the Maya used a ritualized war costume that showed potential relationships with Teotihuacan, leading them to refer to Maya warfare as "Tlaloc-Venus war" (147).

While warfare was both sacred and ritualized, Schele and Freidel suggested that a change occurred in AD 378, when the result of war went beyond the taking of a captive king and extended, through that act of personal conquest, to the taking of an actual kingdom—in this case Uaxactún by Tikal. The subsequent Late Classic period in the central lowlands was then cast in terms of ritualized conquest warfare that was at the same time linked to "political dominance" and loosely to "territory" (Schele and Freidel 1990:452). In their view, the size of ancient Maya polities was compartmentalized and reflected by the distribution of emblem glyphs, not giving way to more global conflicts or control. The unitary divisions of Maya society were seen as being reflected in limited warfare extracting tribute and not in attempts by the victors to substantially alter the societies of the losers; we extend their interpretations and argue here, however, that this warfare did have more significant impacts during the Classic period. Schele and Freidel (1990:380) also cast the Maya collapse in terms of warfare. In their words: "As time went on, the high kings were driven to unending, devastating wars of conquest and tribute extraction" (380)

There has been some disagreement about the details of the Maya warfare model presented in *A Forest of Kings*—mostly revolving around areas that are difficult to prove with extant hieroglyphic texts and archaeological remains. For instance, whereas Schele and Freidel (1990) presented Tikal as the victor in the AD 378 war, Juan Pedro Laporte and Vilma Fialko (1995) argued that Uaxactún actually dominated Tikal and not the other way around—matters of hieroglyphic interpretation that may never be definitively resolved. Juan Antonio Valdés and Federico Fahsen (1995) suggested that the foreign individual (Sihyaj K'ahk') responsible for this successful war was actually buried at Uaxactún, something not contradicted by isotopic analysis of Tikal burials 10 and 48 (Wright 2012:347). Regardless of which site housed this presumed Teotihuacan-based interloper in AD 378, Maya warfare was altered by this event and Maya researchers' views on the nature of Maya warfare shifted, as Schele and Freidel (1990) outlined. David Webster (2000), for example, subsequently argued that Maya war was similar to warfare practiced by other civilizations in that it resulted in economic and political gains for the victor, including the general population. This is something visible in the archaeology of Caracol (D. Chase and A. Chase 2004a). At the time that *A Forest of Kings* first appeared, we had also suggested that Maya warfare impacted the general population in far more than ritual—specifically in terms of economic gain (A. Chase and D. Chase 1989), something noted in the footnotes of the book (Schele and Freidel 1990:442). However, at the time that they wrote, neither we nor Schele and Freidel could not have foreseen the far-reaching impact that Maya ritual could attain through warfare.

Most Maya warfare events are inferred from hieroglyphic texts or from iconography on stone monuments and, less frequently, pottery vessels. Our understanding of Maya warfare derives primarily from interpretations based on these two sources—texts and iconography—as well as from information extracted from ethnohistoric documents. Finding material evidence of warfare in the Maya archaeological record beyond texts is extremely difficult. But, these data do exist in the form of specific artifacts and features recovered and behaviors inferred from these archaeological remains: fortification walls (Demarest et al. 1997; Webster 1976); stone points (Aoyama 2005; Hassig 1992); "skull pits" (Buttles and Valdez 2016; Demarest et al. 2016:177); the burning of central buildings (Cowgill 1988; Inomata and Stiver 1998; Millon 1988), and more. Sometimes, these artifact classes and contexts are correlated with hieroglyphic texts and the iconography on stone monuments (e.g., Scherer and Golden 2014), and other times they are not (Hansen 2008; Webster 1976). However, more nuanced considerations of warfare can also be gained by appropriately conjoining texts and iconography with detailed considerations of archaeological contexts.

In this chapter we further define relationships between history and archaeology, contextualizing both the ritual, organizational, and economic impacts of warfare, and the symbolic materialization of domination and integration, as well as of distribution, disintegration, or dissolution. We argue not only that the wars between Caracol and Tikal and between Caracol and Naranjo are reflected in outwardly visible features—monument construction, or lack thereof, and material evidence of site prosperity and integration—but that evidence for the "subjugation/domination" of these sites by the victorious site of Caracol also may be seen in burials and constructions placed in conquered territory. We similarly argue that the dismantling or dispersal of monuments or other relics can reflect the sharing or disposal of ritual power. We provide an archaeological argument for the subjugation of Tikal that was expressed in the physical interment of Caracol lords in prominent architecture at that site. Furthermore, we suggest that the positioning and acceptance of a Caracol ruler at Tikal may be comparable to patterns and behaviors seen in other historic Colonial contexts. Following the work of Marshall Sahlins (1981, 2008) and others (Hagerdal 2008; Henley 2004; see also Marcus, chapter 4 in this volume), we argue that the concept of a "stranger-king" can help explain the placement and reception of Caracol rulers in what was once both a dominant and foreign polity.

## WARFARE AND CARACOL

When we started archaeological work at Caracol, Belize in 1985, hieroglyphic texts already were being read to indicate that Caracol had engaged in warfare with Naranjo in the early part of the Late Classic period (Riese 1984; Sosa and Reents 1980; Stone et al. 1985). In 1986 our project discovered Altar 21, which recorded that Caracol was involved in an earlier successful war against Tikal (A. Chase 1991; A. Chase and D. Chase 1987, 1989). The recovery of this monument focused our research on analyzing the impact that successful warfare would have had on Caracol. Thus, we temporally ordered the hieroglyphic texts and examined them to determine different kinds of war events (e.g., A. Chase and D. Chase 1998:20, fig. 2). Two star-war events, believed to constitute "all-out war," were evident in the Caracol texts, and Caracol was the victor in both. Tikal was defeated in a star-war in AD 562, and Naranjo was vanquished in a star-war in AD 631. A series of less-understood *jubuuy*, or destruction, events also appeared in Caracol's record prior to the star-war with Naranjo. All of these texts could be contextualized by other data, such as the spatial distance between sites, and, at least for Tikal, archaeology. More than three decades of archaeological work at Caracol also permit the contextualization of the hieroglyphic texts. The AD 562 war between Caracol and Tikal spanned a distance of 76 km, which meant that Caracol would have been challenged to maintain territorial control over that site. Military theory posits that extended territorial control is difficult beyond three days' marching distance or 60 km in the southern Maya lowlands and similar areas (A. Chase and D. Chase 1998; Hassig 1992). That there was also disruption at Tikal following the star-war is indicated in that site's archaeological record through (1) a dynastic upheaval accompanied by monument breakage, resetting, and burial (e.g., Harrison-Buck 2016; Satterthwaite 1958); (2) the cessation of new carved stone monuments for 130 years in Tikal's epicenter (A. Chase 1991; C. Jones and Satterthwaite 1982;

but see Moholy-Nagy 2016); and (3) a decrease in the population of outlying residential settlement at Tikal (Puleston 1974:309; but see Moholy-Nagy 2003), with an accompanying increase in population at Caracol (A. Chase and D. Chase 1989; D. Chase and A. Chase 2000, 2002, 2003b, 2017). That there was an interest in controlling broader political spheres can be seen in Caracol's relationships with Naranjo. With the AD 631 star-war at Naranjo, 42 km distant from Caracol, monument erection related to the indigenous Naranjo dynastic line also ceased (Houston 1991), Caracol apparently placing its own monuments and texts at that site (e.g., Graham 1978, 1980). We believed that Caracol's interest in defeating Naranjo with a star-war was that the site was used as a stepping stone for direct territorial control of Tikal (A. Chase and D. Chase 1998); hieroglyphic texts at Naranjo after this conquest contained passages about Caracol personages, implying that the site may have functioned as a second capital for Caracol for approximately fifty years.

There have been a number of detailed anthropological and archaeological studies of early warfare and its impact on various societies (e.g., Arkush 2000; Keeley 1996; LeBlanc and Register 2003; Nielsen and Walker 2014; Otterbein 1973, 2009; Webster 2000). Because of the record of successful war events at Caracol, we were particularly interested in testing the effects that successful warfare could have had on Maya society with the archaeological data. Keith Otterbein (1973; see also D. Chase and A. Chase 2017) pointed to three specific results of successful warfare: (1) the organizational integration of the victorious society; (2) more prosperity for the victorious society; and (3) an influx of people into the victor's city or polity, drawn there either because of the lure of ritual and economic success or because of having been forcibly moved.

Recognizing these potential outcomes of successful warfare on the victorious population, we tested Caracol's residential settlement archaeologically to document any changes that occurred in the site's residential groups (D. Chase and A. Chase 2000, 2002, 2003a). Because the inhabitants of Caracol placed ceramic vessels within the majority of their ritual deposits (e.g., A. Chase 1994), we were able to tightly date construction and occupation of Caracol's residential groups. Investigations showed all three indicators: integration, prosperity, and population growth. Integration was seen in shared residential group and mortuary patterns—and ultimately in site organization. Material remains in burials and residential groups suggested internal prosperity at the same time that there was a substantial increase in population numbers (e.g., figure 3.1).

Some 70 percent of Caracol's residential groups contain an eastern building that functioned as a shrine or a mausoleum (D. Chase and A. Chase 2004a, 2011, 2017). Most of these buildings followed a standard pattern of ritual

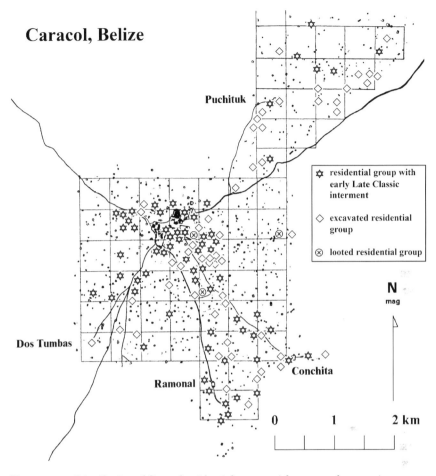

**Caracol, Belize**

Puchituk

Dos Tumbas

Ramonal

Conchita

| | residential group with early Late Classic interment |
| | excavated residential group |
| | looted residential group |

N
mag

0    1    2 km

FIGURE 3.1. *Distribution of Caracol residential groups with excavated eastern interments at the beginning of the Late Classic Period.*

deposition of caches and burials that involved at least one tomb (D. Chase and A. Chase 2004b). Archaeology has revealed that this residential group plan with its associated eastern mausoleum rapidly covered the landscape of Caracol at the beginning of the Late Classic period—coincident with the epigraphically recorded warfare with Tikal and Naranjo. By the end of the Early Classic Period (ca. AD 450–550 at Caracol), interments in eastern buildings at Caracol began to appear, being present in approximately twenty-six residential groups appropriately tested with excavation. During the early facet of the Late Classic period, interments associated with eastern constructions have been documented in seventy-one residential groups (figure 3.1), showing a surge in popularity precisely when the site was engaged in successful warfare. For the late facet of the Late Classic period, at a time when the actual residential settlement for the site covered 200 km$^2$, ninety-five appropriately tested residential groups have produced interments associated with the use of eastern residential shrines. The tombs and interments in these residential groups usually contained not only bodies, but also pottery vessels and other artifacts, such as carved seashell. Ritual caching of finger bowls and faced pottery urns further took place in many of these residential groups (D. Chase and A. Chase 1998, 2001). The market system at Caracol (D. Chase and A. Chase 2014) is projected to have existed during these times and likely functioned to facilitate not only the distribution of ritual containers but also the distribution of quotidian goods such as obsidian, which is present in all of these residential groups, as well as luxury items such as jadeite, which occurs in 41 percent of the groups investigated (D. Chase and A. Chase 2017:225). The occurrence of these ritual goods and imported artifactual materials within most of Caracol's households was interpreted as representing a high level of prosperity for the people living at the site—and one that was not generally found elsewhere in the Maya area (A. Chase and D. Chase 2009).

The rapid spread of this prosperity over the Caracol landscape, as seen in the archaeological data, also indicated a swift population growth on the order of 300 percent at the very beginning of the Late Classic period (A. Chase and D. Chase 1989). While this increase may have been caused by a population influx at the site, isotopic analyses have yet to be run to test this proposition. The residential interments and their contents showed continued prosperity for the site's population even after Caracol had suffered its own star-war defeat at the hands of Naranjo in AD 680. We have previously described the combined "shared identity" and growth in prosperity as "symbolic egalitarianism" (A. Chase and D. Chase 2009; D. Chase and A. Chase 2006, 2017).

The Caracol extensive causeway system may have been an outcome of the site's successful warfare, especially as these roads permitted the effective organizational integration of the site. Apart from the earlier causeways connecting Caracol, Cahal Pichik, and Hatzcap Ceel by the end of the Early Classic period (A. Chase et al. 2014), the majority of Caracol's causeways were built at the beginning of the Late Classic period, precisely the time when the site was engaged in successful warfare. This same causeway system also would have facilitated the deployment of warriors from one end of the site to the other, something directly correlated with the construction of many road systems (Trombold 1991). The causeway system also helped to support a functioning market system for the site (A. Chase and D. Chase 2001a; A. Chase et al. 2015; D. Chase and A. Chase 2014). Three large plazas constituting public space were embedded in the landscape, each approximately three kilometers by causeway from the site epicenter, at the very beginning of the Late Classic period, presumably shortly after the war with Tikal (A. Chase and D. Chase 2001a; D. Chase and A. Chase 2014). The causeways linking the Caracol epicenter to the existing sites of Ceiba and Retiro likely also were built at the same time (A. Chase et al. 2011), thus helping to consolidate and integrate Caracol's huge urban settlement. As the urban settlement grew during the Late Classic, other built causeways expanded Caracol's integrative road and administrative system (A. Chase et al. 2014). Thus, these various archaeological data appear to corroborate all three noted outcomes of successful warfare. Increased site integration was apparent in residential and ritual patterns, as well as in the site's causeway system. Prosperity was noted in the materials present in ritual and household contexts. Finally, population grew substantially.

## EFFECTS OF MAYA WARFARE IN THE ARCHAEOLOGICAL RECORDS OF TIKAL AND NARANJO

Correlating archaeological data with hieroglyphically recorded war events relies heavily upon not only the recovered archaeological record but also upon an interpretation of the severity of the epigraphically recorded conflicts and the associated materialization of such aggression. As the most severe type of Maya warfare, it would appear that a star-war led to the removal of the local ruler and descendants at a defeated site; often, the site was not dynastically "refounded" for an extended period of time. The impact of such a warfare event on the epigraphic record is clear. Tikal did not erect monuments for 130 years after the AD 562 war (A. Chase 1991), and Naranjo did not erect local monuments for 71 years after the AD 631 conflict (Houston 1991). But, such an event also should be detectable in other aspects of the archaeological record. Thus, at Tikal there appears to have been a loss of outlying residential population and a restructuring of that site's settlement pattern (Puleston 1974), while, as noted above, Caracol appears to have undergone a dramatic population increase and site expansion (A. Chase and D. Chase 1989; D. Chase and A. Chase 2002). But, the impact of this successful warfare may also be visible in the epicentral architecture of the defeated sites. For Naranjo, this is implied in the appearance of Caracol monumental texts in association with epicentral architecture. For Tikal, this may in fact be seen in the temples constructed in the North Acropolis during this time period.

We argue here that Caracol's rulers used both their initial star-war victory over Tikal and then subsequently their star-war victory over Naranjo to effectively insinuate themselves into the ritualized fabric of both societies. We believe that this was done through the construction of specific ritual buildings, the symbolic interment of key individuals, and the manipulation of current and previous hieroglyphic texts and monuments. At Tikal, this meant the construction of structures 5D-32–1st and 5D-33–1st in Tikal's North Acropolis and the physical interment of Caracol individuals within their latest tombs (specifically in Burials 23, 24, and 195). This building program in Tikal's North Acropolis was meant to ritually displace the existing site leadership and to establish Caracol's own ritual pantheon.

## Caracol's Stranger-Kings at Tikal

One of the things that has puzzled us after over thirty years of excavation is that we have been unable to locate any of the burials of Caracol's rulers mentioned on its monuments, particularly those of its most noted rulers, Yajaw Te' K'inich II, who spearheaded the Tikal war in AD 562, and his son, K'an II, who waged the Naranjo war in AD 631. This is not for a lack of trying. We have investigated all of the major structures in downtown Caracol and recovered a plethora of tombs (D. Chase 1994; D. Chase and A. Chase 1996, 2011, 2017), many of them dated with hieroglyphic texts (reflecting both death dates and covering activities) that are painted either on tomb capstones or directly on tomb walls (A. Chase 1994; A. Chase and D. Chase 1987). What we can say at this point is that the hieroglyphic dates recovered from Caracol's tombs are not replicated in the carved monument texts, nor can they possibly represent death dates for any of the site's known rulers as they do not match lifespans indicated within the texts (table 3.1; see also A. Chase and D. Chase 1996; D. Chase and A. Chase 2017). It has also been intriguing that many of the primary occupants of Caracol's tombs are women (D. Chase 1994; D. Chase and A. Chase 2017). In the past, epigraphers worked to fit tombs to a given site's monumental record (e.g., Valdés and Fahsen 1995 for Uaxactún). For the reasons outlined above, the assumption of male rulers in tombs or of textually identified individuals in these chambers does not work at Caracol, as gendering the site's tombs has demonstrated that such a supposition is problematic. The woman in the central Structure B19 tomb who died in 9.10.1.12.11 (A. Chase and D. Chase 1987) was initially identified by epigraphers as an arrival from Site Q and the mother of K'an II, being repeatedly called "Lady Batz Ek" (Grube 1994:108; Martin and Grube 2000:91–92, 2008). Based on

TABLE 3.1. Relevant dates from Caracol, Naranjo, Xunantunich, La Rejolla, Tikal, and Dos Pilas.

| Long-Count | Calendar Round | Event | Site/Text |
|---|---|---|---|
| 7.4.17.0.14 | 13 Ix 12 Xul | unspecified action by Naranjo lord | Nar Altar 1 |
| 8.5.18.4.0 | 7 Ahau 3 K'ankin?? OR: 8.5.17/18.4.0 8 Ajaw 8 ? | | Nar St. 25 |
| 8.18.4.4.14 | | | Car St. 20 |
| 9.2.9.0.16 | 10 Cib 4 Pop | | Car St. 13 |
| 9.4.16.13.3 | 4 Akbal 16 Pop | | Car St. 15 |
| 9.5.3.1.3 | 9 Akbal 1 Xul | death date | Car B20 tomb 4 |
| 9.5.3.9.15 | | accession of Wak Chan K'awiil | Tik St. 17 |
| 9.5.12.0.4 | 6 K'an 2(3) Zip | accession of Double Comb *ucab* Tuun K'ab Hix of Q? | Nar St. 25 |
| 9.5.19.1.2 | 9 Ik 5 Uo | seating of Yajaw Te' K'inich II at Caracol | Car Altar 21 |
| | | *ucab* x of Tikal? | Car St. 6 |
| 9.6.2.1.11 | 6 Chuen 19 Pop | axe event against Caracol | Car Altar 21 |
| 9.6.3.9.15 | | katun anniversary of Wak Chan K'awiil | Tik St. 17 |
| 9.6.13.17.0 | | | Tik St. 17 |
| 9.6.8.4.2 | 7 Ik 0 Zip | star-war at Tikal | Car Altar 21 |
| 9.6.12.0.4 | 4 K'an 7 Pax | 1st anniversary of Double Comb | Nar St. 25 |
| 9.6.12.4.16 | 5 Cib 14 Uo | birth of Batz Ek | Car St. 3 |
| 9.6.17.17.0 | 8 Ahau 13 Mac | | Car Altar 21 |
| 9.6.18.2.19 | 9 Cauac 12 Kayab | | Car Altar 21 |
| 9.6.18.12.0 | 8 Ahau ? Mol | action related to Sky Witness of Q | Car St. 3 |
| 9.7.2.0.3 | 2 Akbal 16 Mac | | Car St. 5 |
| 9.7.3.3.17 | 7 Caban 5 Kayab | building of a particular structure | Nar Altar 1 |
| 9.7.3.12.15 | 3 Men 18 Yaxkin | death date | Car B20 tomb 3 |
| 9.7.8.12.12 | 6 Eb 10 Xul | covering of tomb | Car A34 tomb 2 |
| 9.7.10.16.8 | 9 Lamat 16 Chen | arrival x Uxwitza' witnessed by Batz Ek | Car St. 3 |
| 9.7.12.0.4 | 2 K'an 7 Zac | 2nd anniversary of Double Comb | Nar St. 25 |
| 9.7.14.10.1 | 9 Imix 9 Uo | | La Rej St. 1 |
| 9.7.14.10.8 | 3 Lamat 16 Uo | birth of K'an II of Caracol | Nar "Lintel" 1 |

*continued on next page*

TABLE 3.1—*continued*

| Long-Count | Calendar Round | Event | Site/Text |
|---|---|---|---|
| | | | Car St. 3 |
| | | | Car Altar 21 |
| 9.7.19.10.0 | 1 Ahau 3 Pop | ballgame?? | Car Altar 21 |
| 9.7.19.13.12 | 8 Eb 15 Zotz | 1st bloodletting | K'an II |
| | | ucab 4 katun ahau | Car St. 3 |
| 9.8.0.0.0 | 5 Ahau 3 Chen | scattering by Yajaw Te' K'inich II via cherished Lady Moon Bird | Car St. 1 |
| | | katun bleeding by 2nd bloodletting | K'an II |
| | | 3rd katun seating Yajaw Te' K'inich II | Car St. 6 |
| 9.8.0.0.0 | | wooden panels | Tik Bu. 195 |
| 9.8.3.14.4 | 7 Akbal 11 Zotz | split mountain/his skull/waterlily sky house "ko 3 stone place" | |
| | | ucab Yajaw Te' K'inich ? . . . holy | Nar Altar 1 |
| 9.8.5.16.12 | 5 Eb 5 Xul | seating of Yajaw Te' K'inich II (possessed) | Car St. 6 |
| | | seating as "lord bleeder" Flame Ahau | |
| 9.8.5.16.12 | | | Car St. 5 |
| 9.8.10.0.0 | 4 Ahau 13 Xul | seating as "*ba* bleeder lord" Flame Ahau | Car St. 6 |
| | | it was seen by 3-katun bleeder Yajaw Te' K'inich II, water-lily ahau, sibling . . . | |
| 9.8.10.0.0 | | | Car St. 5 |
| 9.8.12.0.4 | 13 K'an 7 Xul | 3rd anniversary of Double Comb | Nar St. 25 |
| 9.9.0.0.0 | 3 Ahau 3 Zotz | | Car St. 5 |
| 9.9.0.4.0 | 5 Ahau 3 Mol | | Car St. 5 |
| 9.9.0.16.7 | 2 Caban 15 Uo | covering of chamber | Car L3 tomb |
| 9.9.2.0.4 | 12 K'an 17 Zip | 3 and ½ anniversary of Double Comb | Nar St. 25 |
| 9.9.4.16.2 | 10 Ik 0 Pop | accession of K'an II ucab TRIAD? witnessed by Batz Ek | Car St. 3 |
| | | | Car St. 22 |
| 9.9.5.13.8 | 4 Lamat 6 Pax | X by K'an II ucab ?-Sky of Q | Car St. 3 |

*continued on next page*

TABLE 3.1—*continued*

| Long-Count | Calendar Round | Event | Site/Text |
|---|---|---|---|
| 9.9.9.0.5 | 11 Chichan 3 Uo | | Car St. 22 |
| 9.9.9.10.5 | 3 Chichan 3 Ceh | arrival of 3-uinal bird at Uxwitza'; it was seen by Batz Ek k'ul-yax-ahau X K'an II hun tan of emblem (not Q) | Car St. 3 |
| | | | Car St. 22 |
| 9.9.10.0.0 | 2 Ahau 13 Pop | K'an II scattered | Car St. 3 |
| | | | Car St. 22 |
| >9.9.12.0.4 | 5-katun Double Comb | | Nar St. 27 |
| 9.9.12.6.6? | | | Car St. 22 |
| 9.9.13.1.9 | | | Car St. 22 |
| 9.9.13.4.4 | 9 K'an 2 Zec | jubuuy Koka' place ah-cab-hi ucab K'an II | Car B16 stucco |
| | | jubuuy "he of Naranjo" | Car St. 3 |
| | | jubuuy his flint/shield | Car St. 22 |
| | | | Nar Step VIII |
| 9.9.13.8.4 | 11 K'an 2 Chen | jubuuy Koka' place ah-cab-hi | Car B16 stucco |
| | | | Car St. 22 |
| | | | Nar Step VII |
| 9.9.14.3.5 | 12 Chichan 18 Zip | verb 3-knot-skull? (ballgame?) | Nar Step VII |
| | | jubuuy | Car B16 stucco |
| | | jubuuy ma-X-kin-??? ucab K'an II sibling of "cauachead" | Car St. 3 |
| 9.9.14.?.? | | | Ucanal Ms. 1 |
| 9.9.17.11.14 | 13 Ix 12 Zac | death | Ucanal Ms. 1 |
| 9.9.18.16.3 | 7 Akbal 16 Muan | star-war over Naranjo by Caracol founder? +[verb] monkey ucab cauachead Q? ox-te-tun-ne he of Chik Naab | Nar Step 6 |
| | | star-war over Naranjo | Car St. 3 |
| 9.10.0.0.0 | 1 Ahau 8 Kayab | witnessed by K'an II | Nar "Lintel" 1 |
| | | K'an II | Car St. 3 |

*continued on next page*

TABLE 3.1—*continued*

| Long-Count | Calendar Round | Event | Site/Text |
|---|---|---|---|
| | | *iwal k'ah* (it was seen) | Car St. 22 |
| 9.10.0.0.0 | | | Nar Step 6 |
| 9.10.1.12.11 | 1 Chuen 9 Sac | death date | Car B19 tomb 1 |
| 9.10.3.2.12 | 2 Eb 0 Pop | star-war / flint and shield | |
| | | Waxaklajuun Ubaah Kan | Nar Step 1 |
| 9.10.4.7.0 | 8 Ahau 8 Tzec | | Car St. 3 |
| 9.10.4.16.2 | 8 Ik 5 K'ankin | 1-katun anniversary of K'an II | Nar Step 10 |
| 9.10.5.12.4 | | | Nar Step 10 |
| 9.10.5.13.4 | 11 Kan 2 Sac | death of Batz Ek | Xun Panel 3 |
| 9.10.7.9.17 | 1 Caban 5 Yaxkin | death of 18-Jog-snake? | Xun Panel 3 |
| 9.10.10.0.0 | ballgame implied | | Xun Panel 3 |
| 9.10.10.0.0 | 13 Ahau 18 Kankin | | Nar Step 1 |
| 9.10.10.0.0 | | | Xun Panel 4 |
| 9.10.12.11.2 | | Flint-Sky-K accession at Dos Pilas | |
| 9.10.16.16.19 | | Jaguar-Paw of Q born | |
| 9.11.5.14.0 | | seating of K'ahk' Ujol K'inich II of Caracol | Car B16 stucco |
| 9.11.5.15.9 | | death of K'an II | Car B16 stucco |
| 9.11.9.16.2 | 12 Ik 0 Mol | anniversary K'an II | Car B19 stucco |
| 9.11.9.16.2 | | anniversary K'an II | La Rej St. 3 |
| 9.11.11.9.17 | | capture of Tah-Mo by Sky-K Dos Pilas | |
| 9.11.19.11.0 | 13 Ahau 13 Cumku | | La Rej. St. 3 |
| 9.11.18.13.0 | 1 Ahau 8 Uo | | La Rej. St. 3 |
| 9.12.0.0.0 | 10 Ahau 8 Yaxkin | | La Rej St. 3 |
| 9.12.7.14.1 | 3 Imix 9 Pop | Star-war Uxwitza'/ Naranjo title | Car B16 stucco |
| 9.12.8.4.9 | 2 Muluc 17 Chen | arrival K'ahk' Ujol K'inich II (?) | Car B16 stucco |
| 9.12.9.17.16 | 5 Cib 14 Zotz | Jasaw Chan K'awiil accedes at Tikal | Tik T1, Lintel 3 |
| 9.12.10.5.12 | 4 Eb 10 Yax | Lady 6-Sky arrives Naranjo | Nar St. 24 |
| 9.12.13.17.7 | | Jaguar-Paw of Q accedes | |

*continued on next page*

TABLE 3.1—*continued*

| Long-Count | Calendar Round | Event | Site/Text |
|---|---|---|---|
| 9.12.15.13.7 | | Smoking-Squirrel of Naranjo born | Nar St. 24 |
| 9.12.19.12.9 | | | Tik Altar 5 |
| 9.13.0.0.0. | 8 Ahau 8 Uo | Giant Ajaw altar at Tikal (w. St. 30) | Tik Alt.14 |
| 9.13.1.3.19 | 5 Cauac 2 Xul | Smoking-Squirrel accedes | Nar St. 22 |
| 9.13.1.4.19 | 12 Cauac 2 Yaxkin | jubuuy kinich-cab | Nar St. 22 |
| 9.13.1.9.5 | 7 Chichan 8 Zac | "shell-kin" event | Nar St. 22 |
| 9.13.1.13.4 | 5 Ix 17 Muan | "shell-kin" event | Nar St. 22 |
| 9.13.2.16.0 | 5 Oc 8 Cumkuu | jubuuy "he of Tikal" was captured/ was born Smoke God K it happened at Caracol? | Nar St. 22 |
| 9.13.3.7.18 | | Jaguar-Paw's flint/shield capture at Tikal | Tik T1, Lintel 3 |
| 9.13.3.15.16 | 13 Cib 9 Kayab | chamber covering; ruler witnessed | Car A3 tomb |
| 9.13.4.1.13 | 13 Ben 1 Zip | | Nar St. 22 |
| 9.13.5.4.13 | 3 Ben 16 Zec | | Nar St. 22 |
| 9.13.6.2.0 | | Shield-K accedes at Dos Pilas | |
| 9.13.6.4.17 | 3 Caban 15 Zec | "shell-kin" captive Kinichil-Cab | Nar St. 22 |
| 9.13.6.10.4 | 6 Kan 2 Sac | "shell-kin" by Shield-jaguar of Ucanal in land of Naranjo Smoking Squirrel | Nar St. 22 |
| 9.13.7.3.8 | 9 Lamat 1 Zotz | ritual carried out by Lady 6-Sky | Nar St. 24 |
| 9.13.10.0.0 | 7 Ahau 3 Cumhu | | Car St. 21 |
| 9.13.10.0.0 | | Lady 6-Sky scatters | Nar St. 24 |
| 9.13.10.0.0 | | | Nar St. 22 |

the archaeological data and on the likelihood that Batz Ek was actually a male regent, we have always challenged this identification (A. Chase and D. Chase 2008; D. Chase and A. Chase 2008, 2017). The newly found Xunantunich Panel 3, by providing the death date for Batz Ek on 9.10.5.13.4, confirms that the B19 locus was not the resting place for this individual (Helmke and Awe 2016a: 9).

We do know quite a bit about the place of Caracol in Maya history from texts, but the identification of physical remains of historically known individuals is generally difficult. Caracol was clearly important in the broader dynastic events of the Classic Period, as can be seen in its connections with both Copán, Honduras, and Tikal, Guatemala. There were epigraphically recorded relationships between Caracol and Copán (Grube 1994; Stuart 2007; Stuart and Houston 1994:23), and it is likely that the founding ruler at Copán, Yax-K'uk'-Mo, originated at Caracol. Not only do stable isotope data indicate that this individual was likely from the Caracol area (Price et al. 2010), but his upper dentition was inlaid with jadeite from premolar to premolar (Buikstra et al. 2004:194) following high-status Caracol patterns (see below). Two Copán monuments (Stela J and Stela 63) also refer to this ruler as Uxwitza' Ajaw, using the primary toponym of Caracol (Martin and Grube 2008:193; Stuart 2007); additionally, a stone bowl from a tomb in Caracol Structure B20 may also record the name K'uk' Mo (A. Chase and D. Chase 1987:20–21, fig. 15; Prager and Wagner 2013), suggesting minimally onomastic ties between the two dynasties, if not outright reference to the same individual. Besides Copán, Tikal also had an early interest in Caracol and its emblem glyphs appear on a number of Caracol's monuments (Stela 6, Stela 15, and Altar 21). Yajaw Te' K'inich II was presumably installed as ruler at Caracol under the aegis of Tikal (likely by Wak Chan K'awiil or Double-Bird) in AD 553 (9.5.19.1.2; text on Caracol Stela 6). After his installation, Caracol Altar 21's texts note that events turned hostile with an "axe event" against Caracol in AD 556 followed by retaliation from Caracol in AD 562 through the promulgation of a star-war against Tikal. This is the event that effectively erased the Tikal dynasty from history for 130 years (A. Chase 1991; A. Chase and D. Chase 1987:33).

What we know about Yajaw Te' K'inich II at Caracol was largely recorded by his son K'an II. Yajaw Te' K'inich II acceded to the throne in AD 553 (9.5.19.1.2). We know that he ruled until approximately 9.8.0.0.0 (AD 593). He is recorded on Caracol Stela 6 as marking this *katun* ending and his presence is noted as well on Caracol Stela 1, where we are told that a youthful K'an II carried out the bleeding ceremony. However, ten years later, in AD 603, he is noted as posthumously witnessing the 9.8.10.0.0 half-katun ceremonies as a water-lily jaguar lord, thus providing us with a rough idea of his death. After a slight interregnum, during which an individual named Flame Ahau is mentioned on Caracol Stela 6 as having been seated to carry out the ritual act of blood-letting (in 9.8.5.16.12 [exactly 6 years and 3 months after the first piercing of K'an II found on Caracol Stela 3]), Yajaw Te' K'inich II's son K'an II, who was born on 9.7.14.10.8 (AD 588), acceded to the throne on 9.9.4.16.2 in AD 618. K'an II is noted as carrying out three jubuuy events against Naranjo in AD 626 and AD 627 (9.9.13.4.4, 9.9.13.8.4, and 9.9.14.3.5) in multiple texts both at Naranjo and at Caracol, seemingly ending the long running reign of the five-katun Naranjo ruler Double Comb. In AD 631 (9.9.18.16.3), K'an II carried out a star-war against Naranjo, presumably bringing the site under his direct control. Apart from the carved stone monuments at Naranjo, other texts at Caracol containing information about K'an II include Caracol Stela 3 (Beetz and Satterthwaite 1981), Caracol Stela 22 (Grube 1994), a buried stucco text in Caana at Caracol (D. Chase and A. Chase 2017:fig. 11; Grube 1994), and a portable slate mace fragment (A. Chase and D. Chase 2001b:fig. 4.5; this type of artifact is known from the Belize Valley [Willey et al. 1965:476–482] and from Copán [Willey et al. 1994:258–259]). The Caana stucco text records the death of K'an II in AD 658 (9.11.5.15.9). A two-katun five-tun anniversary of his accession is noted in a stucco text recovered from Caana's summit (9.11.9.16.2), and another posthumous mention of a two-katun five-tun anniversary of his accession is found on a monument at La Rejolla, Guatemala (9.11.9.16.2).

Based on the extensive archaeological data that has now been accumulated for Tikal and Caracol, we suggest that both Yajaw Te' K'inich II and K'an II were interred at Tikal in the North Acropolis in Structures 5D-32–1st and 5D-33–1st. Knowing that Caracol bested the reigning Tikal dynasty, we believe that they attempted to demonstrate their dynastic rights at Tikal by appropriating the symbolic aspects of the North Acropolis. We think that Yajaw Te' K'inich II is interred in Tikal Burial 195 (figure 3.2) and that K'an II was placed in Tikal Burial 23 (figure 3.3). A dwarf, presumably of ritual significance, was also placed in Tikal Burial 24 (figure 3.4) very shortly after the deposition of Burial 23 and probably in conjunction with the siting of Tikal Stela 31 in the rear room of Structure 5D-33–2nd just before the construction of 5D-33–1st. The placement of this monument in the rear of this room may have been an attempt to resurrect common ties to a Teotihuacan heritage by the Tikal elite. Jasaw Chan K'awiil was originally posited to be the son of the individual interred in Tikal Burial 23 (see W. Coe 1990:540), but this is very unlikely given that the radiocarbon dating of Burial 23 (Coe 1990:843) accords with the AD 658 death of K'an II and that the later Nuun Ujol Chaak is named in Tikal texts as the father of Jasaw Chan K'awiil (Martin and Grube 2000:44). Yet, there appears to have been a concerted effort of some duration to link the refounding of the Late Classic Tikal dynasty to its Early Classic rulers. The ties between Jasaw Chan K'awiil and Yax Nuun Ayiin I ("Stormy Sky") are significant. According to both Clemency Coggins (1975) and William Haviland (1992:79), Jasaw Chan K'awiil accedes to the throne on the 13-katun anniversary of Yax Nuun Ayiin I's earlier accession at Tikal—hardly a coincidence. Martin and Grube (2000:45) point out that the commemoration date on the wooden lintel in Tikal Temple 1 (the mortuary monument for Jasaw Chan K'awiil) was precisely the commemoration date of the 13-katun anniversary of

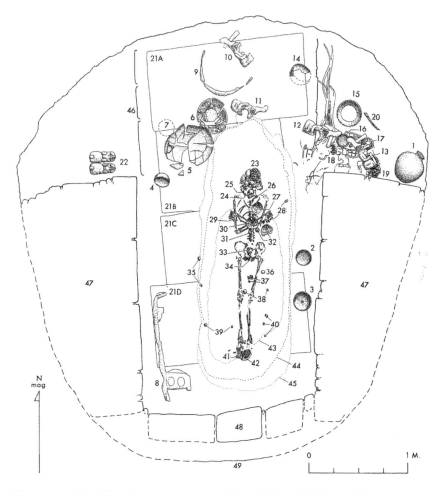

**FIGURE 3.2.** *Tikal Burial 195, the interment of Caracol Yajaw Te' K'inich II (after Coe 1990).*

"the death of Spearthrower Owl, the Mexican overlord and father of Yax Nuun Ayiin I." As discussed below, Jasaw Chan K'awiil also acknowledged Caracol through his formal accession monument.

There are several lines of archaeological data that point to a Caracol origin for early Late Classic tombs in Tikal's North Acropolis. All three individuals recovered in the referenced tombs from Tikal Structures 5D-32 and 5D-33 contain maxillary teeth once inlaid with jadeite and hematite. This was an unusual custom at Tikal. Besides the North Acropolis tombs, inlaid teeth

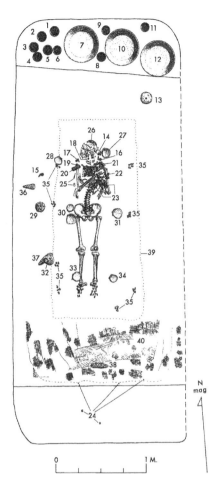

only occurred in two other locations at Tikal—in Burial 193 in Structure 7F-31 and in Burials 147, 149, and 157 all found in Structure 6B-9, leading Marshall Becker (1973, 1983) to suggest that the Structure 6B-1 residential group focused on dentistry. Inlaid teeth, in contrast, are common at Caracol, occurring in fifty-seven residential groups thus far investigated and representing 15.85 percent (*n* =116) of all excavated individuals occurring in the site's burials (D. Chase and A. Chase 2017). The bundled individual in Tikal Burial 195 had inlaid maxillary teeth that extended from premolar to premolar; William Coe (1990:567) notes that all of the inlays seem to have been deliberately removed at the time of death. Both the maxillary inlay pattern from premolar to premolar and the removal of the inlays at death also appears with the bundled individual in the basal tomb beneath the front steps of Caracol Structure B19 (S.D. C4B-3) dated to 9.10.1.12.11. The inlay pattern found in Tikal Burial 23 with maxillary jadeite inlays bracketed by hematite premolar inlays (Coe 1990:539) may resemble the pattern found in the earliest tomb in Caracol Structure B20 dating to 9.5.3.1.3; the individual in this Caracol tomb (S.D. C1H-1) exhibited pyrite inlays in the upper left premolar and the upper right canine with the other inlays in between likely removed at death; however, this Caracol individual also had inlays present on the mandible with canines having a jadeite (left) and pyrite (right) inlay and the inlays on the incisors not being present. Finally, the pattern of inlays found in Tikal Burial 24 may have been replicated in another tomb in Caracol

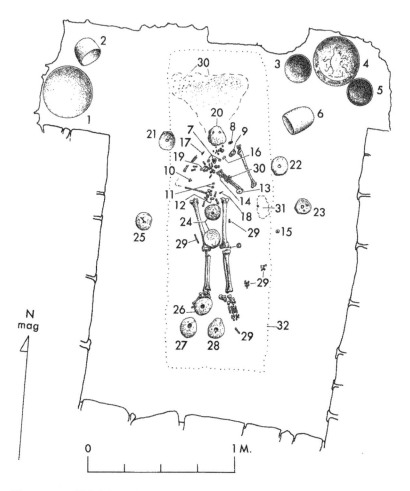

**FIGURE 3.4.** *Tikal Burial 24, the interment of a probable dwarf from Caracol (after Coe 1990).*

Structure B20 (S.D. C1B-3) dating to 9.7.3.12.15; although this tomb had been looted, it yielded a central upper incisor containing three jadeite inlays like the ones in Tikal Burial 24 (Coe 1990:543).

Isotopic analysis of the bone in Tikal Burial 23 was carried out by Lori Wright (2012:349), who concluded that this individual was not from Tikal but had spent his childhood "elsewhere" presumably in a place "located on limestone, but with highland-sourced water," which is an appropriate description for the Caracol landscape if river water to either side of the site was accessed.

This matches earlier archaeological assessments by Coggins (1975:372–380) and Coe (1990:39–540) that the individual was not from Tikal, but was "a foreigner." Coggins made her determination iconographically based on the *ajaw* plates within the burial that she viewed as similar to monuments at Caracol; Coe made his determination based on the inlaid teeth and relative paucity of grave goods in the chambers, as well as the ajaw plates (mirroring the giant ajaw altars from Caracol; bowls decorated with ajaw glyphs are also known from Caracol, e.g., A. Chase and D. Chase 1987, fig. 11). We would also note that a red "disc" was painted on the central capstone of Tikal Burial 23 (Coe 1990:537, fig. 331), which would be consistent with Caracol practice (a red dot is also found on a capstone of Tikal Burial 116 [Coe 1990:852], suggesting a linkage between these two interments, as discussed below). Tikal Burials 24 and 195 have not been tested for stable isotopes, so we do not securely know that they were foreigners to Tikal like the individual in Tikal Burial 23. Based on radiocarbon dating, the placement of the individual in Tikal Burial 23 occurred between 9.11.0.0.0 and 9.12.0.0.0, according to Coe (1990:843); this dating is in agreement with the known death date for Caracol's K'an II (9.11.5.15.9).

Tikal Burial 195 was placed deep under the centerline of Structure 5D-32–1st. A bundled body, another common Caracol practice (e.g., A. Chase and D. Chase 1987:26) was placed into a chamber excavated into bedrock that flooded with water shortly after deposition, an event that mixed some items up but that also preserved perishable artifacts. The bundled body was placed atop four carved wooden panels that recorded the long count date 9.8.0.0.0. Two alabaster sculptures representing agoutis (Moholy-Nagy 2008:fig. 138) were placed in the chamber along with six ceramic vessels, four possibly cardinally oriented K'awiil deity figures, three stuccoed and painted wooden bowls, as well as a ballgame yoke and the remains of a rubber ball. This ballgame association is likely significant given the use of a Caracol ballcourt marker (Caracol Altar 21) to discuss the history of Yajaw Te' K'inich II by his son K'an II. While the individual in Tikal Burial 195 has been identified as "Animal Skull," Simon Martin (2008a) correctly points out that "he has no known stelae and what little information we have comes from texts on unprovenanced ceramic vessels and those found within Burial 195." Martin (2008a:n.p.) further noted that, as "Christopher Jones first suggested, there are good grounds to doubt that Animal Skull descended from the existing royal patriline." Martin (2008a) was intrigued with Tikal Burial 195 because one of the wooden vessels in that chamber preserved part of a text that contained a Caracol emblem (figure 3.5), again something of great importance to this discussion. The placement of the individual in Tikal Burial 195 is of the appropriate date to be Caracol ruler

Yajaw Te' K'inich II, who may have assumed a different name at Tikal, but appears to have retained at least one of his Caracol possessions. One of the footed dishes placed in Burial 195 notes that Animal Skull was a two-katun ruler, which corresponds well with the accession date of Caracol's Yajaw Te' K'inich II.

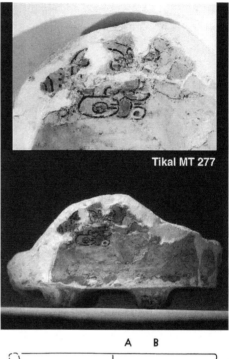

Tikal MT 277

The polychrome plates that were deposited in Tikal Burial 195 also deserve comment. Two plates in this burial name Animal Skull (Culbert 1993:figs. 50e and 51), both of them referring to him as a witness. Although not containing dates, both of these plates are stylistically like others that can be associated with Tikal, but that are Caracol-like in text. Specifically, the nineteenth month of the solar *haab* calendar was known as *kol ajaw* at Caracol and as *wayhaab* elsewhere in the Maya area. During the early Late Classic at Tikal, precisely the name

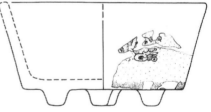

**FIGURE 3.5.** *Caracol emblem on stuccoed wooden bowl in Tikal Burial 195 (after Martin 2008a).*

of *Kol Ajaw* appears on polychrome plates that reference Wak Chan K'awiil and presumably Animal Skull (Christophe Helmke, email June 14, 2018). The linguistic similarity between Caracol and early Late Classic Tikal during this era likely resulted from already established ties between the two cities, especially since Yajaw Te' K'awiil II acceded to office at Caracol under the aegis of a Tikal overlord (Grube 1994:106). However, this linguistic similarity also indicates the strength and impact of the Caracol influence on Tikal at this time (Helmke and Kettunen 2012).

Interestingly, the death of the individual in Burial 195 occasioned a "massive reconstruction of the site center" of Tikal that has been interpreted as a "dynastic overthrow" and "an attempt by usurpers to put their own distinctive stamp on the political and ceremonial heart of the city" (Haviland 1992:73–74), further supporting the idea of a non-Tikal origin for this individual. Whatever the case, Yajaw Te' and Animal Skull may have been one and the same individual or there may have been differentiation between Yajaw' Te and Animal Skull, with the former taking care of business running matters and the latter operating "as a puppet of the city's conquerors" (see Martin and Grube 2000:41). Whatever the case, it is Yajaw' Te who is interred in Tikal Burial 195.

Tikal Burial 24 was interred in Tikal Structure 5D-32 very shortly after Tikal Burial 23. The individual placed in this chamber was described as a "diminutive adult" of approximate 115 cm in stature with a deformed spine (Coe 1990:541–543). Coe (543) posited that this individual was deposited "incidentally" and sees the death of this individual as having occurred very shortly after the death of the individual in Burial 23—"dead master and fatally bereaved, monstrous jester." Because of how unusual the interment of a dwarf is, some researchers are not convinced that a dwarf was actually in this chamber (see summary in Bacon 2007:61). However, after this interment, dwarf iconography, which is very common at Caracol (occurring on Caracol Stelae 1, 4, 5, 6, 8, 9, 11, 19, and 21), becomes evident at Tikal in the carved wooden lintels (Bacon 2007). The layout of nine *Spondylus* shells about the bodies in both Tikal Burials 23 and 24 indicate that the two interments shared common patterns. One of the vessels in Burial 24 was, for Tikal, a "unique" ring-base polychrome dish that is directly representative of the Caracol ceramic tradition and was likely an import from Caracol for the chamber (see Culbert 1993:fig. 42a). Two of the vessels included as special deposits in the fill of construction for Structure 5D-33–1st are also in pure Caracol style (Ca. 201, a cylinder with incised modeled-carved glyphs, and P.D. 235, a short squat cylinder). The inclusion of a dwarf in Burial 24 is further significant, especially as dwarves were believed to be able to function within both the living and lower worlds (A. Chase and D. Chase 1994) and, as noted above, are also extensively portrayed on Caracol stelae (Bacon 2007; Beetz and Satterthwaite 1981).

NARANJO AND ITS MONUMENTAL RECORD

It has long been known that Caracol-related texts occur at Naranjo. These texts, however, are no longer in their original locations. We suspect that one or more ritual buildings were constructed at Naranjo and used by the Caracol victors, but that they were later dismantled because they were not directly associated with ancestral individuals, as at Tikal. However, we believe that these constructions were associated with the carved stone monuments that recorded the deeds of Caracol ruler K'an II in one or more specific locations at Naranjo after he had effectively displaced the earlier dynastic ruler ("Double-Comb") and his line. The Caracol-related stone monuments at Naranjo were later ritually neutralized through being dismantled and nonsensically arranged as a stairway and through pieces of these carvings being spatially distributed to other sites, such as Xunantunich and Ucanal (and probably others), that were under Naranjo's sway toward the end of the Late Classic (e.g., Helmke and Awe 2016a, 2016b). The treatment of these stone monuments and their texts provides a case example of the inchoate power that was vested in these monuments through their texts (and probably images) by the ancient Maya. The subsequent destruction, recombination, and widespread distribution of these texts and monuments may be considered as either representative of attempts to ameliorate their inherent power or to carefully distribute some of the power and symbolism imbued within these stones both to Naranjo's later dynasty and to its allies. The desecration of Maya carved monuments is noted as having involved "repeated, ritualized procedures" in which the "scattering, commingling, or burial of fragments may have been intended to prevent such reuse" (Moholy-Nagy 2016:258).

The recovery of Panels 3 and 4 at Xunantunich during the summer of 2016 by Jaime Awe (Helmke and Awe 2016a, 2016b) emphasize the inherent power of written texts for the ancient Maya. Through moving these texts to Xunantunich, the symbols of Naranjo domination were dispersed, either lessening the power of their message or providing some ritual sustenance to that site, an ally of Naranjo (LeCount and Yaeger 2010). The two large stone panels contain passages related to the Caracol ruler K'an II. Xunantunich has no known recorded connections to Caracol, but these monuments were ritually placed at that site exterior to a building containing one of Xunantunich's buried rulers (presumably transferring to the dead individual or the building that housed him some sort of ritual power). This act also destroyed whatever meaning these panels once had within their original context. That they were moved some distance away from their original location demonstrates that these stones were both decontextualized and "shared." The same process took place with the hieroglyphic stairway at Naranjo (figure 3.6); it contains passages relating to the same Caracol ruler, but placed in a jumbled and decontextualized order that likely combined several different monuments into one. Again, one of these stair blocks was found far to the south at the site of Ucanal,

FIGURE 3.6. *Photograph of the Naranjo hieroglyphic stairway (after Maler 1908).*

where it was associated with that site's ballcourt. While Martin (2000:57–58) argued that these blocks originated at the site of Caracol and were carried to Naranjo as effective spoils of war (see also Helmke and Awe 2016a: 2), it is more likely that the various carved monuments found at Naranjo were part of construction efforts at that site.

K'an II was not the object of the Naranjo war in AD 680; he had already been dead for twenty-two years. The objective target would have had to have been the current Caracol ruler K'ahk' Ujol K'inich. Thus, it should have been his monuments and not those of K'an II that were the focus of subsequent actions—and, indeed, we have no stone monuments for this ruler in the Caracol epicenter. The subject at all of the texts at Naranjo, Ucanal, and Xunantunich is K'an II; therefore, this disbursement pattern would have made more sense if they were coming from Naranjo. That no texts are known for the presumably long-lived ruler K'ahk' Ujol K'inich may indicate that they were purposefully destroyed, whereas it appears that the texts and monuments relating to the dead ruler K'an II had to be treated in a different way.

There are also indications that multiple Caracol-related texts existed at Naranjo and that not all of them were co-located. Examining the stair blocks from Naranjo and Ucanal in more detail reveals that there are stylistically at least two different texts in the stair blocks based on the consistent treatment of day signs as either in or out of cartouches. There is also a sizable Naranjo "lintel" that was likely not a part of any stairway. There are also pieces of another panel recovered "in the debris on top of the Central Acropolis at Naranjo" (Tokovinine 2007:17, fig. 5). Furthermore, in their original context, the panels found at Xunantunich would have been vertically arranged and were likely not part of the Naranjo stairway or arranged on any balustrade; there are clearly more of these vertical panels to be found in the future based on the missing border of the upper cartouche on Panel 3 (Helmke and Awe 2016a: 6, fig. 7).

Finally, the miscellaneous carved stone fragment from Caracol that Martin attributes to the Naranjo stairway was more likely part of a Caracol stela or even a fragmentary stair block from Naranjo that was brought back to Caracol as part of or after the AD 680 conflict. The widespread distribution of these texts that deal with Caracol personages (Yajaw Te' Kinich II and K'an II) at Naranjo, Ucanal, and Xunantunich, however, also provides new insights into Classic period Maya warfare through demonstrating the ritualized aspects of these destructive actions and the power of hieroglyphic writing (and history) to the ancient Maya, especially when positioned by the victor at the subjugated site.

Given that multiple sites exhibited pieces of textual materials relating to Caracol's K'an II, these materials suggest the enormity of impact that the Tikal and Naranjo star-wars by Caracol had in the sixth and seventh centuries. The widespread disbursement of the carved texts suggests a purposeful attempt to either mitigate or share their power (see also Helmke and Awe 2016a, 2016b), thus also supporting how impactful these carved texts were. Although apparently feared by the northern communities that were brought under Caracol's sway, these texts were treated with respect ritually and their inherent power was redirected through subsequent action and ritual. The ritual disbursement of these texts to areas previously held under Caracol's sway after Naranjo's successful star-war at Caracol served to mark the end of the effects of the earlier star-war where Caracol was the victor and to bring balance back to Naranjo's world, as reflected in the establishment of its new dynasty.

### The Effects of Naranjo's Star-War at Caracol

Caracol's hold over Tikal and Naranjo ceased with the Naranjo star-war against Caracol in AD 680 (9.12.7.14.1). The timing of this event was probably sequent to the final construction of Structure 5D-33–1st over the tombs of K'an II and his aide. There has been speculation that the occupant of Burial 23 (K'an II) was the father of the individual in Tikal Burial 116 (Coe 1990:540); however, this is unlikely. It is rather more likely that the individual in Tikal Burial 23 was divorced from the Late Classic Tikal dynastic line because, if the individual in Tikal Burial 116 is Jasaw Chan K'awiil, then the texts record his father as being Nuun Ujol Chak (Martin and Grube 2000). We know from stucco texts at Caracol that the ruler K'ahk' Ujol K'inich acceded to the throne at Caracol in AD 658 (9.11.5.14.0), some twenty-nine days before the death of K'an II. K'ahk' Ujol K'inich was the ruler who was affected by the Naranjo star-war in AD 680. Although K'ahk' Ujol K'inich is recorded as having returned to Caracol in AD 680 (9.12.8.4.9), this star-war ended Caracol's hold on both Naranjo and on Tikal. What eventually happened to K'ahk' Ujol K'inich is not known. However, at Tikal, the effects of the Naranjo victory over Caracol enabled Jasaw Chan K'awiil to establish a new dynastic line. It is suspected that this would not have been the case had the star-war not taken place, for it is likely that K'ahk' Ujol K'inich would have eventually been interred at Tikal like the previous two Caracol rulers.

The first monuments to appear at Tikal after 130 years are iconographically significant in that the altar was carved in Caracol-style with a giant ajaw day-sign in its center to commemorate 9.13.0.0.0 (Tikal Stela 30 and Altar 14; Jones and Satterthwaite 1982:62), again indicating the strength and impact of Caracol influence on Tikal in ritual contexts. Fourteen of these giant ajaw day-sign altars are known from Caracol (Beetz and Satterthwaite 1981:table 2). Also, Lintel 3 of Temple 1 (Structure 5D-1) details events in the life of Jasaw Chan K'awiil and "features a motif most commonly found at Caracol, in this case a dwarf" (Bacon 2007:257). Thus, the new ruler of Tikal, Jasaw Chan K'awiil, appears to have explicitly recognized the ritual impact of Caracol through these paired monuments and the lintel iconography; this recognition likely served to terminate other ritual practices utilized under Caracol's sway (such as the Caracol practice of placing human phalanges in caches; Moholy-Nagy 2008:65). He was also anchored to the earlier foreign-based lords of Tikal through the placement of Stela 31 in the building that housed Burials 23 and 24 and by acceding to the throne on the thirteen-katun anniversary of Stormy Sky's (the individual on Stela 31) earlier accession at Tikal (Coggins 1975; Haviland 1992:79).

While the earlier star-wars by Caracol against Tikal and Naranjo had effectively erased the dynasties from those sites, the Naranjo star-war against Caracol appeared to have had impacts in the global arena, but not within the local population at the site. This may have been because of the direct relationship that Caracol's rulers had with Tikal and Naranjo—and their absence from Caracol. Thus, the star-war at Caracol itself was not as impactful as it was at Tikal and Naranjo, because the ruler may not have been physically located there at the time of the star-war. The stucco text on Caana recorded that the Caracol ruler returned to the site 168 days after the star-war (Martin and Grube 2000; D. Chase and A. Chase 2017), but one is forced to wonder "from where"? Did the attack serve to encourage his return to Caracol from somewhere else? That monument erection continued at Caracol is indicated by a slate stela dating to AD 702. Yet, the political impact of the Naranjo star-war in 9.12.7.14.1, recorded in a buried stucco text on Caracol Structure B16–2nd

(D. Chase and A. Chase 2017:fig. 10), was profound. Even though Caracol's ruler K'ahk' Ujol K'inich, who had acceded to the throne in 9.11.5.14.0 (AD 658), one month before the death of K'an II, rearrived at the site in 9.12.8.4.9 (AD 680), the site's political dominance of the central Petén was over, a fact driven home by both the accession of Jasaw Chan K'awiil at Tikal in 9.12.9.17.16 (AD 681), reestablishing visible rule after an extended hiatus, and the arrival of Lady 6-Sky at Naranjo in 9.12.10.5.12 (AD 682), reestablishing a ruling dynasty at that site as well.

## CONCLUSION

In this chapter we have used history and archaeology to follow up on the interpretations provided by Schele and Freidel in *A Forest of Kings*. In particular, we have reviewed the combined evidence for Maya warfare at the cities of Caracol, Tikal, and Naranjo. These efforts document that the textually recorded warfare did in fact happen, that certain sites and rulers dominated other regions at different points in their histories, and that the impact of warfare can be seen in the archaeological and epigraphic records of both winners and losers. Of special interest is the insertion of rulers from one site to another and the symbolic use of burials to indicate both domination and change in appropriate public and ritual contexts.

While not a necessary component of the previous argument, the concept of "stranger-kings" may help explain the function of Caracol rulers at Tikal. Thus, we suggest that the individuals in Tikal Burials 195 and 24 may be cast as "stranger-kings" at Tikal. Various past and present interpretations support these persons as being of nonlocal origin. But, given the siting of their burials in Tikal's North Acropolis, they have become enmeshed within that site's cosmological ancestors. Sahlins (1981, 2008) originally developed the concept of stranger-kings through his work in the Pacific area to define a concept in which local peoples subjugated themselves to a foreign power, believing that that power was strong enough to resolve some of the tension and conflict that had existed within their own society. Often, stranger-kings also treated their new subjects in a Colonial way for the exploitation of resources that benefited another place; this is argued to have been particularly true for global colonialism (Hagerdal 2008; Henley 2004). The relatively short ruling spans of kings at Tikal prior to Caracol's military exploits suggest that there was substantial turmoil at that site and that any neutral strong outsiders in a position of authority would have been welcome because of the role they could play in resolving conflict. Wak Chan K'awiil acceded to power at Tikal in

AD 537 (9.5.3.9.15); his twenty-five-year rule was ended by the AD 562 star-war. Whereas Wak Chan K'awiil evinced some longevity as a ruler, his defeat was clearly by someone who was stronger and who could bring an end to the rivalry and conflict in the dynastic line at Tikal—Yajaw Te' K'inich II. This is precisely the role of a stranger-king. Whereas Wak Chan K'awiil was ruler for 25 years, Schele and Freidel (1990:454n7) calculated an average span of ruler-ship of only 8 years per king for the 72 years between the death of Stormy-Sky (11th successor) and the accession of Wak Chan K'awiil (21st successor). Thus, the end of the Early Classic at Tikal was clearly a troubled one that was probably rife with conflict between royal families vying for the throne. With Wak Chan K'awiil removed by the actions of Yajaw Te' K'inich II, this Caracol king would have been perceived as an extremely strong overlord, one appropriate for the role of a stranger-king.

The star-war initiated at Tikal by Yajaw Te' K'inich II had severe repercussions for both sites. We can see these results in the archaeological record at Caracol (A. Chase and D. Chase 1989; D. Chase and A. Chase 2017). That it had an impact at Tikal is clearly seen in the 130 years of monument hiatus and also in the "poverty" that is seen in Tikal's general burials dating to this era, at least as reflected in the archaeological record (Coggins 1975:258). However, given what we know about the archaeology of both sites, it would make sense that the two greatest Classic period rulers at Caracol would choose to be interred at a mythical site with greater time depth than their own and that had once housed lords from Central Mexico—a site to which they had once owed allegiance, but that was now under their direct sway. The defeat of Wak Chan K'awiil must have been a shock at Tikal, for he was one of the longest-ruling kings at the site. His subjugation by Yajaw Te' K'inich II would have made the Caracol ruler appear extremely powerful. Given his star-war success at Naranjo, K'an II would also have been an appropriate stranger-king. The defeat of the Caracol king K'ahk' Ujol K'inich by Naranjo not only removed him and the site from global politics, but also provided the opportunity for Jasaw Chan K'awiil to reinsert himself back into the formal Tikal dynasty. Jasaw Chan K'awiil claimed the throne by directly referencing both the stranger-king associated with Teotihuacan through the use of a propitious date for his accession and by referencing the stranger-kings from Caracol through the use of Caracol-related iconography with his initial stela and altar.

*A Forest of Kings* was a major breakthrough volume in conceptualizing the ancient Maya and in suggesting that they could be viewed in much the same way as other historic and contemporary peoples. In addition, however, the history within it remains relevant to current thought and debate in Maya studies.

As expected, continued research brings to light new evidence—whether from texts, excavations, or technical analyses—that help us refine our views of ancient history, religion, and politics. In this chapter we have sought to bring to bear the current state of history and archaeology at Caracol, Tikal, and Naranjo to document the materialization of Maya warfare and to explain the close histories of these sites. It is evident that Maya warfare can be seen not only in historic texts, but also through its impact on both the "winners" and "losers." Key factors in assessing these impacts remain: monument (and monumental architecture) construction and deconstruction; differences in textual terminology; and archaeological evidence for integration, prosperity, and population increase or decrease. We add to these factors, however, the interment of foreign stranger-kings at the defeated sites—an act that clearly demonstrated not only global impact, but also the existence of broader political units, commonly known as "empires," among the ancient Maya. As noted above, we believe that Yajaw Te' K'inich II, the Caracol lord who is credited with the defeat of Tikal, and K'an II, the Caracol lord who conquered Naranjo, are both interred in Tikal's North Acropolis (Burials 195 and 23). These identifications make sense in terms of archaeological and historic contexts and explain both the oddity of these interments at Tikal and the lack of their royal interments at Caracol. Most significant, however, this analysis highlights the nuanced relationships that existed among Maya polities and the degree to which the materialization of ritualized behavior symbolized the conquest, defeat, integration, and dissolution of power and polity among the ancient Maya "forest of kings."

### ACKNOWLEDGMENTS

Archaeological research at Caracol, Belize, has been ongoing annually since 1985 and has been supported by a variety of funding agencies (see D. Chase and A. Chase 2017:232). Recent work at Caracol has been supported by the Alphawood Foundation, the Geraldine and Emory Ford Foundation, and the University of Nevada, Las Vegas. Investigations at Caracol would not be possible without the extensive cooperation and support of members of the Belize Institute of Archaeology (particularly Melissa Badillo, Allan Moore, John Morris, George Thompson, and Brian Woodye). This current chapter has benefited from edits and comments by Christophe Helmke, though we take responsibility for the textual content.

# 4

*People* magazine provides ample evidence that readers enjoy learning about the lifestyles of the rich
and famous. Forty-seven million Americans buy the
weekly magazine to read about royalty (Prince George,
Prince William, and Queen Elizabeth) and celebrity
(Angelina Jolie, Kim Kardashian, and Beyoncé).

Royalty was also the subject of a 1990 book—*A
Forest of Kings: The Untold Story of the Ancient Maya*—in
which Linda Schele and David Freidel provided a
detailed narrative of Maya kings and queens. Schele
and Freidel offered new data that satisfied the public's
growing appetite for information on the ancient Maya,
some years after the door to Maya history had been
opened (Berlin 1958, 1959, 1977; C. Jones 1977; Kelley
1962, 1965, 1968, 1976; Proskouriakoff 1960, 1963, 1964,
1968; J.E.S. Thompson 1962).

Unlike earlier scholars who avoided discussing rulers' personalities and motivations, Schele and Freidel
embraced these variables. Several other topics that they
addressed are worthy of further discussion, including
rulers as agents of change; why some Maya rulers
elected to wear Mexican-inspired warrior costumes;
how Maya usurpers asserted genealogical continuity in
the face of dynastic disruption; and the role played by
competition among factions and lineages during the
expansion of each Maya polity.

*Maya Usurpers*

Joyce Marcus

DOI: 10.5876/9781646420469.c004

## "STRANGER-KINGS" AS AGENTS OF CHANGE

Schele and Freidel's focus on rulers and their motivations was a step forward in our efforts to understand each agent's political strategies. These strategies were important because the cumulative decisions of multiple agents became *processes*. Those processes, in turn, led to the emergence of factional competition and new institutions. By studying Maya rulers' cumulative and repetitive behaviors, we can detect long-term trends and document the rise and fall of polities. The hieroglyphic texts on stone monuments reveal dates and events associated with individual rulers, but the general trends have to be reconstructed by us. Many political transitions took longer than a single ruler's reign. The archaeological record thus provides an important proving ground for social evolutionary theory.

One of the challenges for the Maya was to assert genealogical continuity in the face of dynastic interruption. When a ruling dynasty ended with no heir, there was often a block of time—sometimes days, sometimes years—during which the throne remained empty. During that interregnum multiple claimants might emerge, each hoping to gain sufficient support to take the reins of political control.

A Maya usurper could be a man from the same city but from a different faction or lineage, a man propped up by rulers at other sites, or a warrior with military prowess who claimed to be an outsider or "stranger-king" (e.g., Kathirithamby-Wells 2009; Sahlins 1981, 2008; see also Arlen Chase and Diane Chase, chapter 3 in this volume). Sahlins (1981:115) describes a "stranger-king" as "an outsider, often an immigrant warrior prince whose father is a god or a king of his native land." "These rulers," he goes on to say, "do not even spring from the same clay as the aboriginal people: they are from the heavens or—in the very common case—they are of distinct ethnic stock. In either event, royalty is the foreigner" (112).

Such stranger-kings might claim an exotic origin; they often had to pass through a confirmation process, which might include pilgrimages to other sites, participation in ritual acts of sanctification, entering into a marriage alliance, and military excursions to take captives in battle.

"Stranger-kings" have been described for Southeast Asia (Kathirithamby-Wells 2009). Some were immigrants, some locally born, but all were "men of prowess" who claimed descent from an ancestor that set them apart as foreign. "Foreignness, political genius and marriage alliances with the indigenous ruling elite were shared features of immigrant adventurers within the international trading world of Southeast Asia" (568).

The ideology of usurpers who claim exotic, external origins is well known to scholars studying kingship, inaugurations, and gaps in kingly succession (e.g.,

Feeley-Harnik 1978, 1985; Frazer 1905; Heusch 1997; Hocart 1927; Sahlins 1981, 2008). Those interregna, or transitional periods between reigns, could be full of uncertainty and chaos. Local populations wanted an orderly transfer of power. Such order was often restored by an individual who not only claimed military prowess but also participated in sacred rites that culminated in his coronation as the new king (Marcus 1994).

Usurpers had many challenges: (1) accumulating enough support from the appropriate faction or lineage to prop up their claims; (2) invoking connections to, and establishing alliances with, superior distant sites and cultures; (3) establishing political, sacred, and moral authority; (4) emulating those who had had military successes; (5) suppressing threats from other claimants; and (6) rewarding loyal foreigners and subordinates for their support by inviting them to participate in inaugurations. One can assume that some usurpers had to work long and hard to maintain the support of allies and reestablish the appearance of being a legitimate and sacred successor.

Some Maya usurpers decided to use Mexican-inspired warrior costumes to invoke a foreign origin to legitimize their new dynastic line and enhance their reputation as warriors. As Andrea Stone (1989:164) aptly noted, "One use of the costume was an ideological rallying point for political reorganization. Political factions or troops could be mobilized around a leader claiming a superior foreign pedigree, a type of disconnection strategy which supports political legitimacy and expansionist aspirations."

The Maya adopted symbols of war such as shell-covered mosaic helmets (*ko'haw*); the goggle eyes of the Mexican deity Tlaloc; and rectangular shields, darts, spears, and *atlatls* (see figure 4.1) (Coggins 1975, 1979; Marcus 2000; Nielsen and Helmke 2008; Schele and Freidel 1990; Stone 1989; Stone and Zender 2011; Taube 1992b). Mosaic or platelet helmets appeared at Teotihuacan in the third century AD, at Tikal in the fifth century, and later at other sites (e.g., Piedras Negras, Tres Islas, and Chichén Itzá). Such helmets may have been constructed by sewing perforated rectangles of *Spondylus* to a cloth, which was, in turn, attached to wood or other perishable material. Janet Berlo (1976) suggests that the 209 pieces of perforated *Spondylus* from Burial 5 at Piedras Negras might be the remains of one of these mosaic helmets (W. Coe 1959:fig. 54). As early as AD 225, war helmets and military costumes were worn by sacrificed warriors buried beneath the Temple of the Feathered Serpent at Teotihuacan, and later emulated by the Maya (S. Sugiyama 1989, 1992, 2005). Of all the Tikal royal tombs excavated so far, only the tombs of the fifteenth ruler (a usurper) and that of his son included multiple sacrificial victims.

FIGURE 4.1. *Weapons of war: (a) goggle-eyed warrior holding darts and a knife that pierces a bleeding heart (Atetelco mural, Teotihuacan; redrawn from Headrick 2007:fig. 4.1); (b) goggled-eye warrior wearing mosaic helmet (Burial 10 vessel, Tikal; redrawn from W. Coe 1967:102); (c) warrior wearing mosaic helmet and holding darts (Stela 1, Tres Islas; redrawn from Stone 1989:fig. 4); (d) helmet (ko'haw) (Temple of the Inscriptions, Palenque); (e) warrior holding atlatl and darts (Problematical Deposit 50, Tikal; from Marcus 2003:fig. 13.2).*

## EMULATION

Emulation of foreign styles and the display of nonlocal objects can enhance one's personal prestige and can advertise foreign ties. A leader's motivation to emulate foreign attire worn by a highly regarded warrior is the hope that he will acquire that same regard. Wearing the trappings of highland Mexican warriors could communicate that the Maya leader had military prowess.

Those not in direct line to rule—nobles from other lineages, or lower-ranking nobles from other cities or factions—often emulated prestigious foreigners. Such emulation involved the transfer of prestige, value, and propaganda to the would-be usurper. If in the eyes of the Maya it was the highland Mexican warrior who enjoyed the highest reputation, it makes sense that Maya leaders would adopt their costumes and weapons. Wearing such costumes established these leaders as men possessing military prowess, a key ingredient both for the throne and for political expansion.

## THE IMPACT OF TEOTIHUACAN

Even though Mayanists have been using the phrase "Teotihuacan influence" for many decades, there are problems with the phrase. One problem is that scholars often make the assumption that all nonlocal items had their origin in one city—Teotihuacan—rather than in multiple locales throughout the Central Mexican highlands and beyond (but see Braswell 2003a, 2003b; Demarest and Foias 1993; Foias 1987; Laporte and Fialko C. 1990, 1995; Millon 1973).

A second problem is that many scholars tend to lump the multiple stages of borrowing, copying, and modifying. "Teotihuacan influence" was not a single event, but a long process. Initial borrowing might have occurred during one foreign visit, but that occasion was just the beginning of a multi-era process of incorporation and accommodation in new and different contexts.

The third problem with the phrase "Teotihuacan influence" is that it implies that the Maya were passive recipients rather than active manipulators (e.g., Kidder et al. 1946; Sanders and Michels 1977). The act of incorporating foreign elements into Maya art was a creative and selective process, inspiring numerous scholars to study the way the Maya made those nonlocal elements their own, integrating them seamlessly into local canons and traditions (Borowicz 2003; Braswell 2003a; Coggins 1975; Proskouriakoff 1993; Schele and Freidel 1990:147, 164; Stone 1989). Maya usurpers selected the moment when they would depict themselves wearing Mexican-inspired warrior costumes. The incorporation of these nonlocal elements was a multicentury process (AD 300–1000), resulting in what is sometimes considered a fusion of selected elements creating a hybrid style.

I will now consider the cases of four Maya usurpers who used similar strategies, including the insertion of the word *yax* ("first") in their names as they began new dynastic lines.

**Figure 4.2.** *Green mask from Burial 85, Tikal (drawing by John Klausmeyer from Coe 1967:43).*

Case 1: Yax Ehb Xook, the First Tikal Ruler

Yax Ehb Xook, considered the founder of a Tikal dynasty, may have ruled between AD 50 and 100. The skeleton in Tikal's Burial 85, thought to be that of Yax Ehb Xook himself, was missing the skull and femora. William Coe and John McGinn (1963:32) suggest that these bones were considered sacrosanct and thus held out for some ritual.

Burial 85 included *Spondylus* shell, a stingray spine, and twenty-six vessels typical of the Chicanel phase. It also contained a small green mask with inlaid shell eyes and teeth (see figure 4.2). The mask, which measures only 12.7 cm high, may have been sewn to the cinnabar-impregnated funerary bundle. This mask probably substituted for the missing skull (W. Coe 1967:43; W. Coe and McGinn 1963). The kind of treatment Burial 85 received would be consistent with a person who was a dynastic founder.

The location chosen for the burial of any dynastic founder is significant because it establishes a sacred place to be used as the burial ground for future kings in the same dynastic line. The act of burying Yax Ehb Xook in a bedrock

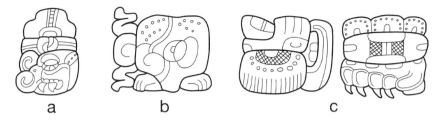

FIGURE 4.3. *Tikal's early texts reveal (a) the name of the fifteenth ruler, Yax Nuun Ayiin I; (b) the name Sihyaj K'ahk'; (c) that Chak Tok Ich'aak died (drawing by John Klausmeyer from Schele and Freidel 1990:figs. 4.18, 4.19).*

chamber with vaulted roof beneath the North Acropolis established that location as a royal cemetery. Later rulers in the same dynastic line continued to be buried there, and even those who wanted to claim dynastic continuity (e.g., rulers 15 and 16, who were from a new dynastic line).

## Case 2: Yax Nuun Ayiin I, Fifteenth Ruler of Tikal

Emulation of Teotihuacan regalia began with Yax Nuun Ayiin I, Tikal's fifteenth ruler (see figure 4.3a). Yax Nuun Ayiin I started a new dynasty at Tikal after the fourteenth ruler had died without an heir. Some depictions of Yax Nuun Ayiin I show him wearing the helmet and military paraphernalia associated with highland Mexican warriors.

Schele and Freidel recognized that Tikal's leaders were active manipulators of nonlocal symbols. When a ruler wore the costume

> of the Teotihuacán warriors, it was because this costume was prestigious and important propaganda to his people . . . Both the son and grandson of the triumphant Great-Jaguar-Paw knew the propaganda value of the Tlaloc complex. They enthusiastically adopted the imagery and its associated rituals, and then quite deliberately commemorated their ancestor's great feat whenever possible on their own public monuments . . . With the enthusiasm of the newly converted, the Maya adopted this ritual and made it their own. (Schele and Freidel 1990:163)

Hieroglyphic texts at Tikal not only reveal the death of the fourteenth ruler (see figure 4.3c), but also the fact that the Tikal throne remained unoccupied for eighteen months. Evidently multiple claimants were competing to get factional and lineage support. The person who emerged was Yax Nuun Ayiin I, a man who decided to use highland Mexican symbolism to assert his military prowess and foreign connections (in effect, a "stranger-king"). He may have added *yax* to his name upon taking office to signify that he was "first" in a new dynastic line.

The fourteenth Tikal ruler died on January 16, AD 378, which corresponds to 8.17.1.4.12 (11 Eb' 15 Mak) in the Maya calendar. This date was recorded not only at Tikal but at other sites as well. The multiple references to that day, and to the associated event, intrigued Tatiana Proskouriakoff, who dubbed it "the arrival of strangers" (Proskouriakoff 1993:4–8; see also Coggins 1975, 1979). On that day (1) a "stranger" with the name of Sihyaj K'ahk' (figure 4.3b) is said to have arrived, and (2) the fourteenth Tikal ruler is said to have "entered the water" (an apparent euphemism for "he died") (figure 4.3c). Some scholars interpret this co-occurrence as evidence that Sihyaj K'ahk' assassinated the fourteenth Tikal ruler (Martin 2003; Martin and Grube 2008:29). If Sihyaj K'ahk' had killed the fourteenth ruler, one might have expected him to assume the Tikal throne the next day, but he did not. Instead, eighteen months later, Sihyaj K'ahk' installed Yax Nuun Ayiin I. Soon thereafter, other lords were installed at a series of Maya cities (e.g., Uaxactún, Bejucal, Achiotal, and Río Azul) (R.E.W. Adams 1999:15; Borowicz 2003:224; Culbert 1991:130; Estrada-Belli et al. 2009; Laporte 2003; Schele and Freidel 1990).

Yax Nuun Ayiin I asserts that he is the son of Spearthrower Owl, whom David Stuart (2000) links to the ruling house of Teotihuacan. Other scholars, however, doubt that such a distant city could put one of its citizens on the throne of Tikal, especially when one considers that not even the Aztecs, with their powerful armies, could control a huge city 1,000 km away.

The hieroglyphic compound "Spearthrower Owl" (figure 4.4) has been variously interpreted as a reference to (1) a Teotihuacan ruler who was the father of Yax Nuun Ayiin I (Stuart 2000); (2) a military title (Braswell 2003a:24; Schele and Freidel 1990:156–157, 449–450; von Winning 1948, 1987); (3) the effigy of a war god carried by Sihyaj K'ahk' (Nielsen and Helmke 2008:469); (4) an important ancestor who developed into a patron deity (468); and (5) the patron war deity of Teotihuacan or one of the major lineages of the city (2008:470). For differing perspectives on Yax Nuun Ayiin I's life and relationship to other Tikal rulers, see James Borowicz (2003), Geoffrey Braswell (2003a), Joshua Englehardt (2013), Francisco Estrada-Belli and his colleagues (2009), Juan Pedro Laporte and Vilma Fialko C. (1990, 1995), Joyce Marcus (2003), Jesper Nielsen and Christophe Helmke (2008), Schele and Freidel (1990), and Stuart (2000).

The simplest explanation is that Yax Nuun Ayiin I was a Maya usurper who cloaked himself in prestigious foreign attire. Haviland says that Yax

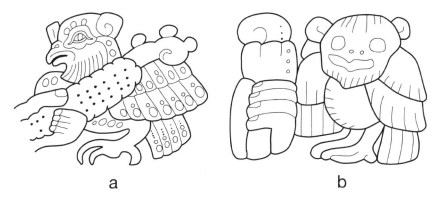

a            b

FIGURE 4.4. *Two examples of Spearthrower Owl compound (drawing by John Klausmeyer from Schele and Freidel 1990:156, 449).*

Nuun Ayiin I grew up at Tikal (cited by Stanley Loten 2007:52), and Braswell (2003a:25–26) suggests that he may have been the child of a female relative of the fourteenth Tikal ruler or someone from a competing lineage at Tikal.

Such intrasite and interlineage jockeying for control may have been brewing long before the fourteenth ruler died at Tikal. Since the various lineages comprising Tikal knew that the fourteenth ruler had no heir, each saw a window of opportunity to seize control (e.g., Braswell 2003a:25–26, Laporte and Fialko C. 1990).

In AD 411, with the accession of Sihyaj Chan K'awiil, we see a ruler interested in reinstating Maya artistic conventions (Borowicz 2003:226). On Tikal's Stela 31, he is shown with his father hovering above him as a protector. "Everything about his headdress connects Sihyaj Chan K'awiil to his ancestors, the old Tikal dynasty, and traditional deities that legitimize rulership" (Borowicz 2003:226).

On both sides of Stela 31 we see Sihyaj Chan K'awiil's father dressed in Mexican military garb. He carries an *atlatl*, feathered darts, and a square shield displaying Tlaloc (see figure 4.5). Schele and Freidel astutely realized that when Maya lords decided to wear Mexican-inspired warrior garb and associate themselves with Tlaloc, those costumes served as important propaganda to their subjects, noting: "If we recall that the Maya utilized their public art for purposes of propaganda, we can see the reasoning behind this costume" (1990:159).

Speaking about the sides of Stela 31, Schele and Freidel (1990:159–160) note that when Sihyaj Chan K'awiil, the sixteenth ruler:

acceded to the throne, he needed to present his father (the forebear upon whom his right to rule depended) in the most powerful light possible. What could be more prestigious than for [the fifteenth ruler Yax Nuun Ayiin I] to appear in the costume worn by [Sihyaj K'ahk'] at the moment of his greatest triumph?

To give the impression that we are seeing [the fifteenth ruler] standing behind his son, [the sixteenth ruler] represented him twice, on opposite sides of the stela. On one side we see the inside of his shield and the outside of his spearthrower; on the other we see the inside of the spearthrower, and the outside of the shield. Upon his shield we see the image of Tlaloc, the goggle-eyed deity that the Maya would come to associate with this particular kind of war and bloodletting ritual.

Few scholars doubt that the lowland Maya had had contact with highland Mexico for centuries prior to AD 445, the year Stela 31 was carved. At Tikal and other sites, there is evidence for trade with highland Mexico with various items imported (e.g., Pachuca obsidian, Thin Orange pottery, and cylindrical tripod vessels). There is evidence of emulation, too, when those nonlocal ceramics were copied using

FIGURE 4.5. *Yax Nuun Ayiin I with mosaic helmet, atlatl, and Tlaloc shield (drawing by John Klausmeyer from Tikal's Stela 31).*

local clays. Excavations in the Mundo Perdido sector of Tikal have exposed buildings in *talud-tablero* style (Laporte and Fialko C. 1990), but they are not exact duplicates of Teotihuacan buildings, because they have different dimensions and *talud*-to-*tablero* proportions. In addition, we now know that the earliest examples of talud-tablero architecture appeared in Tlaxcala, Puebla, the Gulf Coast, Campeche, and Tikal *before* Sihyaj K'ahk' arrived at Tikal. In other words, for more than a century before AD 378, there is evidence that Tikal and the Mexican highlands were in contact (Laporte 2003).

All the monuments carved before AD 378 were later battered, burned, reset in rooms, or moved out from the center of Tikal. It is possible that the ruler Yax Nuun Ayiin I, who started a new dynastic line, ordered that his predecessors' monuments be removed from sight. One stela that was moved from Tikal's central core to a satellite community (Jones and Satterthwaite 1982:108) was missing its uncarved lowest part, presumably because removing that part of the stela lightened the load. Other pre-AD 378 monuments were reset and placed in rooms at Tikal where rituals could be conducted in private (W. Coe 1967, 1990; Jones and Orrego 1987; Jones and Satterthwaite 1982; Just 2005; Martin 2000, 2003).

The monuments of Tikal's sixteenth ruler, Sihyaj Chan K'awiil, show a return to Maya artistic canons: the king is shown in Maya garb; he refers to himself as sixteenth in line; and he features the dynastic founder's name in his headdress. The sixteenth Tikal ruler, like the sixteenth Copán ruler (to be discussed below), invokes the founder in order to legitimize himself and asserts that he is sixteenth in line to suggest that we are witnessing a continuous unbroken genealogical line.

Almost all the texts that refer to the AD 378 event postdate it by several years (e.g., Stelae 4 and 31 at Tikal; the Tikal Marker at Tikal; Stela 22 at Uaxactún). Estrada-Belli and his colleagues (2009:245) note that these texts "present slightly differing narratives on the same historical period by individuals who evidently had different political agendas." One near-contemporaneous text was recorded at La Sufricaya, on the outskirts of Holmul; it was painted during the gap between the death of Tikal's fourteenth ruler and the accession of its fifteenth. When Holmul came under Tikal's control, its royal residence was moved one kilometer from the center of Holmul to La Sufricaya. That royal residence was used for less than a century, circa AD 350 to 450.

One may wonder why Holmul would move the royal residence one kilometer from the site center, only to move it back after less than a century. Evidently a new dynastic line emerged at Holmul, and it needed to start fresh by building its own palace in a new locale. As Estrada-Belli and his colleagues note, the move to La Sufricaya occurred during an era of Tikal control. The palace at La Sufricaya included human figures wearing Mexican-inspired warrior costumes, cylindrical vessels with highland Mexican and lowland Maya motifs, green obsidian blades, and atlatl points.

When Tikal's control over La Sufricaya ended, the Sufricaya palace was buried and its monuments destroyed. In other words, the shift of the palace from downtown Holmul to its outskirts took place when Tikal had control over Holmul and when Tikal evidently favored one of Holmul's lineages over another. After Tikal's defeat at the hands of Calakmul, the La Sufricaya palace was abandoned; the seat of power then returned to Holmul under a royal lineage that was pro-Calakmul and anti-Tikal (Estrada-Belli et al. 2009).

The murals and artifacts from the La Sufricaya palace contribute to our understanding of the political dynamics among cities at different levels of the hierarchy. There was a ripple effect from the top down, from the capital to its subordinate sites. The use of Central Mexican iconography at La Sufricaya thus results not from direct contact with Teotihuacan, but from La Sufricaya's ties to Tikal, whose rulers at that time seem to have been emulating Mexican warrior costumes (Borowicz 2003; Braswell 2003a; Demarest and Foias 1993; Laporte and Fialko C. 1990, 1995; Schele and Freidel 1990; Stone 1989).

Estrada-Belli and his colleagues (2009:254) conclude that "the epigraphy and archaeology of La Sufricaya support the hypothesis that the so-called influx of Central Mexican traits in the southern Maya Lowlands in the Early Classic did not directly emanate from Teotihuacan but was largely related to Tikal's expansion of its political influence at a number of sites, such as Uaxactun, Copan, and Holmul/La Sufricaya." After the La Sufricaya palace was intentionally buried, the site's ties to Tikal ended and Holmul was pulled into the political sphere of Naranjo and Calakmul, two of Tikal's strongest rivals (Marcus 2004a).

CASE 3: YAX K'UK' MO', COPÁN'S DYNASTIC FOUNDER

The first ruler of Copán, who reigned from AD 426 to AD 437, is regarded as a "stranger-king." Later rulers considered him the dynastic founder and mentioned him in their texts. Two of the best-known portraits of this dynastic founder, Yax K'uk' Mo', date to AD 776 (see figures 4.6–4.7). One was found in the inner shrine of Copán's Temple 16, and the other is depicted on the side of Altar Q, a throne-like monument (Agurcia Fasquelle and Fash 2005:236; Marcus 1994). The Altar Q text claims that on September 5, AD 426, a man named K'uk' Mo' took the scepter of office (*k'awiil*) and three days later received his new royal title, K'inich Yax K'uk' Mo' (Martin and Grube 2008). Acquisition of a new name is consistent with his taking the throne (Marcus 2003).

Since K'uk' Mo' was an outsider, he had to legitimize himself by asserting his military experience and prowess. On Altar Q he is depicted wearing a

FIGURE 4.6. *Portrait of Yax K'uk' Mo' from Temple 16, Copán (drawing by John Klausmeyer).*

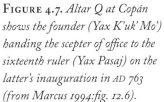

FIGURE 4.7. *Altar Q at Copán shows the founder (Yax K'uk' Mo') handing the scepter of office to the sixteenth ruler (Yax Pasaj) on the latter's inauguration in AD 763 (from Marcus 1994:fig. 12.6).*

rectangular shield on his right forearm and sporting a circle around his eye—a characteristic of Tlaloc, the Central Mexican storm and war god.

Yax K'uk' Mo' behaved in a manner similar to Yax Nuun Ayiin I of Tikal. Both were outside the direct line to rule. Both had to employ creative strategies, because neither could say, "My father was the previous ruler and thus I rule in the same dynastic line."

On Altar Q we read a passage stating that K'uk' Mo' had reached Copán after a trip of five months. In fact, his bone chemistry indicates that he was probably from the Tikal area (Buikstra et al. 2004; Price et al. 2014; Sharer 2003, 2004). Yax K'uk' Mo's skeleton shows that he had survived a number of injuries consistent with past military activity. His battles had left him with three broken ribs (healed), a parry fracture at the midpoint of his right forearm (partially healed), a fractured scapula (partially healed), and a broken fifth metacarpal (Buikstra et al. 2004; Sharer 2003). The rectangular shield on his right forearm probably served to protect his partially healed radius and ulna. By combining AD 437 (his claimed date of death) with biological evidence that he had attained fifty-five to seventy years of age, biological anthropologists have concluded that Yax K'uk' Mo' was in his forties when he became the king of Copán. That he was of noble birth is suggested not only by his cranial deformation, but also by the jade inlays in some of his teeth. While we will never know all the details of Yax K'uk' Mo's life, his story suggests an analogy with other usurpers who used their military skills to take over a throne at some distance from their place of birth. Yax K'uk' Mo' further cemented his position by marrying a noble Copán woman.

On the same day that K'uk' Mo' received his new royal name, he further aggrandized himself by incorporating Quiriguá into his Copán polity. A hieroglyphic text at Quiriguá states that that city's first official ruler took office under the auspices of Yax K'uk' Mo'. This simultaneous installation of rulers suggests that Yax K'uk' Mo' had put someone he trusted in charge of Quiriguá, making the latter city a secondary center in his administrative hierarchy.

As mentioned above, Yax K'uk' Mo' also legitimized himself by marrying an important Copán woman. Her tomb is the richest and most elaborate of all those found at Copán (Sharer 1999, 2003), and her bone chemistry indicates that (unlike Yax K'uk' Mo') she was native to the Copán Valley. The son and heir of Yax K'uk' Mo', known as Ruler 2 of Copán, kept his mother's tomb open in order to make future offerings. This woman's spectacular funerary offerings make sense if she was simultaneously the daughter of a noble Copán family, the wife of Yax K'uk' Mo', and the mother of Ruler 2.

Yax K'uk' Mo' engaged in the kind of ambitious building program typical of a usurper who seeks legitimization (Marcus 2004b). During his short reign (AD 426–437) he constructed platforms and public structures that served as the template and prototype for subsequent rulers. He established a plaza and building complex (the Copán Acropolis) that provided the backdrop for

400 years of royal activities such as inaugurations and funerals. Yax K'uk' Mo' and his successors ultimately administered a state that remained large until April 29, AD 738, the day Quiriguá's ruler turned on Copán and captured the Copán lord. As a result of this victory Quiriguá achieved its independence, and from that time onward embarked on its own ambitious flurry of construction and monument carving. Despite their shrinking realm, later rulers at Copán continued to link themselves to Yax K'uk' Mo', founder of the dynasty.

The AD 426 arrival of Yax K'uk' Mo' at Copán resulted in the founding of a new dynasty and construction of the first palace on new, sacred ground (Stuart and Schele 1986; Traxler 2004). Once established, this new location maintained its significance until the end of the Copán dynasty. Hunal, the structure containing the burial of the dynastic founder, remained the focal point for subsequent superimposed temples (Sharer 1999, 2003).

Copán qualifies as a secondary state, one that split off from a preexisting state rather than arising from a competing set of prestate polities (Marcus 2004b). Some 350 years after the Calakmul and Tikal states had arisen, Copán rose to prominence under a usurper who apparently arrived in the Copán Valley from the Tikal area. He was already familiar with statecraft. Yax K'uk' Mo' used his military skills to take over the throne, arranged an advantageous political marriage to a local princess, undertook a policy of ambitious public building, and launched a campaign of military expansion to legitimize himself. Although he reigned for little more than a decade, this usurper's impact on Copán was so enduring that 350 years later he was still featured on monuments carved for the last couple of rulers of the city.

Yax K'uk' Mo's Tlaloc iconography and military costume helped establish him as a "stranger-king." One consequence was that Copán abandoned its preexisting highland-Guatemala-inspired earthen architecture and adopted stone masonry architecture with strong ties to Tikal (Traxler 2003, 2004).

CASE 4: YAX PASAJ CHAN YOPAAT, THE SIXTEENTH RULER AT COPÁN

In AD 763 the sixteenth Copán ruler Yax Pasaj Chan Yopaat took office (see figure 4.7). On Altar Q he named and depicted the fifteen rulers who had preceded him. Near Altar Q he created a crypt to hold fifteen jaguars, one for each ruler. Yax Pasaj is seated next to the dynastic founder, receiving the scepter of office directly from him (Marcus 1976:fig. 4.48).

The overall impact of Altar Q and the associated crypt with its fifteen jaguars was certainly powerful. Yax Pasaj was asserting: "I am in an unbroken line of rulers that I can trace back to the founder." However, since he was not in fact the son of the fifteenth ruler, his texts featured his mother, who was his most prominent parent. She was a noblewoman from Palenque named Chak Nik Ye' Xook.

Yax Pasaj's monuments constitute a departure from those of previous rulers. Several of his texts were incorporated into the temples and buildings he commissioned. He decorated the last version of Temple 16 with portraits of the founder Yax K'uk' Mo' and with images of Tlaloc (Fash and Fash 2000; Sharer 1999, 2003; Taube 2004c; Traxler 2001).

## TEOTIHUACAN AND THE MAYA

As we learn more about the relationships between the Maya and the Central Mexican highlands, they become far more interesting than any simplistic "Teotihuacan influence" model. Both areas responded to multiple internal and external factors. External factors include visitors and funeral attendees coming from many directions and sites, as well as objects being traded into and out of those regions for centuries (e.g., Demarest and Foias 1993; Laporte 2003; Marcus 2003). Internal processes included emulation of foreign objects, motifs, and iconographic layouts that were adopted and modified over time. The number of ethnic groups that lived along the route between Teotihuacan and the Maya area is so great that we will need decades of excavation at many intervening sites—as well as different types of network, nodal, and Geographic Information Systems analyses—to understand all the trading partners, middlemen, trade routes, and pathways.

Emulation, as well as the long-term process of adapting and modifying foreign elements, needs to be more fully understood if we hope to explain the periodic and sporadic appearance of nonlocal elements in Maya art (e.g., Braswell 2003a, 2003b; Marcus 2003; Taube 2003b; Varela Torrecilla and Braswell 2003). And it is becoming clear that moments of political usurpation often provided the impetus for such emulation.

## COMPETITION BETWEEN ROYAL LINEAGES
## AS A MOTIVATION FOR USURPATION

Not all usurpation was by "stranger-kings"; the usurper could come from another lineage within the same polity. For an example of how deadly such rivalries could be, we need only look at the case of the Xiu and Cocom lineages at the city of Mayapán (Roys 1943, 1962).

The Xiu are said to have staged a revolt against the Cocom, killing everyone from the Cocom ruling house except for one prince who was away on a trading expedition to Honduras. Mayapán shows evidence of this revolt in the form of burning, looting, and destruction. When the son of the slain Cocom ruler returned from his travels, he gathered his subjects and established a new capital at Sotuta, near their old city of Chichén Itzá. Although some of the victorious Xiu celebrated their victory by continuing to reside at Mayapán, they also established a new capital at Mani.

Three generations later, in AD 1536, the current Xiu ruler decided that it was an auspicious time to leave Mani and undertake a pilgrimage to the Sacred Cenote at Chichén Itzá. To reach their destination, however, he and his contingent had to pass through Cocom territory. Thus the Xiu ruler applied for safe conduct from Nachi Cocom, the ruler of Sotuta.

The Xiu ruler undoubtedly feared reprisal by Nachi Cocom, since the former's great-grandfather had led the revolt that killed the latter's great-grandfather. Nevertheless, the Cocom ruler promised the Xiu safe passage through Sotuta. Thus the Xiu ruler, along with his son and forty others, set out for Chichén Itzá.

The Cocom ruler and his retinue met the Xiu a few kilometers southeast of Sotuta. The pilgrims were treated by the Cocom to four days of lavish banquets. Then, at the final banquet on the fourth day, the Cocom suddenly massacred all the Xiu visitors. This act of long-delayed revenge initiated a new round of wars between lineages that helped pave the way for the Spaniards to conquer local polities.

Intense rivalries between royal lineages may have set the stage for earlier Maya usurpations. We have already seen that the political struggle among local Holmul lineages was resolved in favor of the lineage favored by Tikal. We have also seen that the sudden appearance of Central Mexican iconography at La Sufricaya was probably the result of the new lineage being exposed to that material during an accession ritual held at Tikal (Estrada-Belli et al. 2009). Our current data from La Sufricaya, Uaxactún, Río Azul, Copán, and Tikal support the notion that the appearance of Central Mexican traits resulted largely from Tikal's interference on behalf of specific lineages at those cities. As a result, when places such as Holmul came under the sway of Naranjo and Calakmul—two of Tikal's major rivals—the Teotihuacan motifs disappeared.

Similar scenarios may apply to two other usurpers—Yax Nuun Ayiin at Tikal and Yax K'uk' Mo' at Copán—both of whom seem to have needed outside backing. We should be suspicious when we see that a new ruler's accession rite took place at a city other than his own, or when his palace or burial ritual was relocated. Holmul's royal residence, for example, was relocated to La Sufricaya when the lineage favored by Tikal prevailed. Even at

Tikal itself, the burial ground for rulers was moved from Mundo Perdido to the North Acropolis as one dynastic line took over from another (Laporte and Fialko C. 1990, 1995).

## STRATEGIES OF USURPATION

Ten of the strategies used by Maya usurpers or "stranger-kings" included

1. sporting Tlaloc goggles or circles,
2. holding atlatls and rectangular shields,
3. wearing other Mexican-inspired warrior garb, including mosaic shell helmets,
4. taking prisoners,
5. commissioning ambitious programs of construction,
6. commissioning new texts,
7. marrying prominent local women,
8. acquiring new territory through conquest or diplomacy,
9. taking a new name that may include *yax* (first), and
10. traveling to shrines on a ritual circuit before being crowned as king.

Since the four yax individuals (Yax K'uk' Mo', Yax Pasaj Chan Yopaat, Yax Ehb Xook, and Yax Nuun Ayiin) were not in direct line to rule, they faced the challenge of establishing legitimacy when starting a new dynastic line. They used multiple strategies—depicting themselves in Mexican-inspired warrior costumes, establishing alliances with powerful and supportive leaders at other sites, marrying local noblewomen, and making pilgrimages to other sites to participate in sacred rites.

Two of the many important processes were emulation and alliance formation. Emulation was an active, selective, and powerful process. Usurpers emulated others held in high regard, especially military heroes. Alliances and partnerships with many sites (not simply Teotihuacan) were also critical for a usurper to stay on the throne.

The sporadic appearance of Central Mexican motifs in Maya art was once regarded as evidence of intermittent trade or influence. Now we have reason to believe that such motifs were selected by usurpers in need of legitimization, men who chose Central Mexican symbolism to associate themselves with a region famed for its military prowess (Braswell 2003a; Schele and Freidel 1990; Stone 1989, Taube 1992b).

# 5

Twenty-five years ago, Linda Schele and David Freidel published a book (1990) that synthesized epigraphic breakthroughs, comprehensive iconographic analyses, and archaeological data in an approach unique in archaeology at that time. The authors' use of a narrative voice made the tome accessible to a wide audience beyond an exclusively academic readership. It was simultaneously captivating and controversial to some, and it set a new standard for an archaeology that embraced the history of a pre-European people in the Americas as told by its rulers. In the years that have followed, our understanding of the dynamic Classic period has evolved commensurate with new discoveries, enhanced epigraphic readings, more robust ethnographic and ethnoarchaeological analogies, trace element analyses, and an ever-broadening corpus of context-based iconographic material. As these new insights challenge existing understandings of ancient Maya political history and as our interpretations become increasingly nuanced by implementing more sophisticated technological and theoretical approaches, we can still look to *A Forest of Kings* as a hallmark for how to convey features of this ancient corner of the world to a broader public with an effort to frame the narrative in a way that approaches cultural logics of the ancient Maya.

While skepticism in our field is healthy, having the vision to consider interpretive possibilities that test the boundaries of current or accepted knowledge also

*Forest of Queens*

*The Legacy of Royal Calakmul Women at El Perú–Waka's Central Civic-Ceremonial Temple*

Olivia C. Navarro-Farr, Griselda Pérez Robles, Damaris Menéndez, and Juan Carlos Pérez Calderón

DOI: 10.5876/9781646420469.c005

permits innovative and sometimes controversial perspectives; this is what Linda Schele would have called "edge-walking." What results is the kind of challenge that keeps our thinking fresh and our consideration of ancient Maya people worthy of their rich heritage. That we should aim to strike a balance of interpretation that considers multiple lines of evidence and emphasizes continued consultation with Maya people as Schele and Freidel did is another standard they set in this book. In the following chapter, we consider new data on the complex Late Classic relationship between the Kaanul realm, then seated at Calakmul, and El Perú–Waka' (henceforth Waka'). Recent research at Waka' (figure 5.1) underscores the role of royal women of Kaanul from the ways they were memorialized as ancestresses. We argue these queens, consorts, and mothers were key to Kaanul's hegemonic success at Waka' and beyond, a position that has only more recently been emphasized in our literature (Ardren 2002; Baron 2013, 2016b; Freidel 2014b; Freidel and Guenter 2003; Looper and Polyukhovych 2016; Marcus 1973, 1976, 2001; Martin 2008b; Martin and Grube 2008; Reese-Taylor et al. 2009; Teufel 2008). We therefore add our voice to these scholars who have advanced beyond generally androcentric emphases on the roles and actions of kings, situating males as prime movers, actors, and generators of political intrigue. The fact that the epigraphic record registers far more references to powerful males has led researchers, understandably, to see men more vividly in the ancient Maya world. In our view, this fact may influence our perception of the scope of influence the less frequently mentioned royal women of Classic Maya political life may have had. Textual and visual references to mothers and consorts notwithstanding, representations of royal women of undisputable power are far less frequent. Nevertheless, limited mention of powerful women should not precondition our thinking about their political abilities nor limit our ability to discern how they shaped their world. We follow early efforts by Schele and Freidel in *A Forest of Kings*, who brought great royal women such as Lady K'abal Xooc and Lady Six Sky to life. We believe the evidence we discuss here underscores how royal women at Waka', just as men, actively shaped their afterlife narratives in unique ways that framed their own enduring legacies and highlighted their sense of their own political significance. We believe the activities that made a sequence thus far retraced at Structure M13-1 were meaningfully connected, in significant part, to memory work (Mills and Walker 2008) surrounding two important royal women each connected to both the snake and Waka' dynasts.

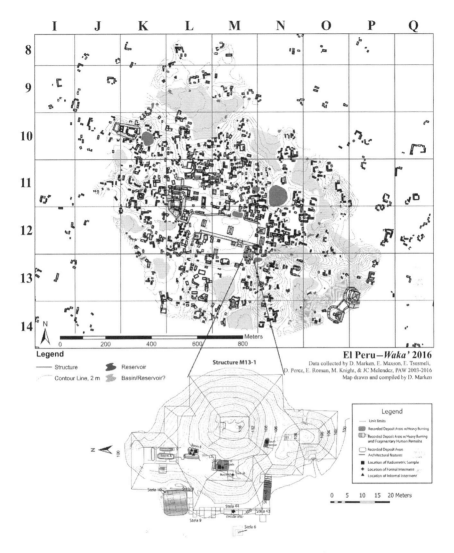

FIGURE 5.1. *Waka' 2016 site map (after Marken et al. 2017:fig. 9.1) with plan of Structure M13-1 (drawing by E. Tsesmeli and modified by O. Navarro-Farr) including excavation units, some exposed architecture, and select excavated features. All images and photographs pertain to the Proyecto Arqueológico Waka'; all images are courtesy of the Ministry of Culture and Sports of Guatemala.*

## A BRIEF HISTORY

In their chapter "Star Wars in the Seventh Century," Schele and Freidel outline the details of the major warring rivals of the period; key figures in this discussion include Tikal, Caracol, Naranjo, and Dos Pilas. Based on exciting breakthroughs in epigraphic decipherments at the time in conjunction with existing iconographic and archaeological data, the authors reference Calakmul's role in the seventh-century wars in the following ways: (1) Calakmul likely inherited the power/status of El Mirador following that site's decline; (2) it was a long-standing rival of Tikal; (3) the ajaw of Calakmul identified as *Cu-Ix* was instrumental in installing Naranjo's Ruler 1 on the throne; and (4) the influence of the Calakmul king was far flung. At the close of this chapter the authors mulled over evidence but ultimately bowed to the constraints of the existing data set. Schele and Freidel were of course correct in surmising that the role of Calakmul in these competing alliances was great; in the last twenty-five years much has come to light about the role of what is now widely referred to as the Kaanul realm. These new insights stem from tremendous breakthroughs in the nuances of decipherment (Martin 2005; Martin and Grube 2008), analyses ranging from chemical composition of ceramics (Blackman and Bishop 2007) to bone chemistry (Piehl 2008, 2009; Price et al. 2007, 2008; Wright 2005), developments in the study of economic systems (Braswell 2010), water and land management (Fedick 1996; Gunn et al. 2002, 2014), paleoethnobotany (Cagnato et al. 2013; Morehart and Morrell-Hart 2015), and the continuing archaeological research at Calakmul (Carrasco Vargas et al. 1999; Folan 1992; Folan et al. 1995), Uxul (Grube et al. 2012), La Corona (Baron 2013; Canuto and Barrientos 2013), Waka' (Navarro-Farr and Rich 2014; Navarro-Farr et al. 2013; Pérez Robles and Navarro-Farr 2013), and a host of other sites bearing data relevant to the Kaanul realm and the events defining the Late Classic now increasingly considered a "Golden Age." Recent evidence from Waka' sheds further light on these events with particular emphasis on the role of royal Kaanul women in the creation and maintenance of its important relationship with that realm. In this chapter, we discuss multiple discoveries at Waka's central civic-ceremonial shrine, Structure M13-1, and evidence from a royal tomb excavated at Waka's Northwest Palace (Lee 2005). Together, these findings undergird our central thesis that royal women were memorialized in these important locales, demonstrating they served a pivotal role in the successful creation and maintenance of the Kaanul regime at Waka'. We do not intend to paint ancient Maya royal women, or indeed ancient Maya women in general, with broad strokes. We do seek to critically examine the long-held default position in our discipline that cedes agency to males without commensurate evaluation of how women contributed in both overt and subtle ways to the creation and maintenance of political and economic structures (see Halperin 2017). The data we draw upon here speak specifically to the political and economic power attributed to Kaanul during the Late Classic and how a line of Kaanul origin royal women made enduring contributions to its memory and power.

Structure M13-1 (see figure 5.1) is one of two true *adosada* shrine pyramids at Waka' (Freidel et al. 2013). Attached fronting platforms, rare in the Maya area, abound at Teotihuacan. The connection noted by Fash and colleagues (2009) between adosadas and new fire ceremonialism at Teotihuacan and, based on architectural and iconographic evidence, at Copán was intriguing to us in view of one other line of evidence at Structure M13-1. Ian Graham's (Escobedo and Freidel 2004; Graham 1971, 1988) documented a well-preserved stela fragment (Stela 9) at this building featuring a ruler standing atop a *kaak witz*, or fire mountain. Stanley P. Guenter (2005) later noted a finely incised text adjacent to that ruler's legs referencing a *wite' naah*—Mayan for fire shrine. Stela 9 fragments had been dragged to Structure M13–1 in antiquity and were recorded in association with dense deposit activities marking the building's final century or so of use. This deliberate behavior involving the movement of this massive fragment with a textual reference to a wite' naah and the building's apparent adosada prompted hypothesizing, following William Fash and his colleagues (2009), that there might be iconographic evidence for a fire shrine atop the Structure M13-1 adosada. Excavations from the 2012 (Navarro-Farr et al. 2013) and 2013 (Pérez Robles and Navarro-Farr 2013) field seasons were designed to test this hypothesis by (1) defining the exterior of the adosada feature, and (2) assessing the adosada's construction history. Excavations yielded rich data including two previously unknown reset Late Classic stelae (43 and 44) each referencing a previously unknown Early Classic royal woman of Kaanul affiliation, Lady Ikoom. Additionally, we discovered a monumental hearth dominating the adosada's summit, which, following its final use, was ritually infilled with a massive deposit of fragmentary modeled stucco facade elements. Finally, in our assessment of the adosada's construction history, we discovered a royal burial, which we believe housed the remains of the Late Classic Kaloomte' K'abel, a princess originating from the dynasty seated at Calakmul who married Waka's then ruler Kinich Bahlam II.

In the following, we discuss these and other related findings and follow with a brief discussion of the features unique to Kaanul power strategies, focusing on the roles of royal women. While acknowledging the contributions of gendered studies to our understanding of its intersection with statecraft, we nevertheless encourage continued work on this front. Preliminarily, we suggest that our scholarly approach to the strategies employed by the snake dynasts of Kaanul might be better framed by (1) the use of gender-neutral language, and (2) a more meaningful acknowledgment of and theorizing about the contributions of royal women as integral to Kaanul strategies of statecraft. We follow Reese-Taylor and her colleagues (2009), positing that this gender-inclusive approach to power acquisition was both deliberate and apparently unique to the Kaanul dynasts, particularly during the Late Classic. This proposition should be tested in future research.

## EARLY DISCOVERIES AT STRUCTURE M13-1

Initial investigation of Structure M13-1 revealed massive and dense surface deposits blanketing the terminal phase architecture; these artifact accumulations, representative of diverse and cumulative ceremonies, were particularly concentrated at the associated plaza floor level on both the northern and southern sides of the building's terminal staircase (Navarro-Farr 2009; Navarro-Farr et al. 2013). The wide range of contents incorporated is discussed elsewhere, as are arguments outlining why they do not constitute de facto refuse or postoccupational squatter's or residential debris (see Navarro-Farr 2009). Ceramic-based dates (Eppich 2009a, 2010) indicate these activities accumulated throughout the Late–Terminal Classic period, roughly AD 780–950. Epigraphically, the Late to Terminal Classic is coeval with the placement of the site's last stela in the late eighth century. The depositional episodes that resulted in these accumulations thus roughly correspond with the decline of the site's royal court. Navarro-Farr (2009) has argued that these performances were conducted under the auspices of an organized but nonroyal authority to ensure the maintenance of balance in the midst of the dissolution of dynastic rule. The deposits are the accumulations of ceremonial residues from at least 150 years and reveal the dynamics of Late to Terminal Classic Wakeños performing during a time of increased uncertainty. Given the significant memory associated with this shrine, as attested by these rich deposits, research during the 2012 season was designed to investigate the building's adosada and its construction sequence to contextualize the motivations of Wakeños for having so richly adorned its base with ritual paraphernalia throughout this period. Excavations focused on exposure of the platform's terminal façade while defining that platform's superstructure architecture, construction sequence, and chronology. It was during these defining excavations that the true breadth and scope of social and ritual memory associated with Structure M13-1 became much clearer. Evidence demonstrated a heavy emphasis on symbolic capital and reliance on organized labor to execute a series of iconographic statements revealed by the careful positioning of fragmentary Late and Early Classic stelae. Work on the exposure of and excavation into the summit of that platform revealed further evidence for ritual activity, buried construction, a royal tomb, and other repositioned monuments and a stela. The context of these findings and a brief review of our current (and provisional) interpretations follow below.

## STELAE 9 AND 43 AND THE CIRCULAR MONUMENT

At the outset of this discussion of data and key findings, it is important to state that comprehensive iconographic and epigraphic readings of these and the other monuments discussed here are still ongoing. Moreover, a great deal of additional discussion involving the context of their placement (both spatially and sociopolitically) is certainly warranted. Nevertheless, a comprehensive discussion of this nature, though necessary, is beyond the scope of this chapter. Therefore, at present, mention is made of the discoveries primarily to thread their significance into the remainder of the key finds discussed herein.

While defining the terminal phase adosada architecture, excavations on the northern and southern ends of this feature revealed nine previously unknown monument fragments, eight of which were reset into the final terrace (figure 5.2). On the north end, we recovered three additional fragments of the Early Classic Stela 9 (discussed above), whose known fragments had been reassembled on the associated Plaza 2 in 2004 (Navarro-Farr 2005). Additional pieces of Stela 9 were discovered atop the plaza floor and set into the northern and northwestern faces of the adosada walls. The recovered fragments each include vivid imagery; on the north face, a small section reveals the profile face of a human figure emerging from a maize plant. The fragment on the northwestern face is so massive, it could scarcely be moved (it was encountered having fallen forward, and a crew of eighteen men with a makeshift tripod and crank was required simply to restore the monument fragment to a standing position). This fragment was the uppermost section featuring a massive headdress with a bird at its center—likely representing a back-rack (figure 5.2a) that would have adorned the standing ruler.

A circular monument (figure 5.2b) was also discovered beneath the final central staircase fronting the adosada. It may be associated with an additional semiexcavated circular monument revealed in a tunnel investigation that appears smaller but is still only partially exposed. We have yet to define that monument nor do we understand its relationship (if any) with the circular

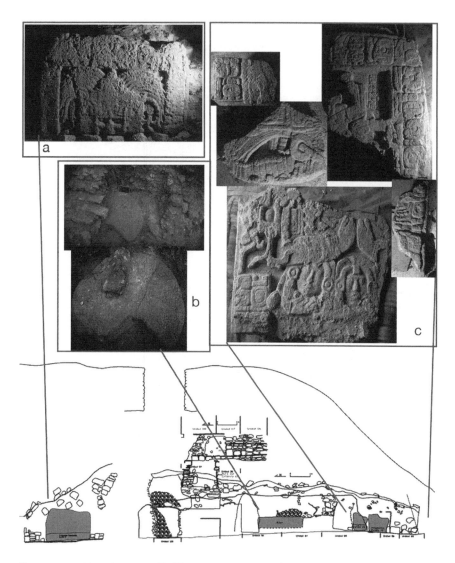

**Figure 5.2.** *East-facing profile (drawing by J. C. Pérez) of Structure M13-1's terminal adosada wall: (a) upper section of Stela 9 seen reset into upright position (photos by F. Castañeda); (b) circular altar including a view of in situ terminal phase stair risers overlying the monument (photos by F. Castañeda); (c) fragments of Stela 43 seen adorning the south and southwest basal faces of the terminal adosada walls (photos by F. Castañeda and S. Guenter). All images and photographs pertain to the Proyecto Arqueológico Waka'; all images are courtesy of the Ministry of Culture and Sports of Guatemala.*

monument described briefly here. We posit that both circular monuments were placed prior to the construction of the final stela-adorned adosada and, therefore, possibly in association with the construction of Structure M13-1 Adosada Sub I. The exposed circular monument beneath the final stair risers yielded hieroglyphic texts that were rather eroded, necessitating their photography by night. We have yet to complete a reading on this monument, though its form and its close proximity to the other circular monument suggest a calendric function, though that is speculative.

Five additional stela fragments were concentrated on the south end of the adosada, adorning the southwest and south terrace walls; these all correspond to the previously unrecorded Stela 43 (figure 5.2c). The two largest fragments were found positioned side by side adorning the terminal adosada terrace wall facing west near the south end of that wall. These fragments feature a ruler's torso with arms bearing a ceremonial bundle with hands in the crab-claw position. The ruler wears a belt with two jade masks (a third is missing). An open serpent maw is seen emerging from the ceremonial bundle with the section corresponding to what was originally seen emerging from the serpent's maw having been snapped off at some earlier time. The open maw was positioned to be juxtaposed with the image on the adjacent stela fragment reset upside down so that the water lily nibbling fish motif on the headdress can be seen emerging from the ancestral serpent figure. Two additional fragments of this monument were recovered on the south face of this terminal adosada wall. One of these two was recovered adorning the base of the south-facing wall. This fragment had been considerably thinned such that only the carved surface remained and was set into the wall against the underlying ballast. The image was affixed in place with a generous layer of plaster and surrounded by carefully cut stones along the top. This piece featured part of the ruler's headdress, neck, and earspool (see figure 5.2c). The other, a much smaller block, was retrieved from excavation of surrounding collapse and included the fringed edges of feathers pertaining to the end of a feathered headdress as well as a glyph block and the number 14. Although retrieved from surrounding collapse, due to its position wedged into a nearby tree root, it is likely that it too had been set deliberately into an upper section of the south-facing final terrace wall that had subsequently collapsed due to the intervening root. The fifth fragment was the smallest piece and was discovered in the collapse surrounding the southwest corner of the terminal adosada.

Preliminary analysis indicates this stela dates to AD 702. The figure composite itself, though fragmentary, features a standing male ruler facing toward his left (see Castañeda 2013 for more on this), who is likely K'inich Bahlam

II. Although this name does not survive on any of the known fragments, he was the king ruling on this date. The dedicatory date of the stela in the ancient Maya calendar was 7 Ahau 3 Cumku (January 20, AD 702) and commemorates the day 7 Ahau. Two earlier iterations of 7 Ahau were also commemorated in the text of Stela 43, including the *katun* endings 7 Ahau 3 Xul (August 29, AD 317) and 7 Ahau 3 Kankin (December 3, AD 573). The 573 date is also associated with a woman named on the stela as Lady Ikoom. At the time of discovery of Stela 43, this reference to Lady Ikoom was too isolated and decontextualized to permit a more solid determination of who this woman was. We could only presume that she was likely an important female figure in the larger dynastic history of Waka'. We would come to learn much more about her later in our investigations. These fragments also show that the stela was dedicated under the suzerainty of the snake king, Yuknoom Took K'awiil, whose rule extended from AD 702 to AD 731 (Martin and Grube 2008).

These massive monument fragments were repositioned to either adorn the adosada façade at the building's base or, in the case of the circular monuments, may have been placed in dedication to an earlier phase of the adosada. Together, they exhibit some of the most colossal efforts on part of the Late and Late–Terminal Classic populations (the latter of which may not have been acting under the authority of the royal court in the post AD 801 period) to manipulate architecture and reshape material narratives vis-à-vis their positioning as described above. The significance of these and other components of the archaeological record of this final built phase and the rituals associated with them warrant much lengthier discussions elsewhere.

### STRUCTURE M13-1 ADOSADA SUMMIT EXCAVATIONS

The intervention of this building, initiated via the summit of the final adosada platform, was a nearly three-month-long process that yielded several striking discoveries further illuminating the long use-life of the building and its deep ceremonial significance. The summit of the platform was used as a monumental hearth, a true fire shrine, which underscored the significance of the Stela 9 fragment referencing a wite' naah (figure 5.3). The complication is one of chronology. The wite' naah reference on Stela 9 dates to the sixth century. The dating of the monumental hearth is more complicated, as the stratigraphic position of the feature with respect to the earlier phases suggests construction and use of the space and feature spanned the eighth-ninth centuries. However, radiocarbon dates from wood samples retrieved from the fire shrine's various burning layers indicate dates spanning the early to middle

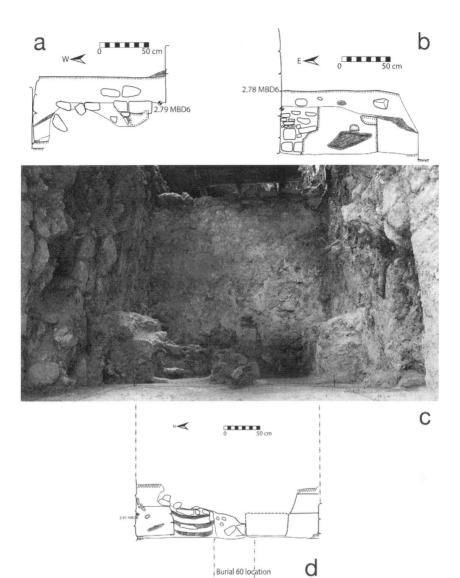

FIGURE 5.3. *Fire Shrine—three views: (a) illustration of north wall of fire shrine interior (drawing by O. Navarro-Farr); (b) illustration of south wall of fire shrine interior (drawing by O. Navarro-Farr); (c) excavated fire shrine looking west (photo by J. C. Pérez); (d) illustration of east wall of fire shrine interior including location of burial 60 (drawing by O. Navarro-Farr). All images and photographs pertain to the Proyecto Arqueológico Waka'; all images are courtesy of the Ministry of Culture and Sports of Guatemala.*

seventh century (Cagnato 2015). One possibility for the unusually early dates of the fire shrine is the old wood effect. Clarissa Cagnato (2015) has noted many wood fragments featured paint layers. The suggestion is that the burned items may constitute relics that would not only explain the old wood effect but constitute an intriguing proposition. This time difference between the use of the fire shrine and the sixth-century textual reference to a wite' naah on Stela 9 is significant in that it reveals eighth-ninth century Wakeños understood and drew upon this much earlier reference. In other words, we believe those who replaced this Stela 9 fragment in this location understood its significance in relation to fire ceremony and endeavored to connect this textual reference with activities on the Structure M13-1 adosada summit. We also believe the choice to build this late shrine atop the same platform encompassing an important royal burial (discussed below) demonstrates how these findings are linked and suggest the interred was inextricably tied to this fire shrine.

The fire shrine, itself utilized multiple times, was subsequently sealed, or "terminated," by being completely infilled with façade fragments of modeled stucco. The fire shrine had also been dedicated with the intrusion burial (Burial 60) of a rather humbly adorned individual whose remains were rather poorly preserved. In spite of the scarcity of observable evidence, Erin Patterson (2013) determined the individual was likely a middle-aged adult. Additionally, the lack of cranial elements, with the exception of twelve teeth, suggested to Patterson that the cranium was removed at some point following interment. The teeth, though relatively few in number, indicated the individual's health was relatively good.

The entire fire shrine platform was built over a previously existing and exposed set of stairs leading to a double-chambered set of narrow I-shaped rooms. We recorded the easternmost of this two-room space, dubbing it Structure M13-1 Adosada Sub I. Below, we encountered the buried staircase corresponding to the earlier Structure M13-1 Adosada Sub II, which housed the interment of one of Waka's most celebrated rulers.

## BURIAL 61

In exposing the façade of the buried Adosada Sub II, excavators encountered a chamber filled with collapsed debris of a naturally collapsed floor from above. After stabilizing the area, we cleared and screened the debris and encountered a series of flagstones forming a cyst within a four-sided masonry chamber. This chamber was built into the staircase fronting the façade of Structure M13-1 Adosada Sub II just north of that building's centerline. Following the creation

FIGURE 5.4. *Photogrammetric composite image of Burial 61 (image created by F. Castañeda). All images and photographs pertain to the Proyecto Arqueológico Waka'; all images are courtesy of the Ministry of Culture and Sports of Guatemala.*

of this chamber and the accompanying mortuary ceremony, Structure M13-1 Adosada Sub I was constructed. We return to this construction activity later.

Buried in this built chamber were the remains of an adult of advanced age interred with a considerable amount of carved jades, shell, numerous perishable artifacts, and various ceramic offerings that Keith Eppich (2012) dates to the early to mid-eighth century (figure 5.4). An exhaustive description of the tomb contents is impossible presently, so we will proceed with a summary of key components of the assemblage as well as brief descriptions of the layout and mortuary patterns we think bear a strong resemblance with Calakmul Structure II Tomb 4 (henceforth referred to as CSII-T4).

It is important to begin the discussion of mortuary evidence associated with Burial 61 with the disclaimer that the comprehensive cleaning, restoration, and analysis of these materials are ongoing and that any current hypotheses based on the present evidence are necessarily provisional. That said, we lay out some patterns that resemble those seen in CSII-T4 and that such resemblances may suggest cultural affiliation. One of the largest vessels is a polychrome flat-based plate with a large kill hole that was placed painted side down over the individual's upper left torso; its positioning suggests the interred was wielding a shield. Its form and design are Late Classic (Eppich 2012) and noted on stylistic basis to bear close resemblance with Calakmul assemblages (Dorie Reents-Budet, personal communication, 2012). The interior rim includes a decorative band of cormorants similar to some Kerr collection vessels that were produced between the seventh century and early eighth. This vessel also bears striking resemblance in terms of its composition, painting style, and iconographic motif to a vessel included among the offerings associated with the CSII-T4 interment believed to be that of Yuknoom Yich'aak K'ak' (Carrasco Vargas et al. 1999), ruler of Calakmul between AD 686 and AD 695, who may have been K'abel's brother. In general, we believe the ceramic assemblage, which included a series of stacked bowls covered with stucco painted in Maya blue, various black-slipped Late Classic bowls, a black-slipped Chilar Fluted cylinder vessel, and the large plate bearing cormorant iconography typical of Calakmul also resemble ceramics included in CSII-T4 and *may* distinguish her as a Kaanul affiliate.

We also recovered a small figurine worn by frequent use face down in the pelvis. It may represent a fetish for divinatory practices. Red cinnabar paint surrounds the creature's neck, possibly referencing the God Akan (Grube 2004a), one of the city's patron deities (Guenter 2005, 2014c), in an act of self-decapitation. Numerous jade and shell beads and other ornaments were found near the chest and throughout the headdress area. Among these was a small jade head located near the chest and a tubular bead near the right arm. This long tubular jade bead incorporates a carved mirror motif Stuart characterizes as "a more general marker of shining and resplendent surfaces" (2010a:291) and tentatively reads the logogram as *LEM* with the Mayan root "to shine" (291). The left arm and hand were flexed and positioned over the chest beneath the overturned shield-like polychrome platter. Conversely, the individual in CSII-T4 is arranged with the right forearm crossed over the chest and the left arm over the abdomen (Carrasco Vargas et al. 1999); in mirror opposition to the arrangement in Burial 61.

A small alabaster jar carved in the form of a shell features the emerging head and arm of an aged human figure and the texts engraved proved key to identifying the interred. A series of four glyphs appears from atop the jar, starting from its tiny lid and continuing down the back side. Stanley Guenter (see Navarro-Farr et al. 2013) reads the first as *yotoot*, or "the house of." The second glyph references the original vessel contents. Unfortunately, the second sign is not currently deciphered. The vessel owner's name appears in the two final glyphs: the first translates as "Lady Water lily hand." The final glyph is a feminine version of the Calakmul emblem glyph. The reading is of Ix Kan Ajaw, or "Great Serpent Lady," and the identification is the name Lady Water Lily Hand as a princess of Calakmul (Navarro-Farr et al. 2013, 2016). This is an alternative form of writing Lady K'abel, as both names consist of water lilies sustained by a hand and they are both named as princesses of Calakmul. The personal nature of this vessel suggests that the remains in Burial 61 are of the same Lady K'abel. Moreover, the presence of a large *Spondylus* bivalve over the pelvis mimics the *xoc* shell seen on Lady K'abel's waist on her Stela

34 portrait, now in the Cleveland Museum of Art (see Acuña 2014:fig. 3.3b). Unfortunately, the deterioration of the pelvis prevented definite sexing (Patterson 2013). Erin Patterson (2013) noted the remains yielded ambiguous traits and scored the nuchal crest as a five on the Jane Buikstra and Douglas Ubelaker (1994) scale, a more robust expression of that element. Nevertheless, Patterson notes (2013), the robusticity present on select elements such as the nuchal crest and the linea aspera can just as likely have resulted from a particularly active female as from a male (itself an interesting pattern). Patterson (2013) determined the individual was advanced in age, based on dental wear, cranial suture closure, and arthritic lesions.

The cementing of the vessels onto the funerary bench surface indicated the chamber was built immediately prior to burial. This fortuitous circumstance permitted the recovery of impressions of perishables such as a woven mat and bolts of fabric covering the newly cemented dais wall. This illustrates the treatment of the body and the arrangement of the deceased, which involved a wooden bier set atop a low masonry bench. The individual was then wrapped in bolts of fabric, set atop the bier, and then laid atop the bench, again similarly to the individual in the CSII-T4 interment. The body was adorned in jade, shell, beaded garments, and headdress including a small mosaic jadeite mask and an arrangement of perforated *Spondylus* plaques, which also included a smaller stone mosaic arrangement. Obsidian blade fragments appear throughout. Analyses of these materials are currently pending.

Further elements of this ruler's mortuary tableau recovered in laboratory investigations also warrant mention. Chemical analyses of the sediments from the tomb (Loughmiller-Cardinal and Cagnato 2016) indicate a high concentration of mercury (He) or cinnabar throughout the chamber, accounting for the sediments' reddish color and that of the bones themselves. These analyses also indicate the presence of *Zea mays* (Loughmiller-Cardinal and Cagnato 2016), underscoring the importance of this food stuff. A vessel placed to the western end of the chamber near the ruler's feet revealed well-preserved iconography featuring a Teotihuacan-affiliated motif of a war serpent incorporating jaguar and butterfly elements (Van Oss 2016). Royal mortuary complexes associated with Kaanul rulership are also noteworthy for the frequent inclusion of jadeite mosaic funerary masks (Carrasco Vargas 2000). Damaris Menéndez's reassembly of a jadeite mosaic embedded in the ruler's headdress revealed the inclusion of a small-scale jadeite mosaic face (roughly the size of a human hand) adorning the headdress. Preliminary analysis of jadeite materials from Burial 61 (Melgar Tísoc and Andrieu 2016) indicates the same methods of production appear to have been used for Calakmul origin jadeite pieces, another point underscoring Burial 61's ties to Kaanul. Certainly, the mortuary patterns discussed here on the whole are not necessarily unique for Classic Maya funerary ritual (Eberl 2005; Fitzsimmons 2009; Welch 1988), and we do not intend to assert as much. Nevertheless, there are certain similarities of content and arrangements between Waka's Burial 61 and the CSII-T4 interment. These suggest to us that K'abel sought, quite deliberately, to arrange her afterlife performance in ways that were either meant to reflect her elevated Kaanul pedigree or her close association with the individual in CSII-T4, believed to be Yuknoom Yich'aak K'ak'. In any event, we can be certain that she (1) had a hand in controlling her own afterlife narrative, and (2) chose how she wished to be remembered by her people at Waka'.

## STELA 44

Stela 44 (figure 5.5) was reerected to be built into the staircase fronting Structure M13-1 Adosada Sub I, the two-chambered I-shaped narrow rooms discussed earlier built atop Sub II and the intrusive Burial 61 chamber. In fact, the final tread of that staircase covered what was once the face of Stela 44, which had been removed deliberately in some previous period. We know, from the excavations of its base, that the stela was not original to that locale and had been reset in its current position as part of the construction effort to both seal and build around the Burial 61 chamber and create Structure M13-1 Adosada Sub I. The monument discovered in this context, Stela 44, dates to the sixth century AD. Stanley P. Guenter deciphered the preserved glyphs on the upper sides of the monument (Pérez Robles and Navarro-Farr 2013; see also Martin and Beliaev 2017). The text, while partial, provides a new chapter in Waka's history. Because the city was important in the regional political and military struggles of the great kingdoms of the lowland Maya, the text also reveals more about regional politics in the Classic Period.

We interpret the repositioning of Stela 44, set on an angle through the plaza floor, as a caching event in dedication to the construction sequence that saw the interment of Burial 61 and established a new centerline for the Structure M13-1 Adosada Sub I. The front of the stela is much eroded but depicts a forward-facing king cradling a ceremonial bundle, a typical sixth-century pose for Waka's stelae. Stela 44 was dedicated in AD 564, during the hiatus at Tikal (Freidel et al. 2017; Pérez Robles and Navarro-Farr 2013). Waka' experienced a nearly coeval hiatus though the discovery of this monument has shortened that period. Tikal's King Jasaw Chan K'awiil ended the hiatus by defeating his rival, the snake king Yuknoom Yich'aak K'ahk', in AD 695 (the likely occupant

FIGURE 5.5. *Stela 44-2 views: (a) complete view of Stela 44 in situ; (b) close-up view of standing ruler with hands in "crab claw" position carrying a bundle (photos by J. C. Pérez). All images and photographs pertain to the Proyecto Arqueológico Waka'; all images are courtesy of the Ministry of Culture and Sports of Guatemala.*

of CSII-T4). The full details and implications of the new evidence from Stela 44 are too vast to enumerate fully here, and analyses are still in progress. Thus, what follows is a brief summary of what we think currently.

Stela 44 was dedicated by a Wak Dynasty king named on that monument as Wa'oom Uch'ab Tz'ikin (Freidel et al. 2017; Pérez Robles and Navarro-Farr 2013). This king came to the throne in AD 556, presumably right after the death of the other man named on the monument who we presume to be his father, so-called king Chak Took Ich'aak Wak Ahau, Great Fiery Claw. The name Chak Took Ich'aak was a famous Tikal royal name, attached to two major kings of *that* dynasty who ruled in the fourth and fifth centuries. We think it is likely that the Wak king Chak Took Ich'aak, father of Wa'oom Uch'ab Tz'ikin, was named after these famous Tikal kings. From this we surmise that both he and his predecessor were vassals of Tikal. Stela 44 also indicates Wa'oom

Uch'ab Tz'ikin's accession was witnessed by a woman named Ikoom; the same queen was named on the recovered Stela 43 fragments. Here, Ikoom also bears the royal epithets Sak Wayis and K'uhul Chatan Winik. These titles are also closely associated with the snake kings (Martin 1993, 1997, 2008b). We therefore think it likely that Lady Ikoom was a princess of or affiliated with Kaanul. Given her prominence in the text of Stela 44, it is likely that she was the queen consort of the named Waka' King Chak Took Ich'aak and the mother of King Wa'oom Uch'ab Tz'ikin.

In sum, we have a king at Waka' whose father is named for the Tikal king who was killed and replaced under the aegis of Sihyaj K'ahk'. This same Wak Dynasty king married a Kaanul affiliate princess. She likely represents the first of numerous Kaanul princesses to rule at Waka', including Kaloomte' K'abel, who died in the early eighth century and whose burial this cached stela memorialized. Perhaps most important, it appears her marriage to the Waka' ruler once loyal to Tikal represents a turning point in this political alliance from Tikal to Kaanul. That pivotal change is therefore attributable not only to the brokered marriage, but to the actions of Lady Ikoom herself. Stela 44's history is partial, but it clearly conveys the Waka' dynasty's enduring loyalty to the snake kings. This makes sense when considering Waka' held a strategic stronghold on the royal road (Freidel et al. 2007) used by the snake kings to conquer Tikal and much of Petén in the seventh century. That brief imperial golden age faded in AD 695 with the defeat and death of the snake king, Yuknoom Yich'aak K'ahk', overlord and probable brother to Kaloomte' K'abel. She died less than a decade later, but her husband recalled Lady Ikoom and his undying loyalty to the snake kings on Stela 43. We believe K'inich Bahlam II regarded Lady Ikoom as his ancestress.

The newly discovered history recorded on stelae discovered in association with Structure M13-1 Adosada Sub I indicates Queen Ikoom preceded Kaloomte' K'abel by at least two centuries and also hailed from Kaanul. We believe her remains were those from a royal tomb excavated in 2004 (Lee 2005, 2012) in the Northwest Palace Acropolis. Although we did not know about the historical Queen Ikoom at that time of those excavations, Eppich (2011) correctly discerned that the royal woman's tomb dated to the sixth century AD had been ritually reentered during the mid–late eighth century. Such activities were not uncommon as acts of reverence and invocation of sacred memory associated with a divine ancestor (McAnany 1995). Reentering Queen Ikoom's tomb was a testament to her enduring influence. Eppich (2011) also made the case that her tomb reentry ceremony was tied to ritual activities carried out in a grand gallery of rooms fronting the palace that were later covered by a staircase.

## ON KAANUL, WOMEN, AND STATECRAFT

We have robust evidence permitting closer view of the memory work associated with two powerful Kaanul-origin royal women who called Waka' their home. To discuss the role of these women and how they engineered power during the complex political intrigue of Kaanul's Late Classic golden age, the enumeration of some signature Kaanul characteristics is germane. First, throughout the Classic period, this realm was seated in different locales that may have originated in the Mirador heartland during the Preclassic (Hansen and Guenter 2005), moved to Dzibanché in the Early Classic (Martin 2005), then to Calakmul during the golden age of the Late Classic (Martin 2005). Second, emblem glyphs for these realms transition from bat to snake and back to bat in the mid-eighth century (Martin 2005). Finally, a key feature well documented by the epigraphic record is the practice of marrying Kaanul princesses off to lords of junior allies and/or subordinate polities to anchor their allegiance, a practice known as hypogamous marriage. While this has been noted as characteristic of marriage patterns in various Mesoamerican contexts of royal alliance (Marcus 2001), it has also been noted that the practice, among the Classic Maya, is exemplary of exogamous marriage (Martin 2008b). The end goal, whatever term is best suited, was for royal heiresses of Kaanul to marry key dynasts throughout Petén, particularly along the important north-south trade artery connecting the Kaanul heartland all the way south to Cancuén, along which Waka' was just such a site.

These patterns lead us to speculate that perhaps it was the fluid nature of the Kaanul realm that made it so successful in aggregating power. This very term "fluid" is used by Martin (2005) to capture Kaanul's idea of city state or polity as not necessarily being geographically tied or linked. We agree that this fluidity in terms of the seat of their regional base and of their emblem glyph is a key Kaanul feature. We would argue that another similarly fluid characteristic is how power was shared and distributed in a way that was not dependent upon or restricted by gender. Specifically, we refer to the institutional perception that power could be brokered through the actions of its male *and* female court members. This perception points to a power not limited by a strictly binary view of gender or by patriarchy as has been identified as characteristic of much of the rest of Classic Period Maya dynastic structure. In fact, we argue the expansion of the Kaanul influence was made possible in part through women and the attendant bonds fostered through motherhood and marriage alliance. The use of marriage diplomacy (after Teufel 2008) by Kaanul was widespread, and the daughters of the snake married rulers at Hix Wiitz, Yaxchilán, La Corona, and, of course, at Waka'. We further contend that these distinct contributions to statecraft have been underemphasized (but see Ardren 2002 and Reese-Taylor et al. 2009 as notable exceptions). Of the many marriages, we now know of four queens of probable Kaanul pedigree who married Wak' dynasts. They are, in chronological order of their rule, Queen Ikoom, Kaloomte' K'abel, an anonymous wife of King Bahlam Tz'am (who succeeded K'abel and her husband Kinich Bahlam II), and Queen Pakal. After Queen Pakal and her husband (also unknown), Waka' has one more ruling pair, Aj Yax Chow Pat and his unknown wife, but their reign was brief and we have no evidence that this wife was also affiliated with Kaanul. To reiterate, of these four, remarkably, we have discovered tombs with evidence linking the interred with two of these historical figures, Burial 8 from the Northwest Palace Acropolis (Lee 2005, 2012) likely corresponding to Queen Ikoom and Burial 61 (Navarro-Farr et al. 2013) of Kaloomte' K'abel.

A bias in our thinking of royal women of Kaanul and, indeed across the Classic lowlands, as subordinate or meaningful *only* or *primarily* in terms of their relationship to a male peer or senior is a reflection of the patriarchal structure reflected in the documentation we have on ancient Maya royal life. Such a bias is not surprising, again, given the nature of certain epigraphic data that best reflect how ancient Maya royals talked about themselves. We acknowledge this structure is well documented in Classic Maya life and do not here intend to negate that. Our position rests in the biases *we* as researchers hold. We argue that to understand women strictly from the confines of such a system is to, perhaps unwittingly, render them passive and acquiescent to such structures rather than conceiving of them as agential, powerful, and savvy in their own right. Our goal is to work to change that perception, beginning with royal women of Kaanul who are fairly well represented both archaeologically and epigraphically at Waka'. We invite dialogues from scholars involving research about both ancient royal and nonroyal Maya women from other sites and, indeed, across Mesoamerica. The steps toward meaningful inclusivity in our thinking may be small, but we believe they are well worth taking.

## CONCLUDING REMARKS

Previous research on the significant ritual activity enacted on Structure M13-1 after the decline of Waka's royal court led to musings on the nature of social memory associated with this building. This was a question the senior author often pondered over in numerous and extensive field conversations with David Freidel. This work gives depth and context to those understandings. Late and Terminal Classic era Wakeños understood the importance of their city's long-enduring alliance with the snake realm and how Kaloomte' K'abel and Lady Ikoom were proud emblems of that alliance. Today these findings not only resonate with archaeologists and interested publics but, most important, with Maya people today and the communities within which and among whom we work. Through these narratives, which David and Linda initiated years ago, we proudly continue to participate in the process of sharing these enduring legacies.

## ACKNOWLEDGMENTS

Our ongoing work as members of the Proyecto Arqueológico Waka' (PAW) is at the invitation of and supported by the Instituto de Antropología e Historia de Guatemala (IDAEH), the Ministerio de Cultura y Deportes, and the Departamento de Monumentos Prehispánicos (DEMOPRE). Our project benefits from the support of the Waka' Foundation, Jerry Glick and the Jerome E. Glick Foundation, the Department of the Interior of the United States, the GeoOntological Society of San Francisco, the National Geographic Society, the Foundation for the Cultural and Natural Patrimony of Guatemala, and generous private benefactors. This research was supported generously by the Fundación Patrimonio Cultural y Natural Maya (PACUNAM), the Alphawood Foundation, the Hitz Foundation, the University of New Mexico's Division for Equity and Inclusion, the University of New Mexico's Department of Anthropology, and the College of Wooster. We are deeply grateful for the support and valuable input from all members of the PAW research team, including David Freidel, Francisco Castañeda, Keith Eppich, Damien Marken, Michelle Rich, Erin Patterson, Clarissa Cagnato, and Jennifer Loughmiller-Cardinal.

# 6

*Statecraft in the City of the Centipede*

*Burials 39, 38, and Internal Alliance Building at El Perú–Waka', Guatemala*

Michelle Rich and
Keith Eppich

[Shield-Jaguar] married her not because of her mother's relatives but because her father was member of a powerful noble lineage . . . Temple 23 was his effort to forge a grand compromise: to honor Lady Xoc and the principle of internal alliance while building support for the child of the foreign alliance. (Schele and Freidel 1990:270–271)

The monuments of Yaxchilán tell a story of marriage and alliance-building. There are two kings in this tale, a father called Shield Jaguar (Itzamnaaj Bahlam III) and his son known as Bird Jaguar IV. Over the course of the eighth century, both kings faced the same challenge: the need to accommodate the noble families of the city while building alliances with foreign powers. This balancing act played out on the stone monuments they raised. Shield Jaguar took Lady K'abal Xook as his wife, because she was from a potent local family with past royal connections. He honored her through public ritual and marked this honor in monumental art. In the famous lintels of Yaxchilán, it is Lady Xook who pulls a bladed rope through her tongue to let blood. It is Lady Xook who summons the war serpent Waxaklajuun-Ubaah-Kan. It is Lady Xook who dresses her royal husband for battle. It is another wife, however, Lady Ik' Skull of Calakmul, certainly married to bolster an alliance with the powerful Kaan state, who bears his heir and successor. Headed to war, Shield Jaguar needed the ritual magic of one wife and the political might and connections of the other.

DOI: 10.5876/9781646420469.c006

Similarly, Bird Jaguar followed his father's path. He married several women, including local women from the noble lineages of the city and foreign queens from distant kingdoms.

As described at length by Linda and David in chapter 7 of *A Forest of Kings*, "Bird-Jaguar and the Cahalob," the two kings solved their problem through careful diplomacy. They shared the supernatural charisma of their office by inviting other actors onto the ritual stage. By extending the royal prerogatives of sacred ritual, they deliberately constructed internal alliances within the city, binding those other actors to the king. Furthermore, they memorialized these mutual performances in the monumental narratives of the city itself. The art of Yaxchilán depicts queens performing ritual magic and vision rites by themselves and together with their kings. The kings are also depicted alongside local lords—uncles and brothers through marriage—conducting sacred ritual and preparing for war together. These particular monuments were artistic achievements of the highest caliber that concretized the political decisions of these two rulers in an elaborate visual statement. The marriage rites, ritual bloodletting, and conjuring acts commemorated on these public monuments served as a mechanism of internal alliance building, reinforcing the stability and importance of the bond between nobles. The maintenance of local ties was especially important when the kings welcomed foreign brides, building necessary connections to the great powers of the Classic Maya world, but in so doing introducing potentially threatening or competing interests into the kingdom.

While the artistic solution pursued by Yaxchilán's rulers seems unique, the problem faced by these two kings was not. Classic city-states possessed potent elite lineages, and such noble families seemed to require a certain degree of wooing. At Copán, William Fash (1991) describes a similar problem. The sixteenth king, Yax Pasaj, had to include noble lineages in complex power-sharing arrangements. Fash argued that Yax Pasaj extended royal perquisites to non-royal and cadet lineages, and the elite families emulated royal art, monuments, lifestyles, and distinctions. Stephen Houston and David Stuart (2001) have pointed out that some subroyal nobles possessed considerable autonomy from their divine lords. Some of those nobles gain considerable prominence in the epigraphic record, particularly in the seventh and eighth centuries. They note that cadet lineages may lead to fissioning or political rupture within the polity, and they echo *A Forest of Kings* by writing "the role of women as alliance-builders through marriage and the need to fortify connection with underlings through a heightened emphasis—a nimbus extended to nonregnal lords—in surviving examples of monumental art" (2001:76). Successful statecraft in the Classic world, it seems, consisted of any given ruler's ability to build and maintain internal alliances with local elite. There were apparently different strategies for doing this, including the novel solutions employed at Yaxchilán and Copán, and archaeological research at Waka' suggests yet another. At this site in central Petén, Burials 38 and 39 suggest that shared funerary rituals and gifts of high-quality ceramics may be evidence of internal alliance building. It is not merely that the two burials are similar, but in many aspects they are identical. If the story of Yaxchilán revolves around the use of public ritual and exquisite monumental art to secure intrapolity alliances, the story at Waka' centers on funerary ritual and gifted ceramic art to do the same.

## THE EL PERÚ–WAKA' REGIONAL ARCHAEOLOGICAL PROJECT (PAW)

El Perú–Waka' is in the Laguna del Tigre National Park near the junction of the San Juan and San Pedro Mártir Rivers in the western portion of the department of Petén, Guatemala. Archaeological investigation of the ancient center began under the codirection of David Freidel and Hector Escobedo in 2003. Field research and laboratory analysis conducted by the El Perú–Waka' Regional Archaeological Project (PAW) has been ongoing since that time, but has varied annually in size and scope. In the years since 2012, there has been a renewed focus on excavation. The investigations undertaken by PAW demonstrate a complex and shifting history for this Classic Maya center. It was occupied for the duration of the Classic period, from roughly 300 BC to AD 1000. The emblem glyph of the site changed over the course of its long occupation, but in the Early Classic it contained the goggle-eyes and toothed fang of the giant tropical centipede (Guenter 2007b). The ancient city was *Wak-*, referencing the *Scolopendra* species, examples of which may grow up to a foot long and possess venom known to cause death in humans (Guenter 2007b). For the modern world, the site is known by the hyphenated El Perú–Waka' but to the Classic Maya, this was Waka', the "City of the Centipede."

The city consists of a dense urban core surrounding by a far-ranging and unevenly clustered settlement (figure 6.1). It centers on the long concourse of Plaza 1, one of the largest plazas in the Maya world, which is surrounded by pyramids, palaces, patio groups, temples, and all the ruined splendor of an ancient Maya city. Waka' apparently had its origins as series of scattered farmsteads in the Late Preclassic before coalescing in the second and third centuries AD into a ritual center, which is still poorly understood archaeologically. The site expanded dramatically in the Early Classic, attaining its current size and shape by the end of the third century. Featuring prominently in the

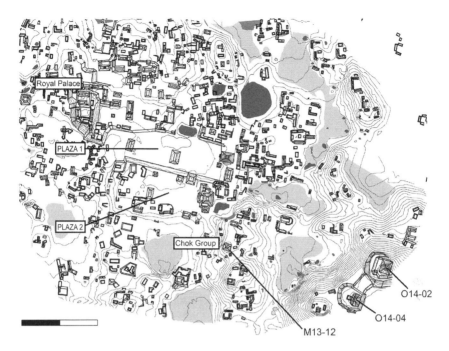

**Figure 6.1.** *Urban core of El Perú–Waka' (drawing by Damien Marken and Evangelia Tsesmeli).*

epigraphic record of the Maya region, Waka' served as an important western conduit for persons and commerce flowing to and from central Petén. It held a strategic position along the east-west route of the San Pedro Mártir and the north-south axis of the Great Western Road, placing it at an important economic and political crossroads (Demarest and Fahsen 2003; Freidel et al. 2007; Woodfill and Andreu 2012). In this location, Waka' participated in all the great historical events of the Classic period. The Early Classic city received the Entrada of Sihyaj K'ahk' in the late fourth century and became a full participant of the "New Order" cities of the fifth century (Freidel et al. 2007; Grube and Martin 2001; Guenter 2014c; Martin and Grube 2008). Like the other New Order cities, Waka' experienced a major downturn in the sixth century, one that featured the destruction of many of the Early Classic monuments and perhaps even partial abandonment (Guenter 2014c; cf. Sharer et al. 2005). There is a ninety-three-year epigraphic hiatus between AD 564 and 657 during which there is no current evidence of Waka's rulers raising monuments, construction activity is muted, and urban settlement apparently disrupted.

The hiatus ends with the reign of the city's greatest king, K'inich Bahlam II, the Long-Lived. He reasserted centralized control for the remainder of the seventh century and the first half of the eighth, when the city attained its maximal population. Damien Marken (2011) conservatively estimates a population of around 7,000 individuals at this time, though the actual number is likely to have been much higher. Waka' closely aligned itself with the great northern city of Calakmul and became the indispensable junior partner of the hegemonic rule of the Kaanul Snake-kings. Eventually, a series of misfortunes ravaged the city, including a major defeat by Tikal in 743. Despite revivification efforts, Waka' appears to have undergone a dissolution of centralized authority at the end of the eighth century. The settlement pattern changed dramatically at this time with the population surging inward, nucleating in the defensible city core and abandoning much of the urban periphery (Eppich 2015; Marken 2011, 2015). During the last century and a half of the city's occupation, there is no real evidence for an obvious royal presence or even centralized rule of any kind. The end of Waka' came slowly and irregularly, with ragged abandoned patches in the site core. The final human presence in the city is evidenced only by the remains of Terminal Classic ceramics used in small ceremonies, and by AD 1000, Waka' appears wholly abandoned.

However, the historical moment with which we are concerned dates to the mid-seventh century AD, on or around the year 657, when Waka's rulers raised Stela 1 in front of the great pyramid we call Structure O14-04. This date stands as a major turning point for Waka', marking the end of the epigraphic hiatus and the ascension of the city's greatest ruler, K'inich Bahlam. This is the beginning of a real "golden age" for the City of the Centipede, with large construction projects across the site core and an expansion of settlement through the kingdom. Politically, this is the moment when Waka' embraced its alliance with Calakmul. K'inich Bahlam married Lady K'abel, who was likely either the daughter or granddaughter of Yuknoom Ch'een the Great, the *kaloomte'*, "emperor," of Calakmul. She is a figure of enormous importance at Waka'. On the city's stelae she was depicted as the equal of her royal husband in an artistic tradition that portrays status with brutal honesty (Marcus 2006). Superiors were placed high on monuments, looking down on their social inferiors, who were portrayed in submissive postures, kneeling before or placating their superiors. On Stela 34, Lady K'abel carries a flapstaff scepter and shield, wears a plumed headdress, and stares her husband on the adjacent Stela 33 in the eye (see Schele and Freidel 1990:274; Tate 1992:84; Wanyerka 1996). Lady K'abel and K'inich Bahlam ruled the city for the next sixty-odd years, vigorously cementing the alliance between Waka' and Calakmul.

But, in 657, all of that lies in the future. In 657, these monarchs would have been very young, in their early twenties or even in their teenage years. The fledgling king K'inich Bahlam must have faced a formidable political problem. Set against a backdrop of war, he had to convince his city to accept a Snake Princess of Calakmul as royal coruler. The great military campaigns marking the rise of the Calakmul hegemony were still underway, and to accept this princess is to take sides in a conflict that had already broken royal families and smashed ancient cities (Grube and Martin 2001; Martin and Grube 2008). In *A Forest of Kings*, Linda and David described this era as "Star Wars in the Seventh Century." And in 657, this young king wants to marry the grand-daughter of the emperor.

## BURIALS 38 AND 39: A TALE OF TWO TOMBS

In 2006, Eppich and Rich discovered Burials 38 and 39, respectively, and the similarities between the two interments were readily apparent. Located in ceremonial architecture within a residential compound, Burial 38 was that of an individual of secondary elite status (figure 6.2), whereas Burial 39, situated in one of the largest civic-ceremonial funerary pyramids at the site, was the final resting place of an epigraphically unknown ruler of Waka' (figure 6.3). The ceramics in the mortuary assemblages place both burials within the site's Early-to-Late Classic transition, roughly AD 500–700, overlapping with the epigraphic hiatus. Both masonry tomb chambers were located in ritual architecture contexts, had analogous mortuary assemblages, shared roughly comparable layouts, and demonstrated evidence for reentry during the Late-to-Terminal Classic period.

### Architectural Contexts and Associated Stelae

Burial 38 was placed along the centerline axis of the northern-oriented Structure M13-12. At six meters tall, this building is the largest in the Chok Group, and features an extensive frontal platform—or *adosada*—covered with midden-like votive deposits. Two construction phases were identified, dating to the Early-to-Late and Terminal Classic periods. The earlier phase featured a smaller structure of similar height, which was constructed atop Burial 38. Terminal Classic modifications demolished the earlier staircase, replacing it with a larger and wider stair. Overall, archaeological evidence is consistent with the interpretation of this structure as an ancestor shrine. The tomb chamber itself measured 2.3 × 0.9 × 0.8 m and is oriented on an east-west axis,

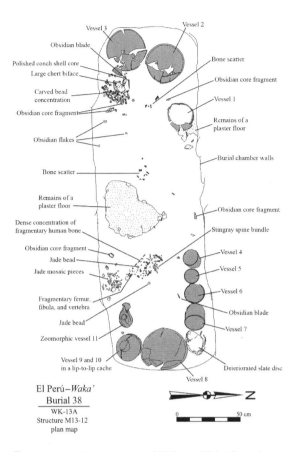

Vessel 3
Vessel 2
Obsidian blade
Polished conch shell core
Large chert biface
Bone scatter
Obsidian core fragment
Carved bead
concentration
Vessel 1
Obsidian core fragment
Obsidian flakes
Remains of a
plaster floor
Burial chamber walls
Bone scatter
Remains of a
plaster floor
Obsidian core fragment
Dense concentration of
fragmentary human bone
Stingray spine bundle
Obsidian core fragment
Vessel 4
Jade bead
Vessel 5
Jade mosaic pieces
Vessel 6
Fragmentary femur,
fibula, and vertebra
Obsidian blade
Jade bead
Vessel 7
Zoomorphic vessel 11
Vessel 9 and 10
in a lip-to-lip cache
Deteriorated slate disc
Vessel 8

El Perú–*Waka'*
Burial 38
WK-13A
Structure M13-12
plan map

N
0                    50 cm

**FIGURE 6.2.** *Plan drawing of El Perú–Waka' Burial 38
(by Keith Eppich).*

perpendicular to the centerline of the building. A stela fragment was also buried on the centerline of the building, one of a half-dozen badly eroded broken
monument fragments scattered across the front of the structure.

Located in the Mirador Group, the imposing Structure O14-04 sits on
an eight-meter-high basal platform. It is a composite pyramid comprising
a four-meter-high adosada, with front and lateral staircases, which abuts a
curved and terraced twelve-meter-nigh pyramid. A two-room masonry shrine
was constructed atop the adosada, in addition to another masonry superstructure at the pyramid's summit. A causeway connects Structure O14-04 to the
even larger pyramid, Structure O14-02. Primary construction occurred in the

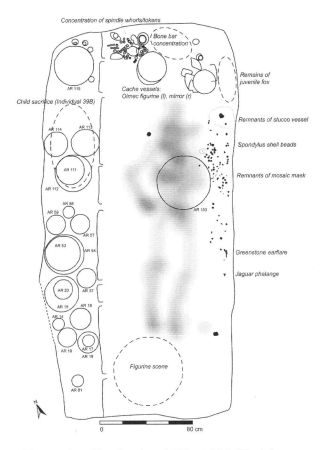

Concentration of spindle whorls/tokens

Bone bar concentration

Remains of juvenile fox

AR 115

Child sacrifice (Individual 39B)

Cache vessels: Olmec figurine (l), mirror (r)

Remnants of stucco vessel

AR 114   AR 113

Spondylus shell beads

AR 111

Remnants of mosaic mask

AR 112

AR 58

AR 59

AR 153

AR 57

AR 53   AR 54

Greenstone earflare

Jaguar phalange

AR 20   AR 37

AR 15   AR 16

AR 14

AR 17

AR 19   AR 18

Figurine scene

AR 81

N

0                 80 cm

**Figure 6.3.** *Plan drawing of El Perú–Waka' Burial 39. Shaded image denotes general location of human skeleton remains. Objects in the mortuary assemblage obscured by other objects or skeletal material are not included. Ceramics are depicted whole, but were broken in situ when the tomb was infilled after ancient reentry (drawing by Michelle Rich, Jennifer Piehl, and Varinia Matute).*

Early Classic period, with Late and Terminal Classic modifications. Structure O14-04 is oriented north-northwest, and is, interestingly, directly facing the Chok Group and Structure M13-12. The Burial 39 vaulted masonry chamber measured 3.3 × 1.7 × 1.2–1.4 m, with the long axis perpendicular to the building's centerline axis. It was located underneath the shrine room and inside the adosada, directly on top of an unexplored staircase. Rather than being an earlier substructure, these may be the basal treads of the pyramid's staircase—the upper portion of which is still visible behind the shrine room while the lower portion of which was encased by the adosada construction. Stela 1 is positioned in front of Structure O14-04 and is notable because it ends the ninety-three-year epigraphic hiatus at Waka. The inscriptions are poorly preserved, but it possesses a legible date of 657 (9.11.5.0.0) (Guenter 2005, 2014c). The stela is fairly traditional in that it depicts a standing king, and one remaining clue to his identity is a jaguar element in the headdress that alludes to K'inich Bahlam II.

Although structures M13-12 and O14-04 are both ritual structures, there are notable differences in these architectural contexts. The Chok Group is residential in function, and Structure M13-12 serves as a residential-ritual shrine within that compound. This group is also significantly closer to the site center and appears to be integrated more effectively as evidenced by remnants of a long staircase that link it to Plaza 2. Conversely, the spatially distinct, topographically elevated, and physically restricted Mirador Group is composed of only monumental and ritual architecture, and Structure O14-04 is a civic-ceremonial funerary pyramid containing multiple interments. The masonry chambers of Burials 38 and 39 also exhibit differences, with less ornate Burial 38 having a flat slab roof and a plastered floor surface, compared to the more elaborate vaulted roof and bench/alleyway in Burial 39. The long axis of the chambers also differs, with Burial 38 oriented east-west. This is in opposition to Burial 39, where the long axis of chamber is oriented slightly east of north. Finally, a carved stela was erected in front of Structure O14-04, where Structure M13-12 possessed only the upper portion of a stela placed in the building's later staircase, a monumental fragment that may not even be original to the building.

## INTERMENTS, MORTUARY ASSEMBLAGES, AND LAYOUTS

The person in subroyal Burial 38 was buried with eleven whole vessels dating to the mid-seventh century. While several of those vessels had glyphic texts, they were poorly preserved and largely illegible, yielding only part of a name, "Chak K'in (human head)-ta?," which may or may not have pertained to the interred individual. The vessels were arranged as if placed around a supine human figure, however, skeletal remains were almost nonexistent. All major skeletal elements had been removed from the tomb, leaving the individual represented only by several small scatterings of fragmentary human bone. Clues to the orientation of the interred individual were present in the form of teeth and cranial fragments located at the chamber's western end. Also at this end, a total of 108 small, flower-like spindle whorls of stucco, basalt, bone, and shell were tightly clustered as if they had been bundled or strung together. This clustering also contained a conch shell core, a large chert biface, and obsidian blades. At the opposite end of the chamber was an empty lip-to-lip cache on one side and a deteriorated slate disk on the other. This is almost certainly the backing for a pyrite mirror. A faceless zoomorphic vessel in the shape of a small dog was located adjacent to the lip-to-lip cache. Near that, also at the edge of the chamber, a concentration of ninety-six jade tesserae, including a shaped nose, provide evidence for the inclusion of a jade mask. Next to that was a concentration of fragmented human bone, and a grouping of six to eight stingray spines, which suggests they also were bundled or wrapped in a perishable container. Scattered chert and obsidian cores, blades, and debitage appear to be associated with the Terminal Classic reentry.

Burial 39 contained the remains of an adult individual of advanced age oriented with the cranium to the northern end of the chamber. This person was laid in extended supine position on a masonry bench, bordered on the west by a narrow alley. The skeletal remains were poorly preserved, but the individual was complete. Markers of sex and age were absent on the pelvis, making definite sexing impossible, but several lines of inconclusive evidence based on the mortuary assemblage and other clues have been explored, leading to plausible interpretations that the individual could be *either* male or female. Surprisingly, fragmentary remnants of woven fabric wrapped around the deceased were preserved in direct association with the skeletal remains. The mortuary assemblage consisted of impressive elite artifacts signifying the wealth of Classic period rulers, including thirty-three ceramic vessels; a remarkable narrative figurine scene comprised of twenty-three ceramic figurines; various greenstone artifacts including three sets of earflares and a pendant representing a human figure with a removable eyepatch; *Spondylus* shell beads, small carved shell ornaments, and miniature mosaics; and numerous other artifacts. Of the vessels, twenty-four were located in the alley to the west of bench, while nine were on funerary bench. Ten vessels have painted or incised inscriptions, naming at least three individuals (see Guenter 2014c:158). None of these correspond with the partial name on the Burial 38 vessel, and none of these names can be associated with any certainty to the person buried in the tomb. A total of sixty small, flower-like spindle whorls of shell, ceramic, basalt, and limestone were tightly clustered as if they were bundled or strung together and placed at the north end of the tomb. This clustering also contained a perforated Atlantic Cowrie shell tinkler, bivalve shells with large centrally located perforations, two plain bone pins or spatulas, small vessels, and obsidian blades. Next to this were lip-to-lip cache vessels containing a remarkable Olmec-style heirloom figurine, and a second set of lip-to-lip cache vessels containing a square pyrite-encrusted mirror. Adjacent to this were the skeletal remains of a juvenile canid. A concentration of 151 jade tesserae, including small obsidian disks and mother-of-pearl fashioned to look like eyes, indicate a mosaic mask was laid next to the individual. The deceased's chest was covered by a large, inverted plate laid over the aforementioned greenstone pendant and a cluster of nine stingray spines. Scattered chert and obsidian cores, blades, and debitage appear to be associated with the later reentry.

### Late-to-Terminal Classic Reentry

Both tombs were reopened and reentered. In this, they are not unique. Of the six tombs known from the city, three were reopened during the same historical era. This was likely associated with the attempts to revive centralized authority at the site in the late eighth century and early ninth. The revivification efforts of the last kings involved opening these tombs in what are likely *och k'ak* ceremonies. As described by David Stuart (1998), such ritual involved opening the resting places of the honored dead, filling them with smoke and incense, and ritually manipulating the contents, usually the bones themselves. Stuart cites ample archaeological evidence for such activity. At Waka', burials 8, 38, and 39 were all reentered around AD 801, give or take a few decades. The ancient Maya opened the tombs, manipulated the contents, and sometimes removed skeletal elements. Upon resealing said tomb, they often left additional offerings to these interred ancestors.

For Burial 38 in Structure M13-12, this activity was accompanied by substantial architectural modification. The Maya of the Chok group largely demolished the older version of the structure, reducing it to its rubble core. They completely removed the lower third of the pyramid's staircase and lifted away most of the roofing slabs of Burial 38's tomb chamber. They reentered the tomb, and small flecks of charcoal indicate a ceremony incorporating fire or censing was conducted. They took most of the skeleton, leaving only scattered cranial fragments, teeth, and fragmentary phalanges to indicate that a body once lay there at all. Other bones they collected and placed in the center of the small chamber. Most notably, they removed the bones of the appendicular skeleton and the skull itself. Upon departing, the chamber was totally infilled, the old roofing slabs unceremoniously tumbled into this new construction fill. As the newcomers filled the tomb, however, they left offerings. Mixed into that infilled chamber were 2,527 obsidian artifacts, flakes, blades, and core fragments; 445 chert flakes and broken bifaces; and a ceramic bowl, carefully positioned between two of the slabs, at the level of the old roof. Mixed into all this were hundreds of flecks and chunks of burned carbon. The ceramic bowl is of a type very common at the site in the early ninth century, thus providing a date for this reentry event.

Burial 39 was reentered when the Maya cut through a 10 cm thick plaster floor dating to the Late Classic that formed the floor of the shrine room constructed atop the adosada. After the tomb had been reaccessed, the western side of the tomb's vault and all of the capstones appear to have been intentionally collapsed into the chamber before the chamber was purposefully and entirely infilled, over the original contents of the Burial 39 mortuary assemblage. Consequently, the roof of the chamber was never rebuilt, but some of those vault stones appear to have been actually laid over the skeletal remains of Burial 39's original interment. The chamber's fill matrix contained signs of burning, and there were concentrations of obsidian blades and cores worked and broken in situ, and pottery was smashed in situ. This "reentry fill" inside the chamber also contained modeled stucco fragments and various faunal remains, including among others *Bufo marinus* (giant toad), *Odocoileus virginianus* (white-tailed deer), and a *Testudines* (turtle) carapace fragment. A total of 2,561 artifacts were recovered in the fill of the 3.3 × 1.7 × 1.2–1.4 m chamber. The artifact categories represented in this total were ceramic sherds (11%), chert (47%) and obsidian (11%) chipped stone and tools, faunal bone (15%), fragments of sculpture and decorative elements made of stucco (8%), and shell (8%). Additionally, evidence suggests the shrine room above the tomb was also infilled, as if to seal it off from further use.

Despite the fact that the reentry events in both tombs occurred during the same era, there are several key differences between them. In Burial 38, all major skeletal elements of the interred individual were removed, whereas in Burial 39, the skeletal remains were left intact and covered by the flat slates that originally comprised the chamber's vault roof. Additionally, during the reentry, a child sacrifice was added at the north end of the Burial 39 alleyway. So, in terms of the treatment of ancestral remains and human offerings, the reentry associated with Burial 38 was essentially extractive, while the reentry associated with Burial 39 can be conceptualized as additive. At present, we have not formulated an adequate explanation for the difference in the reentry treatment of these two interments tethered together so very clearly by their analogous mortuary assemblages and layouts. The manners of reentry and of infilling are similar and may have been conducted by the same group of Maya.

The motives probably involve the changing social dynamic at the city in the early ninth century and the collapse of centralized rule, resulting in a more decentralized political order. For our purposes here, it does not really matter. What matters is that the historical events of 657 involving K'inich Bahlam II, Lady K'abel, and the internal alliances they built are remembered some 150 years after the fact. If the purpose of such funerary ritual is to concretize a collective memory of past actions, the reentries of the tombs clearly show that these "memory-making" rituals succeeded (see Inomata 2006; Navarro-Farr and Rich 2014; Van Dyke and Alcock 2003). They succeeded brilliantly.

## EXPLORING SHARED MORTUARY CERAMICS

What does it mean that Burials 38 and 39 have the nearly identical vessels? In the world of the Classic Maya, high-quality ceramics served as tokens of esteem and political power. They were not just drinking cups or expressions of artistic achievement, though they were that as well. High-end polychromes depicted scenes of gods, kings, history, and myth. They often bear glyphic dedications texts declaring both the function of the vessel and the name of the lord who commissioned it (Stuart 2005a). These vessels come largely from specific workshops, ones directly associated with palace compounds (Ball 1993; Foias 2004; Halperin and Foias 2010; Reents-Budet et al. 2000). Rulers sponsored the production of this ceramic art, displaying their own generosity, wealth, and refinement. These vessels appear in feasting and funerary contexts and were likely expressly made for feasts and funerals. Lisa LeCount (1999, 2001), in particular, constructed an argument proposing that these vessels reflect social and political relations present in ancient Maya polities. The vessels were made to be given away, commissioned by royal actors and gifted to subordinates during feasts. Subsequent research has largely confirmed her ideas (Eppich 2007, 2009b; Foias 2000; see also Reents-Budet 1994). In this way, the feast and the ceramic art functioned as something to be given away, thrown away even, to highlight the wealth of the ruler. They were objects made to be gifted in these instances of Classic Maya "potlatching" (Rathje 2002). They could not easily be regifted or sold, serving as inalienable objects (Weiner 1992). Thus, such vessels moved from the royal workshop to the ruler, were gifted by the ruler, and then, as we understand from an archaeological perspective, included in funerary assemblages.

The royal character of the ceramics from Burial 39 is quite clear (figure 6.4). The images on the vessels include plumed gods, sacred shells, and floral scrolls, and are executed using a complex multislipping technique known from the

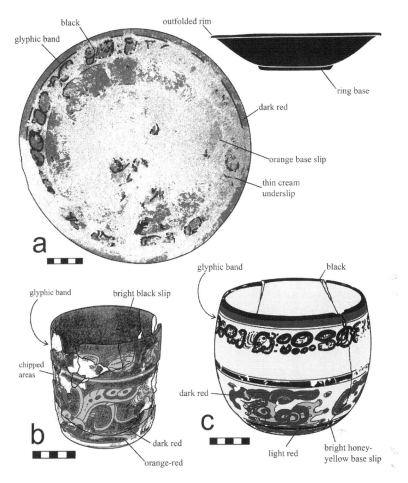

**Figure 6.4.** *Three Vessels from Burial 39: (a) deep-bottomed bowl/dish with polychrome designs in red and black on orange; (b) vertical-walled small cylinder vase with red, orange, and black polychrome designs executed in reserve; (c) highly glossy bowl with designs in black and red on a bright honey-yellow base slip (drawing by Keith Eppich).*

Classic Maya. Some of the pieces are probably foreign, using artistic styles not native to the traditions of Petén. Many of the pieces show little to no use-wear and were likely made specifically for inclusion in the royal tomb. Some of the vessels are clearly local and are known from other contexts at the site. And undoubtedly, the ceramics from Burial 39 are echoed in Burial 38 (figure 6.5).

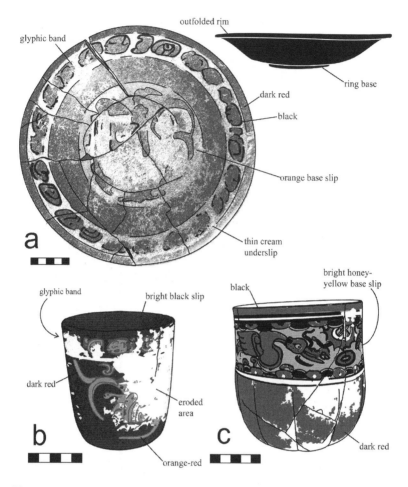

**Figure 6.5.** *Three Vessels from Burial 38: (a) deep-bottomed bowl/dish with polychrome designs in red and black on orange; (b) vertical-walled small cylinder vase with red, orange, and black polychrome designs executed in reserve; (c) highly glossy bowl with designs in black and red on a bright honey-yellow base slip (drawing by Keith Eppich).*

Burial 39 possesses two broad, deep-bottomed dishes with polychrome designs executed in red and black on an orange base slip. An unusual attribute of these vessels is that the glyphic band is placed directly on the cream underslip. This is an artistic effect, designed to mute the color around the glyph to make the glyph even more lustrous. This same technique, on the same type of form, also appears in Burial 38, which also has two examples of the same ceramic. All four vessels are virtually identical. A black-slipped drinking cup, more specifically a small cylinder vase with an unusual design, was also included in the Burial 39 mortuary assemblage. The design consists of red and orange glyphs and floral elements executed in reserve, surrounded by a glossy black slip. The ancient artisans painted the ceramic black, but left blank areas and drew in the red design elements afterward. This is an unusual design technique that makes it striking that Burial 38 also has the same exact design executed on the same type of vessel form. In fact, Burial 38 possesses two such vessels as well as a flat-bottomed bowl with, again, designs executed using the same technique. The technique is the same; the forms are the same; the floral elements are the same. In fact, the calligraphy is exactly the same on the individual glyphs, and it is very likely that the same royal scribe who painted glyphs on the Burial 39 cylinder vase also painted them on the Burial 38 vessels.

The remaining vessels from the two tombs are not identical, but show strong similarities. Such vessels are likely the products of the same royal ceramic workshop. Burial 39 possesses a beautiful bowl with designs in black, dark red, and light red executed on a highly glossy honey-yellow base slip. Similarly, Burial 38 contains a curved-bottomed vase featuring a cormorant, executed in black and red on the same style of highly glossy honey-yellow background. Both tombs include these products of royal artisans, possibly even the products of the same ceramic artist. To see royal ceramics placed in a nonroyal context is striking, especially vessels of such quality and present in such quantity. It is unlikely that such close similarity is accidental. Someone, in the ancient past, made a conscious decision to place them in these contexts.

## MATERIAL MARKERS OF INTERNAL ALLIANCE BUILDING AT WAKA'

In comparing and contrasting Burials 38 and 39, considered nonroyal and royal respectively, we have demonstrated these interments share a striking number of characteristics linking them together. But who were these people? It is possible the individuals in Burials 38 and 39 were closely biologically related. It is possible they were tied together through marriage. It is possible they were connected through an elaborate, hierarchically organized political system. Because of these possibilities, the person interred in Burial 39 may have, while living, extended royal prerogatives to the person interred in Burial 38, whose mortuary assemblage is an anomaly in the currently known archaeological record at Waka'. Most subroyal burials documented at Waka' contain one, two, maybe three high-quality vessels, those of the superlative, palace workshop variety. Those vessels documented in other burials certainly have not been identical to vessels in a high royal burial, as we see in this scenario. Together, these notions suggest some level of intrapolity alliance building, materially reinforced as in the monumental program invoked at Yaxchilán under Itzamnaaj Bahlam III and Bird Jaguar IV.

So who is the royal personage in Burial 39? Given the date of Stela 1 in front of Structure O14-04 and the date of the ceramics in the mortuary assemblage, we can safely assume that this individual directly preceded K'inich Bahlam II. It is quite possible this person was one of his parents. Because we are unable to securely sex the skeletal remains, we are unsure if the interred may have been his mother or his father. But, regardless, the selection of objects for placement in a tomb is a deliberate and intentional act perpetuating an identity held in life, or, perhaps alternatively, crafting a new one in death. Because ancestor veneration was an integral component of Classic period Maya life, we must consider that beyond practices and rituals dealing with the dead for the duration of the funeral, such veneration incorporated the commemoration of ancestors throughout the life of the survivors (McAnany 1995:10–11). In this way, identity is derived from shared remembrance, from collective social memory that provides people an image of their past and a design for the future (e.g., Alcock 2002:1; Fentress and Wickham 1992). Social identity can be contrasted with individual identity, which is bound up in concepts of personhood. C. Fowler (2004:7) defines personhood as the contextually understood, constantly changing condition or state of being a person and indicates that persons are "constituted, deconstituted, maintained and altered in social practices in life and after death." We do not know, exactly, who these people were while they lived, but we do know that they were intentionally and purposefully linked in death. Their posthumous personhood was forever connected and, indeed, still is today. Fowler (2004:79–81) also provides a valuable discussion addressing the importance of rites of passage in shaping personhood. These ritual processes delimit dramatic changes in personal identity *due to a shift in relations with other persons*. Personhood and identity can be negotiated through everyday practice, but can also be perceived as a community affair in which public performances play a vital role, such as funerals.

While the overarching purpose of a funeral is to commemorate the dead, funerals are also for and, perhaps most important, constructed by the living. That ceramics of this quality and in this quantity are present in Burial 38 must have involved the decision making of a royal actor. It remains unknown if the Burial 38 individual acquired these royal vessels during life, and was then buried with them in death, or if the vessels were gifted during mortuary ritual. Because we will likely never be able to address this dilemma, we turn our attention to the most prominent royal actor we can identify, K'inich Bahlam II. As he was married to a Calakmul princess, that type of potent internal alliance building must have been crucial, like at Yaxchilán, in the face a powerful nonlocal queen from the Snake Kingdom. Internal alliance building between kings and lineage heads was important and served as a crucial mechanism for statecraft inside Classic city-states. Whether this road was already paved for K'inich Bahlam II through royal prerogatives previously extended to the person in Burial 38, or he began to forge it himself in the shadow of death, by furnishing a nonroyal grave with products of the royal workshops in 657, is unknown. Some 150 year later, in the turbulent times of the collapse of Classic period dynastic kingship, both Burials 38 and 39 were reentered, and after rituals were enacted, the chambers were entirely infilled. At that point our data show that the person in Burial 38 was an ancestor collected, to possibly relocate or physically carry with during the tumult of the Terminal Classic, whereas the person in Burial 39 was either protected with—or held down by—vault stones from her or his own tomb chamber.

## EPILOGUE

In the first pages of *A Forest of Kings*, Schele and Freidel (1990:16) describe themselves as "historians of the ancient Maya," as they set about the intricate task of telling the ancient Maya past via a fresh perspective. To set the stage, they summarized background information, and then ambitiously collated detailed evidence available at that time, employing multiple lines of inquiry: archaeology, epigraphy, iconography, and ethnohistory. They also interwove colorful narratives that brought those complex and intriguing data sets to life. Our examination of Waka' Burials 38 and 39 endeavored to do the same, by interweaving multiple lines of evidence to examine the use of mortuary ritual and gifted ceramic art to secure intrapolity alliances between the royal ruling elite and nonroyal lineage heads. In the years since the publication of *A Forest of Kings*, many of the specific details presented in the volume have been revised through the hard, ongoing work of dedicated researchers, but a number of the fundamental principles presented in the book still ring true. Appealing to multiple audiences, this seminal and provocative book certainly impacted the nature and direction of ancient Maya studies. As it says in the *Popol Vuh*, there was a magic book that could show war and death, famine and feuds, past and future (Tedlock 1985:219). Perhaps *A Forest of Kings* is one such book.

## ACKNOWLEDGMENTS

The authors would like to thank Linda Schele and David Freidel for their pioneering and inspirational collaborative work, the Instituto de Antropología e Historia (IDAEH), and the past and current directors and members of PAW, as well as our many affiliated collaborators. We are grateful for the funding provided to PAW by the Jerome Glick Foundation and Judy Glick, and funding to Michelle Rich through a National Science Foundation Graduate Fellowship and a research grant from the Foundation for the Advancement of Mesoamerican Studies, Inc. (FAMSI), all of which facilitated the archaeological fieldwork and laboratory analyses on Burial 39 reported on herein.

# 7

With the publication of *Forest of Kings*, Linda Schele and David Freidel (1990) helped realize the promise of the keen insights of Tatiana Proskouriakoff (1960, 1963, 1964, 1993) and usher in an era of epigraphy as biographical, even literary, history. The publication of *Forest of Kings* in 1990 followed two decades of tremendous progress in the decipherment of Classic Maya texts, driven forward by growing knowledge of dynastic sequences (Haviland 1977; Houston and Mathews 1985; Jones 1977; Mathews 1988; Mathews and Schele 1974) and revolutionary understandings of the structure of the inscriptions (e.g., Stuart 1987). The rulers of Palenque, Yaxchilán, Tikal, and other kingdoms had begun to emerge from the hazy past, while epigraphers revealed evidence of interdynastic conflicts and détente.

Although some of the details of decipherment from 1990 may no longer hold, the innovative telling of that history, and we think particularly the integration of historical texts with the architectural landscape of Yaxchilán itself, was prescient and has helped to define archaeology, epigraphy and art history in the Usumacinta region since. Moreover, Schele and Freidel's book took a largely academic discourse and made it more accessible to a broader public, foregrounding the passions, political machinations, and desires of these ancient characters. Kings, queens, and nobles did not just do things—they wanted things; they were angry, jealous, and competitive. The "Forest

*Revisiting Bird Jaguar and the* Sajal *of the Yaxchilán Kingdom*

Charles W. Golden and
Andrew K. Scherer

DOI: 10.5876/9781646420469.c007

of Kings" was not populated by the inscrutable and mysterious Maya. These Maya were fascinatingly human.

Indeed, human wants and desires are at the core of the chapter titled, "Bird Jaguar and the Sajal of the Yaxchilan Kingdom" (Schele and Freidel 1990:252–305). It is a real "Game of Thrones," a multigenerational tale of palace intrigue, alliance, and warfare. With the death of the powerful ruler Shield Jaguar the Great (now known as Itzamnaaj Bahlam III) in AD 742, rival queens and competing lineages vied to control networks of power in the royal court. The young prince who would become Bird Jaguar (or Yaxuun Bahlam IV, as we might call him now), fought off half-brothers and other claimants to ascend the throne as a victorious warrior king in AD 752 (Josserand 2007; Mathews 1997; Proskouriakoff 1963:163–164, 1964:180; Schele and Freidel 1990:262–305). To bolster his claims to rulership, Yaxuun Bahlam IV became a great patron of architecture and sculpture; he quite literally reshaped history through the dedication of numerous monuments and the selective destruction, curation, and conspicuous presentation of older monuments that he had reset in new buildings in the city center.

Yet, Yaxuun Bahlam and his successors did not reach the pinnacle of authority alone. Instead, they relied on interkingdom alliances sealed through marriages, and the political and military support of a class of lords within the kingdom known as *sajal* (called *cahal* by Schele and Freidel, using then current readings) to achieve and maintain the reins of power (Stuart 1985). These sajal were noble courtiers, war captains, and rural governors. It is their role in the Yaxchilán kingdom as evidenced in the epigraphic record—particularly during the reigns of Itzamnaaj Bahlam III, his son Yaxuun Bahlam IV, and his grandson Itzamnaaj Bahlam IV—that has especially informed our field research over the past decade and a half. Across the broken landscape of the Upper Usumacinta region Yaxchilán's kings fought, danced, and feasted alongside their loyal lieutenants as they sought the upper hand against the dynasts of neighboring Piedras Negras and other kingdoms (Chinchilla and Houston 1993; Golden et al. 2008; Houston and Stuart 2001; Jackson 2013; Parmington 2003; Scherer and Golden 2009; Tokovinine 2005).

In this chapter we focus on the relationship between Yaxchilán's paramount rulers, the *k'uhul pa' chan ajaw*, "holy split-sky lord," and their subordinate sajal across that broader landscape (Martin 2004). As Schele and Freidel noted, sajal were likely members of the ruler's extended family or members of otherwise politically powerful factions in the court. However, they were also the creatures of the ruler, ultimately dependent on him for their authority. Sajal were crafted physically and morally: first in childhood by their families through transformations of the head and face, and then through adornments, regalia, and performance with the *k'uhul ajaw* in dance, warfare, and the presentation of tribute, particularly captives. Such transformations empowered sajal to become the manifestation of royal authority throughout the greater landscape of the kingdom.

In turn, it is this close connection between the sajal and the person of the ruler that made these nobles such emblematic captives, objects to be accumulated by enemy lords. To begin to fully address these transformations and relationships in this chapter we will first discuss the crafting of personhood among the Classic Maya, highlighting especially the importance of the head and face. We will then examine how the sajal as a being was completed through performances that were central to the political messages depicted on the monuments of the Yaxchilán kingdom (figures 7.1–7.2).

## THE BODY, THE HEAD, AND BEING HUMAN

Sajal, including male and female members of the court, were born into illustrious families, but birthright alone did not make a sajal. Young Maya lords began as *ch'ok*, a term that identifies them as "sprouts" in a quite literal, vegetal sense. These were unripe beings in the process of becoming (Houston 2009:154–163; Schele 1992:141–142). As the rich discussion by Stephen Houston (2009) of Classic period youths makes clear, *ch'ok sajal* did not simply age into adulthood. To achieve full potency as an ally and aid to the king, the sajal of Yaxuun Bahlam needed to be transformed. Maya sovereigns did not merely supervise ritual or political events; they worked them and cultivated them as one would work and cultivate the agricultural field (Stuart 2005a, 2011:2; 2005a; Taube 2003a:464). So, too, the bodies of subordinate nobles were cultured beginning in childhood, first by their families and then by their kings to serve the sovereign and the dynast. The physical creation of the sajal, required first of all the creation of the head and visage of a sajal,—called *baah* in the inscriptions of the Classic period (Houston Stuart, and Taube 2006:62-72). This was a process enacted in daily practice and through intermittent rituals.

To say that the head and face were central to notions of Maya personhood is more than to simply recognize a general human interest and focus on facial recognition. For the Maya of the Classic period, as in many modern communities, the head and face *are* the person (Houston and Stuart 1996; Stuart 1996). They are parts that stand for the whole, and in particular they represent the aspect of potential personhood that is accessible and malleable. In this sense, the physical body stands in contrast to the spiritual co-essences that were and

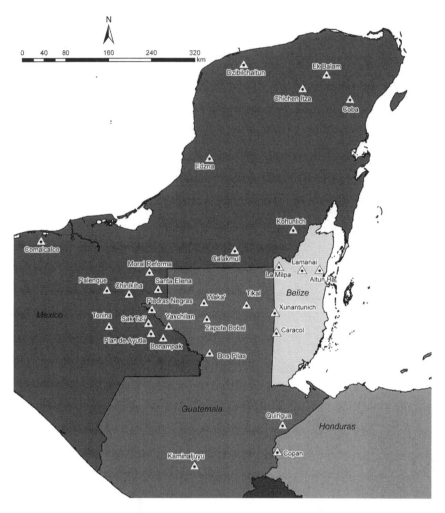

**Figure 7.1.** *Location of the Usumacinta River region including Yaxchilán and its neighbors inset in a modern political map (drawing by Charles Golden).*

remain critical components of personhood. For lack of a better translation we might call these souls, but they are quite different from Judeo-Christian understandings of souls in which the soul is the intrinsic essence of a person, perfectible through prayer, penance, and performance. Maya souls help define a person, but they are not the person, and in contemporary understandings multiple souls may inhabit a single body.

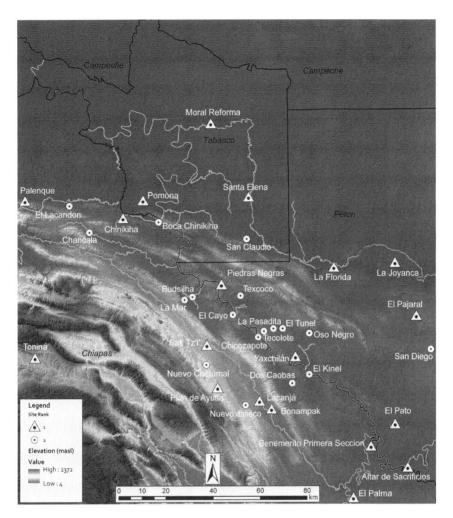

FIGURE 7.2. *Regional map of the region encompassing Yaxchilán and its neighbors (drawing by Charles Golden).*

For the contemporary Maya, and perhaps also the ancient Maya, the union of body with co-essences began at birth and continued throughout childhood, constituting a critical part of personhood (Groark 2009, 2010; Houston and Stuart 1989; Pitarch 2011; Scherer 2015:12). In the Classic period animate life force, wind, and breath are idealized in concept of *ik'* (Houston and Taube 2000:267), and one class of spiritual co-essences are identified in Classic period texts as *way* (Houston and Stuart 1989). Although the relationship between way and the individual remains a matter of debate, there is some sense that these essences relate to matters of power, witchcraft, and illness (Calvin 1997; Grube and Nahm 1994; Helmke and Nielsen 2009; Stuart 2012a).

Most pertinent for our discussion is that a good argument can be made that the ancient Maya, like their modern descendants, understood souls as external entities of immutable character that could become untethered to lived bodies while dreaming, through fear, as a result of intoxication, or in death. In contrast, the body is mutable and perfectible. In its form and comportment, one's corporeal self is the very essence of morality or its opposites (Guiteras-Holmes 1961; Houston, Stuart, and Taube 2006; Pitarch 2011; Scherer 2015:11–49; Vogt 1970; Vogt and Stuart 2005).

Tzeltal understandings of bodies offer a useful analogy for considering Classic Maya bodies, especially in light of important linguistic parallels. Among the Tzeltal, the "flesh body" (*bak'etal*) comprises all parts of the body understood as connected to the circulatory-respiratory, animating systems. It is that which makes the being only *potentially* human, and it is something shared by all animals. What makes a human truly human is the "presence body" (*winkilel*). The presence body is the complete body, the flesh body plus "the figure, the body shape, the face, the way of speaking, of walking, of dressing" (Pitarch 2011:98) The presence body is perceived by others as biomoral, a social being capable of engaging in interpersonal action. Both of these aspects of the body are "fabricated" over the course of life, fed by food and by social interaction (Pitarch 2011: 100).

During the Classic period, humans were described as *winik*, a term that suggests the nuanced significance of "animate, sentient being" similar to Pitarch's description of the Tzeltal *winkilel* (Houston, Stuart, and Taube 2006:11). Texts make clear that captives, on the other hand, have been reduced to *baak*, literally bones. They have become beings that are no longer fully human, no longer winik, but rather mere objects. As Houston (2001) points out, in Classic period art, baak are dehumanized, likened to animals through their nakedness and uncontrolled emotions.

In Classic period texts, it was the head, the face, the self, the *baah* that were cultivated, ripened, and fundamentally the focus of humanization. The Classic period Maya have long been noted for realistic depictions of human individuals, with a focus on portraiture on polychrome pottery and carved stone sculpture that is arguably rivaled in the Americas only in the modeled pottery of the contemporary Moche culture of South America. This intense concern by Maya artists with the face was not merely an artistic style, but reflected the deep concern with the self, the intrinsic being, of the subject depicted. The baah was the image and the reality of personhood (Houston, Stuart, and Taube 2006). Thus, for instance, images of Maya deities are given individuality by their faces, headdresses, and other features and adornments of the head that are partible and can stand in for the whole deity when combined with other imagery (M. Coe 1973:54; Houston, Stuart, and Taube 2006:16–17; Houston and Taube 2000:283; Martin 2015). This emphasis on the synecdochic function of heads and faces is also evident in the Maya tradition of dancing with masks: appearing with the faces of gods, Maya lords and ladies made these beings copresent (Grube 1992; Looper 2009).

Ethnographic observations echo this need for the self, for the head, to see and to be seen in order to achieve human intersubjectivity. "One is what one shows to others," writes Pitarch (2011:5). So, for instance, in the masked dance of the Rabinal Achi, a performance that dates to the sixteenth century if not earlier, the dominant Rabinal lord demands that his enemy be brought into his presence and be known through a reported invocation:

> Now bring him in here, sir, this brave, this man . . . in my teeth, in my face. I have yet to look him in the teeth, yet to look him in the face . . . to see how brave he may be, how manly. (Tedlock 2003:91)

## CRAFTING THE BAAH, SHAPING THE SAJAL

The transformation of the head and face over the life of humans echoes the framing and shaping that took place as the gods worked to perfect humans (not always successfully) at the dawn of creation (Christenson 2007). In the Popul Vuh—a sixteenth-century K'iche document but one that likely has resonances with Classic period religion (Christenson 2007)—the act of creation is explicitly described using the verbs to frame (*tz'aq*) and to shape (*b'it*). Through this process of assembly, humans gained the ability to speak, see, listen, walk, and manipulate things. They became winik in the parlance of the Classic period. That is, to perceive and have mobility are fundamental to being human, and perception is rooted in attributes of the head (Houston, Stuart, and Taube 2006:58–72). As in the Classic period, and as in Maya language communities through today, the Popol Vuh emphasizes the connection between self and visage, as for the K'iche to appear as human is to be human, "then they looked like people therefore; people they became" (Christenson 2007:156).

Yet, our best evidence for the crafting of ancient heads and selves comes not from ancient inscriptions, imagery, and ethnohistoric analogy, but rather from the mortal remains accessible to us as the fragmented skeletons encountered in excavations. As a number of scholars have suggested, the act of crafting Classic period bodies began immediately after birth with the shaping of the head, the first framing and shaping of the baah (Duncan and Hofling 2011; Geller 2011; Scherer 2018; Tiesler 2011, 2013). Such shaping was not a simple one-time act, but required daily practice in the wrapping, unwrapping, and compression of the infant head until age two or three, when the cranium lost its plasticity and achieved its final form (Tiesler 2011). Among the Maya of the western kingdoms, the tabular oblique form—creating the elegant and elongated profile so pronounced in royal portraits at Yaxchilán and its neighbors—was the dominant head shape (Scherer 2018). The form demonstrates the western Maya's perceived affinity to maize and the supernatural beings that embody this precious crop. Moreover, the crania of western elites and commoners alike were crafted in this form.

Once the head was formed, childhood between the period of weaning and puberty was a liminal phase in which the body learned the regulation of proper bodily movement and control (Ardren 2011). Entry into social adolescence involved the first bloodletting as evidenced in artistic depictions, most famously on Panel 19 from Dos Pilas. There, a youthful lord of Dos Pilas enacts his first bloodletting overseen by his father and supervised by emissaries from the court at Calakmul, to which the rulers of Dos Pilas were subordinate (Houston 1993:115; Martin and Grube 2000:61). The age at which such ritual initiations took place likely varied widely, and could happen as early as five years old, determined as much by political needs as by physical maturation (Stuart 2008; also Houston, Stuart, and Taube 2006:131–132).

Social adolescence likely ended with the carving of teeth into adult, and fully human, forms (Houston, Stuart, and Taube 2009:163–165). Just as the binding of the head began the crafting of the Maya self, the modification of the teeth was another important milestone, if not the final rite in the process. Although the anterior permanent teeth (the most commonly modified) are in place by about age ten, Andrew Scherer's analyses of a large sample of skeletons from the Usumacinta region indicate that the youngest people to have modified teeth are between eighteen and twenty years old at the time of death. This would suggest that as individuals approached the completion of their first *winikhaab* (often called *katun* in the academic literature)—their first set of twenty years—they were transformed and became yet more complete and more human. Nearly 60 percent of those individuals with modified teeth have their incisors filed into an *ik'* or "t-shape" that indicates an enlivening spirit.

Thus, cranial shaping, bloodletting, and dental filing formed an often painful sequence of rites whereby the Maya shaped and marked the body from infancy to adulthood (Geller 2006; Houston and Scherer 2010). These acts of transformation were not without serious risk. At the site of El Kinel, Guatemala—a rural center subordinate to the dynasty of Yaxchilán—a young woman died between the ages of sixteen and twenty, quite possibly as the result of an infection resulting from a dental inlay process that penetrated into the pulp chamber of an incisor (Scherer et al. 2014). So, too, Vera Tiesler (2011) has documented lesions on the skulls of children that may be the result of serious complications from daily head wrapping and compression. Such injuries may have required surgeries, and occasionally they resulted in death.

Rulers and nobles were always in the process of becoming. At what age, precisely, the unripe ch'ok sajal of Yaxuun Bahlam IV became complete beings with fully adult bodies, we cannot say (Houston 2009). Moreover, once physically formed the adult body still needed to be crafted as a being of authority through dance, battle, and bloodshed in the palace and temples of Yaxchilán and on the battlefield with its enemies.

## FRAMING THE SAJAL THROUGH VISION AND MOVEMENT

These transformations of the sajal through performance are encoded in monuments and architecture. Indeed, one of the critical observations made by Schele and Freidel (1990) was that the monuments of Yaxchilán must be understood in relationship to their architectural settings. Yaxchilán and its subordinate centers are famed for their exquisite lintels depicting sajal and ruler engaged in performance together. These were often placed three to a building, each above the doorway entrance to an interior room space, and frequently forming a narrative across the set. We would like to extend their important insight to note that we must also understand the architectural settings of monuments at hinterland sites in spatial relationship across the landscape to the polity capital. We must consider how urban center and border outpost together operated to construct a lived space that frame the actions of the Yaxchilán sajal directly under the watchful gaze of his king. For the sajal and other courtiers were empowered in the -*ichnal*—the visual, perceptual field, the agentive and supervising presence—of the ruler (Houston 2006:141-142; Houston et al. 2006 :173-175).

The Yaxchilán king would likely have visited hinterland sites in person, but our personal experience and computer modeling of viewsheds also indicate that Yaxuun Bahlam IV could have gazed out to the north from the South Acropolis at Yaxchilán and seen many of the noble palaces that housed these monuments (Golden and Davenport 2013; Scherer and Golden 2009). Among these palaces were the central reception buildings at borderland sites including Tecolote, La Pasadita, Chicozapote, and Oso Negro. Indeed, even the famed Structure 1 at Bonampak, though not visible from Yaxchilán, was nonetheless nearly identical to the central structures of Tecolote, La Pasadita, and Chicozapote. Such structures were built to royal specifications by masons and adorned with murals by artisans sent to the hinterlands from the dynastic center by Yaxuun Bahlam IV and his successors (Golden 2003; Golden and Scherer 2013; Golden et al. 2008; Scherer and Golden 2009, 2014). These palaces vary in some features, but are remarkably similar in terms of room spaces and architectural details (Scherer and Golden 2012:71).

Other than the more distant Bonampak, La Pasadita is perhaps the best known of these sites, having yielded at least four carved lintels that looters ripped from its buildings in the 1960s or 1970s. Such looting brought about the collapse of La Pasadita Structure 1, and the destruction of its remaining mural paintings (Doyle 2015; Golden 2003; Kamal et al. 1999). There are four lintels that depict the sajal Tiloom, two of which we are able to link securely to Structure 1 from the fragments of the lintels still on site. Two of the four depict the Tiloom in the company of Yaxuun Bahlam IV. In the earliest of these, Tiloom performs a scattering ritual with Yaxuun Bahlam, while in the second Tiloom delivers a captive prince from Piedras Negras to his overlord. The third lintel marks a political transition, with Tiloom presenting a helmet-like headdress to Itzamnaaj Bahlam IV, the enthroned heir of Yaxuun Bahlam IV (Doyle 2015), while a fourth lintel depicts Tiloom alone, engaged in a vibrant dance.

Although the scenes depicted on these monuments may have taken place at Yaxchilán itself, the emplacement of the monuments at La Pasadita suggests instead that they occurred at the latter site or somewhere nearby. The implication is that the Yaxchilán king made regular visits to these sites to participate in ritual events and oversaw military campaigns. There may be a tendency to see the lintel that depicts Tiloom dancing by himself as an outlier, freeing the sajal from his overlord's gaze. Yet, we argue that the intervisibility of the South Acropolis at Yaxchilán and Structure 1 at La Pasadita meant that Yaxuun Bahlam IV and his heir were always copresent with Tiloom through the -ichnal of the ruler.

We can see this royal oversight even with individuals who would seem to have their own power bases, including members of the royal family such as Lady Great Skull Zero, wife of Yaxuun Bahlam IV and her brother, both of whom are sajal and appear together on Lintel 14 at Yaxchilán. Lintel 14 is one of a set of three carved lintels in Structure 20. Yaxuun Bahlam is very much present on the other two lintels of Structure 20, his -ichnal ever present and supervising these images and activating the space and performance. Similarly, although the famed mural text from Structure 1 of Bonampak would seem to describe the victory and authority of Bonampak's own ruler, in fact it heavily concerns the Yaxchilán king Itzamnaaj Bahlam IV overseeing the accession of the Bonampak ruler. Bonampak Lintel 2 beneath which one passes to enter the central room makes the k'uhul ajaw of Yaxchilán yet more present, depicting him in the process of taking a captive (Martin and Grube 2008:136).

Thus, the ruler's literal oversite, his -ichnal, and his joint performance of rituals and warfare with his sajal formed and empowered those sajal, even as the image and self of the king were also shaped. The resultant bodily comportment, the performance of self, might be encompassed by a term like "habitus" (Bourdieu 1977), if we want to put it in European academic terms. It seems most reminiscent to us, however, of the framing and the shaping of the flesh body and the presence body among the modern Tzeltal Maya of Chiapas, as described above. Although the precise meaning of the sajal title is elusive, it may refer back to the body of the noble and its relationship to that of the k'uhul ajaw. *Ajaw* would seem to be a title derived from "he who shouts," a powerful, authoritative body. Sajal, on the other hand, may denote one "who fears" (Stuart 1993:329–330), or perhaps a "small person" (Tokovinine 2005:47). Alternatively, based on modern Tzeltal and Chontal cognates (e.g., Tzeltal—*sajal k'op*, "whisper") we speculate that the term may imply "one who whispers," as a title that pairs well with "he who shouts" (Keller and Luciano G. 1997:209; Polian 2015:562–563; Slocum et al. 1999:103).

We can turn to Yaxchilán's neighbor and great rival Piedras Negras for another potent glimpse into the modeling and the making of sajal. There, on Stela 5, a figure named K'an Mo' Te' appears as the *baah teem sajal*, the "head throne *sajal*," his role emphasized by this image, serving his lord on the dais above and created in that position through his presence in the -ichnal. His service to the king shaped his role and his being. He is remembered years later on Panel 3 as a *baah sajal*, the "head sajal," still seated front and center at the foot of his lord, yet another Piedras Negras king, in his -ichnal (Martin and Grube 2008:149; figure 7.3).

There is another intriguing statement regarding the embodiment of both king and *sajal* on Panel 3. Seated to the bottom right of the Piedras Negras king is a figure whose name has been effaced, but who is associated with a fine line inscription that presents an unusual incidence of reported first-person speech: *awinaken Yokib*. The text literally reads something like "I am your person, Yokib," where Yokib is the dynastic title born by rulers of Piedras Negras (Bíró 2011:294; Stuart et al. 1999:11–19).

**Figure 7.3.** *Panel 3 from Piedras Negras showing (a) K'an Mo' Te' baah sajal; and (b) an unknown lord making first-person statement,* awinaken yokib—*"I am your person, Yokib"' (painting by Mary Louise Baker, Courtesy of the Penn Museum, Image #176733).*

One could read this in a European sense as a pledge of loyalty to an overlord, and it may indeed have this implication (Bíró 2011:294). Yet, we would suggest that the sculptor did not intend this statement as merely a statement of fealty by the sajal to the person of the ruler per se. Rather, in some sense it is a statement that this sajal—like his counterparts in the Yaxchilán kingdom—is the product and offspring of, the creation and creature of, the dynasty as embodied in the king.

Perhaps the most fascinating series of lintels is the set of looted sculptures known as the Palmer collection, about which Alexandre Tokovinine (2005; see also Jackson 2013:37–41) has written in detail (figure 7.3). Although we cannot yet link these monuments to any documented archaeological site, they nonetheless reveal the key relationship of k'uhul ajaw and sajal, presenting a retrospective political history that spans the period that brought Yaxuun Bahlam IV to power. On what is surely meant to present the earliest piece of the narrative (figure 7.4a), Itzamnaaj Bahlam III (Yaxuun Bahlam's father) stands to the viewer's right. The king carries a spear and is said to wear, and is shown wearing, the same jaguar headdress that he receives from his wife on Lintel 26 at Yaxchilán. He is accompanied by a ch'ok sajal named Ajkamo', who carries an axe and a drum. Ajkamo' is a young warrior, who claims four captives and holds the title of *yajawte'*, "spear-lord."

On what would appear to the second lintel in the series (figure 7.4b), Ajkamo' stands on the right and goes unnamed, but is clearly identified by

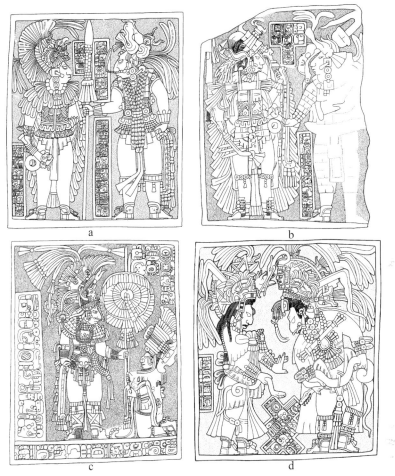

**FIGURE 7.4.** *Four-looted lintels from an as-yet-unidentified hinterland site in the Yaxchilán kingdom (from Mayer 1995:74–79, pl. 253–259).*

his regalia, including the same drum and axe that he wields in the first monument. On the left is a ch'ok ajaw—the unripe prince of Yaxchilán. Although this prince carries an unfamiliar preaccession name, the other titles attributed to the figure—particularly "he of twenty-captives"—make it clear that this is indeed Yaxuun Bahlam IV at about AD 726, before he took the throne. The text suggests that the action portrayed on the monument is the presentation of a mask representing the "old deer god," one of the patrons of Yaxuun Bahlam (Tokovinine 2005:42).

The third lintel in the series jumps ahead to AD 750 (figure 7.4c), and shows Ajkamo' kneeling before Yaxuun Bahlam. A mirror-imaged text (Matsumoto 2013) describes the actions undertaken by Ajkamo' as the adornment of the same headdress worn by Itzamnaaj Bahlam in the first monument of the series. Intriguingly, Itzamnaaj Balham had been dead for some eight years by this time, and Yaxuun Bahlam IV was still two years from officially ascending to the throne. Nonetheless, in an unreversed text below the figures, the monument's carver accorded to Yaxuun Bahlam the full regnal titles of the holy lord of Yaxchilán.

In the fourth and final monument (figure 7.4d), the action takes place in AD 767. Image and inscription make clear that Yaxuun Bahlam and Ajkamo' are here engaged in performing a snake dance. Standing to the viewer's left is Ajkamo', who is now afforded the title of *aj-k'uhuun* (Jackson and Stuart 2001). Although the meaning of this title is debatable, and individuals so named likely performed multiple courtly roles, it is intriguing that one of the possible readings is "he of the holy headband," likely referring to the ceremonial *amate* bark-paper headband worn by Maya rulers (Jackson 2013:68; Jackson and Stuart 2001:222; Stuart 2012b). On the right stands the Yaxuun Bahlam IV, now undeniably in his full glory as uncontested ruler of the kingdom.

Across these four lintels we can see the joint transformation of ruler and ruled, and the focus on crowns, mask, and the image and self of the ruler. On the one hand, the transformation of Ajkamo' from ch'ok sajal to aj-k'uhuun may be a matter of aging and maturing into a series of new positions (Tokovinine 2005). Yet, just as individuals did not simply age from ch'ok into the full ripeness of adulthood (Houston 2009), neither did one simply change positions with the acquisition of years. Rather, it was the performances recorded and remembered on these monuments that shaped Ajkamo' and his kings.

Of central interest in these monuments considered as a group are the headdresses—not just those that are worn, but those that function as the focus of action and text. In the first monument, the young Ajkamo' is engaged with Itzamnaaj Bahlam III and his jaguar crown. In the second scene, Ajkamo' presents a mask to Yaxuun Bahlam IV that depicts and makes copresent a deity closely associated with the king. In the third lintel the jaguar crown that once belonged to his father is now the possession of Yaxuun Bahlam and is adorned by Ajkamo'. Finally, although the imagery focuses on dance, Ajkamo' is named by a title—aj-k'uhuun—explicitly concerned with the royal headband. Such head adornments frame and shape the *baah* of the ruler. Therefore, thus just as performance with the k'uhul ajaw shaped the sajal, so too the noble lord, in the guise of sajal and aj-k'uhuun was needed to form the king.

## YAXUUN BAHLAM IV AND THE SAJAL OF
## THE YAXCHILÁN KINGDOM

As much as the monuments and buildings of the Yaxchilán kingdom empha-size a king who oversees his subordinates, they also point to the importance of cooperation and shared performance throughout the space of the kingdom. In *A Forest of Kings*, Schele and Freidel (1990) vividly paint a picture of the politi-cal machinations that may have brought Yaxuun Bahlam IV to the Yaxchilán throne after a ten-year interregnum. Yet, the system that the Yaxchilán dynasty established in this contentious process was—at least rhetorically—a relatively stable one. When Yaxuun Bahlam acceded in AD 752, he took control of essen-tially the same kingdom that his father had governed, and his son, Itzamnaaj Bahlam, inherited this same territorial unit largely intact in AD 768, thanks in no small part to lords such as Ajkamo', who bridged the transition. There must have been a political shake-up among the magnates of the kingdom with each transition, yet there was no obvious fracture. It is likely not a coincidence that sajal who served at the throne in Yaxchilán itself were rhetorically over-shadowed by governors of hinterland centers who served to create a relatively stable political landscape that extended from the dynastic seat to the edges of the kingdom, and permitted the extension of royal military power far beyond those borders.

For Yaxuun Bahlam, most important of all was his loyal ally K'an Tok Wayiib, a lord named as the baah (head or first) sajal on monuments from both Yaxchilán itself and also from a monument formerly without prove-nience recovered about a decade ago in the town of Retalteco, Guatemala (Houston, Golden et al. 2006). Recently acquired local information strongly suggests that this monument was in fact taken from Tecolote, the largest of Yaxchilán's border sites positioned along the territorial boundary with Piedras Negras (Golden and Scherer 2013; Golden et al. 2008; Scherer and Golden 2009). K'an Tok Wayiib likely administered the edge of the kingdom around Tecolote and, along with his peers—including Tiloom at La Pasadita, and Ajkamo'—served to project royal power along and across the border.

It is hard not to see the polysemy of baah when used to describe a sajal. On the one hand, it is an ordinal; this is the "head" sajal, first among a category of lords, and ranked above all others. He is presumably the right hand of the ruler. On the other hand, the term takes on a subtly different significance in Maya worldview. For the head does not merely lead the body, but it is the very image and being of the body as a whole. A baah sajal is both the ultimate sajal, but also represents the ideal of what a sajal should be. He is the very image, the being, and self of sajal-ship.

As monuments from throughout the kingdom attest, maintaining this stability was in no small part the result of the k'uhul ajaw performing the boundaries of the kingdom alongside his border lords themselves, through performances recorded on monuments placed across the kingdom. There are certainly physical, functional markers of the border along the northern limits of the Yaxchilán kingdom: Walls and hilltop redoubts cross from east to west, comprising part of an architectural landscape that includes the palaces of border lords at sites such as La Pasadita and Tecolote (Golden et al. 2008; Golden and Scherer 2013; Scherer and Golden 2009, 2014). These features constituted a formidable martial landscape and gave the impression of permanence.

Yet these durable material features alone were insufficient to project the authority of the king and the solidity of his kingdom. Rather, it was the personal performance of the ruler and his courtiers that was required to constitute, activate, and perpetually maintain and redefine the limits of the kingdom and the bounds of its moral community. These public performances required spaces built to royal specifications. Masons followed architectural templates from the dynastic center and were deployed to the hinterlands, where they built palaces that still stand today, virtually identical in form and dimension at places such as Bonampak, El Chicozapote, Tecolote, and La Pasadita. The king deployed royal artisans to these border palaces, where they painted murals and installed carved monuments that depicted the ruler of Yaxchilán and his subordinates dancing, scattering offerings, dominating captives, and receiving them as tribute. The texts on these monuments are not necessarily or centrally concerned with the biographic history of the sovereign and sajal, but instead aided the body of the ruler and the sajal in expanding and maintaining the moral space-time that centered the kingdom and created place from space (Monaghan 1998; Stuart 1998:375).

It was the dyad of k'uhul ajaw and sajal that was required, and the ruler created his partners, investing them with the power to perform. Such inscribed monuments were particularly potent because they united the image and self of the ruler and sajal in *perpetual* performance, an ongoing act of creating the landscape (Davenport and Golden 2016; Golden 2010; Golden and Scherer 2013; Gossen 1974b:398–399; Houston and Stuart 1998; Houston, Stuart, and Taube 2006:72–81; Hull 2003:375–376; Scherer and Golden 2014; Stuart 1996). The ever-present, ever-living bodies of the ruler and his subordinate were depicted as the epitome of controlled, human behavior, and they danced, fought, and performed the limits of the territory into being.

## POSSESSING THE SAJAL, POSSESSING THE LANDSCAPE

The creation of the bodies of sajal as powerful companions for the k'uhul ajaw also made them important captives. Sajal and other subordinate lords taken in warfare were not just symbols of victory; they were captive pieces of the self of the defeated kingdom and its rulers. The rulers of Yaxchilán and their ascendant sajal stand (or sit) in elegant contrast to their twisted and writhing captives. These are animalistic beings from outside the moral landscape of the kingdom (Houston, Stuart, and Taube 2006:202–226; Taube 2003a). Stripped of their lordly humanity, their human souls perhaps scared right out of them, they were reduced and transformed into baak; they became amoral flesh bodies and no longer moral and fully human winik. They were possessions who served as metonyms of their places of origin, the person of the enemy ruler, and the material landscape of the defeated enemy kingdom.

Perhaps the best example involves the polity of Namaan (centered on modern La Florida, Guatemala) on the San Pedro Mártir River, an essential route of travel into and out of the Sierra del Lacandón. In AD 681, Itzamnaaj Bahlam III took the captive Aj 'Nik, a seemingly minor noble within the hierarchical structure of the Namaan kingdom centered on La Florida. This captive became such an important touchstone in the career of Itzamnaaj Bahlam III that he bears the title "Master of Aj 'Nik" in thirty-two different inscriptions (Martin and Grube 2008:124).

The capture of Aj 'Nik was so significant because it was a critical strike by Itzamnaaj Bahlam III prior to his accession against the person and landscape of his nominal superior, Ruler 2 of Piedras Negras, in the twilight of that king's rule. Aj 'Nik was in some sense a "minor lord," otherwise unknown in the texts. Yet, his capture was a powerful sign that Yaxchilán's forces could exercise power across on the far side of the Piedras Negras domain. This was a crucial travel route for people moving to and from Piedras Negras and central Petén, and thus threatened access to the east and imperiled the flow of goods into the Piedras Negras kingdom (Golden and Scherer 2013; Golden et al. 2012; Scherer and Golden 2014). As much as this victory may have threatened movement across the landscape, it also represented the acquisition by Itzamnaaj Bahlam of a lord who had been carefully crafted by the ruler of Namaan. The capture of Aj 'Nik removed a body that might have helped to perform, bring into being, and maintain the Namaan kingdom and moral community.

The importance of such a blow was further underscored by the betrothal of K'inich Yo'nal Ahk II of Piedras Negras to Ix Winikhaab Ajaw, a princess of the Namaan dynasty. This is one of the most celebrated marriages in the epigraphic record, made famous particularly by Piedras Negras Stela 3, and was apparently orchestrated by Ruler 2, who supervised a prenuptial rite for the couple only days before his death in AD 686 (Martin and Grube 2008:145; Stuart 1985). The prevalence of sculpture featuring Lady Katun Ajaw at Piedras Negras must be seen as a rhetorical conflict against the numerous references to the captured Aj 'Nik.

Payback, however, was forthcoming. On Stela 8 from Piedras Negras, the Yaxchilán king's victory is turned on its head. Here a lord from Piedras Negras, subordinate to the same K'inich Yo'nal Ahk married to Lady Katun Ajaw of Namaan, takes captive a sajal from Yaxchilán. The capture phrase was clearly directed as a pointed barb to the person of Itzamnaaj Bahlam III, naming the captive as "his *sajal*, the guardian of Aj 'Nik.'" This is more than just a tit-for-tat, pawn-for-pawn statement. It is a performance intended to undercut the power of the claims laid by Itzamnaaj Bahlam upon the person and the landscape of Namaan and Piedras Negras.

Thus, considering the creation and crafting of sajal in performance with their overlord, and the extension of royal power across the landscape through the dyadic pairing in image, text, and person of *k'uhul ajaw* and *sajal*, it becomes clear that the claims of Yaxchilán's rulers to captives were more than just the bellicose rhetoric of military strong men. The audacious boasts of Yaxuun Bahlam IV to be "he of twenty captives," the special "affection" that Itzamnaaj Bahlam III and IV had for certain prisoners, and the delivery of groups of captives as tribute were not indicative of warfare spiraling out of control or a particularly aggressive kingdom. Instead, the change in being, as captive lords became baak, represented the final logical transformation of these bodies into objects of power, inalienably linked to the landscape and person of the overlord who had created and perfected him or her—objects of power now possessed by Yaxuun Bahlam, his father, and his son.

## CONCLUSION

In concluding, we end where we began, with an appreciation for the keen insights and vivid prose of *A Forest of Kings*. Weaving together the then state-of-the-art decipherments, Linda Schele and David Freidel (1990) painted a picture of palace intrigue that still captivates after twenty-five years. Critically for us as researchers working in the Yaxchilán kingdom, Schele and Freidel connected the dots of history and politics by linking the inscriptions to the architectural landscape in which they were set. By expanding that perspective, by considering the past three decades of advances in decipherment, exploring the political landscape as the setting for the monuments as part of a broader set of political performances, we can better see Yaxuun Bahlam IV as the great patron of Yaxchilán. He expanded the power and authority of the dynasty, building on the patterns established by his father, Itzamnaaj Bahlam, and passing them along to his son of the same name. Critical to this expansion were the sajal of the Yaxchilán kingdom, noble lords who supported the king's ambitions, brought him to the throne, and waged his battles, but who were also crafted by the king and were ultimately his creations.

# 8

*Macaw Mountain
and Ancient Peoples of
Southeast Mesoamerica*

WENDY ASHMORE

In *A Forest of Kings*, Linda Schele and David Freidel captivated readers with substance and inference about multiple Maya cities and their inhabitants. For Copán, they focused on long- and short-term developments culminating in the death of its last effective king, Yax Pasaj Chan Yopaat, whose death effectively coincided with the end of both dynastic rule and social cohesion at Macaw Mountain, Copán. Extraordinary finds and ideas have come to light since that 1990 publication, things the authors could not have known when they wrote. The time is right to explore briefly some theoretical, substantive, and methodological advances for interpreting people's lives and practices in culturally diverse societies of what are now parts of Guatemala, Honduras, and El Salvador. Freshly discriminating models and innovative analytic methods continue to enrich greatly our understanding of people, politics, and lived experience at Classic Maya Copán and its vexing subordinate Quiriguá, as well as a growing range of their neighbors, whether allies, foes, subordinates, or other. Much remains as told in *A Forest of Kings*, and as its authors foresaw in their prologue, at least as much has augmented the narrative in the subsequent twenty-five years.

As I reexamined *A Forest of Kings* for this essay, two comments struck me at the outset, one by Linda Schele and one by David Freidel. With respect to when they were writing in 1989, Linda remarked, "This time of discovery is not yet over, for the decipherment of the

DOI: 10.5876/9781646420469.c008

Maya writing system, the study of their religion and politics, the excavations and analyses of the remains of their lives are not yet finished. In truth, they are barely begun" (Schele and Freidel 1990:14). In his personal note, David tells us that in response to receiving his early article on Cerros, Belize, Linda "called me up from Austin and said, 'David, you're right for all the wrong reasons. We have to talk'" (16).

Both comments are pertinent to this essay and to reconsidering ideas about Copán and southeast Mesoamerica a quarter century after their book was published. Each quotation embodies, in my view, the dynamism and energetic collaboration that pervade Maya studies today. We all know that inquiry is never truly completed, but the outreach, generosity, and constructive critique in expressions quoted are growing hallmarks of today's study of the ancient Maya and their neighbors. And David's comment made me smile, recalling that I, too, had been the fortunate (and surprised) recipient of that kind of call from Linda, when my article on site-planning principles came out, in 1991. I have never been quite so happy on hearing such bluntly stern-yet-encouraging criticism. Open collaboration invites just such supportive critique.

Working from Linda and David's collaborative spirit, I highlight aspects of the last quarter century of research at Copán, and at Quiriguá and nearby places in southeast Mesoamerica. That is, the Copán focus is the conjunctive approach so impressively successful in research there. For Quiriguá and the southeast, multiple independent projects have collectively created a mosaic of understanding, across people, polities, and cultures.

## COPÁN

In 1975, at the behest of the Instituto Hondureño de Antropología e Historia (IHAH), Gordon Willey, Bill Coe, and Bob Sharer (1976) proposed multi-faceted programs of archaeological research and preservation at and around Copán, the plan originally envisioned for work from 1976 to 1981. The proposal instead gave rise to a *series* of multiyear Copán Archaeological Projects, each with its own goals and theoretical standpoint, some continuing to this day. In 1991, Bill Fash and Bob Sharer assessed the achievements of the work to that date, urging expanded pursuit of a conjunctive approach, integrating diverse perspectives and data sets—from epigraphy, to settlement archaeology, excavation, iconographic study, geomorphology, and bioarchaeology—"in a cross-cutting and self-correcting strategy" for a fuller understanding of ancient Copán (Fash and Sharer 1991:170).

Of course, as Schele and Freidel acknowledged, all of this research was well afoot when they wrote *A Forest of Kings*, in which their chosen case study for Macaw Mountain—a sacred place to ancient Copanecos—was the rule and demise of Copán's final effective king, Yax Pasaj Chan Yopaat. What has happened in the quarter century since that 1990 volume publication is virtual fulfillment of the ambitious research plan Fash and Sharer outlined only a year later. Especially striking to me is the Copán Acropolis Project, in which Fash solicited teams led individually by Sharer, Ricardo Agurcia, and Will Andrews, to pursue mutually complementary investigations that would illuminate how the seat of authority in the Copán polity—that is, the Acropolis—came to be, and how the actions of ancient kings and nobles shaped and were shaped by political, economic, and ritual dimensions of Copán history. The goals certainly echo Linda's words, that discovery had barely begun. And the same goals offered ample opportunities for the new insights to be right, for all the *right* reasons. Conjunctive and collaborative stances remained key tenets in all that ensued.

A major goal for the Acropolis inquiry was establishing "the historical reality of the first 11 [of the 16] Copán rulers recorded in Copán's texts, and the scale of constructions in the Acropolis associated with these initial rulers (contemporary with the Acbi ceramic complex [AD 400–650])" (Fash and Sharer 1991:172). Were the earliest kings portrayed on Altar Q historical individuals or legendary, even mythical, personae? (figure 8.1).

Sharer's Early Copán Acropolis Project (ECAP) addressed exactly that, through a series of remarkable tunneling excavations that documented architectural establishment and growth of the axis mundi and heart of the Copán city and polity. Earlier tunneling efforts had taken place in the 1930s and again in the 1970s. From those tunnels as well as in the massive river erosion cut that was the modern Acropolis's eastern facade, it was evident that ancient Copanecos had created, modified, and terminated Acropolis construction, fortunately within an extraordinarily stable matrix that proved invaluable for modern archaeological tunneling. Excavators from ECAP documented not only the sequence of building programs, but also a series of buried hieroglyphic monuments and royal tombs, most prominently including the remains of the Copán dynasty founder, K'inich Yax K'uk Mo', and slightly later in ancient time, those of a royal woman, most likely the founder's wife. These initial rulers had *indeed* existed (figure 8.2).

Concurrent tunneling programs by Fash's team at Temple 26 (Str. 10L-26) and the Hieroglyphic Stairway, and by Agurcia's team at Temple 16 (Str. 10L-16), as well as Andrews' team's aboveground excavations just south of the

FIGURE 8.1. *Copán Altar Q, west side looking northeast, showing founder K'inich Yax K'uk' Mo' (left of center) transferring authority to the sixteenth ruler, Yax Pasaj Chan Yopaat, the two facing each other across a pair of glyphs for the date of the latter's accession (photo by author).*

Acropolis (Group 10L-2), together fully complemented ECAP, providing evidentiary glue that united the earliest, middle, and latest developments at the Acropolis, and in these, multifaceted traces of temporality in dynastic circumstances and strategies (Sharer et al. 1999; see also Ashmore 2015; figure 8.3). From the fifth-century buildings, offerings, and sculpture beneath temples 16 and 26; to sixth-century Rosalila structure, with its intentionally preserved polychrome stucco façade and chert eccentric offerings; to the seventh-century tomb of Smoke Imix, Ruler 12; and the eighth-century residential complex that housed Yax Pasaj and his retinue—these and ECAP investigations have supported a greatly enriched narrative of Copán's royal history. And while far from certain, it is even possible that the final resting place of Ruler 13, Waxaklajuun Ubaah K'awiil, might have been encountered a kilometer due north of the Acropolis (Ashmore 1991, 2013, 2015).

State-of-the-art bioarchaeological study has revealed the origins, life experiences, diet and health of royal families and of their subjects (Buikstra et al. 2004; Price et al. 2010; Storey 2005). At the same time, settlement studies, within and beyond the urban core, have produced not only substantial

**Figure 8.2.** *Cutaway view of sequential construction overlying the Copán axis mundi, culminating in Structure 10L-16, whose frontal, western stair is visible at right. Note earliest fifth-century construction with founder's tomb, and anciently preserved sixth-century Rosalila (Image 526714; copyright © Christopher Klein/National Geographic Creative).*

and significant findings but also the grounds for continued debate about their interpretation (Canuto 2004; Manahan and Canuto 2009; Webster 2005). Ample publication—in Spanish, English, and other languages—has characterized work at Copán, and two edited volumes bring many of these collaborative accomplishments together: *Understanding Early Classic Copan* (Bell et al. 2004a) and *Copán: The History of an Ancient Maya Kingdom* (A. Andrews and Fash 2005). In light of all that has been learned from the impressively intricate work accomplished, I suspect we are all relieved that actual research did not adopt Bill Coe's original proposal, to trench the Acropolis deeply, from east to west, to complement the north-south river cut (Willey et al. 1976:14)!

Of course, research at other Classic Maya polities and capitals has similarly yielded conjunctively attested histories in recent years, and as known for multiple of the centers discussed in this symposium, Copán was *not* the absolute first case. At Tikal, for example, Clemency Coggins's 1975 dissertation and multiple publications by Christopher Jones (1977, 1991) have linked rulers, monuments, tombs, and royal construction programs. Still, the degree

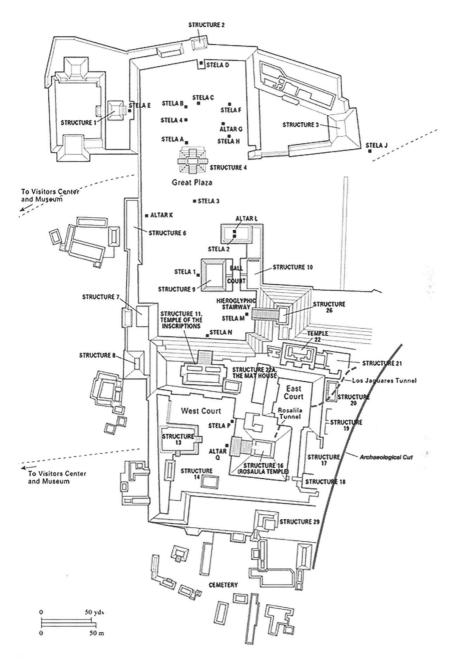

**FIGURE 8.3.** *Copán principal Group (plan with structure labels: Acropolis, 26, 16, Group 10L-2).*

of *explicit collaboration in conjunctive programs* at Copán has become a prime model for work elsewhere. Paraphrasing Linda, the best was yet to come, and is still underway.

## SOUTHEAST MESOAMERICA

In *A Forest of Kings*, Schele and Freidel touch on polities elsewhere in southeastern Mesoamerica, principally at Quiriguá. The latter is famous for, among other things its king's AD 738 capture and decapitation of Copán's Ruler 13, Waxaklajuun Ubaah K'awiil, or 18 Rabbit. A major archaeological project at Quiriguá took place in the late 1970s, and it documented construction histories, settlement patterns, and ceramic complexes that previous inquiries had scarcely touched (Sharer 1978). The final two of six monographs reporting that work are nearing completion at the University of Pennsylvania. Since Linda and David wrote, however, new and quite substantial work has taken place, including conservation and fresh excavations by José Crasborn and his colleagues at the Guatemalan Instituto de Antropología e Historia (IDAEH), the excavations revealing a hieroglyphic bench in the East Group (Marroquin et al. 2010); detailed analysis of the Quiriguá epigraphic record by Matt Looper (1999, 2003), a former student of Linda's; and reconsideration of existing Quiriguá data and interpretations, stimulated in part by vigorous research at Copán and its neighbors (Ashmore 2007, 2009; Sharer 2002; Sharer and Traxler 2006, 2009). A prominent example is Mary Bullard and Bob Sharer's forthcoming pottery analyses, which have been greatly refined through Sharer's direct engagement with Copán ceramics. For instance, our understanding of a simple, white-painted ceramic type, rare at both Quiriguá and Copán, gains from availability of contexts for its occurrence at both sites. One squat cylinder of this type recovered from a cenotaph chamber at Quiriguá also exhibited Teotihuacan-like *tau*-shaped feet, a material reference to that interregional giant, whose actions and renown had such profound effects across much of Mesoamerica (Braswell 2003b; Carrasco et al. 2000; figure 8.4). Put simply—both the foot form and the pottery type's elite contexts at Copán suggested that the vessel and the otherwise vacant chamber were meant to commemorate a member of a prominent Quiriguá family (Ashmore 2013:110).

Beyond Quiriguá and Copán, substantial research since 1990 has enriched immensely our understanding of societies in this culturally diverse region. Many of the investigators involved gnash their teeth at the "Mayoid" or other Maya-related labels given to the places they work. These scholars' research in

FIGURE 8.4. *Vessel 13N/48-1 from Quiriguá Structure 3C-2. Height 8.9 cm, diameter 15.0 cm (photo by author).*

the last quarter century has long since earned recognition of the region as a set of social and cultural entities in their own right (Joyce and Hendon 2000; Schortman and Nakamura 1991; Schortman et al. 1986; Urban and Schortman 1986, 1988; Urban et al. 2002). Consensus thought today identifies dynastic rule at both Copán and Quiriguá as intrusive from distant Maya places, especially Tikal. Indigenous peoples and cultures were present before and after subjugation by the Maya intruders. The life histories of the indigenous groups identifies autonomous, if *sometimes* Maya-influenced, trajectories of local polities and people.

Since *A Forest of Kings* was published in 1990, multiple, mutually independent projects in northwestern and west central Honduras have yielded compelling evidence for local autonomy, each society engaging to variable degree with adjacent and more distant peers, *sometimes* including Copán and Quiriguá, but *only* sometimes. Working closest to those Maya centers, Ed Schortman and colleagues continue consideration of the regional effects of Quiriguá's king killing Copán's Waxaklajuun Ubaah K'awiil, focused principally on culturally distinct capitals along both sides of the sierra that separated them, a set of polities responding to their abrupt "liberation" from four centuries of intrusive Maya hegemony (Schortman and Ashmore 2012; Schortman and Nakamura 1991). Early in the new millennium, Marcello Canuto and Ellen Bell (2003) undertook study of the El Paraíso Valley, at the highland summit of a route, arguably a major one, connecting Classic Copán and Quiriguá, revealing signatures of influence from both sides of the aforementioned sierra, and importantly, signatures of *indigenous, non-Maya culture.*

Farther afield, however, and not always *very* far, projects in the Chamelecón, Ulúa, Comayagua, and other river drainages continue to affirm the autonomy of culturally diverse polities and to outline their quite distinctive life histories (Dixon 1992; Joyce and Hendon 2000; Schortman and Urban 1994; Urban and Schortman 1986, 1988; Urban et al. 2002). Since 1990's *A Forest of Kings*, the cases have grown ever stronger. From this I join colleagues in urging that although the kinds of conjunctive approaches undertaken explicitly at Copán are powerful sources for understanding, the latter polity cannot be fully comprehended without comprehension of dynamics across the larger region in which the Maya polities are embedded. I daresay colleagues working in Maya and other parts of the region would agree.

### DISCUSSION/CONCLUSION

Extraordinary finds and ideas have come to light since *A Forest of Kings* was published in 1990, many of them things Schele and Freidel could not have known when they wrote. Freshly discriminating models and innovative analytic methods continue to enrich greatly our understanding of people, politics, and lived experience at Classic Maya Copán and its vexing subordinate Quiriguá, as well as a growing range of their neighbors, whether allies, foes, subordinates, or independents. Much remains largely as told in *A Forest of Kings*, and as its authors foresaw in their prologue, at least as much has augmented the narrative in the subsequent twenty-five years. Collectively, we're still working hard to get more and more things right, and this time for the right reasons.

### ACKNOWLEDGMENTS

I am grateful to Travis W. Stanton and M. Kathryn Brown for inviting my participation in this volume and in the 2015 Society of American Archaeology (SAA) symposium that preceded it. Individually and jointly, Linda Schele and David A. Freidel have advanced Maya studies tremendously, and *A Forest of Kings* is a particularly influential contribution. My debt is immense to them and to all those whose work and ideas are represented in this chapter, with apologizes for any and all errors in my account. Use of first names herein is for the relative informality of the symposium, citing collegial friends. Tom Patterson has kept me focused and offered helpful comments, always astutely critical as the essay came together.

## 9

*A Forest of Kings* had a significant impact on the field, as well as among public audiences, when it was published in 1990 (Schele and Freidel 1990). At the time, David Freidel was in the first stage of a long-term project at the site of Yaxuná, Yucatán (Selz Foundation Project). While chapter 9 of *A Forest of Kings* focused primarily on Chichén Itzá, Freidel's work at Yaxuná helped to shape the narrative of the struggle for political supremacy over the northern Maya lowlands among a series of cities and political confederations during the latter part of the Classic period. Freidel began his project at this site with two primary objectives in mind (see Stanton et al. 2010). First, given the previously reported evidence of a large Preclassic occupation at Yaxuná (Brainerd 1958; J. Thompson 1954), he was interested in understanding the development of early Maya society in the northern lowlands, only just recently researched in earnest by E. W. Andrews V (1988; Andrews V et al. 1984) at Komchén in the early 1980s. Second, Freidel was intent on testing the hypothesis of Anthony Andrews and Fernando Robles Castellanos (1985) that Yaxuná was a strategic site that was militarily contested by several cities during the latter part of the Classic period, specifically Cobá and Chichén Itzá. The narrative laid out in *A Forest of Kings* went on to shape interpretations of regional Maya politics in the central portion of the northern lowlands throughout the course of Freidel's project and made a significant impact on the literature (Ambrosino 2003, 2007; Ambrosino

*Borderland Politics*

*A Reconsideration of the Role of Yaxuná in Regional Maya Politics in the Latter Part of the Classic*

TRAVIS W. STANTON,
ALINE MAGNONI,
STANLEY P. GUENTER,
JOSÉ OSORIO LEÓN,
FRANCISCO PÉREZ RUÍZ, AND
MARÍA ROCIO GONZÁLEZ
DE LA MATA

DOI: 10.5876/9781646420469.c009

et al. 2003; Freidel 1992a, 2007; Suhler 1996; Suhler et al. 1998). Subsequent work by the Instituto Nacional de Antropología e Historia (INAH; Toscano Hernández and Ortegón Zapata 2003), the Proyecto de Interacción Política del Centro de Yucatán (PIPCY; Loya González and Stanton 2013, 2014; Magnoni et al. 2014; Robles et al. 2011), other projects working in the central northern lowlands (e.g., Vallejo and Manahan 2014), and original members of the Selz Foundation project (Johnstone 2001; Shaw and Johnstone 2001, 2006) has begun to change our understanding concerning how polities in the region articulated with one another in the absence of hieroglyphic texts bearing on intersite relations. In this chapter we argue that many of the data from Yaxuná that were once used to argue for direct confrontations between a Puuc-Cobaneco alliance and Chichén Itzá are actually separated in time. Moreover, we argue that Yaxuná and some other important sites in the region were subjected to gradual abandonment processes that likely greatly contributed to the urbanization processes at the Itzáe capital as well as the growth of a few larger regional towns likely allied to Chichén Itzá during the final portion of the Classic period.

## MAKING SENSE OF REGIONAL NORTHERN POLITICS IN THE 1980S

During the 1980s, the potential of hieroglyphic inscriptions to better understand intersite relationships during the Classic period was still beginning to be appreciated. *A Forest of Kings* was the first major book manuscript to attempt to synthesize the known data and, using a conjunctive approach, create regional histories for the Maya. In the northern lowlands, however, this endeavor was, and continues to be, exceedingly difficult (see Loya González and Stanton 2013). There are frustratingly few hieroglyphic inscriptions in the north that make mention of other sites and the hieroglyphic record is generally in poor shape compared to the southern lowlands. Andrews and Robles Castellanos' (1985) answer to this problem was to employ a method out of the pages of culture history research to attempt to understand how the large polities of the end of the Classic period and beginning of the Postclassic articulated with one another. By assuming that the distribution of artifact styles, in this case ceramics, was a reflection of political influence, they mapped out the political reach of the Puuc confederation (likely headed up by Uxmal toward the end of the Classic period), Cobá, and Chichén Itzá (figure 9.1). Using primarily the distribution of Slate Ware ceramic styles, Andrews and Robles Castellanos hypothesized that that a standoff occurred between the growing Terminal

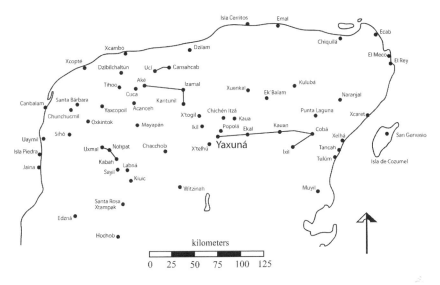

FIGURE 9.1. *Map of the northern Maya lowlands (image created by Travis Stanton).*

Classic political powerhouses of Cobá and the Puuc cities. Cobá's domain was thought to extend to Yaxuná due to the causeway (Sacbé 1) that connected the two cities (Villa 1934). As Chichén Itzá was established and grew, the Puuc cities waned and were engulfed in an Itzáe state. Cobá continued to remain a regional power for a time, and Andrews and Robles Castellanos (1985) hypothesized that the Itzáe encountered "massive resistance" at Yaxuná from Cobá forces. Yet Cobá's political influence was eventually diminished, and by AD 1000 programs of monumental construction were terminated and the causeways at that site were abandoned.

While there are questions concerning the use of ceramic styles to map political influence (Stanton and Gallareta Negrón 2001), the method is an interesting one to consider given the more recent work on Classic period market economies (Dahlin et al. 2007; King 2015). It is probable that there is a complex correlation between sociopolitical influence emanating out of cities and the reach of the products (and the idea of these products) in their markets. With this issue aside, Freidel's work at Yaxuná resulted in a continued elaboration of Andrews and Robles Castellanos's model (Freidel 1992, 2007; Schele and Freidel 1990; see also Shaw and Johnstone 2006). *A Forest of Kings* built off of this work to suggest that Yaxuná was a border town between the Terminal Classic Cobá and Puuc states. Initial work at Yaxuná indicated that it was not a city with an overlay of Cobá architectural traits, but that a combination of characteristics from both the western and eastern portions of the peninsula was present, with a heavy emphasis on Puuc-style exterior designs (Suhler et al. 1998). In this narrative, Sacbé 1 was interpreted as a response by Cobá to the threat of Chichén Itzá, but in conjunction with help from the Puuc. These ideas were further expanded by David Freidel and other students on the project in later publications (e.g., Ambrosino 2007; Freidel 2007), but the theme of a Puuc alliance with Cobá against the expanding threat of Chichén Itzá remained central.

## SUBSEQUENT RESEARCH ON THE SOCIOPOLITICS OF CENTRAL YUCATÁN

Since the completion of the Selz Project there has been fairly continuous work at Yaxuná and across its hinterlands, Lourdes Toscano excavated in the Puuc Group at Yaxuná from 1997 to 2002 and performed salvage work along the road between Yaxuná and Chichén Itzá in 2005. Since 2007 PIPCY has conducted research in a roughly 500 km² area to the southwest of Chichén Itzá including Yaxuná. Salvage work around Chichén Itzá and other sites in the region—such as X'togil, Abán, Kaua, and Kantunil conducted by José Osorio León and Francisco Pérez Ruíz—has been ongoing for decades as well. Coupled with several reevaluations of the Selz Project data by Dave Johnstone, Tatiana Loya González, Justine Shaw, and Travis W. Stanton (see Johnstone 2001; Loya González and Stanton 2013, 2014; Shaw 1998; Shaw and Johnstone 2001, 2006), the new data have presented a more nuanced picture of the centuries leading up to the founding of Chichén Itzá and the subsequent process of massive urbanization in the central northern lowlands.

REDATING SACBÉ 1 AND THE SEVENTH-CENTURY COBÁ CONNECTION

The first important realization that eventually led to a reconfiguration of the narrative outlined by Schele and Freidel (1990) occurred when the Selz Project was still conducting research at Yaxuná after *A Forest of Kings* was published. Dave Johnstone (2001; Suhler et al. 1998), the project ceramist, identified Arena Red as a diagnostic of the Late Classic Yaxuná III Complex (dated by Suhler et al. 1998 to AD 600–700/750 and AD 550–700 by PIPCY; see table 9.1). Given the association of this ceramic type with Sacbé 1 (the causeway to Cobá) gleaned from excavations of the terminus building and a portion of the causeway itself, Johnstone was able to redate the causeway to this period of this complex and, thus, prior to the foundation of the Itzáe state. This redating

**TABLE 9.1.** Ceramic chronology of Yaxuná.

| Chronology | Ceramic Phase | Common Ceramic Groups |
|---|---|---|
| AD 1400 | Yaxuná V | Mama |
| AD 1350 | | Panabá |
| AD 1300 | | Navulá |
| AD 1250 | | |
| AD 1200 | | |
| AD 1150 | **Hiatus** | **Hiatus** |
| AD 1100 | | |
| AD 1050 | Yaxuná IVb | Dzitás |
| AD 1000 | | Sisal |
| AD 950 | | Dzibiac |
| AD 900 | | |
| AD 850 | | |
| AD 800 | Yaxuná IVa | Muna |
| AD 750 | | Teabo |
| AD 700 | | Ticul |
| | | Sisal |
| AD 650 | Yaxuná III | Arena |
| AD 600 | | Chum |
| AD 550 | | Chuburná |
| | | Batres |
| | | Maxcanú |
| | | Sabán |
| AD 500 | Yaxuná II | Xanabá |
| AD 450 | | Polvero |
| AD 400 | | Sabán |
| AD 350 | | Sierra |
| AD 300 | | Dos Arroyos |
| AD 250 | | Oxil |
| | | Aguila |
| AD 200 | Yaxuná Ic | Xanabá |
| AD 150 | | Sierra |
| AD 100 | | Polvero |
| AD 50 | | Alex |
| 0 | | Sabán |
| | | Ucú |
| | | Dos Arroyos |

*continued on next page*

TABLE 9.1—*continued*

| Chronology | Ceramic Phase | Common Ceramic Groups |
|---|---|---|
| 50 BC | Yaxuná Ib | Sierra |
| 100 BC | | Flor |
| 150 BC | | Ucú |
| | | Zapatista |
| 200 BC | | Tamanché |
| 250 BC | | Sabán |
| 300 BC | | |
| 350 BC | Yaxuná Ia | Juventud |
| 400 BC | | Dzudzuquil |
| | | Pital |
| 450 BC | | Ucú |
| 500 BC | | Achiotes |
| 550 BC | | El Llanto |
| 600 BC | | |
| 650 BC | | |
| 700 BC | | |
| 750 BC | | |
| 800 BC | | |
| 850 BC | | |
| 900 BC | | |
| 950 BC | | |
| 1000 BC | | |

was understandable considering that the preserved dates on monuments at Cobá are restricted to the seventh and eighth centuries AD (see Guenter 2014a) and that the contemporaneous Palmas Complex at Cobá is the most represented at the site (Robles Castellanos 1990). The ceramics found on the causeway itself implied that the causeway was abandoned prior to the end of the Yaxuná III Complex, and thus before the rise of Chichén Itzá, bringing Andrews and Robles Castellanos (1985) chronological sequence into question.

Subsequent work by PIPCY has continued to refine the ceramic sequence, and a total of 93 C-14 samples have been analyzed from diverse stratigraphic contexts across the site from the Middle Preclassic to the Terminal Classic. This work has resulted in significant changes to our understanding of the Yaxuná III Complex (Stanton and Magnoni 2016). Beginning with the end of the Early Classic, there is now sufficient evidence to suggest a relatively smooth transition from the Flaky Ware tradition to the Slate Ware tradition. Flaky Wares, such as Xanabá Red, are the most popular slipped ceramics in the northwestern and central portion of the northern lowlands during the Terminal Preclassic and Early Classic. While Teresa Gallareta Ceballos and Fernando Robles Castellanos (2012) have suggested that it may date as early as the Middle Preclassic, this ware became immensely popular during the rise of Izamal at the end of the Preclassic. Johnstone (2001) restricted this ware, identifying only ceramics from the Xanabá Group, to the Late Preclassic and all but the tail end of the Early Classic. The sixth century, where he placed the appearance of many of the so-called Middle Classic types found in the Oxkintok sequence of Carmen Varela (1998), as well as the first Slate Wares in his Yaxuná IIb Complex, was not reported by Johnstone to have Flaky Ware material. It is not until the Late Classic, after the appearance of Slate Ware material, that Johnstone identified Arena Red in the sequence.

Excavating in a massive three-meter-deep trash pit on the North Acropolis in 2009, we began to get different picture of the ceramic sequence during the latter portion of the Classic (Marengo 2013; Stanton and Marengo Camacho 2014). Given that a large portion of the deposit was protected by a rock shelter, the preservation of the material was much better than that of most of the material Johnstone had to work with; this is an important point, as Flaky Ware ceramics are usually heavily eroded given their friability. To sum up briefly, we found that the Flaky Ware material extended into Johnstone's Late Classic Yaxuná III Complex as part of the Chuburná Group (Gómez 2012). In fact, the Chuburná and Arena groups made up the bulk of the Yaxuná III slipped assemblage. It is clear in the stratigraphy that Slate Ware material was not present at the beginning of Johnstone's Late Classic Yaxuná III Complex, defined primarily by the presence of Arena Red. Slate Ware ceramics eventually appeared in the stratigraphy over the course of Yaxuná III, sharing forms with the late material in the Chuburná Group. Over time, the Flaky Ware material disappeared in favor of the typical range of Slate Ware ceramics we have been comfortable calling Cehpech since the publication of the pottery of Mayapán by Robert Smith (1971). The Middle Classic Maxcanú Group is also ever present in the Yaxuná III Complex deposits (see Varela Torrecilla 1998), as is the Batres Group, common at Cobá (Robles Castellanos 1990). The ceramic associations for the Yaxuná III complex have been supported by other excavations at Yaxuná, and the current C-14 chronology suggests an AD 550–700 range. Given the terminal deposits on the causeway, this chronology would place the date of the abandonment of Sacbé 1 prior to AD 700 and before clear

Puuc-style construction appears at the site, supporting Johnstone's redating of this causeway from the Yaxuná IVa to Yaxuná III Complex.

The possibility of a seventh-century date for the construction of Sacbé 1 is appealing given what we currently know about the epigraphy of Cobá. Building off of the separate analyses by Stuart (2010b) and Sven Gronemeyer (2004) separate analyses of identifiable rulers at Cobá, Guenter (2014a; see also Reese-Taylor et al. 2009) has proposed that a woman *kaloomte'* from Cobá ruled from about AD 640 to AD 681. This Lady K'awiil Ajaw was a bellicose queen, and her surviving iconographic corpus depicts her standing over twelve captives. Guenter argues that she either incorporated Yaxuná into a seventh-century conquest state or she consolidated Cobá's gains during her reign. In any event, the archaeology at Yaxuná demonstrates that the causeway could have been constructed during her reign or even prior to it, but that it was no longer in use soon after her reign was over, suggesting that Cobá's political reach did not extend to Yaxuná after AD 700; the last securely dated monument (Stela 20) at Cobá dates to AD 780 (Guenter 2014a).

The Arrival of Puuc Cultural Traits

At some point during the first part of the seventh century, not long after Lady K'awiil Ajaw's death, Slate Ware ceramics were fully adopted at Yaxuná and the slipped ceramic assemblage lost many of the Yaxuná III types, such as Chuburná Brown, Arena Red, Maxcanú Buff, and Batres Red. Major changes in architecture and site settlement are also noticeable around this time, with Puuc-style stone carving appearing at numerous architectural groups, some of which diverge from previous site-planning principles, while other of which were targeted to refurbish ruined buildings from earlier periods (Stanton and Freidel 2005). All of the variants of Puuc-style architecture at Yaxuná have been associated with Cehpech-style Slate Ware material, Yaxuná IVa Complex studied by Johnstone (2001), except the terminal deposits on Str. 6F-68, a *popol nah* (council house) on the North Acropolis. We have taken these data to indicate that any sort of "influence" from the Puuc region at Yaxuná postdates the possible political control of the site by the rulers of Cobá.

Where we can most clearly see the development of these new western cultural influences at Yaxuná is in the Puuc Group, a series of structures immediately to the south/southwest of the North Acropolis (figure 9.2). Using a seriation of architectural styles based on his experience working around Kabah and using his excavation data gathered on Toscano's project, Gustavo Novelo

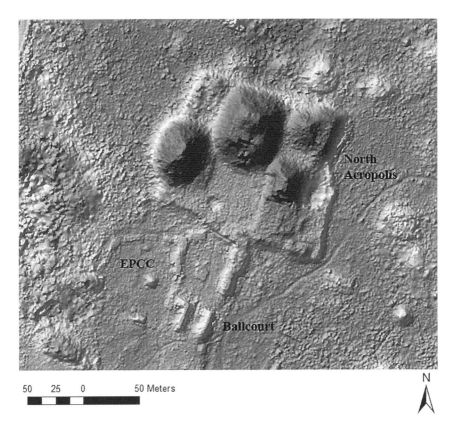

50  25  0          50 Meters

N

FIGURE 9.2. *LiDAR image of the North Acropolis of Yaxuná showing the EPCC (image created by Travis Stanton).*

Rincón (2012) has pieced the chronology of the complex together. In its final state the complex is a polygonal group forming an Early Puuc Ceremonial Complex (EPCC) defined by Nicholas Dunning (1992). These groups are polygonal arrangements of buildings replete with ramps and masonry towers covered with stucco that would have approximated very large stela. In addition to the ramps present at Yaxuná are two towers with anthropomorphic figures, which have not been published. The only known ballcourt at Yaxuná, dating to the Terminal Classic, is also found here. The EPCC has been interpreted as an administrative center and is reported throughout the Puuc region; well-excavated examples include the ones from Labná and Chac II (May Ciau 2000; Smyth et al. 1998). To our knowledge the Yaxuná example is only one of two

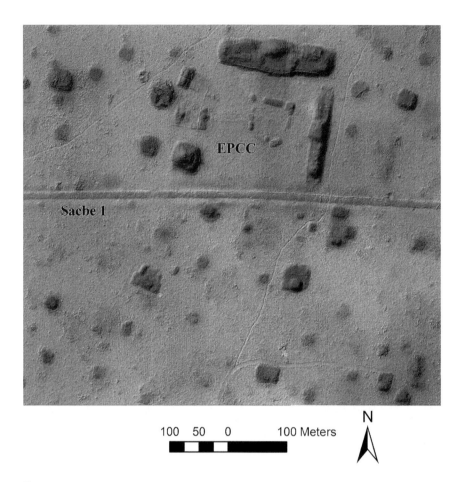

100  50  0        100 Meters   N

FIGURE 9.3. *LiDAR image of Kauan (image created by Travis Stanton).*

reported outside of the western part of the peninsula, the other recently identified on LiDAR imagery along Sacbé 1 to Cobá at the site of Kauan (figure 9.3).

Novelo Rincón (2012) demonstrates an accretion of architecture in the Puuc Group, starting with Early Puuc styles and ending in a fine veneer masonry style that he equates with the construction of a popol nah at Yaxuná, Str. 6F-68, only one of two architectural complexes at Yaxuná in which the Selz Project reported Sotuta ceramics (Suhler 1996). While much of the stone-working style at the Puuc Group and 6F-68 looks "Puuc," as Freidel and his students noted during the 1990s there is a mix of architectural techniques from the eastern and western portions of the peninsula (Suhler 1996; Suhler et al. 1998).

Supporting this notion, Novelo concludes that local style of construction was used to support a Puuc aesthetic.

While we are inclined to agree with Andrews and Robles Castellanos (1985) as well and Schele and Freidel (1990) to see the political hand of Cobá in the central portion of the peninsula, albeit much earlier than had been argued by those researchers, the question of "Puuc-ness" at Yaxuná is a bit more complicated. Using the presence of an EPCC at Yaxuná as evidence of a form of direct administration from the Puuc region, Novelo supports the idea of a local population whose control switched from Cobá to the Puuc kingdoms around AD 700. In fact, he makes a case that the EPCC at Yaxuná is evidence for the presence of an administrator from the Puuc and sees some migration from the west to Yaxuná. While this may be the case, the data are not particularly clear, and there is a lot more going on regionally at this time for which to account, such as settlement at Ikil, Popolá, and X'telhú. In any event, analysis of both stable isotopes and dental morphology of a sample of thirty-two individuals dating to Yaxuná III and Yaxuná IV contexts do not provide much evidence of movement of people from the Puuc region to Yaxuná or even close biological affinities (Price et al. 2018; Tiesler et al. 2017). Thus, while the presence of an EPCC is suggestive of a close cultural tie between Yaxuná and the Puuc region during the late eighth and ninth centuries, the nature of this relationship remains unclear.

In our collective regional surveys of the area, we have found few sites that date to the Preclassic and even fewer that appear to date to the Early Classic; Yaxuná is by far the largest of the early communities. We only begin to see development of a larger materially identifiable population across the landscape during Yaxuná III. Sites such as Ikil and Popolá (both characterized by small scatters of pre-Yaxuná III ceramics), where we have conducted large-scale test pit programs, appear to be small villages during Yaxuná III, and our surface collections at other sites suggest that many small villages may have been founded at this time, though their number and size were much less than for Yaxuná IVa. By the time Slate Ware became the dominant slipped ware in the region around AD 700–750, there was an explosion of growth. Numerous new communities were founded, and we see a tremendous increase of rural settlement—too much to be considered a product of local populations. In tandem, however, we also see a number of larger settlements develop in the region. While we do not have the chronological control at the sites as Novelo does for the Puuc Group, we can see that Puuc-style stonework associated with Cehpech-style ceramics characterize sites such as Ikil, X'telhú, X'togil, Rancho Alegre, Ceh' Yax, X-Panil, and Popolá, many of which have some form of carved monuments (Magnoni et al. 2014). Yet the trend is clear: there is a much larger population living on the landscape at this time, and there is a much more developed settlement hierarchy.

Archaeologists have long argued both X'telhú and Popolá to have been satellite sites whose *sajaloob* paid tribute to the lord of Yaxuná (Freidel 2007; Schele and Freidel 1990; Magnoni et al. 2014). In fact there are nearly identical range structures at both sites that depict seated lords and possible tribute in a series of panels. While X'telhú has some larger central architecture, which may date earlier, Popolá has virtually none (Johnson 2012), a pattern seen at other Terminal Classic sites in the region such X-Panil and X-auil despite sizable settlement at these communities. Yet there are other contemporaneous communities, such as Rancho Alegre and X'togil, with larger site centers dating to this period, which neither have panels, nor range structures such as those reported at Popolá and X'telhú.

Surface survey and salvage work by INAH at X'togil has revealed substantial occupations during both Yaxuná IVa (AD 700/750–850/900) and Yaxuná IVb (AD 850/900–1000). Located off to the west of Chichén Itzá, X'togil occupies an area between the last known segment of Sacbé 3, the causeway that passes Cumtún headed out to the west from the Itzáe capital (González de la Mata et al. 2006), and Kantunil, a site with a substantial Sotuta (Yaxuná IVb) occupation that was the endpoint for a causeway headed south out of Izamal. Given this location and the chronology of occupation, X'togil may have been on the road between Chichén Itzá and Izamal, communities implicated in each other's affairs in ethnohistoric documents (Roys 1933).

Ikil, where PIPCY has conducted a substantial amount of fieldwork, is a site boasting a large pyramidal structure (Str. 1) that was originally constructed with two staircases, most likely during Yaxuná IVa, and later modified into a radial structure (Robles et al. 2011) probably during Yaxuná IVb (figure 9.4). The basal façade of the palace has the same size and form of elements as the basal façade of Str. 6F-68 at Yaxuná, suggesting that the same masons were responsible for their manufacture. Interestingly, the hieroglyphs in the lintels indicate that there was a local ruler at the site, possibly suggesting some level of independence during from Yaxuná and other centers, likely during the early eighth century.

The two lintels from Str. 1 clearly form a single, cohesive text. In the last half century, these lintels have been subjected to a number of epigraphic analyses (Andrews IV and Stuart 1968:73; Bíró 2003; Graña-Behrens 2006:113; Grube 2003; Grube and Krochok 2007:209–210; Stuart 2005a:151–152). These earlier studies established the basic message of this text. Lintel 1 describes the dedication of something, probably the shrines in the upper room of Str. 1, in honor of a royal woman (and, perhaps, another individual). Lintel 2 records that this

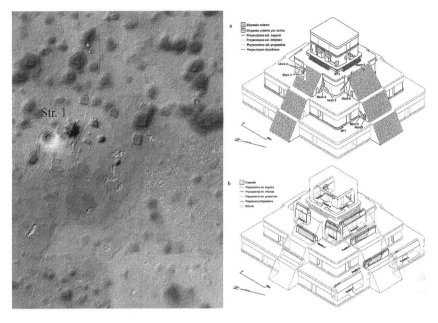

**FIGURE 9.4.** *LiDAR image of Ikil and architectural reconstruction of Str. 1 (LiDAR image created by Travis Stanton and isometric drawings by Amparo Robles).*

dedication was carried out under the auspices of a male ruler or a series of elite individuals. While there is still much debate about certain aspects of the text, and while we cannot read all of the signs, we can present the following general translation of the text:

> This is the dedication of the [shrine] of the royal woman, Lady Six (Sky?) Lord, Lady (Deer Metate?) Yal Chan Took', One Lord . . . This work was overseen by Chak Tzi . . . , Ballplayer Sky Flint, Ukit Maap(?), K'ahk'? To . . . Lord. . . .

The text is clearly dominated by names and titles; sixteen of the twenty glyphs consist of names or titles, and the remaining four glyphs provide a standard dedicatory expression (Glyphs 1 and 2), state what it was that was actually dedicated (Glyph 3), and credit the ruler who commissioned this construction (Glyph 11). The third glyph describes what was dedicated, perhaps a *waybil*, or "sleeping place/shrine" (Grube and Krochok 2007:210) of a local deity, though the spelling is quite unusual. Whatever this word, it likely refers to the niches of the structure themselves, which would have functioned in the same way as the inner shrines of the Cross Group temples at Palenque, certainly labeled as waybil for the patron gods of that city (Houston 1996; Stuart 2005b, 2006).

While the shrines at Palenque were dedicated to deities, Ikil Lintel 1 states that the owner of these possible shrines was a female of royal status, presumably a historical queen. Glyphs 4–6 are likely a common elite female title, "Lady Six Sky Lord," while Glyph 7 may be a personal name or perhaps a title indicating her place of origin.[1] The final two legible glyphs on Lintel 1 are names and/or titles, but do not include the expected female identifier IX/IXIK and so could refer to this woman or could be the name of a male companion.

The long list of names and titles on Lintel 2 could all pertain to one individual, but it is possible that a series of names is given, just without any of the normal relationship glyphs separating them. Glyph 14 is the title of a ballplayer while Glyph 16 is Ukit, a very common part of many names from Late/Terminal Classic northern Yucatán. Glyph 19 appears to be an Emblem Glyph, though the reading of the Main Sign is anything but clear. The final glyph, Glyph 20, has been said to be the Emblem Glyph of Ek' Bahlam (Bíró 2003:3), but there is no clear *ajaw* title in this glyph (Bíró's suggestion that the two last hieroglyphs read AJAW-wa is unconvincing, as this would not be the normal or even a recognized way of spelling this title, at Ikil or elsewhere), and there is an unexplained first sign to this glyph that does not ever appear in the Ek' Bahlam Emblem Glyph. This final glyph is probably an otherwise unrecognized title but probably has no reference to Ek' Bahlam at all.

In short, then, the two lintels of Ikil Structure 1 are fairly typical of Late Classic texts from across the Maya world in recording the dedication of a monument in honor of local elite lords/ladies, and gives credit to the lord who commissioned this work and as well as a long list of names and titles. Unfortunately, none of these names appears in other texts, and we have not yet recognized the ancient emblem glyph of the site. We can say, though, that at least one lord of Ikil was wealthy and powerful enough to commission an accomplished artist to carve two lintels with a legible hieroglyphic text, a fact that highlights the importance of this site in understanding the history of north-central Yucatán.

Moving on from Ikil, we find that one center we do not understand very well for this eighth- and early ninth-century period is Chichén Itzá; corresponding to that site's Yabnal Complex (AD 600–800; Pérez de Heredia Puente 2012). The idea of sequential Maya and Toltec phases at this city forwarded by Alfred Tozzer (1957) and other archaeologists affiliated with Carnegie Project (e.g., Brainerd 1958) has been roundly criticized (e.g., Schele and Mathews 1998). In fact, the designation of an earlier pure Maya Cehpech phase is now controversial. Pérez, however, has now reported pure Cehpech deposits from the Cenote Sagrado (lacking stratified contexts), the Three Lintels Group, the lower platform of the Caracol, the first platform of Las Monjas (Brainerd 1958), and deep below Initial Series Group; it appears that there is a pre-Sotuta community at the site. The published Yabnal Complex Slate Wares look very much like the Yaxuná IVa material in terms of their surface appearance, decoration, and in many cases forms; however, Eduardo Pérez de Heredia Puente (2012:384–385) reports *molcajete* forms and slips tending toward more cream to buff tones in the Say Slate Group, indicating that materials he defines in this group may be contemporaneous with what the PIPCY project has defined as late Muna Slate: Var. Cafetoso found at Ikil and Str. 6F-68 at Yaxuná dating to after AD 800. Yet while the evidence of this earlier occupation at Chichén Itzá is slim, it is also deeply buried at the site, leaving archaeologists to see very little of what the community looked like prior to AD 850. This situation begs the question as to what Chichén Itzá might have looked like, and what role it could have played in the eighth-century sociopolitical landscape, when many of Yaxuná's ruined buildings were refurbished and an apparent Puuc administrative complex was constructed. Was preurban Chichén Itzá a vassal of Yaxuná? Was it, and all of the other burgeoning communities, part of a patchwork of relatively independent smaller sites that included Yaxuná? These questions are difficult to answer with the current data, but will be critical for future work in terms of defining the articulation of the early process of urbanization of Chichén Itzá with changes in site settlement systems starting in the latter part of the ninth century. In any regard, while there is a distinct possibility that Yaxuná and other sites in the region were politically and socially impacted by the Puuc phenomenon to the west, at the present time there is little concrete evidence of actual direct control or migrations. What we can say, however, is that the evidence for Puuc "influence" postdates the abandonment of Sacbé 1 and influence from Cobá.

The Rise of Chichén Itzá

By the end of Yaxuná IVa, Yaxuná itself experienced a great demographic decline (Ambrosino 2007; Suhler 1996; Toscano Hernández and Ortegón Zapata 2003). Sotuta-style Slate Wares have only been reported from a small vaulted structure (Str. 6F-9) off the southern edge of the North Acropolis, on terminal deposits at a popol nah (Str. 6F-68), and in a small area of the site core centered at the Puuc Group, where several of the structures were refurbished. At this time Yaxuná had become a small village amidst the ruins of the ancient center. Several researchers have suggested that it was a small agricultural community that paid tribute to the lords of Chichén Itzá (Suhler 1996; Toscano Hernández and Ortegón Zapata 2003), which at this time had become the massive metropolis for which it is famous.

Regional survey to the south and west of Chichén Itzá by INAH and PIPCY has revealed a pattern of settlement much different from that reported for the previous period. Most of the regional centers were abandoned or greatly reduced in population. A considerable number of small hamlets, often located near cenotes, dotted the landscape, but in the overall population paled in comparison to the previous period. The only sizable towns outside the immediate urban area of Chichén Itzá that have been reported are Ikil and X'togil (Robles Castellanos et al. 2011); Str. 1 at Ikil was likely made into a radial pyramid at this time with the addition of two more staircases that would have made it look more like the Castillo at Chichén Itzá. Small communities, —but demonstrating finely cut architecture, sculpture, and on occasion hieroglyphic texts—appear closer to the Itzáe capital and in some cases are connected to the city via causeways (Anderson 1998; González de la Mata et al. 2006). Other, more established communities such as Abán and Yaxuná, both sites occupied continuously from the Middle Preclassic to end of the Terminal Classic, show a substantial decrease in population at this time and appear to be small hamlets or villages located among the ruins of once substantial centers.

Farther to the northeast, as Daniel Vallejo Cáliz and T. Kam Manahan (2014) report, existed a somewhat similar situation for Xuenkal. Although this site was home to a flourishing craft production industry (Ardren et al. 2010), the site had diminished in population as Sotuta-style ceramics made their appearance. Vallejo and Manahan convincingly argue that the several platforms used only during the period of Cehpech pottery styles were gradually abandoned, indicating that as Chichén Itzá was undergoing its massive process of urbanization it drew in people from the surrounding communities who wished to participate in the vibrant economic, social, and ritual renaissance occurring at this city.

While there are not comparable studies of abandonment processes at structures dating to Yaxuná IVa, at Yaxuná there is one particular context that has been argued to date to the transition to Yaxuná IVb. Str. 6F-68 is a three-room range structure built in the late Puuc style that was appended on to the south side of 6F-4, an Early Classic temple that was in ruins at the beginning of the Terminal Classic. The floor deposits of the structure included numerous broken pottery vessels and evidence of intense burning. Given that the ceramics on the floor and in front of the building were a mix of "Cehpech" and "Sotuta" styles and that the North Acropolis was fortified during this period, several of the Selz

Project members have argued that this structure was ritually terminated after an attack by warriors from Chichén Itzá (Ambrosino 2007; Ambrosino et al. 2001, 2003; Ardren 1999; Suhler 1996; Suhler and Freidel 1998); this attack led to the depopulation of Yaxuná and the abandonment of its monumental architecture.

The question of whether Yaxuná was attacked is a difficult one to answer, as the evidence is circumstantial. Yet something happened near the transition from Yaxuná IVa to IVb that led people to leave the city and abandon Str. 6F-68, and most likely other structures across the site, in this state. Interestingly, excavations of a wide number of residential contexts at Ikil indicate that Slate Ware ceramics stylistically similar to the mixed Cehpech-Sotuta material found at Str. 6F-68 are common throughout the site; Sotuta-style ceramics are never recovered in pure lots. In fact, much of the Slate Ware material from the site of Ikil exhibits a mix of attributes on single vessels; for example, over 30 percent of the molcajete forms (a Sotuta Complex attribute) have Cehpech-like slips. The ceramic assemblage on the floor of Str. 6F-68 is nearly identical to the contexts at Ikil in this respect, indicating that the ceramics found in this abandonment context at Yaxuná might not have been brought by the Itzá for the purpose of conducting a termination ritual, but were in circulation at Yaxuná at the time the building was abandoned and terminated; given that nearly all contexts at Ikil have mixed Cehpech- and Sotuta-style ceramics and the fact that several basal facade elements of Str. 1 at Ikil and Str. 6F-68 at Yaxuná are exactly the same size and shape, we believe Sotuta ceramics were available to people at Yaxuná close to the date Str. 6F-68 was built. This introduction may suggest that Yaxuná was already integrated to some degree into the growing economy of Chichén Itzá while it was still a major community. In fact, a late Yaxuná IVa context not associated with Sotuta-style Slate Ware material contains the cremated remains of an individual—a mortuary pattern typical of Central Mexico—leading Vera Tiesler and her colleagues (2017) to argue that ideological influences from Chichén Itzá were present at Yaxuná earlier than had been previously contemplated. This presence may mean that broader social changes in the region reflected at Chichén Itzá had already begun to impact other communities in the region. Returning to Str. 6F-68, one notes that the one burial encountered beneath the floor of the structure had been entered during the abandonment process, the grave goods and skull removed (some teeth still remained), and the entry hole burned. While these data have been interpreted as an act of ancestor desecration (Ambrosino 2007), it is also possible that, regardless of whether Yaxuná was actually subjected to a violent event at this time, people removed the ancestral heirlooms to take with them as they left the city, maybe to live at Chichén Itzá itself (Tiesler et al. 2017).

## CONCLUSIONS

The narratives of political struggles for power in the northern lowlands towards the end of Classic period outlined in *A Forest of Kings* and subsequent publications were ambitious. Given the lack of hieroglyphic inscriptions treating the topic of intersite relationships in the northern Maya lowlands, material and contextual evidence were relied upon for understanding how polities such as Chichén Itzá, Cobá, and Uxmal interacted. As was predicted by Andrews and Robles Castellanos (1985) and Schele and Freidel (1990), Yaxuná, with its central location in the north, has provided numerous data bearing on such interaction. As with all archaeological interpretations, the ones presented here will likely change as new data on these centers come to light. Our interpretation of the available evidence to date indicates that Yaxuná underwent a series of radical changes from the beginning of Yaxuná III to the end of Yaxuná IVb, changes that were directly related to a series of outside influences, first from Cobá, then from the Puuc, and last from Chichén Itzá, whose urbanization process first reduced Yaxuná to a village and ultimately caused its abandonment. Very little material from the subsequent Hocaba ceramic Complex of the Postclassic has been reported for any of the sites in our survey area outside of Chichén Itzá itself.

## ACKNOWLEDGMENTS

We thank the Consejo de Arqueología of the Instituto Nacional de Antropología e Historia for granting the permits to conduct this research. This research was generously supported by the National Science Foundation (#1623603), Fundación Roberto Hernández, Fundación Pedro y Elena Hernández, the Selz Foundation, Jerry Murdoch, and the University of California, Riverside. This chapter benefited from comments from two anonymous reviewers, though the final product is the sole responsibility of the authors. Finally, we thank the communities in the municipalities of Tzinum and Yaxcabá for allowing us to conduct research on their land.

## NOTE

1. Péter Bíró (2003:3) suggests that the main sign of Glyph 6 is an upside down **IK'** wind glyph infixed with **ku**, thus providing an emblem glyph for this woman that he reads as *Iik'* or *Ik'u* and that he relates to the modern toponym, Ikil. There are many problems with this reading, however. The internal details of the main sign are poorly preserved, as a break through the entire lintel has split Glyph 6 in half. What

Bíró sees as an upside down **IK'** sign with an infixed **ku** syllable, I suggest is just the remnants of the internal details of the **CHAN** sign, and can be compared to a certain **CHAN** logogram occurring at the bottom of Glyph 8 on Lintel 1. In any event, there is little reason to believe the toponym Ikil is ancient, as it is neither attested in native chronicles nor by early travelers (Andrews IV and Stuart 1968:71). Due to his reading of this hieroglyph, Bíró suggests that this woman was a local queen of Ikil. Guenter finds it much more likely that, as with most royal ladies mentioned in ancient Maya texts, she was nonlocal and would have most likely married a local lord of Ikil.

# 10

## In Search of Paradise

### Religion and Cultural Exchange in Early Postclassic Mesoamerica

KARL A. TAUBE

When my colleague Travis Stanton kindly invited me to submit a chapter to this volume concerning *A Forest of Kings*, I enthusiastically accepted, as this work is a watershed contribution to the study of the ancient Maya as well as a steady source of inspiration for many of us in the field. In this popular and widely cited volume, Linda Schele and David Freidel (1990) seamlessly joined archaeological fieldwork with the most recent insights concerning Maya epigraphy and art, an approach adopted in many subsequent studies since the publication of *A Forest of Kings* to the present (e.g., Fash 1991; Houston et al. 2015). As coauthors, Schele and Freidel were a consummate match, with Freidel being a highly trained and experienced field archaeologist of the Maya lowlands and Schele being one of the preeminent experts on ancient Maya writing and iconography. In this book, the authors demonstrated that at the point of its publication in 1990, we were already dealing with true history pertaining to ancient Maya sites and their texts and imagery, much like ancient Old World civilizations, including Mesopotamia, Egypt, and Shang dynasty China. *A Forest of Kings* firmly established that the Classic Maya had a very highly developed concept of rulership as well as detailed records of dynastic history, including such matters as royal birth and accession, as well as marriage and battles to name a few.

One of the last chapters of *A Forest of Kings* concerns Chichén Itzá, which in many ways is distinct in

DOI: 10.5876/9781646420469.c010

terms of detailed historical records appearing on carved stone monuments, which are notably rare at the site. In addition, many glyphs appearing with "Toltec"-style figure have logographic glyphs that appear to be entirely distinct from Maya canons of hieroglyphic writing. Nonetheless, the amount of carved sculpture placed on buildings is remarkable and has no parallel neither in the Maya region nor with its contemporary in Central Mexico, this being the site of Tula, Hidalgo. During the Early Postclassic, Chichén Itzá was one of the most important polities in Mesoamerica. As noted by Schele and Freidel (1990:348), "all of Mesoamerica knew of Chichén Itzá as a valuable ally or a formidable enemy." In addition, the art of Chichén Itzá is filled with images of warfare and sacrifice, including battle murals from the Upper Temple of the Jaguars, armed warriors and the arraignment of captives; what can be derived with certainty from these public monuments is that the government of Chichén Itzá carried out successful campaigns against its enemies. Although my study addresses militarism and warfare at Chichén Itzá, I take a slightly different tack in discussing how the cult of war related to concepts of the soul and the afterlife, which can also relate to beliefs found earlier at Teotihuacan and with the Contact period Aztec.

Since the sixteenth-century documentation of Mexica, or Aztec, religious beliefs and practices, it has been known that they conceived of a number of afterlife realms, including a flower-filled paradise of the sun. By no means for everyone, this celestial region was restricted to heroic warriors who were slain in battle or by sacrifice as well as women who died in childbirth. According to the Florentine Codex, the souls of warriors were transformed into beautiful birds and butterflies who drank the sweet nectar of beautiful flowers: "They changed into precious birds—hummingbirds, orioles, yellow birds, yellow-birds blackened around the eyes, chalky butterflies, feather down butterflies, gourd bowl butterflies, they sucked honey [from the flowers] there where they dwelt" (Sahagún 1950–1982, bk. III: 49).

In Tlaxcala, jewels, birds, and other esteemed items embodied the souls of deceased nobles, in striking contrast to commoners:

> Those of Tlaxcala had that the souls of lords and officials became mist and clouds, birds of rich plumage of various types and stones of high value. And that the souls of the common people were turned into weasels, smelly beetles, and nasty animals that cast a very stinking urine and into other thieving animals. (trans. by author from Mendieta 1980:97)

In this study, I note that precious jewels also appear in Early Postclassic Maya imagery pertaining to the spirit world, both as falling or floating elements in scenes of paradise, but also as jewelry worn by spirit beings inhabiting this world as signs of their regal and heroic nature.

In an important and far-reaching essay, Jane Hill (1992) notes that the concept of a floral paradise, or "Flower World," is widespread among Uto-Aztecan-speaking peoples, including the Huichol, Yaqui, O'odham, and Hopi, as well as the Aztec. In addition, similar concepts of paradise were present among still more ancient cultures of Mesoamerica, including Teotihuacan, whereas in the case of the Aztec, butterflies and precious birds symbolized the souls of heroic warriors (Berlo 1983, 1984; Headrick 2007:135–138; Taube 2000, 2005, 2006). In fact, the Aztec explicitly related Teotihuacan to the fiery dawn emergence of the sun to the heroic dead. The Florentine Codex account of the people of Teotihuacan states that they addressed their deceased with the following prayer of exhortation:

> In this manner they spoke to the dead when one had died . . . 'Awaken! It hath reddened; the dawn hath set in. Already singeth the flame colored cock, the flame-colored swallow; already flieth the flame colored butterfly. (Sahagún 1950–82, bk. 10:192)

In a number of studies, I note that the Classic Maya also had a solar floral paradise, including the concept of Flower Mountain, an ancestral place offering access to the heavens (Taube 2005, 2006, 2010a, 2010b, 2015). Along with being identified with the sun, it was also the abode of the Maya Maize God as well as royal ancestors, who are often portrayed apotheosized as the maize deity or the sun god, beings commonly portrayed at Flower Mountain, with sun being reborn on a daily basis and the maize deity once a year as green, growing maize sprouting from the earth. Moreover, I argue that many ancient Central Mexican concepts pertaining to the solar paradise, including its relation to the east as well as such precious items as jade and the quetzal, concern the Maya region, which is not only due east of Central Mexico, but also provides the most esteemed forms of wealth, jade, and quetzal plumes.

It is increasingly clear that Flower Mountain was very much present at Teotihuacan, and appears in Teotihuacan-style murals, in vessel scenes, and on ceramic censers from the Escuintla region of south coastal Guatemala (Taube 2005, 2006). The great Temple of Quetzalcoatl (also widely known now as the Feathered Serpent Pyramid), located on eastern side of the Street of the Dead, is an architectural portrayal of this sacred mountain, with plumed serpents surging through massive, open blossoms (Taube 2004b, 2005, 2006, 2010b). However, the presence of butterflies in Central Mexican concepts of paradise is in striking contrast to Classic Maya art, where generally butterflies are absent aside from intentional evocations of Teotihuacan (see Franco C. 1961:198, 244). Unlike Teotihuacan and Aztec butterflies with elaborately decorated wings, Classic Maya insects tend to be skeletal and generally unwholesome creatures with fleshless skulls, rickety limbs, exposed vertebrae, and ribs as well as explicit death symbols, including extruded eyeballs and "death collars" motifs fitting for the dark underworld and night rather that the diurnal paradise of the sun.

Clearly, the Aztec did not receive their beliefs concerning butterfly warrior souls and the flowery paradise directly from Teotihuacan, as there are some 600 years between the demise of this Classic city and the founding of Tenochtitlan in the early fourteenth century. The Early Postclassic site of Tula is a far more likely and immediate source for the origins of the Aztec solar paradise. It is well known that the inhabitants of Tula traced much of their cultural heritage to the Toltecs of Tollan, and the site of Tula is filled with evidence of Aztec offerings as well as looting (López Luján 2003; López Luján and López Austin 2009). However, just as the Aztec regarded Tula as a canonical source of many of their traditions, it is likely that the Toltecs similarly considered still earlier Teotihuacan as their immediate *cultura madre*. In comparison with such Epiclassic centers as Xochicalco, Cacaxtla, and Teotenango, the monumental art and architecture of Tula is the most similar to that of Teotihuacan (see Mastache et al. 2002:92). One clear example of this continuity is the iconography pertaining to war and sacrifice. Although it has received relatively little comment, the warrior butterfly complex known for the Aztec and Teotihuacan was fully present at Tula as well as Chichén Itzá.

Although the monumental art of Tula constitutes a major source of information concerning Early Postclassic beliefs of the afterlife realm of heroic warriors, the roughly contemporaneous site of Chichén Itzá—situated virtually due east of Tula—is the most illuminating on this subject, with elaborate scenes pertaining to paradise and the afterlife. In Mesoamerica, the solar paradise pertains to the east, the place of the dawning sun, the morning star, and the source of the rain-bringing spring and summer winds (Taube 2010a, 2015, 2017). Although many traits for Aztec and Toltec concepts of paradise were also present at Teotihuacan, other motifs and themes pertaining to Postclassic Central Mexican conceptions of paradise probably derived from the Classic Maya (Taube 2010b). Clearly enough, given its close cultural links to Tula, the great site of Chichén Itzá would be a logical cultural source of Maya-related imagery appearing in Postclassic highland Mexico.

## FLOWER MOUNTAIN IN YUCATÁN

Mention has been made of the ancient Maya concept of Flower Mountain, a primordial paradise closely related to the souls of ancestors. In the Maya region, it is of great antiquity, and graphically appears in the North Wall mural from the Late Preclassic site of San Bartolo in the northern Petén region of Guatemala (Saturno et al. 2005:14–18, fig. 12). Dating to roughly the first century BC, the scene features a zoomorphic mountain covered with flowering plants as well as wild beasts. The widely open maw of this mountain is clearly a cave with its vertical canine as an undulating stalactite. Similar cave maws are also known for Late Classic Maya portrayals of Flower Mountain and recall Chenes and Río Bec temple doorways as the fanged mouths of great zoomorphic faces, a convention also known for Temple 22 at Copán. According to Claude Baudez (1999:57), the frontal faces and the long-snouted heads appearing on the corners of structures of Chenes, Río Bec, and Puuc all portray a being commonly referred as the Cauac Monster: "los mascarones representados en torno a las puertas, en los ángulos y en las fachadas de las estructuras de Río Bec, Chenes y Puuc, son una variante del monstruo de las tierra, *cauac*."[1] This interpretation is in striking contrast to the widespread belief that such long-snouted masks in the Puuc as well as Chichén Itzá portray the Maya rain god, Chahk, an identification made in 1908 by Eduard Seler (1902–1923:IV:209–210). At that time, little was understood of the relative age of ancient Maya images. It is now clear, however, that examples of Chahk with long, pendulous noses appear only later in the Late Postclassic, such as in the pages of the Codex Madrid. For the Classic and Early Postclassic period, Chahk has a much blunter, muzzle-like snout, including Late Classic examples from the Puuc site of Mulchic (see Taube 1992b:fig. 8a).

The identification by Baudez (1999) of the long-snouted zoomorphic masks appearing on Río Bec, Chenes, and Puuc facades being representations of the "Cauac Monster" pertains directly to an earlier decipherment by Stuart (1987:17–18) establishing this being as a zoomorphic hill or mountain, termed *witz* in ancient Maya script. Dedicated in AD 715, Copán Temple 22 constitutes a clear link between Classic Maya "Witz Monsters" and the later architectural masks of the Yucatán Peninsula (see Fash 1991:122–123). Not only do stacked witz heads frame the corners of the Copán temple—a widespread theme in Río Bec, Chenes, and Puuc architecture—but the central doorway has an open, toothy maw, recalling later temples in the Río Bec and Chenes regions.

Many Classic Maya "Witz Monsters" have a prominent blossom in the center of the brow to denote them as Flower Mountain (Saturno et al. 2005; Taube 2004b). Similarly, for both the Puuc region and Chichén Itzá, the so-called Chahk mask facades are indeed Flower Mountain, again with a central flower just above the snout (Taube 2004b:85–86). In addition, Puuc-style facades of Flower Mountain often have a pair of short crossed bands on the face (figure 10.1a–b). As is the case of the "Kawak markings" appearing on Classic witz heads, including Copán Temple 22, they mark the masks as faces of stone, in other words mountains (figure 10.1a–b). Identical crossed bands on two glyphs for stone appear in the text from the Temple of the Hieroglyphic Jambs at Chichén Itzá, one being the sign for a stone altar and the other simply the glyph for stone, or *tun* (figure 10.1c–d). The tun glyph also serves for the day name Kawak, appearing in the Postclassic codices like a stylized face with the crossed bands on the "cheek" (figure 10.1e). The Postclassic crossed bands may derive from the undulating crossed lines appearing in the sign for the day name Etz'nab', denoting hard stone such as flint. Although rare outside of Yucatán, the crossed band sign appears on a fragmentary panel found near Structure B at Tula, quite possibly a form of the Maya Witz Monster, with portions of the brow and earspool discernable at the lower right corner of the relief (figure 10.1).

Although one can trace the Witz Monster from Late Preclassic and Classic Maya imagery to Puuc-style facades of the Terminal Classic and Early Postclassic periods, examples appearing in the Late Postclassic codices are quite different (figure 10.2a–d). Although displaying the Cauac markings and crossed bands found on earlier examples of witz heads, they are far more anthropomorphic, and display the visage of an old, chapfallen man. For Structure 16 at Tulúm, this being appears at the corners of the cornice, quite like earlier examples of witz heads appearing on Late Classic buildings of Yucatán as well as Copán Temple 22 (figure 10.2e). The large corpus of witz heads from Chichén Itzá provide an important bridge between the Classic and Late Postclassic forms of this motif, as many examples bear human features, including the form of the eyes and nose. In addition, most have a blossom on their brow to denote them as Flower Mountain (figure 10.2 f–g). For the two illustrated examples, warriors in Toltec-style military regalia stand atop this place-name, probably to link Flower Mountain to heroic beings (for full scenes, see Taube 2004b:fig. 15b–c). At Chichén Itzá, an especially elaborate form of the human mountain motif appears on the columns from the Lower Temple of the Jaguars, where it merges with a cleft turtle shell containing the Maize God, clearly denoting the mythic mountain of sustenance from which maize first emerged (figure 10.2h).

Along with the mask facades of the Puuc region and Chichén Itzá, Flower Mountain also appears with Chenes-style architecture, here with axially

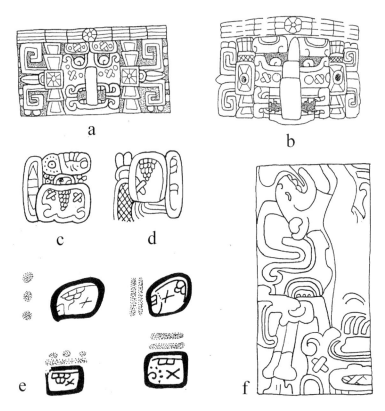

FIGURE 10.1. *Flower Mountain and Postclassic Maya portrayals of stone
with crossed bands (drawings by author): (a) Flower Mountain with blossom
on brow and crossed bands on face from the Temple of the Warriors, Chichén
Itzá (from Taube 2004b:fig. 14b); (b) Flower Mountain from Osario Temple,
Chichén Itzá (from Taube 2004b:fig. 14c); (c) glyphic sign for altar, Temple of the
Hieroglyphic Jambs, Chichén Itzá (from Grube and Krochock 2007:fig. 7); (d)
glyphic sign for TUN, or stone, Temple of the Hieroglyphic Jambs, Chichén Itzá
(from Grube and Krochok 2007:fig. 7); (e) Postclassic examples of the Kawak
glyph, upper, Codex Dresden, lower, Codex Madrid; (f) fragmentary panel with
possible witz mask with crossed-bands (after de la Fuente et al. 1988:no. 149).*

oriented doorways as the frontal open maw of the mountain (Taube 2004b,
2010b, 2013). Michael Coe (2005:172–173) notes that the Chenes-style stucco
facade at Ek' Bahlam is Flower Mountain, in this case with many round blossoms on the brow and cheeks (see Vargas de la Peña and Castillo Borges

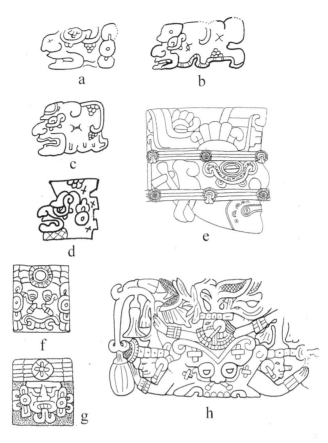

FIGURE 10.2. *Postclassic portrayals of anthropomorphic witz heads (drawings by author). (a) witz head, Codex Dresden, p. 66b; (b) witz head, Codex Dresden, p. 34c; (c) witz head, Codex Dresden, p. 41a; (d) witz head, Codex Madrid, p. 11c; (e) witz head on corner of Structure 16, Tulúm (from Taube 2010a:fig. 28a); (f) witz head, Upper Temple of the Jaguars, Chichén Itzá (from Taube 2004b:fig. 15b); (g) witz head, Mercado, Chichén Itzá (from Taube 2004b:fig. 15c); (h) witz head merged with split turtle carapace with emerging Maize God, Lower Temple of the Jaguars, Chichén Itzá (after Seler 1902–1923:5:317).*

2001:lámina 14). The interior of this structure contained the burial chamber of Ukit Kan Le'k Tok'. The vault capstone of the crypt depicts the ruler as the Maize God, again linking this being of life and resurrection to Flower Mountain (see Vargas de la Peña and Castillo Borges 2001:lámina 18). In the

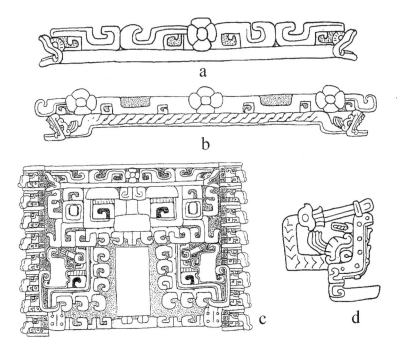

**Figure 10.3.** *Portrayals of plumed serpents and flowers on Flower Mountain facades appearing in Late Classic Chenes architecture (drawings by author): (a) bicephalic plumed serpent with clouds and central blossom on back, El Tabasceño (see figure 3c); (b) bicephalic plumed serpent with clouds and blossoms on back, Hochob (reconstruction by author after Seler 1916:fig. 20); (c) Flower Mountain facade, El Tabasceño (from Taube 2004b:fig. 13); (d) plumed serpent with floral tail as zoomorphic breath of witz facade, Hochob (from Taube 2010b:fig. 25c).*

Chenes area proper, structures at El Tabasceño, Hochob, and Manos Rojas display prominent flowers on the brow of the Witz Monster to identify it as Flower Mountain (figure 10.3; for Manos Rojas, see Gendrop 1983:fig. 76). For all three cited sites, the mountains also have feather-crested serpents running across their brows (figure 10.3a–c). While the Central Mexican plumed serpent tends to be a rattlesnake with quetzal plumes covering its entire body, the ancient Maya preferred to depict this being as a snake with simply feathers on its brow, much like the crest of the male quetzal (figure 10.3a–d; see Taube 2010a:figs. 24c–h, 25). As in Central Mexico, the Maya serpent embodies the living force of breath and wind. Thus whereas Witz Monster facades in the Yucatán typically have breath scrolls emerging from the corners of the mouth, the Hochob facade has feather-crested serpents with floral tails instead, though breath scrolls do emerge from the creatures' mouths (figure 10.3d).

In her initial study of Flower World, Hill (1992:125) noted that one of the most basic metaphors shared with Uto-Aztecan groups as well as other peoples is a floral road of the sun, as in this twentieth-century account for the Tzeltal Maya: "el sol se levanta en la mañana en el oriente, sube en el cielo por una vía florida hasta llegar a su apogeo al medio día"[2] (Holland 1961:168) Among the nearby Tzotzil of Zinacantán, a feathered serpent serves as the vehicle of the sun: "At dawn the sun rises in the east preceded by Venus, the Morning Star, a large plumed serpent called *Mukta ch'on*" (Vogt 1969:89). In ancient Mesoamerica, the flower road is embodied by the plumed serpent, which often has a floral tail or blossoms on its body, including the cited serpents on the witz facades from Hochob and El Tabasqueño (figure 10.3a–c, see also Taube 2010b:172–175). For El Tabasqueño Structure 1, a bicephalic feathered serpent carries S-shaped *muyal* cloud scrolls atop its body, indicating that this being is the vehicle of rain clouds as well as the sun, both originating from the east. The Yucatec Maya of Quintana Roo regard the east as the cardinal direction of primary importance due to its clear relation to rain:

> It is there that the rain gods assemble to make their decisions before going out to water the earth, and it is from that direction that the first thunders sound to announce the coming of the rains. (Villa Rojas 1945:155)

In addition, Villa Rojas also notes the local concept that the east was identified with the realm of heaven: "According to some beliefs, La Gloria, dwelling place of God and of the principal winds, is also in the east" (155). The earliest known example of Flower Mountain exhaling a plumed serpent appears in the aforementioned North Wall mural from San Bartolo, where the Maize God and other figures stand atop the back of the creature, which also bears a prominent yellow flower and exhales two more from its snout, denoting as the floral road (see Saturno et al. 2005:fig. 12).

Clearly enough, the San Bartolo serpent emerging out of a mountain maw in profile could translate into two serpents exiting the corners of the mouth if viewed frontally, as has been discussed for the breath elements on witz facades in Yucatán as well as Early Classic Maya examples of zoomorphic mountains exhaling pairs of serpents (see Saturno et al. 2005:figs. 13a, 16c; Taube 2004b). The celebrated and roughly coeval EVII-sub pyramid at Uaxactún had plumed serpent balustrades on all four sides with their upturned throats displaying rows of feathers, much like the feathered serpent scene at San Bartolo (Saturno et al. 2005:fig. 17b). These sculptures constitute early forms of the later plumed serpent balustrades known for Central Mexico and Postclassic Yucatán, including the famed northern stairway of the Castillo at Chichén Itzá. Rather than being mere architectural ornament, the serpents serve as symbolic roads or vehicles for ascending or descending sacred architecture (Taube 2002). In addition, although in terms of humanly functional architecture the pair of serpents flank a stairway, it is more than likely that the entire composition denotes a feathered serpent as the symbolic "road" for ascending or descending sacred architecture.

## BUTTERFLY SYMBOLISM IN EARLY POSTCLASSIC MESOAMERICA

Among the most striking images shared in the monumental sculpture of Tula and Chichén Itzá is a frontally facing crouching figure with large claws and a long bifurcated serpent tongue wearing an elaborate zoomorphic helmet headdress, goggles, and a butterfly nosepiece (figure 10.4e–f). According to Eduard Seler (1902–1923:5:366), the figure constitutes a form of Quetzalcoatl, and to the present the identity of this being continues to be a source of much debate. Whereas Ignacio Marquina (1951:865) describes it as the "hombre-pájaro serpiente" (man-bird snake), for Tozzer (1957:123) it is a "Jaguar-Serpent-Bird." More recently, I (Taube 1992b) termed this being the War Serpent, a creature incorporating serpent, feline, and butterfly traits that often appears in earlier Classic period art as a shell platelet helmet headdress in Teotihuacan and Maya iconography (see also Taube 2011, 2012). An Early Classic Teotihuacan–style censer lid from Xico in the valley of Mexico clearly depicts this same clawed being, here with the feathered eyes of Teotihuacan butterflies as well as probable symbolic antennae atop the head (figure 10.4b). The Classic and Early Postclassic being is probably an ancestral form of the Xiuhcoatl based on the concept of a caterpillar, the pupate form of butterflies before metamorphosis (Taube 2000, 2012). Among the Classic Maya, the War Serpent is strongly reptilian and is named Waxaklajuun Ubaah Chan, or "18 Images its Snake" in Classic Maya inscriptions (Freidel et al. 1993:308–310). However, the Teotihuacan version is typically more feline and although still a supernatural amalgam of animals it should perhaps be considered more a "War Jaguar" than a serpent being at this site.

A Thin Orange Teotihuacan vessel depicts the feline "War Serpent" with a prominent bifurcated tongue and feathered eyes backed by long quetzal plumes (figure 10.4a). Both this Early Classic figure and that from Xico lack the goggles known for the Early Postclassic examples of Tula and Chichén Itzá. However, Joseph Ball (1974:7) described an important Early Classic style

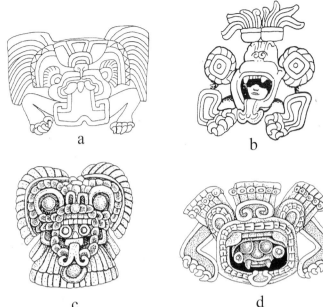

**FIGURE 10.4.** *Classic and Early Postclassic portrayals of War Serpents (drawings by author): (a) Feline War Serpent with bifurcated tongue, detail of Early Classic Thin Orange vessel (after Solís 2009:no. 58); (b) Early Classic War Serpent, detail of Early Classic censer attributed to Xico (from Taube 2000:fig. 9.11b); (c) Early Classic bundle figure wearing War Serpent platelet headdress, Becán (after Ball 1974:6); (d) Late Classic Tlaloc figure wearing War Serpent platelet headdress, Cacaxtla (after photograph courtesy of Andrew Turner); (e) goggled figure wearing War Serpent headdress, Tula (from Taube 2000:fig. 9.11d); (f) goggled figure with War Serpent headdress, Chichén Itzá (from Taube 2000:fig. 9.11e).*

example discovered within the well-known Teotihuacan "host figure" from Becán, Campeche (figure 10.4c). Appearing as a warrior mortuary bundle with a mirror on the chest, the figure not only displays the goggled eyes and long bifurcated serpent tongue, but also wears the shell platelet form of the War Serpent helmet headdress (for similar mortuary bundles wearing War Serpent headdresses, see Taube 2000:figs. 10.2b, 10.20a–b, e–f). Ball (1974:7) compares the Becán figure to the much later examples from Tula and Chichén Itzá (e.g., figure 10.4e–f). A ceramic *almena* sculpture from Late Classic Cacaxtla provides an excellent link between the Early Classic Teotihuacan and Maya forms of the War Serpent, with the helmet headdress having the platelet shell armor found with the Becán example (figure 10.4d). Moreover, with its prominent fangs as well as goggled eyes, the being in the Cacaxtla creature's maw is clearly a form of Tlaloc, suggesting that the other goggled beings at Tula and Chichén Itzá may also allude to this deity. Rather than a form of the plumed serpent, the crouching figure at Chichén Itzá and Tula is a distinct being who can be readily traced to the symbolism of deceased warriors at Early Classic Teotihuacan.

Mention has been made of the stylized butterfly nosepieces found on Early Postclassic War Serpents of Chichén Itzá and Tula. Given the widespread relation of breath to the soul in Mesoamerica, these nosepieces may well denote the butterfly souls of heroic warriors. Of similar form, the winged breast pieces worn by warriors at Chichén Itzá and Tula were long ago identified as butterflies by Seler (1902–1923:5:298). Thus, just as there are stylized butterflies on the nose as possible symbols of the breath essence of life, they also cover the chest and hearts of warriors. Similar but more explicit butterflies with horizontal "ribs" appear in the Codex Borgia (see fig. 10.10, top left). Clearly enough, the Early Postclassic butterfly warrior imagery at Tula and Chichén Itzá constitutes an important thematic link between warrior butterflies of early Teotihuacan and those of the Late Postclassic Aztec. However, there has been notably little discussion of butterflies in Early Postclassic Mesoamerica. Three relief panels from Tula portray winged insects with segmented abdomen, short antennae, and probable speech or song scrolls emerging from their open mouths, clearly denoting supernatural beings, as in real life butterflies are notably silent in this regard (figure 10.5e–g). Although these creatures have been identified as bees (de la Fuente et al. 1988:193–194), the undulating wing segments behind the abdomens are those of butterflies rather than bees. The early Colonial Codex Borbonicus also portrays butterflies with a prominent forelimb, including at least one example with a downturned abdomen (figure 10.5a). For the drum supporting the famed Aztec sculpture of Xochipilli,

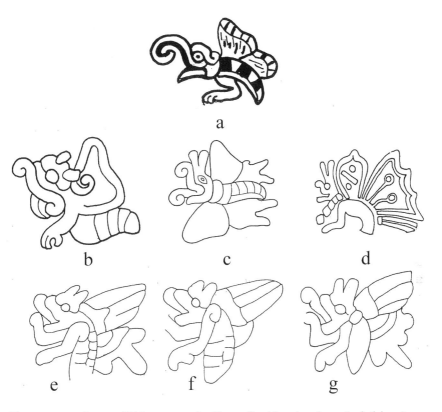

FIGURE 10.5. *Aztec and Toltec portrayals of butterflies (drawings by author): (a) early Colonial butterfly and down-curving abdomen, Codex Borbonicus, p. 5; (b) Aztec butterfly, detail of drum supporting seated Xochipilli (after Beutelspacher 1988:fig. 207); (c) Aztec petroglyph of butterfly from Acalpixca (after Franco 1961:pl. 20); (d) Aztec sello of butterfly wearing necklace (after Franco 1961:pl. 5, no. 2); (e–g) Toltec butterflies appearing on carved stone slabs, Tula (after de la Fuente et al. 1988:no. 135)*

there are butterflies with similarly segmented abdomens and short antennae as well as the forelimb (figure 10.5b). In addition, an Aztec petroglyph from Acalpixca, near Xochimilco, portrays a butterfly with comparable antennae and undulating lower wing segments (figure 10.5c). A Postclassic ceramic *sello* has horn-like antennae as well as a forelimb and a partially depicted down-turned abdomen, recalling the forelimbs and abdomens of the Tula butterflies (figure 10.5d). The sello butterfly also wears a necklace, which, as José Luis Franco C. (1961:230) notes, is notably rare with portrayals of Mesoamerican butterflies. Rather than an ordinary butterfly, this is a supernatural being probably portraying a warrior soul.

For two of the Tula butterfly sculptures, lines cross the abdomen, surely alluding to the segmented bodies of insects, including the aforementioned example at Acalpixca (figure 10.5b–d). However, the Toltec butterflies also have segmented elements running down their backs suggesting vertebrae, with the more frontal lines then being ribs. In other words, the creatures appear to partly skeletal. Although this could well relate to Classic Maya portrayals of insects, it probably denotes these creatures as the souls of deceased warriors, a theme that will be further discussed for a vessel scene from Isla de Sacrificios, Veracruz.

At Chichén Itzá, explicit butterflies appear on the sculpted balustrades of the North Temple in the Great Ballcourt (figure 10.6a). In the scenes, butterflies and birds sip the nectar of blossoms from a vine wrapped around a floral tree, a scene strongly reminiscent of the Florentine Codex description of the Aztec solar paradise, where the souls of warriors become brilliant birds and butterflies that drink from flowers. In fact, Frances Berdan (personal communication, 2011) notes that the two lower birds in the illustrated jamb are supernatural composite creatures, with the heads of hummingbirds but the long, flowing tails of male quetzals (figure 10.6a). Flowering vines and birds also appear on sculptured panels from the Castillo Viejo at Chichén Itzá, along with repetitive basal texts stating, "it is in the image of the flowers of his grandfather" (Schmidt et al. 2008:7). According to Schmidt and his colleagues (2008:10), these texts allude to flowers of the ancestors as well as paradise, with the Castillo Viejo being a form of Flower Mountain: "The notion of flowery paradise as ancestral abode strengthens the flower mountain interpretation of Maya pyramids and enhances our understanding of ancestral lineage as living natural flora" (10). The Castillo Viejo panels also have quetzals and other birds sipping the nectar of the flowering vines (11–12). However, the east jamb at the entrance of the temple has an especially interesting detail. Along with a quetzal, there are two butterflies with forelimbs and downturned abdomens, quite like the examples discussed for Tula (figure 10.6b).

Discovered during the excavation of the Temple of Chac Mool within the Temple of the Warriors, a series of carved stone blocks portray the floral paradise in brilliant polychrome (figure 10.7). The two reconstructed portions display a probable parrot and two yellow butterflies with forelimbs and segmented abdomens. Not only do these creatures have long quetzal tails in brilliant green, but they also emit song or speech scrolls, recalling the examples from Tula. Singing and with quetzal attributes, these butterflies are clearly supernatural beings and probably portray souls in paradise.

**Figure 10.6.** *Portrayals of floral paradise with birds and butterflies at Chichén Itzá (drawings by author): (a) flowering tree with vine—note four birds and two butterflies near base; detail of balustrade relief from the North Temple of the Great Ballcourt, Chichén Itzá (after Tozzer 1957:fig. 184); (b) flowering vine with flying quetzal bird and two butterflies, enlarged detail of butterflies to right, east jamb of Castillo Viejo, Chichén Itzá (after Schmidt et al. 2088:11).*

Aside from on monumental sculpture from Tula and Chichén Itzá, butterflies also occur on Early Postclassic drinking vessels. A pyriform vase from the site known as Chak Mool or Santa Rosa on the south-central coast of

FIGURE 10.7. *Fragmentary polychrome reliefs of supernatural butterflies and a flying bird in the floral paradise—note song scrolls and quetzal tails of butterflies; reliefs discovered during excavations of the Temple of the Chac Mool, Chichén Itzá (drawing by author after Morris et al. 1931:pl. 19).*

Quintana Roo has seated butterflies on its annular stand (figure 10.8a; see Romero Blanco 2002). Although the term "pyriform" alludes to a pear shape, this is clearly not the case for Mesoamerica, and it is more than likely that it alludes to a floral bud, which would be entirely appropriate in terms of the surrounding butterflies at the base. Along with prominent wings extending from their backs, the butterflies also have the goggle eyes commonly found with them at Teotihuacan. Along with the Chak Mool vessel, José Osorio León, and María Rocío González de la Mata (personal communication, 2011) kindly showed me a very similar butterfly from the base of a fragmentary pyriform vase found in the eastern area of Chichén Itzá close to the cave of Balankanché (figure 10.8b). As in the case of the Chak Mool vessel, the butterfly is seated and has goggle eyes and in addition wears a bracelet. Acquired by the British Museum in 1844, an Early Postclassic pyriform vase from Isla de Sacrificios, Veracruz, portrays a very similar butterfly wearing a bracelet, though in this case the creature appears on the rim rather than the annular

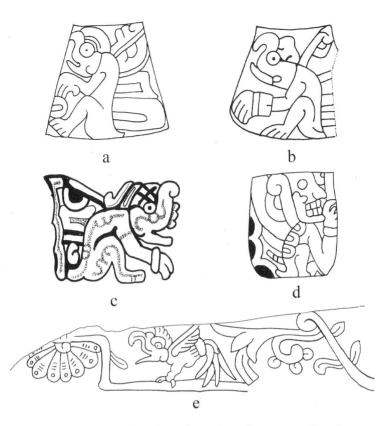

FIGURE 10.8. *Early Postclassic butterflies and paradise imagery of vessels from the northern Maya lowlands and Isla de Sacrificios (drawings by author): (a) seated butterfly on base of Fine Orange pyriform vase from Chak Mool, Quintana Roo (after Romero Blanco 2002:51); (b) Seated butterfly on base of fragmentary Fine Orange pyriform vase, Chichén Itzá (drawn from photo by author); (c) butterfly on rim of pyriform vase, Isla de Sacrificios (drawing by author from vessel on display in the British Museum); (d) seated skeletal butterfly, base of pyriform vessel, Isla de Sacrificios (after du Solier 1943:78); (e) quetzal on flowering vine, detail of vessel from Isla de Sacrificios (after du Solier 1943:76).*

base (figure 10.8c). Another pyriform vessel from this island has a base having a butterfly with a bracelet, though in this case it is skeletal, with a fleshless head and clearly delineated vertebrae (figure 10.8d). In addition, an Isla de Sacrificios vessel portrays a quetzal with flowering vines, quite like aforementioned scenes at Chichén Itzá (figure 10.8e). Located offshore of coastal

Veracruz, Isla de Sacrificios is in many ways the most eastern area for peoples of the Gulf Coast or Central Mexico, unless they still could travel far further to the Caribbean shores of the eastern Yucatán Peninsula, that is, the present state of Quintana Roo. The cited Isla de Sacrificios vessels are obviously related to Sotuta ceramics from Chichén Itzá, which also display a broad array of floral imagery on their rims (see Brainerd 1958:figs. 77, 82, 83, 87). Oddly enough, there has been no study as of yet concerning floral imagery and symbolism on Sotuta ceramics. According to Bey and Ringle (2007:394), the pyriform vessels at Chichén Itzá were for "elite drinking bouts, particularly of cacao." The Early Postclassic consumption of cacao may have often concerned the evocation of the illustrious dead, the butterfly and avian souls of heroic warriors. In a similar vein, I (Taube 2010a) have noted that many later Mixteca-Puebla polychrome ceramics bear butterfly and flower imagery, probably pertaining to warrior souls and the solar paradise.

## THE WIND GOD EHECATL-QUETZALCOATL
## AND THE MYTHIC ORIGINS OF MUSIC

In Aztec thought, music was a central component of the solar paradise. Along with singing birds, flowers were a common symbol of music. Miguel León Portilla (1963) noted that a basic Nahuatl *difrasismo* for poetry was *in xochitl in cuicatl*, meaning "flower and song." Page 4 of the Aztec Codex Borbonicus portrays the god of music, Xochipilli, emitting a large song scroll marked by a flower and the *ilhuicatl* sky band (for discussion of *ilhuicatl* motif, see Houston and Taube 2000:276–278). These elements denote the song scroll as floral and celestial, both being basic qualities of the solar paradise. The famed Aztec sculpture of a masked Xochipilli portrays him seated atop a drum ornamented with flowers and butterflies (see Alcina Franch et al. 1992:364). His body is covered with flowers, suggesting that he is nothing other than the floating music emanating from the drum, which is also decorated with butterflies as well as music. According to John Bierhorst (1985), the early Colonial *Cantares mexicanos* were to conjure heroic souls from the celestial paradise. While some of the songs exhibit clear Christian influence, many of them also mention both the eagle and the jaguar, the patrons of the two major Aztec military orders dedicated to the sun (see Bierhorst 1985:135, 151, 183, 185–187). Seler (1902–1923:5:364) noted that in Aztec thought, men of the eagle and jaguar orders were "courageous warriors who ended their lives in battle or as captives on the sacrificial stone." In other words, they were the heroes par excellence of the solar paradise.

Several pages in the Codex Borgia portray the mythic origins of music, such as is described in early Colonial sources pertaining to the Aztec (Taube 2001:114–115, 2004a). According to the *Histoire du Mechique*, Tezcatlipoca sends the wind across the sea to the house of the sun to obtain musicians to cheer humans after the sacrifice of the gods at Teotihuacan: "To this said the god Tezcatlipoca: 'Wind, go through the sea to the House of the Sun, which has many musicians and trumpeters with him, who serve him and sing'" (trans. by author from Garibay 1979:111).

Similarly, in an account by Mendieta (1980:80), a follower of Tezcatlipoca crosses the sea to obtain musicians and instruments from this solar realm:

> They say that the devotee of Tezcatlipoca (who was the main idol of Mexico), persevering in his devotion, came to the coast of the sea, where he appeared in three ways or forms, or called him and said: "Come here guy, because you are so my friend, I want you to go to the House of the Sun and bring from there singers and instruments so that you can make a celebration for me" (trans. by author).

As I have noted elsewhere, it is likely that pages 35 to 38 of the Codex Borgia portray Tezcatlipoca and Quetzalcoatl obtaining a sacred bundle containing music from Tlalchitonatiuh, a moribund aspect of the sun god (Taube 2001, 2004b). On Codex Borgia page 35, Quetzalcoatl and Tezcatlipoca, who oddly wears the duckbill mask of the wind god Ehecatl-Quetzalcoatl, takes a burning bundle featured prominently on the following page. Displaying eagle down balls, crosshatching, and crenelated edging, the textile wrapping of this bundle is a basic costume element of Quetzalcoatl in the Codex Borgia, especially in his guise as Ehecatl (e.g., Codex Borgia pages 19, 51, 56).

On Codex Borgia page 36, a great column of ash spiraling out of the burning bundle carries precious birds, butterflies, flowers, and musical instruments as well as five images of a flying, but seemingly lifeless, Quetzalcoatl with shut eyes (figure 10.9d). On page 38, the ash stream ends with the same Quetzalcoatl figure, but now clearly alive with widely open eyes emerging from the open beak of Ehecatl-Quetzalcoatl (figure 10.9c). This apparent portrayal of the rebirth of Quetzalcoatl from a burning mortuary bundle is strongly reminiscent of the Aztec *Anales de Cuauhtitlan*'s account of the death and resurrection of Quetzalcoatl following his journey from Tula to the lands of the east, quite possibly Yucatán, where he cremates himself upon reaching the furthest shore:

> They say that as he burned, his ashes arose. And what appeared and what the saw were all the precious birds, rising into the sky. They saw roseate spoonbills,

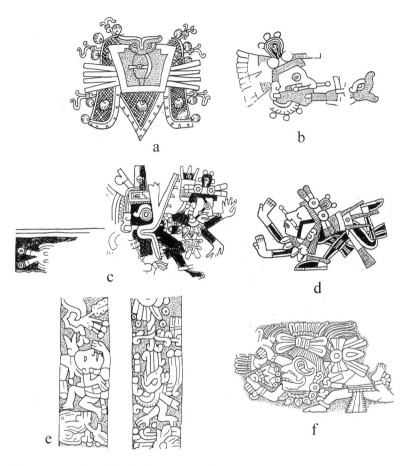

FIGURE 10.9. *Late Postclassic scenes pertaining to music and supernatural flight (drawings by author): (a) burning bundle containing red zoomorphic flute, Codex Borgia, p. 36; (b) Xochipilli playing red zoomorphic flute, Codex Borgia, p. 37; (c) Quetzalcoatl emerging out of music stream embodied by Ehecatl, Codex Borgia, pp. 37–38; (d) Quetzalcoatl flying in music stream, Codex Borgia, p. 36; (e) human figure and bird rising in floral bands on ends of Aztec wooden* teponaztli *(after Saville 1925:pl. 32); (f) Ixtlilton, Aztec god of dance, flying on side of Aztec ceramic drum replicating form of* teponaztli *(after Alcina Franch et al. 1992:no. 75).*

cotingas, trogons, herons, green parrots, scarlet macaws, white-fronted parrots, and all the other precious birds. And as soon as all his ashes had burned, his ashes arose. They saw the heart of a quetzal rising upward. And so they knew that he had gone to the sky, had entered the sky. (Bierhorst 1992:36)

Similarly, a pair of Late Postclassic spearthrowers depict the plumed serpent rising from a pool of water in the maw of the earth deity Tlaltecuhtli (see Saville 1925:pl. 11). The emerging feathered serpent bears a chain of hummingbirds and flowers on its back, and I interpret the entire scene as Quetzalcoatl emerging at dawn as the floral road rising from the eastern sea (Taube 2010a:176).

Along with the precious birds, the Codex Borgia column of wind-borne ash also contains flowers, butterflies and articles of music and dance, including turtle and ceramic drums, a pair of avian flutes, rattles, a conical dance cap, and a prominent dance staff (figure 10.10). In many respects, this stream encapsulates the Flower World complex first discussed by Hill (1992), who notes that it is frequently expressed through music among Uto-Aztecan speakers of Mesoamerica and the Greater Southwest. In the Codex Borgia episode, an especially important detail is the red element atop the bundle on page 36, which has an open zoomorphic mouth exhaling the entire column of ash. I (Taube 2001) identify this device as a flute, the same instrument played by Xochipilli as the god of music on the following page 37 of the Codex Borgia (figure 10.9a–b).

Scenes of precious birds, flowers, and flying figures are also on Aztec drums as forms of the Borgia column wind and music. The visible ends of an Aztec *teponaztli* feature bands containing flowers, a flying human figure, and a quetzal, much like the Borgia stream (figure 10.9e). Whereas the central scene on one side of this drum portray an intertwined eagle and jaguar—surely alluding to the Aztec military orders, the other features the sun rising out of a probable Tlaltecuhtli maw into the sky. This celestial realm has four armed warriors, probably warrior souls in the celestial solar paradise (see Saville 1925:plates 30–32). Still another wooden teponaztli has flowers on its ends and a central dancing or flying male with shut eyes, recalling the five images of Quetzalcoatl in the Codex Borgia stream of ash (see Couch 1988:no. 53). Among the Classic Maya, there is a strong relation of music and dance to flight, with plumed dancers often merging into birds (see Taube 2009a). As with the flying Quetzalcoatl figures in the Codex Borgia bundle scene, the Aztec dancer's eyes are shut, possibly to indicate a "false death" of trance or fainting. An Aztec ceramic drum of teponaztli form portrays a god of dance, Ixtlilton, in the very same position as the flying Quetzalcoatl figures in the Codex Borgia wearing an identical shell necklace (figure 10.9f). Although not an actual wooden teponaztli, this object was probably a ceramic drum having leather stretched over its large orifice on the back as the sounding surface (see Alcina Franch et al. 1992:no. 75).

The Late Postclassic flying figures under discussion recall reclining and evidently celestial males appearing in earlier Toltec-style art of Tula and Chichén

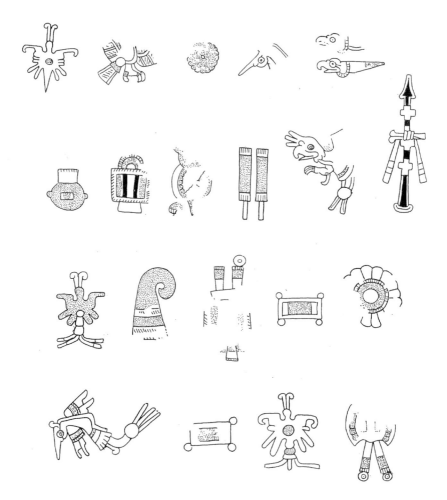

**FIGURE 10.10.** *Items of music and dance appearing in stream of music issuing out of zoomorphic flute, Codex Borgia, pp. 36–37 (drawings by author).*

Itzá, including reliefs from the Palacio Quemado at Tula, which Cynthia Kristan-Graham (1999:171) suggests may portray deceased warriors and kings (figure 10.11e–f). In Sala 2 of this complex, the figures fly before petalled *cuauhxicalli* vessels resembling open flowers, much as if these heroic beings were about to sip the precious "nectar" of sacrificial blood (see Mastache et al. 2009:figs. 13–14). In fact, a common motif in Postclassic solar and war iconography is gods and the souls warriors wielding their spearthrowers or darts as symbolic *popotes* to drink blood, much like the proboscises of butterflies or the

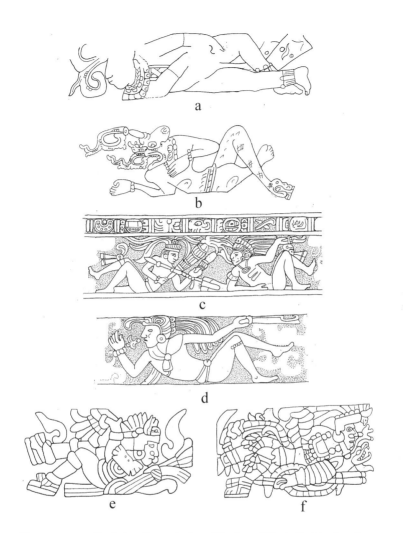

FIGURE 10.11. *Reclining figures in Late Classic and Early Postclassic art (drawings by author): (a) reclining figure with death costume elements and cranial torch of K'awiil from Hieroglyphic Stairway of Temple 26, Copán (after Gordon 1902:pl. 5); (b) K'awiil in reclining pose, detail of Fine Orange vessel from Kohunlich (after Velázquez Morlet 1995:35); (c) reclining warriors on Pabellón vessel (after Werness 2003:fig. 1.48); (d) reclining warrior with spearthrower on Pabellón vessel (after Werness 2003:fig. 1.34); (e) reclining Toltec warrior with flames, Tula (after de la Fuente et al. 1988:no. 106); (f) reclining Toltec warrior riding feathered serpent (after de la Fuente et al. 1988:no. 108).*

long beaks of hummingbirds (Taube 2009b:103). Clearly enough, as the central chamber and court of the Palacio Quemado, Sala 2 may have been a place of music and dance to conjure the beings flying above, much like the band of music and dance encircling the burning bundle on Codex Borgia, page 36.

Although reclining "flying warrior" figures in prone or supine positions are relatively common in Early Postclassic Toltec art, they remain unknown for Xochicalco, Cacaxtla, or still earlier Teotihuacan. Rather than being of earlier Central Mexican traditions, this motif may well derive from the Classic Maya. Dating to the eighth century AD, a number of risers from the Hieroglyphic Stairway of Temple 26 at Copán portray human figures reclining on their sides, recalling the bound captives in similar positions on stairway risers at Tamarindito (see Green Robertson et al. 1972:pl. 4). One individual in this pose at Copán wears regal jewelry along with a clear "death collar" and a loincloth marked with the Kimih "division sign" for death (figure 10.11a). He also displays the cranial torch of K'awiil appearing with royal ancestors, including the columnar Stela 11 from Copán Temple 18 as well as with K'inich Janaab Pakal on the Sarcophagus Lid from the Temple of the Inscriptions at Palenque. A Terminal Classic Fine Orange ceramic sherd from Kohunlich, Quintana Roo, portrays K'awiil in a very similar reclining pose, indicating that it relates to not only captives, but to far wider-ranging concepts of deceased individuals and gods (figure 10.11b). Moreover, Terminal Classic Fine Orange ceramics from such Pasión sites as Ceibal and Altar de Sacrificios often portray warrior figures in similar pose (figure 10.11c–d). In terms of their proportions and accoutrements, some appear to be strongly "Toltec" in appearance, and arguably perhaps some of the convergence of Terminal Classic Maya and Central Mexican "Toltec" may derive from this region, long recognized for its clear celebration of Central Mexican traditions at Ceibal. In addition, as shallow bowls, many Pabellón Modeled-Carved vessels were probably used for drinking cacao or pulque, much as George Bey and William Ringle (2007) posit for vessels at Chichén Itzá, as mentioned above.

At Ceibal, one of the most striking monuments displaying both Maya and Central Mexican iconographic conventions is Stela 3, dominated by a curious stone element topped by flowers, arguably a form of Flower Mountain backing and looming over the central human figure (see Graham 1996). Whereas the uppermost register displays a pair of Tlaloc rain gods, below the central scene there are two musicians perhaps conjuring the highland Mexican rain gods above through music. Although otherwise entirely human, the right individual displays a clear duckbill strongly suggesting Ehecatl-Quetzalcoatl, the wind god of Central Mexico (figure 10.12b). Due to a glyphic decipherment

a

b

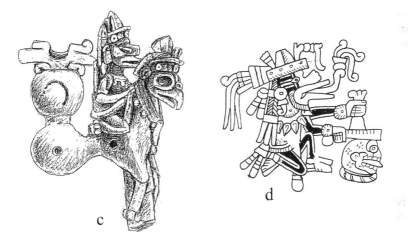
c

d

FIGURE 10.12. *Music and duckbilled deities in ancient Mesoamerica: (a) Late Preclassic Maya dancing duckbilled figure with song scroll, detail of West Wall of Las Pinturas Sub 1A, San Bartolo (detail of drawing by Heather Hurst, from Taube et al. 2010:fig. 32a); (b) duckbilled deity shaking rattle, Seibal Stela 3 (drawing by author after Graham 1996:7:17); (c) ceramic flute portraying Ehecatl riding atop bird (drawing by author of object on display in the Museo Regional de Tapachula, Chiapas); (d) Mixtec wind deity 9 Wind playing bone and scapula rasp atop skull resonator, Codex Vienna, p. 24.*

by David Stuart of a text from Yaxchilán, it is now clear that the Classic Maya also had a duck wind deity. This being is of great antiquity in southeastern Mesoamerica, and appears in the murals at Late Preclassic San Bartolo, along with the jadeite Tuxtla Statuette, Olmec pendants, and probably even an Early Formative Locona ceramic vessel from coastal Chiapas (figure 10.12a; see Taube et al. 2010:48–49; Taube 2018).

Known as Ehecatl to the Aztec and 9 Wind among the Mixtec, the duck-billed wind god of highland Mexico does not appear until the Late Postclassic in highland Mexico, suggesting it was indeed introduced from southeastern Mesoamerica. At present, I am unaware of any imagery pertaining to such a being in the known corpus of Early Classic Teotihuacan. Among the ancient Maya, there is another anthropomorphic wind god who often displays a large flower on the brow and *ik'* sign wind markings on his face and body (see Taube 2004b:73–74, figs. 2–3). Appearing epigraphically as the head variant of the numeral 3 and the patron of the month Mak, he is also embodies music—sound being carried by air and wind (Taube 2004b). As has been noted for Ceibal Stela 3, the duckbilled wind deity is also a musician, and two Late Classic Maya figures portray him with a turtle shell drum (see Taube and Taube 2009:fig. 9.11a–b). For the West Wall at San Bartolo, the Late Preclassic duckbilled wind deity sings and dances with small flying birds emitting song scrolls as well (see Taube et al. 2010:101). Possibly of Aztec manufacture, a remarkable Late Postclassic gray ceramic whistle in the Museo Regional de Tapachula, Chiapas, portrays Ehecatl riding atop a large-beaked bird (figure 10.12c). In the Mixtec Codex Vindobonensis, 9 Wind emits an elaborate song scroll while sounding a bone rasp atop a human skull (figure 10.12d). Clearly enough, the Mesoamerican duckbilled wind god of music corresponds closely to the aforementioned episode in the Codex Borgia, where the moving stream of flowers, butterflies, and accoutrements of music and dance is the body of Ehecatl, who carries the reborn Quetzalcoatl emerging from his open beak (figure 10.9c).

Dating to the end of the Classic period, the duckbilled deity on Ceibal Stela 3 clearly resembles examples of Ehecatl and 9 Wind in highland Mexico, and it could be argued that this was the region from which the Late Postclassic derived. However, a much larger and very significant corpus of examples occurs at Early Postclassic Chichén Itzá as well, of still somewhat later date and with obvious cultural connections with Tula of Central Mexico. In these relatively late examples as well as with all the already discussed eastern Mesoamerican forms, the head tends to be entirely human aside from the projecting bird bill, which resembles a buccal mask that could be readily donned by entertainers as well as priests. In his early study of the iconography of Chichén Itzá, Seler illustrates an avian atlantean figure of this duckbilled wind god (figure 10.13a). This figure readily recalls a pair of Aztec atlantean Ehecatl-Quetzalcoatl sculptural supports for a dais or throne (figure 10.13b). The Late Classic Maya site of Dos Pilas, Guatemala, has two exquisitely carved duckbilled wind deities serving as dais supports, demonstrating that this theme can be readily traced to the Classic Maya (see Finamore and Houston 2010:no. 26).

At Chichén Itzá, excavations and restoration work directed by Peter Schmidt have uncovered many other Early Postclassic examples of the duckbilled wind deity, or Ehecatl-Quetzalcoatl. Sixteen panels from the upper facade of the Osario Temple feature him with a bird mask while usually grasping in both hands rattles, a turtle shell, and other drums amidst falling cacao pods and jewels (figure 10.13c; see Schmidt 2007:175). The pair of long pendant elements hanging from the sides of the belts are trait of dancers both at Chichén Itzá as well as Late Postclassic Central Mexico, including the Codex Vaticanus B (see Taube 1994). The figures have tall cloth headdresses with a large central blossom, recalling the floral brow-piece of the aforementioned human Maya wind god.

Still more elaborate portrayals of the duckbilled being occur in facades from the Initial Series Group, also excavated and reconstructed in a project directed by Peter Schmidt (figures 10.13d-e, 10.14a; see Schmidt 2003, 2007; Schmidt et al. 2018). In these facades, the deity wears the cloth turban headdress found not only with the aged being often referred to as God N or Pahuahtun, but also with the aforementioned duckbilled musician on Ceibal Stela 3 (see figure 10.12b). In reliefs from the Temple of the Owls, the wind god strikes a ceramic drum, clearly denoting him as a musician (figure 10.13d). Nearby reliefs from the House of the Phalli have the same duckbilled deity dancing and apparently singing while striking a drum (figure 10.13e). In this case, the entire face is avian, with the large round eyes resembling the bald, macaw-like orbits found with Muscovy ducks (*Cairina moschata*). However, still more remarkable are the backgrounds behind the series of duck wind gods, which are filled with cacao as well as falling or floating regalia related to public performance and dance, including headdresses, pectorals, jade jewelry, and dance fans, recalling the stream of objects appearing in the aforementioned Codex Borgia stream of music and dance motifs embodied by Ehecatl, which Seler (1963:2:32) describes as "objetos que parecen simbolizar todos ellos la preciosidad y el adorno"[3] (see figure 10.11).

Another structure in the Initial Series Group, the House of the Shells, displays massive and complex friezes of Ehecatl holding onto undulating, flowering vines, recalling the suggested scenes of paradise from the fragments from

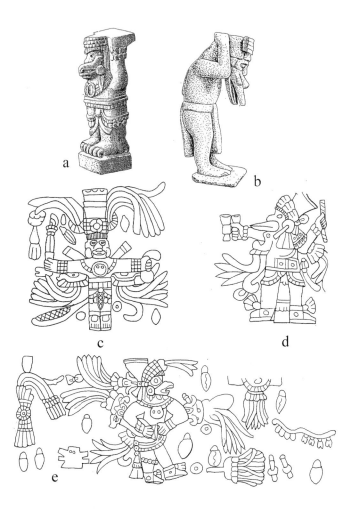

FIGURE 10.13. *Portrayals of Ehecatl at Early Postclassic Chichén Itzá and for the Late Postclassic Aztec (drawings by author): (a) Ehecatl atlantean sculpture with apparent taloned eagle feet, Chichén Itzá (from Seler 1902–1923:5: 277); (b) Aztec atlantean sculpture of Ehecatl (drawing by author after Nicholson and Keber 1983:no. 21); (c) Ehecatl dancer grasping musical instruments, Osario Temple, Chichén Itzá (from Taube 2004b:fig. 14d); (d) Ehecatl musician striking double-chambered drum, detail of relief from the Temple of the Owls, Chichén Itzá (after Schmidt 2003:fig. 44); (e) Ehecatl playing music with floating elements of dance costumes and precious items, including jade ornaments and cacao, detail of relief from the House of the Phalli, Chichén Itzá (after Schmidt 2003:fig. 31).*

**FIGURE 10.14.** *The avian theme of rebirth and paradise (drawings by author): (a) Ehecatl wind god emerging with flowering vines out of cracked egg, detail of relief from the House of the Snails, Chichén Itzá (after Schmidt 2003:fig. 36); (b) quetzal bird descending to drink from open blossom, detail of relief from the House of the Shells, Chichén Itzá (after Schmidt 2003:fig. 36); (c) quetzal wearing necklace while drinking from a blossom, Chichén Itzá (after Schmidt 2003:fig. 36); (d) quetzal drinking form a vessel as an open flower, Codex Borgia, p. 3.*

the Temple of Chac Mool excavations as well as the Old Castillo at Chichén Itzá (figures 10.6b, 10.7, 10.14a, c, f). The facade features a series of deities emerging from a large, round form with an upper, open cleft having oddly uneven edges. Considering the obvious avian nature of most of the emerging figures, the round element is clearly a freshly broken, open egg. In previous research, I (Taube 2000:309) suggested that the warrior mortuary bundles of Central Mexico were the "chrysalii or cocoons of warrior butterfly souls." However, as has been noted, the souls of heroic warriors were not only butterflies, but birds as well, and in this context what better metaphor for rebirth and resurrection than a bird freshly emerging from its open shell?

## CONCLUSIONS

*A Forest of Kings* provides a detailed a graphic account of militarism and warfare at Chichén Itzá, but at that time, there was little interest and discussion of Mesoamerican concepts of the afterlife, including the paradise realm of warrior souls. While Early Classic Teotihuacan and sixteenth-century Aztec concepts of the afterlife realm of heroic warriors have been well documented, the obviously intervening period of the Early Postclassic (AD 900–1250) encompassing both Chichén Itzá and Tula has received surprisingly little scholarly interest. This omission is all the more puzzling when one considers the detailed Aztec accounts of the journey of Quetzalcoatl to the east and his death and resurrection, as previously noted for the *Anales de Cuauhtitlan*. In addition, Diego de Landa also mentions the coming of K'uk'ulkan to Chichén Itzá, and not only does he state that this is the same being known as Quetzalcoatl, but also that "he arrived from the west" (Tozzer 1941:22–23). Obviously, highland Mexican peoples would associate his journey with the eastern shores of Veracruz, such as the Isla de Sacrificios, but still further lies the eastern coast of Yucatán, now the state of Quintana Roo of contemporary Mexico. For what we now know concerning glyphic texts of direct and politically altering Early Classic events with Teotihuacan at such major Classic Maya sites as Tikal and Copán, the interaction between these regions was direct and powerful enough for Late Classic Maya rulers to proudly proclaim their Central Mexican ancestry and affiliations. But of more relevance here is that in highland Mexico, the Maya region as the source of wealth and abundance was never forgotten. As I have often mentioned, the Borgia Group of highland Mexican codices consistently depict the east as the place of jade, quetzals, and, of course Tonatiuh, the vibrant sun god rising from the eastern dawn (see Taube 1994). Still another item of wealth from the Maya region is cacao, and it is likely that at Chichén Itzá, the ritual imbibing of cacao concerned the conjuring of and communion with the souls of warriors. Thus not only do floral imagery and supernatural butterflies appear on drinking vessels, but monumental reliefs at Chichén Itzá portray cacao pods with floating jewels and other elements pertaining to paradise, a motif that I have termed the "rain of flowers" (see Taube 2004b).

Clearly enough, Quetzalcoatl relates closely to concepts of the eastern paradise, including him being an eastern god of the dawn and the embodiment of vivifying forces of breath and wind, the vehicle for rain-bearing clouds, music, and the souls of the heroic dead. I would argue that the cultural relationship between Chichén Itzá and Tula during the Early Postclassic relates closely to their geographic orientation, with Chichén Itzá being almost due east of Tula, the place of the dawning sun and the paradise realm of warrior souls. At Chichén Itzá, a plumed serpent figure is commonly paired with an obvious embodiment of the sun, or Tonatiuh in Central Mexico (see Miller 1977; Taube 1994). In addition, a jade plaque from the Cenote of Sacrifice at Chichén Itzá features the armed sun god atop the plumed serpent as his vehicle (see Finamore and Houston 2010:no. 65). In a number of publications, I (Taube 1992a:140–143, 1994) suggest that the Late Postclassic sun deity of highland Mexico, Tonatiuh, is based on the concept of a Maya king. In addition, in the present study I mention that plumed serpent balustrades, reclining supernatural warriors, and duckbilled wind gods may derive from the Maya region.

Aside from themes of possible Maya origin, other components of the Postclassic solar paradise complex surely derived from Early Classic Teotihuacan, including the crouching War Serpents appearing in the monumental art of Chichén Itzá and Tula. In addition, the appearance of butterflies in monumental sculpture at Chichén Itzá is also of Central Mexican origin, as although the concept of warrior souls as butterflies is widespread at Teotihuacan it has no immediate correlate in Classic Maya imagery. In this regard, it important to note the appearance of a Teotihuacan-style butterfly from an Early Classic mural at Xelhá, Quintana Roo, virtually on the eastern Caribbean shore, as well as similar Teotihuacan butterflies appearing on ceramic vessels from Altún Ha in eastern Belize (see Taube 1992b:fig. 18b–c). In addition, it will be recalled that Early Postclassic pyriform vases from both the Isla de Sacrificios, Veracruz, and the coastal Quintana Roo site of Chak Mool bear portrayals of supernatural butterflies. Among contemporary Yucatec Maya of Quintana Roo, brilliantly colored butterflies are identified with the east:

> It is also believed that the butterflies acquire the vivid colors of their wings in some place in the east, and that is why the small, discolored butterflies which one sees flying eastward during last days of May return months later with wings covered with polychrome adornment . . . It is well known that the ancestors

of the present day Maya are in hiding somewhere in the east, awaiting the moment when they may return to their land and resume their ancient grandeur. (Villa Rojas 1945:155)

Not only does this account describe the east as a place of renewal for butterflies but also as the realm from which the souls of the ancient ancestral Maya will be reborn to return in all their ancient glory.

## NOTES

1. "The masks represented on the doors, corners, and facades of Río Bec, Chenes, and Puuc structures are a variant of the Earth or cuauc monster" (translation by Travis Stanton).

2. "The sun rises in the east in the morning, rising in the sky via a flower road until it reaches its apex at mid-day" (translation by Travis Stanton).

3. "Objects that seem to symbolize preciousness and adornment" (translation Travis Stanton).

## 11

The book, *A Forest of Kings* (Schele and Freidel 1990), has a special place in my own personal history because I literally became a Mesoamerican scholar during the research and writing of the text. When I took my first graduate seminar with Linda Schele, I was planning to study contemporary American art. Taking the class as a requirement, I entered a classroom filled with perhaps thirty people, only ten of whom were actually enrolled in the class; the rest were profoundly dedicated to Mesoamerican research—an intimidating situation that impressed upon me my then outsider status. The subject of the course was caches, a term that Linda never defined to those of us new to Mesoamerican research, and it was definitely a trial-by-fire type of learning.[1] On that first day, she wrote the names of a few Mesoamerican sites on the blackboard and told each of the participants to pick one. I chose Chichén Itzá, because it was the only one that sounded familiar, so I reasoned that there must have been a great deal of research written about the site. However, this assumption was quite mistaken, for in the late 1980s the majority of information still came from the Carnegie Institution of Washington, which excavated the site for twenty years beginning in 1924.[2] Further, the Maya-Toltec connections promoted by Tozzer (1957) and Samuel Lothrop (1952) framed much discussion of Chichén Itzá, but these publications were by then thirty years old.

*Empire at Chichén Itzá Revisited*

Annabeth Headrick

DOI: 10.5876/9781646420469.c011

Ultimately, it was both a terrifying and exhilarating experience, in which, as a young graduate student, I came to new insights, several of which made their way into *A Forest of Kings*, one in the form of a footnote, a milestone for a first-year graduate student.[3] Linda, and ultimately David A. Freidel, led me into a world in which research was collaboration, many voices played a role, and there were so many unpenetrated realms to investigate. This approach, I must say, was a welcome thing from the more formal hierarchy in the then-traditional fields of art history, and I was hooked.

Chichén Itzá, that first Maya site I ever studied, always intrigued and perplexed me. It is a site where fundamental questions of who lived there and what the nature of the city's political organization was have challenged scholarly inquiry. I eventually spent my early career on the city of Teotihuacan (Headrick 2007), but the original attraction to this topic was not Teotihuacan's substantial importance in Mesoamerica, but the city's ability to ultimately explain issues encountered at Chichén Itzá. Chichén Itzá is not a place where neat categories of ethnicity necessarily apply, and it demands a broad knowledge of Mesoamerica to tease apart its complex history.

In their chapter on Chichén Itzá in *A Forest of Kings*, Linda and David challenged the dominant narrative of the city's foreignness (Schele and Freidel 1990:346–376; see also Karl Taube, chapter 10 in this volume). Instead of seeing the site as a Maya city subsequently conquered and rebuilt as a Toltec city, they pulled from the then-emerging scholarship of settlement pattern archaeology, noting that the raised causeways, or *sacbeob*, effectively linked the various architectural groupings into a unified whole.[4] Furthermore, they followed the partial overlap model for Yucatecan ceramics, wherein the so-called Toltec ceramics at least partially overlapped with the Puuc Maya ceramics, indicating at least some contemporaneity of the two traditions (A. Andrews and Robles Castellanos 1985).

In addition, Schele and Freidel pointed out the epigraphic and iconographic evidence for a Maya identity at the site. The most obvious data supporting this are the presence of Maya hieroglyphic writing, especially a group of three Puuc-style structures, including the Temple of the Four Lintels.[5] These buildings included lintels over their doorways carved with fairly extensive hieroglyphic texts. Within this writing, use of the word *ajaw*, or lord, serves as confirmation that Classic Maya traditions of kingship had survived in the Yucatán Peninsula. At least on these three buildings, the naming of lords functioning as rulers appeared to be a system that had persisted into the Epiclassic. Granted, these carved lintels on domestic structures were more modest and private proclamations than the "forests of kings" seen on the public stelae of the Classic period. In those splendid monuments of an earlier time, the portraits of rulers and their aggrandizing statements of personal achievements endured to posterity in the main plazas. Yet because the rulers still touted their actions on the lintels at Chichén Itzá, Schele and Freidel noted that the system had transformed, but the origins, the traditions, were still recognizable. These lintels, along with a hieroglyphic frieze from the Casa Colorada, also seemingly listed a string of individuals with the title, ajaw. Combining this textual evidence with traditions documented by the Spanish at the time of the Conquest for systems of shared governance, they put forward an argument for *multepal*. Essentially, their argument was that at Chichén Itzá the institution of ajaw had transformed so that several lords cogoverned the site, seemingly reaffirming its Maya identity even as the structures of Maya political power altered.[6] More recent epigraphic research has seriously challenged the argument for multepal. Ideas about coruling lords began to crumble as Stuart (Stuart et al. 1999:177) put forward that the houses to which such lintels belong were more likely "owned" by deities than by humans. Shannon Plank (2004) developed these ideas and reanalyzed the hieroglyphs, revealing that a number of the supposed human lords were indeed deities and that the Maya conjured their presence through burning rituals.[7] Marc Zender (2004) further noted that some of these individuals were fire priests who assisted the ruler in the burning rituals. Thus, it now appears that in the period represented by these Puuc structures with their hieroglyphic lintels, the system of the singular ajaw had persisted at Chichén Itzá, and the shared governance did not appear to be among a group of Classic-style lords. Instead, a stronger case for shared governance comes from the sculpture and murals of the Temple of the Warriors (figure 11.1), a later structure built in the International Style.[8] Here, the military, perhaps building upon traditions of Central Mexico, exerted a powerful presence in the social, economic, and political structure of Chichén Itzá.[9]

Schele and Freidel saw the Temple of the Warriors as a place where a more anonymous and collective ajaw could share their power with the greater population at Chichén Itzá. As they noted, the warriors sculpted on the numerous columns fronting the temple proper wear military emblems adopted by the Maya from Teotihuacan (see Taube, chapter 10 in this volume, for additional discussion of warriors at Chichén). Warriors carved and painted on Column 17 and Column 40 from the Northwest Colonnade (figure 11.2) include year signs and Tlaloc masks in their costume and prominently brandish atlatls and their darts. This imagery entered Early Classic Maya iconography through Tikal and other Teotihuacan-friendly cities, and in the Late Classic these cities increasingly mythologized their Teotihuacan origins and used such

FIGURE 11.1. *The Temple of the Warriors, Chichén Itzá (photo by author).*

bellicose imagery to advertise their identity, which was diametrically opposed to the Maya-centric identity of the Kaan kingdoms allied with Calakmul (Stuart 2000). Thus, Linda and David noted that this foreign imagery at Chichén Itzá was not new to the Maya; it had been filtered through a Maya lens for 500 years when it came from the Maya region into the iconography of Chichén Itzá. Much more is now known about the 11 Eb date, when Atlatl Owl orchestrated a coup d'état at Tikal, and the deep ideological and economic divisions between Tikal and Calakmul.[10] Chichén Itzá can be situated into the story of this old animosity, and its celebration of Teotihuacan imagery puts it firmly in the camp of Tikal and Copán, as Chichén Itzá proclaimed its affiliation with the ancestral Tollan of Central Mexico, Teotihuacan (see also Taube, chapter 10 in this volume).

Certainly, some of the Central Mexican imagery entered the visual vocabulary of Chichén Itzá via the Maya, but the Temple of the Warriors extends this embrace of Central Mexico because it reveals that the people of Chichén Itzá adopted forms of social organization that do not have their origins in Classic Maya history. As much as the Maya of Tikal and Copán embraced the military-oriented Tlaloc ideology of Teotihuacan, the actual warriors who fought the battles of the Classic kings continued to act more like independent contractors. Vessels such as Kerr 638 (figure 11.3a) celebrate individual identities and accomplishments. The victorious warriors accompanying their almost naked captives wear Tlaloc goggles, but each man's costume differs in its individual elements. Likewise, on Yaxchilán Lintel 8 (figure 11.3b), successful rulers and their vassals advertise their individual military exploits as each takes physical possession of his own captive. Classic Maya military strategies never adopted the more collective organization of Teotihuacan's military

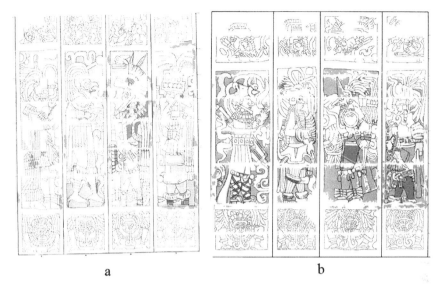

a          b

FIGURE 11.2. *(a) Column 17, Temple of the Warriors, Chichén Itzá; (a) Column 40, Northwest Colonnade, Temple of the Warriors, Chichén Itzá (after Morris et al. 1931:pl. 59 and 106).*

orders, such as that depicted in a mural from the Atetelco apartment compound (figure 11.4). Here, similarly clad canine warriors deny their individuality to some degree and walk in processions celebrating their shared identity (Headrick 2007:72–89).

The Temple of the Warriors exhibits an interesting blend of these two traditions. On the one hand, as Schele and Freidel pointed out, the sculpted colonnade has the effect of portraiture, with differently costumed figures (figure 11.2). There is an amazing array of individuals with star skirts, shell pectorals, or skull masks distinguishing one from the other, and a number of individuals have glyphs (such as figure 11.2a, third figure from the left) that identify them personally (Kristan-Graham 1989:197–200, Lincoln 1986:154; see also Taube, chapter 10 in this volume). This variety echoes the individuality of Late Classic Maya warriors on ceramics. Yet on the other hand, these warriors process in a grand hall meant to subsume these individuals into a collective whole. Furthermore, the hypostyle hall itself is a new innovation that affords this communal identity a physical space and reaffirms the unity of the individual actors. In this way, the Maya at Chichén Itzá thoroughly merged their strategies of individual warrior identities with the unified mentality of Central

FIGURE 11.3. *(a) Procession of warriors and captives, rollout photograph of a Late Classic Maya vase, Justin Kerr, Justin Kerr Maya vase archive, K-638, Dumbarton Oaks, Trustees for Harvard University, Washington, D.C.; (b) Lintel 8, Yaxchilán (Drawing by Ian Graham © President and Fellows of Harvard College, Peabody Museum of Archaeology and Ethnology, PM 2004.15.6.5.8).*

Mexican traditions. The grouping of individual warriors under a common roof, I would suggest, is a nod toward Central Mexican collective military strategies, but the Temple of the Warriors has an even more obvious reference to forms of military organization developed earlier at Teotihuacan.[11]

The animal imagery found on the substructure of the temple proper argu-ably derives from the mascots of Teotihuacan's military orders (figure 11.5a). In a detail of a mural from the White Patio, part of an apartment compound at Teotihuacan, a feline and a canine have hearts, dripping with blood, before their mouths. As I have argued elsewhere (Headrick 2007:72–89), the feline and canine reference animal mascots of two military orders. While it is still likely

**FIGURE 11.4.** *Detail of the reconstruction of the South Portico murals by Augustin Villagra, White Patio, Teotihuacan (photo by author).*

that these animals served as symbols of sociopolitical groups at Teotihuacan, the recent faunal analysis by Nawa Sugiyama (2014, 2017) of animals cached inside Teotihuacan's Pyramid of the Moon has amended our understanding of these animal images. She explains that the Teotihuacanos captured such animals alive and held them in zoos, confirmed by evidence that these animals had diets that included maize. Thus, the hearts positioned before the mouths of the felines and canines at Atetelco may suggest that Teotihuacanos fed the hearts of sacrificial victims to their zoological captives, a practice that likely terrified the enemies of the city.[12] Several hundred years later at Chichén Itzá, relief sculptures at the Temple of the Warriors (figure 11.5b) portray a feline, a bird, and other animals that clutch hearts in a redux of the Classic period ritual. Although archaeology at Chichén has not yet resulted in similar evidence of captive animal curation, the sculpted façade indicates that the Itzáe may have engaged in similar practices or at least sustained the memory of these dramatic performances at Teotihuacan. In addition, the astounding number of warriors and ritual participants who stride along with serpents

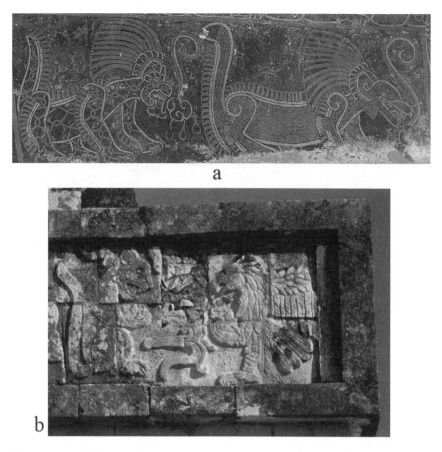

FIGURE 11.5. *(a) Mural of feline and canine with bleeding hearts in front of their mouths, lower talud wall, West Portico, White Patio, Atetelco, Teotihuacan; (b) relief sculpture of feline and bird with hearts clutched in their paw and talons, substructure of the Temple of the Warriors, Chichén Itzá (photos by author).*

arching over their heads in the art of Chichén Itzá appears to be an Early Postclassic revival of Teotihuacan's tradition of serpent-costumed figures. For example, a dais in the Temple of the Warriors Northwest Colonnade (figure 11.6a) shows warriors with atlatls and atlatl darts who have spectacular serpents writhing behind their bodies, and these mirror earlier images of figures processing with feathered serpent headdresses at Teotihuacan (figure 11.6b). In chapter 10 in this volume, Taube posits that the feathered serpent symbolized a floral road of the sun also traversed by warriors, a belief probably held by

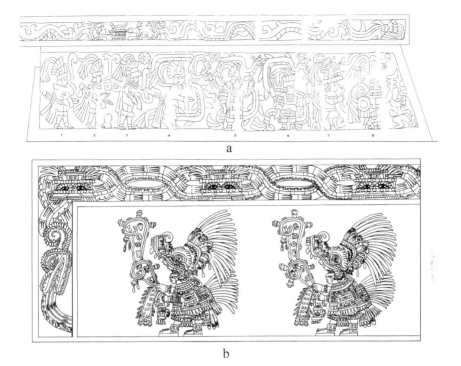

a

b

FIGURE 11.6. *(a) Detail of processing warriors with serpents arching behind them, north side of the dias from the Northwest Colonnade, Temple of the Warriors, Chichén Itzá (after Morris et al. 1931:pl. 26.); (b) Teotihuacan figures in serpent headdresses, Room 2, Tepantitla, Teotihuacan (after Miller 1973:fig. 173).*

both Teotihuacan and Chichén warriors. Thus, Schele and Freidel's emphasis on the Maya foundations of Chichén Itzá withstands the tests of time, but to my mind we should integrate into this model a greater recognition of the contributions of Central Mexican social structures, some of which are unprecedented in the Maya region during the Classic period.

Another significant aspect of Linda and David's understanding of Chichén Itzá was their recognition that the city practiced strategies of incorporation when it came to captives obtained through warfare. To explain incorporation, they used images such as Column 37 of the Northwest Colonnade (figure 11.7). As they so rightfully noted, these captives with their bound hands exhibit one significant and critical difference from their Classic Maya counterparts. In Classic Maya art, such as the East Court of the Palenque

Figure 11.7. *Column 37, Northwest Colonnade, Temple of the Warriors, Chichén Itzá (after Morris et al. 1931:pl. 103).*

Palace (figure 11.8, see also figure 11.3), captives often appear virtually naked, stripped only to their loincloths, and strips of paper filling the holes where these elites once wore jade earflares. At Chichén Itzá the difference is remarkable because the captives still wear elaborate attire. Several have sumptuous cloaks over their shoulders, and many sport earflares and other jewelry, including feline and bird pectorals. Schele and Freidel's explanation for this is that rather than profoundly humiliating their captives, the Itzáe

**Figure 11.8.** *Captives from the East Court, Palace, Palenque (photo by author).*

might have invited their foes to join the cause, thereby incorporating them into the empire.

However, there may be other explanations for the festive finery displayed by the captives. Sacrificial practices documented at Teotihuacan can provide insight onto the elegant apparel worn by the captives on Column 37. Mass sacrificial offerings found in the foundations and around the Temple of the Feathered Serpent as well as large caches from the Pyramid of the Moon demonstrate that Teotihuacanos frequently deposited their victims arrayed in splendid costumes. Numerous men sacrificed at the Feathered Serpent Pyramid died wearing complex shell and bone necklaces and slate-back mirrors. They also had clusters of projectile points near their bodies, suggesting that bundles of atlatl darts were placed next to them to convey the offering's militant symbolism (S. Sugiyama 2005, 2017). At the Moon Pyramid the individual sacrificed in Burial 2 wore greenstone earflares and a necklace, while the regalia of three individuals in Burial 3 included greenstone earflares, a necklace, and a nose plaque, as well as shell earflares and a necklace (López Luján and Sugiyama 2017; S. Sugiyama et al. 2004; S. Sugiyama and López Luján 2007). In contrast to the buried offerings at Teotihuacan, the majority of extant sacrificial remains at Chichén come from the Sacred Cenote, where costume and skeletal material probably separated from each other in the watery matrix and through the excavation of these materials by dredging (Coggins 1984:24–26). Nevertheless, a remarkable amount of greenstone and gold jewelry emerged from the cenote, and it is likely that these elements adorned the bodies of the people thrown into the watery pool.[13] In this way the sacrificial individuals of Chichén would resemble those of Teotihuacan by having gone to their deaths not in a simple loincloth but with great finery ornamenting their bodies. Another interesting parallel between the two cities and their offering practices are the atlatl, atlatl darts, projectile points, and fending sticks recovered from the cenote (Coggins and Shane 1984:46–47, 49, 100, 103–104). Such military implements could have accompanied sacrificial victims into the water and served to project a military context for the sacrifice, just as the projectile points at the Feathered Serpent Pyramid conveyed militarism at Teotihuacan. The parallels of sacrificial victims potentially dressed in opulent costumes that included elite status items along with weaponry conveying warfare symbolism indicate that the Itzáe could have maintained sacrificial practices established at Teotihuacan. Both cities may have preferred to display their captives as militarily strong elites with access to wealth, and through this display those conducting the sacrifices projected their own valor and economic contributions by capturing and dispatching such worthy foes.

The captives on Column 37 (figure 11.7) provide evidence that the Itzáe used their sculptural art as a more permanent means of documenting the high status of their captives even after their bodies and regalia sunk to the bottom of the cenote. One captive wears a diadem that markedly resembles the headdress of Postclassic Central Mexican rulers and elites, and another dons the paired feathers, or *aztaxelli*, of Central Mexican warrior-priests of the Postclassic period.[14] Thus, instead of incorporating their captives into their political system as they expanded, the Itzáe, an alternative explanation might be, wanted to better advertise the status and identity of their various captives as well as the far-reaching nature of their military exploits, in this case, possibly all the way into Central Mexico.

While Schele and Freidel identified incorporation as a strategy of Chichén Itzá, they also noted that trade was an important factor in the city's success. Examination of one captive donning a prominent round pectoral (figure 11.7) further elucidates the nature of resource acquisition at Chichén Itzá. Comparison to the city's material culture indicates that this is probably a gold pectoral.[15] Archaeological examples of such pectorals are well known, for they are the gold disks that the Itzáe deposited in the Sacred Cenote.[16] In particular, if we look to the gold disks, such gold pectorals may also be a statement of the vast extent of Chichén Itzá's military exploits, perhaps in an effort to expand the types of exotic materials the elites and warriors at this city could wear on their bodies to advertise their power and successes. One of these gold disks from the Sacred Cenote,

**FIGURE 11.9.** *Drawing of Gold Disk G, Sacred Cenote, Chichén Itzá (after Lothrop 1952:fig. 35).*

Disk G (figure 11.9), displays Itzáe warriors, who likely functioned as traders as well, riding in a dugout canoe pursuing a befeathered individual on a raft who appears on the left side of the disk (Lothrop 1952:51; Shatto 1998:218–220). As John Hoopes (personal communication, 2013) has pointed out, the figure on the raft prominently wears a gold pectoral, suggesting not only that the man himself was not the only target of the military pursuit, but also that the flashy gold worn around his neck may have been the resource that the Itzáe desperately wanted to acquire.[17] Thus, by leaving their captives richly attired in their memorialized images, the elite warrior-merchants of Chichén Itzá may have advertised the resources that their military and trading exploits brought into the empire. Quite simply, the gold pectoral heralds the foreign and exotic shiny gold that Chichén Itzá's military-traders brought into the economy of the site.[18]

Viewed altogether, this one column announces a great deal about the role of the military at Chichén Itzá. Recognizing some of the headdresses as Central Mexican indicates that the military took captives and perhaps garnered resources from the lands to the west, something Taube also entertains in this volume. Furthermore, considering that these same headdresses were status markers, for both warriors and elites, they tell viewers of potential political conquests made by the Itzáe, or, at the very least, they document the high status of their captives. The presence of the gold pectoral proclaims the economic contributions made by Chichén Itzá's warrior-merchants and reveals the city's ever increasing international reach as its military traders acquired these resources from ever more foreign realms.[19]

While the Temple of the Warriors is one of the few pre-Columbian structures with a modern name that is largely accurate (the structure did celebrate its military with their weapons prominently displayed), images such as one mural from the upper temple reinforce evidence that the military had an important economic role. The mural graced a large room with long benches that accommodated a council of assembled individuals, something distinct from the smaller benches reserved for rulers in Classic period structures. In this mural (figure 11.10), warriors stand in canoes passing by a coastal town, demonstrated by the presence of stingrays and crabs in the water.[20] By including this scene on the walls of the room, the mural reminded the assembled leaders of the vast reach of Chichén Itzá's military merchants, ever willing to traverse the ocean to bring in increasingly exotic sources of wealth, such as the gold pectorals some warriors wear on the sculpted columns of the temple. The intersections between warfare, trade, and the acquisition of economic resources was ever more complex at Postclassic Chichén Itzá, and overall, it is these warrior-merchants, rather than multiple kings, who shared in the power and prestige of Chichén Itzá's social order.

As a footnote to my original footnote in *A Forest of Kings*, I certainly now accept that the early date I proposed for the Osario text was inaccurate, but this reminds me of yet another lesson learned from Linda. Sitting on the couch in her house one day, we discussed criticisms she received about her frequent reversals of earlier statements; that is, scholars repeatedly queried her about changing her mind, revising her ideas, and contradicting her prior proposals. Linda looked at me and exhorted me to be flexible and to remember that models change as we get new information. If you do not, she said, you get left behind. I have often wondered what enjoyment she would derive from the

FIGURE 11.10. *Mural depicting a coastal scene as reconstructed by Ann Axtell Morris, Temple of the Warriors, Area 31, Chichén Itzá (after Morris et al. 1931:pl. 159).*

new discoveries and proposals made since her death, and, indeed, the discussions that challenge David and her ideas in this very text.

## NOTES

1. Not wanting to repeat this pattern of withholding information, I will explain here that a cache is the term for an offering buried within a structure that, while ultimately hidden from view, seems to have served the purpose of ensouling a building, space, or object.

2. Today, the most efficient means of accessing the Carnegie material is from the compiled publications found in John Weeks (2012). For the original reports, see esp. Earl Morris and his colleagues (1931), H.E.D. Pollock (1936), and Karl Ruppert (1935, 1952).

3. In the nature of scholarly growth, I have modified my position stated in that footnote (Schele and Freidel 1990:500n26). While I originally held that the Osario preceded the Castillo, new research on the chronology and epigraphy of Chichén Itzá (Braswell 2012; Braswell and Peniche May 2012; Graña-Behrens et al. 1999) make a compelling argument that the Osario was the later building and was constructed during the Early Postclassic (Headrick 2018).

4. Charles Lincoln's (1990) contemporaneous dissertation shared many of these arguments about settlement pattern archaeology at Chichén Itzá. He argued that architecture labeled as Toltec and Maya stood together and formed unified architectural groupings. Thus, the integration of the architectural styles contradicted models wherein one style replaced another.

5. Much of this argument replied on the epigraphic work of Ruth Krochock (1988).

6. Schele and Peter Mathews (1998:197) also embraced the idea of *multepal*. On the other hand, Lincoln (1990) developed an argument for dual kingship.

7. For more on such burning rituals see Stuart (1998).

8. Geoffrey Braswell and Nancy Peniche May (2012) have a current discussion of Chichén Itzá's chronology, and Cynthia Kristan-Graham (2011:453) offers additional discussion of the social implications of colonnaded halls such as the Temple of the Warriors.

9. Rafael Cobos (2011) adds to this discussion by arguing that the architecture built during the later phase of Chichén Itzá indicates increased social complexity at the site even as a paramount ruler still maintained centralized power. Likewise, relying largely on the content of the Temple of the Warriors murals, De Luna Lucha Aztzin Martinez (2005) stresses the increased importance of individuals involved in the military and trade to Chichén Itzá's social structure.

10. Simon Martin and Nikolai Grube (2000) provide a concise discussion of the Tikal and Calakmul (Kaan) animosities.

11. For discussion of the Central Mexican strategies of military orders developed at Teotihuacan, see Annabeth Headrick (1996, 2001, 2007) and Saburo Sugiyama (2005). Finally, for another perspective on Central Mexican influence at Chichén Itzá, see Peter Schmidt (1998).

12. In earlier work (2007), I argued that these hearts suggested shamanic transformation and cannibalism, but Nawa Sugiyama's excellent analysis offers a more compelling argument.

13. Mary Ellen Miller and Marcos Samayoa (1998) argued that the cenote sacrificial victims wore many greenstone ornaments, affording them Maize God-related status.

14. See Cecelia Klein (1987:320) for a discussion of the aztaxelli and its appearance on warriors and priests.

15. When discussing the murals of the Upper Temple of the Jaguars, Aztzin Martinez (2005:56) identifies a similar pectoral as a gold disk. Furthermore, in a personal communication with John Hoopes (2013), he identified a round pectoral on a figure depicted on Chichén Itzá Disk G as a probable gold pectoral, which spurred me to identify these gold pectorals elsewhere (Headrick 2015).

16. For studies on these gold pectorals, see Clemency Coggins and Orin Shane (1984) and Lothrop (1952).

17. An expanded discussion of this image and Chichén's excursions abroad appears in Headrick and John Hoopes (in press).

18. Coggins and Shane (1984), Antonio Jaramillo Arango (2016), Lothrop (1952), and Elizabeth Paris and Carlos Peraza Lope (2013) provide perspectives on metal and trade at Chichén Itzá.

19. Aztzin Martinez (2005) makes similar arguments about the relationship of trade and military activities at Chichén Itzá and the increased social standing of these individuals.

20. Some of the earlier discussions of this mural appear in Aztzin Martinez (205), Sylvanus Morley and George Brainerd (1983:421), Morris and his colleagues (1931:398), and Rahilla Corinne Abbas Shatto (1998:220–224).

# 12

*Closing the Portal at Itzmal Ch'en*

*Effigy Censers and Termination Rituals at a Mayapán Ceremonial Group*

Marilyn A. Masson,
Wilberth Cruz Alvarado,
Carlos Peraza Lope, and
Susan Milbrath

DOI: 10.5876/9781646420469.c012

The publication of *A Forest of Kings* book in 1990 broke new ground in immeasurable ways, as reflected in the contributions of this book. For Marilyn Masson, as for many doctoral students at University of Texas–Austin at the time that *Forest* and *Maya Cosmos* were published, the excitement generated by Linda Schele and David Freidel's collaborations was transformative, given the explosion of international and interdisciplinary sharing of information and ideas at that time. Doctoral students in art history and archaeology, as well as professional colleagues, attended Linda's seminars and even her undergraduate lecture hall classes, which were ablaze with new discoveries and ideas as she absorbed and processed the latest developments in the field. The synthesis exhibited in Linda and David's works was truly pathbreaking for the field of archaeology, and it provided models and methods for ways to draw on dry, descriptive reports in the libraries, along with new hieroglyphic texts and ethnohistorical analogies, to generate new syntheses of significance to comparative anthropology.

This chapter pays homage to the contributions of Linda Schele and David Freidel by offering a modest effort to reconstruct religious rituals at a Postclassic Maya monumental group and to interpret them in the broader context of capital city of Mayapán's late political history. Our approach draws on Linda and David's arguments regarding sacred geography, especially patterns of ensouling or activating monumental features that allowed for communication with otherworldly entities and the essential responsibility of ritually terminating these portals at the end of their use. Specifically, we analyze and compare the ceremonious breakage and deposition of ceramic deity effigy censers as part of the closure of an outlying hall and temple complex at Postclassic Mayapán, the Itzmal Ch'en Group.

## ITZMAL CH'EN IN THE CONTEXT OF MAYAPÁN'S ABANDONMENT

The termination rites of the rapidly abandoned Itzmal Ch'en group at the urban site of Mayapán reflect broader processes of decline at the city during the fourteenth century AD, some 50–150 years before its ultimate collapse. Mayapán was the largest Maya political capital of the Postclassic period (AD 1150–1450), the center of a regional confederation in northwest Yucatán. The Mayapán polity endured frequent and severe droughts that led to famine, unrest, warfare, and some outmigration from AD 1310 to AD 1400, prior to large-scale war and abandonment in the mid-fifteenth century AD 1441–1461 (Kennett et al. 2015; Masson and Peraza Lope 2014a; Russell 2013; Tozzer 1941:36n178). The city recovered briefly when moisture levels returned for a period of about twenty years in the early fifteenth century, but unfavorable conditions returned, and the weakened polity was destroyed by factional war. Archaeological indicators of the polity's unraveling include termination deposits, mass graves, destruction, and other abandonment rites that mostly yield (AMS) dates between AD 1310 and 1400 (Peraza Lope et al. 2006), including the events at Itzmal Ch'en that are the focus of this chapter (Peraza Lope and Masson 2014a; Delgado Kú et al. 2020).

The Itzmal Ch'en locality represents the largest outlying ceremonial group beyond the monumental center at Mayapán, near the far eastern Gate H of the walled city (figure 12.1). At Itzmal Ch'en, two fourteenth-century events (Peraza Lope et al. 2006) include a mass grave of burned, dismembered, and chopped human remains that was deposited along the southwestern edge of the group's platform (Paris et al. 2017). A second event, the focus of this chapter, involved a careful rite of effigy censer breakage that resulted in deposits of sherds from multiple vessels placed in discrete concentrations over a colonnaded hall and temple. These censers lay on the surface of the final floors of the buildings and plaza surfaces near the foundations, beneath collapsed rubble. In this chapter, we report the results of an effigy-censer refitting project that aids in reconstructing aspects of ritual practice at Itzmal Ch'en, including the tally and identities of deities once housed in its public buildings. We also

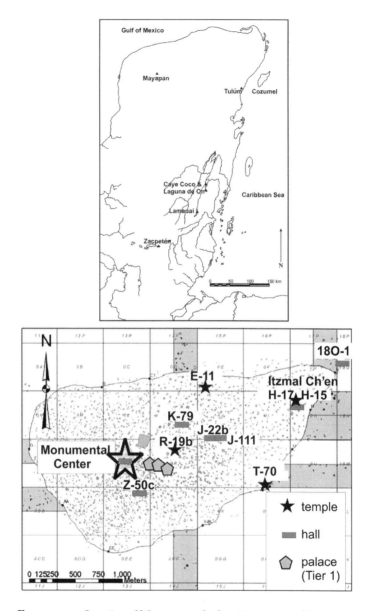

Figure 12.1. *Location of Mayapán and other sites mentioned in text in the Yucatán Peninsula; also, location of Itzmal Ch'en and other ceremonial architecture within (or near to) the walled city of Mayapán (map by Marilyn Masson).*

assess the spatial configuration of deliberate destruction and deposition signaling the termination of these edifices' sacred capacities.

A primary goal of the refitting project was to determine whether pieces of the same censers were deposited at the Itzmal Ch'en temple and the hall. Refits may have provided one indication of absolute contemporaneity of the events at the two buildings, but no matches were present. Censer refits were confined to the areas on or around each individual structure. Refitting was undertaken by Wilberth Cruz Alvarado and Luis Flores Cobá, who have pieced together dozens of ceramic effigies from the site center. Although effigy censers were also broken and strewn amidst the human remains of Itzmal Ch'en's mass grave (adjacent to the colonnaded hall), these were in a higher state of fragmentation and were not discretely distributed in concentrations. No refits were attempted from the mass grave, and it is not known whether sherds from broken vessels at the temple or the hall examples are also present in this burial.

While it is unclear whether the violence resulting in the mass grave preceded or followed the effigy-censer breakage rituals of the hall and temple, AMS dates reveal that all three contexts at Itzmal Ch'en signal abandonment of this public facility 50–150 years before the city's collapse (Peraza Lope et al. 2006; P. Delgado Kú et al. 2020). Similarly dated features in the site center reveal that Mayapán's urban landscape from the late fourteenth to mid-fifteenth centuries included war-torn, abandoned houses and buildings that were never again rebuilt or utilized (Masson and Peraza Lope 2014a:figs. 8.2–8.3). At the epicenter, reports describe burned and collapsed roofs, multiple mass graves, smashed effigy censers, and ceremoniously abandoned houses, mostly during the fourteenth century (Adams 1953; Masson and Peraza Lope 2014a; Peraza Lope et al. 2002; Peraza Lope and Masson 2014a, 2014b:fig. 2.2; Serafin 2010; Serafin and Peraza Lope 2007).

## ABANDONMENT RITES AND TERMINATION RITUALS

The concerted ritual and violent activities at Itzmal Ch'en attest to its importance as a symbolically charged location in Mayapán's urban setting. The locality has remained sacred to the present day and, until recently, was the designated place for Cha Chaac ceremonies performed by residents of the nearby town of Telchaquillo. Rituals determine sacred domains (Swensen 2015:331) and may also desacralize them. Breaking or "killing" ritual objects is a prevalent cross-cultural practice with considerable time depth (Lorenzen 2003:65; Mock 1998:5; Swensen 2015:337). One approach to understanding the social context and function of secondary monumental groups or other elite buildings is to analyze their abandonment, especially when this activity was purposeful and ritualized, falling into the category of "termination ritual" (e.g., Garber 1986:117; Mock 1998; Schele and Freidel 1990:127; Stanton et al. 2008). Termination rites were sometimes preludes to events of renewal that represent new beginnings, as for the Aztec New Fire ceremony (Mock 1998:9; Swensen 2015:337). In other words, the distinction between dedication and termination rituals can be blurred, particularly when these events mark part of the same process (Joyce 2011:545). Postclassic Maya effigy-censer installation and destruction were also sometimes cyclical and were closely tied with calendrical passages, as we discuss below.

Termination rituals may also represent final acts that signal the abandonment of architectural groups or settlements, although abandonment processes can be incremental (Stanton et al. 2008). Reverential and desecrating acts of termination may not always be associated with warfare (Pagliaro et al. 2003:76). In some cases, monumental nuclei of Mesoamerican centers were abandoned first, accompanied by the exodus of elites, with lingering occupation of settlement zones, as for Aguateca (Inomata 2003), Dos Pilas (Palka 2003), and elsewhere (Stanton and Magnoni 2008:5). The Itzmal Ch'en temple and hall deposits fit the category of a planned event, lacking evidence for haste or duress (Canuto and Andrews 2008:260). In contrast, the mass burial reflects a violent event, with its haphazard deposit of desecrated bones in a shallow grave (Paris and Russell 2012; Paris et al. 2017; Vidal Guzmán 2011).

Evidence for censer-smashing rituals is commonly observed across the Postclassic Maya area, and these deposits reflect several distinctive types of behavior, including termination, pilgrimage, in situ breakage, funerary contexts, or occasions that called for their substitution with new effigies (D. Chase and A. Chase 1988:72; Howie et al. 2014:41–45; Lorenzen 2003:143–145; Milbrath and Peraza Lope 2013:209–210; Pugh and Cecil 2012:317, 322; Rice 2009:300–301; J.E.S. Thompson 1957:601–602). Contact-era sources indicate that effigies were manufactured to resemble specific gods who were patrons of calendrical intervals, particularly, the *katun* and *wayeb* (Chase 1985:119–121; Milbrath and Peraza Lope 2013; Rice 2004). Other intervals or events commemorating sacred geography called for effigy replacement (e.g., D. Chase 1986, 1988; Graff 1997; de Landa 1941:136–169; Lorenzen 2003:143–145; Russell 2000; Thompson 1957:602). Sometimes the transfer of responsibility from one effigy to another was gradual, resulting in the temporary installation of effigy pairs (Rice 2009:301; Tozzer 1941:168–169). Two recently found pairs at Zacpetén include male and female entities within a small temple (Pugh and Rice 2009:148). A male-female pairing is also present at the Itzmal Ch'en temple, as we discuss below.

Replacement called for ceremonious discard of effigies no longer in use, as is known for the Lacandon Maya (McGee 1998:45) and Postclassic Maya sites (Masson 1999:298, 2000:238; Milbrath and Peraza Lope 2013:213; Russell 2000). Sometimes censers were ground up to make other censers, as indicated by Colonial period sources documented in Yucatán (Milbrath and Walker 2016) and also at Lamanai (Howie et al. 2014:44). Materials were sometimes taken to a designated locality distant from the original context. On the shores of Laguna de On, Belize, concentrations of incomplete censers were deposited around the sides of an altar; each concentration included sherds from different effigy vessels (Masson 2000:78, 238; Russell 2000). In contrast, at Mayapán's public buildings, censers are often found at or close to their original context of use.

Pilgrimage destinations in the hinterlands (Walker 1990) as well as at caves or shrines (Masson 2000) frequently have deposits of ritually discarded materials (that were first used elsewhere); other items may represent primary-use objects brought, used, and discarded in situ. Certain abandoned cities sometimes were incorporated into Postclassic pilgrimage circuits, as in the case of Cerros, where effigy censers and altars were constructed atop Preclassic buildings (Milbrath and Walker 2016). During the Contact period, processions were undertaken to circumambulate political territories. These pilgrimage rites incorporated caves, buildings at earlier archaeological sites, and other landmarks (Rice 2004; Roys 1967). Pilgrimages were often undertaken during times of duress, to make offerings at sacred localities. The most dramatic example is the (disastrous) Xiu quest to travel to Chichén Itzá's cenote following climatic hardships of early sixteenth-century Yucatán (Tozzer 1941:54n270), culminating in their massacre (at Otzmal) by their enemies, the Cocom.

Broken censers may also be present in ritual middens along with other ceremonial garbage (e.g., Mock 1998:10; Shook 1954). All of the contexts described above for effigy-censer recovery are present at Mayapán's site center, including ritual breakage and careful placement of incomplete vessel fragments at new locations (e.g., Milbrath and Peraza Lope 2013:210). Examples of nontermination depositional contexts for effigy censers abound in the literature. They can be broken in situ, ritually discarded and replaced, or left at a building during postabandonment pilgrimage journeys (e.g., D. Chase and A. Chase 1988:72–74; Pugh and Rice 2009:163, 168). Mayapán's monkey scribe effigy was found facedown in shallow soils behind Temple Q-58. It was broken but complete, and it has been fully restored (Milbrath and Peraza Lope 2003b). Additional Mayapán examples of restorable censers are reported from Hall Q-81 by Winters (1955:385), who suggests they were left, whole and in situ and were smashed by roof fall after abandonment; abundant examples are further illustrated by R. Smith (1971) and reported by others (e.g., Milbrath and Peraza Lope 2003b, 2013:210; Shook and Irving 1955:144). Some effigies at Zacpetén were probably left in an activated state on the surface of Temple 602, broken later by roof collapse. Other contexts from this site suggest intentional breakage and termination (Pugh and Rice 2009:147–154).

Effigy censers are most often found in broken states. Modeled clay head-dresses and body ornamentation are particularly prone to fragmentation. Remains visible on the surface may also have attracted collectors; faces, for example, are commonly missing (Walker 1990). Curation of faces and removal of them from their original contexts were practiced by residents of Mayapán (Thompson 1957:601–602). Effigies lacking distinct deity attributes may represent ancestors or other heroic figures while others clearly indicate formal, recognizable deities (Masson 2000:239; Nielsen and Andersen 2004:fig. 4; Peraza Lope and Masson 2014c).

Although many behaviors account for the recovery of effigy censer fragments, their ritual breakage is often interpreted as the result of intentional destruction and disempowerment of ritual objects at contexts at Mayapán and elsewhere (e.g., Masson 2000; Russell 2000; Sampeck 2007:307). Smashing, mixing, and deposition in discrete concentrations suggest that the effigy vessels were purposefully deactivated. It is widely noted that effigy censers represented conduits or portals through which practitioners could communicate with otherworld beings (Milbrath and Peraza Lope 2013:211). Burned offerings, including incense, could generate smoke that aided ritual specialists in conjuring supernatural beings (Freidel et al. 1993:216, 246–247; Rice 1999:25–27). These functions were identified among Contact period Maya peoples and have considerable pre-Columbian time depth for effigy and noneffigy censers (Rice 1999; Walker 1990).

At Itzmal Ch'en, we argue, the broken and rearranged effigy sherds represent a termination ritual that would have disempowered the objects and the architecture on which they were found. The presence of a single piece of greenstone in one concentration at both the hall and temple attests to a coordinated, standardized effort at this pair of buildings at Itzmal Ch'en. One eroded greenstone chisel was placed in a single concentration in front of the altar at Hall H-15 (table 12.1) and the other, a chunk of raw material, was in a concentration on the eastern bench of Temple H-17's upper room (table 12.1). These inclusions reflect parallel rites (Masson and Peraza Lope 2014c:fig. 6.23; Peraza Lope and Masson 2014a:fig. 3.11). Each piece was found with the fragments of particularly important personages, including a female urn at the temple (Effigy #5) and with Effigy #7 at the hall. The inclusion of

**TABLE 12.1.** List of concentrations with refits (effigies #1, 2, 4–7) and other distinctive entities (effigies #3, 8–13).

| Effigy # | Structure | Description | Grid Square | Lot | Strata | Level |
|---|---|---|---|---|---|---|
| 1 | Temple H-17 | Death god (torso, head gear, jaw) | 11-K | 5355* 5352 | I I | 3 3 |
| 2 | Temple H-17 | Unidentified entity (crude paste, unusual headdress, arm frags) | 11-K | 5355* 5352 | I I | 3 3 |
| 3 | Temple H-17 | Unidentified entity with stacked jewel on headdress | 11-K | 5352 | I | 3 |
| 4 | Temple H-17 | Unidentified entity (red paint, two arms and feet, cape, proboscis on headdress) | 11-K | 5355* 5352 | I I | 3 3 |
| 5 | Temple H-17 | "Female" urn on box (no breasts, proboscis on headdress, one hand and foot); concentration 5386 contained a piece of greenstone | 13-L | 5385 5386* | I I | 2 2 |
| 5 | Temple H-17 | "Female" urn on box (same as above) | 12-K | 5276 | I | 3 |
| 5 | Temple H-17 | "Female" urn on box (same as above) | 13-K | 5367* 5374 | I I | 2 3 |
| 5 | Temple H-17 | "Female" urn on box (same as above) | 12-L | 5295 | I | 2 |
| 6 | Temple H-17 | Male urn on box (torso with striped/painted braided cloth, shell discs, arm fragment) | 8-K | 5395 | I | 2 |
| 6 | Temple H-17 | Male urn on box (same as above) | 12-L | 5295 5450 5290 | I III | 2 3 |
| 6 | Temple H-17 | Male urn on box (same as above) | 13-L | 5385 5386 | I | 2 |
| 6 | Temple H-17 | Male urn on box (same as above) | 13-K | 5374 | I | 3 |
| 6 | Temple H-17 | Male urn on box (same as above) | 11-J | 5315 | I | 2 |
| 6 | Temple H-17 | Male urn on box (same as above) | 12-K | 5276 | I | 3 |
| 7 | Hall H-15 | Unidentified entity (with foot, arm, body, headdress frags) | 6-K | 4171* | I | 2 |
| 7 | Hall H-15 | Unidentified entity (same as above) | 5-K | 4157 | I | 2 |

*continued on next page*

TABLE 12.1—*continued*

| Effigy # | Structure | Description | Grid Square | Lot | Strata | Level |
|---|---|---|---|---|---|---|
| 8 | Hall H-15 | Unidentified entity with proboscis miter (from concentration with greenstone) | 10-K | 4220* | I | 3 |
| 9 | Temple H-17 | Unidentified entity (crude non-local? paste, maize ear adorno, head-dress, arm) | 11-K | 5350* | I | 2 |
| 10 | Mass grave | Female (one torso with breasts, *quechquemitl*) | 20-F | 4094 | III | 1 |
| 11, 12 | Mass grave | 2 death god maxillae | 20-E | 4301 | I | 4 |
| 13 | Temple H-17 | Female (one cape fragment and arm) | 11-K | 5352 | I | 3 |
| 14 | Temple H-17 | Unidentified personage with nonlo-cal paste | 11-J | 5315 | I | 2 |
| 14 | Temple H-17 | Unidentified personage with nonlo-cal paste | 11-K | 5350 | I | 2 |
| | | | | 5352 | I | 3 |

* signifies concentrations identified in field. Lots 5386 (temple) and 4220 (hall) contained eroded greenstone objects.

greenstone or other precious stones with smashed censers has been reported at other Postclassic Maya archaeological sites (Lorenzen 2003:73), and broken or smashed greenstones were often part of termination rituals (Garber 1986).

## ITZMAL CH'EN'S FUNCTIONS AS A CEREMONIAL GROUP

Mesoamerican research has long been concerned with how replicated, out-lying monumental features such as the Itzmal Ch'en group functioned within urban landscapes. Were they part of coordinated urban planning that deliv-ered state ideology, ritual, or other administrative functions to urban zones? Or were they sponsored by precocious secondary elites who had the resources and influence to construct monuments for the purposes of subgroup goals? Outlying monumental groups can develop from both processes. The individ-ual characteristics of the Itzmal Ch'en and other groups reveal conformity to state norms as well as idiosyncratic deviation (e.g., D. Chase 1992; P. Delgado Kú 2004; P. Delgado Kú et al. 2012a, 2012b; Hare et al. 2014:188; Masson and Peraza Lope 2014b; Peraza Lope and Masson 2014a:144). Like temples, halls exhibit patron-specific programs of stucco and limestone human, deity, and animal sculptures, and multiple episodes of mural and column fresco painting (Delgado Kú 2009; Masson and Peraza Lope 2014b; Milbrath and Peraza Lope 2003b; Peraza Lope 1999). These features reveal that public buildings were staging grounds for formal rotations of patron gods timed with calendrical ceremonies that integrated religious and political bureaucracies (Love 1994; Masson 2000; Rice 2004).

## ETHNIC AFFILIATIONS

The city's multiple colonnaded hall and temple groups represent investments built by leaders of Mayapán's confederated polity (D. Chase 1992; Hare et al. 2014:188; Peraza Lope and Masson 2014b, 49, 144; Proskouriakoff 1962:90), as has been suggested for other northern sites (e.g., Cobos 2004; Freidel and Sabloff 1984:182). The Itzmal Ch'en group has been considered a candidate for a facility controlled by the Kowoj family, named in the chronicles as the guardians of the east gate (Pugh 2002; Roys 1962). Our investigations reveal artifacts suggestive of multiple ethnic ties, as is often the case at major architectural groups of this cosmopolitan city (Peraza Lope and Masson 2014a).

Affiliations may have also shifted through time. For example, a stucco plaza altar at the group (H-18a) originally featured feathered serpents but was remodeled to represent an Aztec-style Earth Monster (Milbrath and Peraza Lope 2003a:fig. 20). Perhaps this transformation is tied to violent site intrusions such as those discussed here for Itzmal Ch'en. If so, disruptive contact with Aztec-related groups may have occurred earlier than Susan Milbrath and Carlos Peraza Lope originally proposed (2003a:25–31), given the late fourteenth-century abandonment of Itzmal Ch'en.

## ACTIVITIES

Halls embodied political "houses" (Ringle and Bey 2001; Roys 1962:65), as for the contemporary Postclassic *nimja* edifices of the capital of K'umarcaaj/Utatlán in Guatemala (Carmack 1981). Diverse activities hosted at or near to halls and temples of Mayapán's site center included feasting, food preparation, crafting, censer and figurine making and use, and, probably, investiture (Masson and Peraza Lope 2014c; Peraza Lope and Masson 2014a:107, 2014b:79, 83–84; Peraza et al., n.d.). At Utatlán, bride-price bestowal and marriage also occurred at nimja (Carmack 1981:11). There are twenty-two halls at epicenter of Mayapán, and at least seven additional halls exist within or beyond the city walls (figure 12.1, Peraza Lope and Masson 2014b:72; Russell 2007).

Mayapán-style halls were emulated at other major contemporary towns across the peninsula (e.g., Freidel and Sabloff 1984:157; Masson and Peraza Lope 2014b; Pugh 2002; Rice 2009; Sanders 1960). Such outlying groups served as administrative and ritual nodes and served as way-finding markers for pedestrian traffic and, perhaps, as ritual stations for calendrical celebrations (Hare et al. 2014). Open plaza areas have also been recognized as multifunctional spaces, at times used as public squares, pedestrian thoroughfares, landmarks, places to replicate the ritual or political activities of the state across an urban landscape, or marketplaces (A. Chase and D. Chase 2003; Dahlin et al. 2010; King 2015; Lynch 1960; Shaw 2001). No elite residences are present near Itzmal Ch'en; such dwellings are located closer to downtown. The Itzmal Ch'en group would have been easily entered from all sides, between buildings or from the southwestern staircase. The nearby *cenote* (that shares the group's name) is one of the largest water-bearing features at the city (figure 12.1), and it would have drawn visitors passing through the city wall via Gate H; stone-lined lanes guided pedestrians further from the cenote toward the site center (Hare et al. 2014:fig. 4.6; A. Smith 1962:fig. 1). House H-11 (figure 12.2), next to the cenote and the monumental group, would have served as a custodial house like those next to temples of the site center (Masson and Peraza Lope 2014c:348).

Formal occasions also account for significant quantities of ordinary (utilitarian) debris. Archaeological studies of feasting have long recognized that the use of public buildings results in ceramic and faunal debris that overlaps in kind (if not quantity) with domestic assemblages. At Mayapán and Xochicalco, most stages of ceremonial preparations (including food) took place at the ritual destination (Cyphers and Hirth 2000). Animals were brought in their entirety to be butchered, along with cooking, water, and storage vessels (as well as serving dishes); *metates* and *manos* were sometimes present at public edifices (Masson and Peraza Lope 2013; Peraza Lope and Masson 2014a:119–123). Crafting also occurred in and around temples and colonnaded halls (Masson and Peraza Lope 2014c; Masson et al. 2016). Some of the debris derives from ritual economy production activities in making or preparing goods essential to ceremonies; for example, figurine and effigy censer making took place at specific buildings in the monumental zone (Peraza et al. n.d.).

## ARCHITECTURAL FEATURES OF ITZMAL CH'EN

The rapid and ceremonious abandonment of Itzmal Ch'en allows for special opportunities to evaluate the social identity of the group's patrons as well as casual, ritual, and violent activities conducted there. Three construction phases

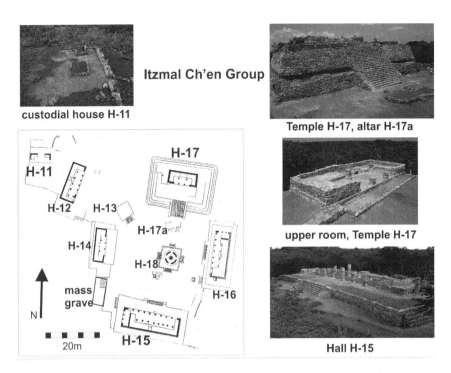

FIGURE 12.2. *Map of the Itzmal Ch'en ceremonial group (modified by author from Proskouriakoff 1962:fig. 1), and photos of three fully excavated and consolidated structures (House H-11, Temple H-17, Hall H-15).*

are recognized for Hall H-15 and Temple H-17. Idiosyncratic attributes of the temple include its exceptionally wide dimension, rounded corners, and niches built into the western face (Delgado et al. 2012a). Proskouriakoff (1962:127) noted that the temple was paired with a frontal plaza shrine, as are serpent temples, while its upper room exhibits the plan of a typical oratory. Unusual characteristics at halls in the site center sometimes suggest ethnic affiliations (Milbrath and Peraza Lope 2003a; Peraza Lope and Masson 2014a; Ringle and Bey 2001:286). One of the striking characteristics of the Itzmal Ch'en group is the wide range of deities (and/or deified ancestors) represented in the ubiquitous sculptural assemblage, most of which resemble examples from the site center. Although serpent sculptures depicting Mayapán's mythical founding hero, K'uk'ulkan, are more abundant than other personages at this temple, the group clearly served a diverse range of ritual events (Masson and Peraza Lope 2014a).

The Itzmal Ch'en temple is one of the largest built in the Maya area during the Postclassic period (figure 12.2); its substructure reaches a height of 8 m, and its broad base measures 27.5 m wide by 19 m deep. In front of the temple, a plaza-level statue shrine (H-17a) is present, near a large slab carved with the hollow eyes and skeletal teeth of the death god (Delgado Kú et al. 2012b; Peraza Lope and Masson 2014a:136). The Carnegie project excavated the plaza's central round building (H-18) that was probably dedicated to K'uk'ulkan/Ehecatl, but later, its adjacent plaza altar (H-18a) was remodeled to represent the Earth Monster (Milbrath and Peraza Lope 2003a:fig. 20). A burial shaft within the H-18 shrine contained a conch shell horn (Chowning 1956; Masson and Peraza Lope 2007). In the upper room of Temple H-17, a stone table altar was reported by the Carnegie investigations, supported by stucco effigies of probable ancestral personages (Delgado Kú et al. 2012a:fig. 2.269; Thompson 1955). Other sculptures were thrown down on the surface of the temple and its base that had originally decorated the upper facade, room, or niches on the temple's west side. Forty stone sculptures were present on or around Temple H-17 (Cruz Alvarado 2012; Peraza Lope and Masson 2014a:128, fig. 3.7), of which twelve were serpents. Others included anthropomorphic deities such as an old god emerging from a turtle, a female, and an Itzamna figure, as well as two monkey effigies, three turtles, two birds, and various human statue or geometric fragments. Cached behind the altar of the interior, upper temple room was a turkey sculpture, a chert knife, and a censer fragment depicting maize foliage (Peraza Lope and Masson 2014a:132). Although the turkey sculpture is relatively unique, many of Mayapán's public buildings feature small animal sculptures.

Hall H-15 of the Itzmal Ch'en group was large (19.5 × 5.7 m) and much decorated (figure 12.2). The transverse (western) room had a large serpent head that would have descended from the beam and mortar roof. The façade of the hall was decorated with recycled Puuc mask stones and human figure sculptures (Delgado Kú et al. 2012b). Small animal sculptures decorated the exterior frontal (northern) wall of the hall, including a dog, serpent, jaguar, and turtle (Peraza Lope and Masson 2014a:130). An Itzamna effigy vase was recovered within the hall's central altar (2014a:fig. 3.12).

### EFFIGY CENSERS AND TERMINATION RITES AT ITZMAL CH'EN

Analysis of the effigy censers at Itzmal Ch'en provides new insight into their role in termination rites at this group. We specifically focus on the analysis of concentrations of smashed censers. Refitting efforts reveal careful mixing and dissembling of individual vessels, and the personages identified between concentrations. This work developed from earlier research on pottery from Itzmal Ch'en that included type-variety analysis and the identification of vessel form for all diagnostic sherds (Cruz Alvarado et al. 2012). Large quantities of effigies are present at the Itzmal Ch'en contexts (as for other public buildings at Mayapán) compared to domestic structures investigated at the city (Peraza Lope and Masson 2014a:figs. 3.4–3.5). Specifically, Ch'en Mul effigy sherds represented 57 percent of 46,738 Postclassic sherds from Temple H-17, 32 percent of 8,549 Postclassic sherds from Hall H-15, and 72 percent of 19,336 Postclassic sherds from the Itzmal Ch'en mass grave (Cruz Alvarado et al. 2012:tables 15.2, 15.4, 15.8).

Full horizontal excavation at the hall and temple in 2008–2009 recovered these materials from interior and exterior spaces of the buildings, with concentrations identified within the roofed space and/or next to the foundations. The most obvious concentrations were mapped, photographed, and separately collected in the field (Delgado Kú et al. 2012a, 2012b), and others were identified during analysis and photography of the ceramic collection. Most concentrations had at least twenty (sometimes much more) effigy censer sherds, including diverse pieces from all parts of the human body and/or regalia. Figures 12.3 and 12.4 illustrate concentrations identified in the field (dark gray) and other locations from which diagnostic effigy censer fragments seemed to cluster (light gray, identified in lab analysis). Although we have limited our discussion to concentrations of effigy censers from Temple H-17 and Hall H-15 that were identified via lab and fieldwork (Peraza Lope and Masson 2014a:130, 134–135), we acknowledge that the definition of "concentration" is difficult for all but the most obvious piles of censers documented over the surfaces exposed in the field. While overall ubiquity of effigy censers at these structures results in abundant fragments in the buildings' general vicinities, all thirty concentrations at the temple and all six at the hall (indicated on figures 12.3 and 12.4) stood out for having a cluster of especially diagnostic effigy fragments representing diverse portions of ceramic personages. Notably, these sherds were not from fill, but from within the final layers of soil over the plaza or building floors of the group. Refits were possible between concentrations identified from both the lab and field, lending credibility to the idea that most concentrations were part of the same termination event. In other words, smaller concentrations of effigy censers (not recognized in the field) are less likely to be general debris and are more likely related to the same effigy-smashing activities that heralded the cessation of the ceremonial group's use.

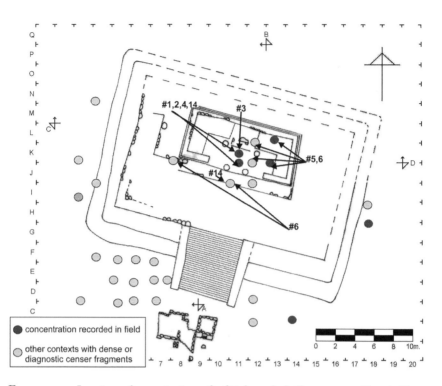

**Figure 12.3.** *Locations of concentrations of refitted smashed effigy censers at Temple H-17. Numbers and arrows indicate locations of refitted censers listed in table 12.1 (drawing by Marilyn Masson).*

It is probable that more partially reconstructible censers are represented at the temple and hall than have been identified thus far. A prior estimation of the minimum number of individuals (MNI) for the temple is fifteen effigies, based on a count of effigy noses (Peraza Lope and Masson 2014a:130). The list of fourteen partially refitted and matched effigies in table 12.1 is less than this tabulation of noses, identified for the temple, hall, and mass grave. Multiple concentrations held sherds from effigies #1–2 as well as #4–7 and #14. Six of the cross-concentration refits are from the temple, and one is from the hall. Effigies #3 and #8–13 were recovered from single lots, though it is important to remember that these are incomplete vessels for which remaining sherds are surely located elsewhere around the buildings. Three of the personages on this list are represented by a single fragment (#10, #11, #12). They were added to the table to expand the MNI estimation derived from refitting and related efforts,

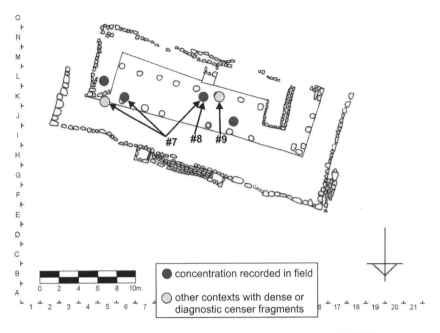

FIGURE 12.4. *Locations of concentrations of smashed effigy censers at Hall H-15. Numbers and arrows indicate locations of refitted censers listed in table 12.1 (drawing by Marilyn Masson).*

and they were likely part of censers represented by (nonfitting) fragments with matching paint, headdress elements, and paste. A list of additional concentrations from which no refits were identified is provided in table 12.2. Of these, only two were identified and recorded in the field; the remainder includes clusters of effigy sherds observed in the lab.

Nine of the fourteen effigies listed in table 12.1 are from the temple (#1–6, #9, #13, #14), two are from the hall (#7, #8), and three derive from the mass grave (#10–12). Two of these examples, limited to death god maxillae from the mass grave (#11, #12, table 12.1) may be associated with other dispersed face fragments. An effigy from the temple may have been of nonlocal origin (Effigy #14), based on distinctive paste attributes (figure 12.5). It derives from three concentrations that also included portions of other entities (figure 12.3, table 12.1). The entities and their characteristics are described below.

Effigy #1 from Temple H-17 is a death god (figure 12.6), indicated by the cut out torso and rib cage, resembling a stucco death god on the frieze of the first version of the Temple of K'uk'ulkan (Peraza Lope and Masson 2014b:80), as

**TABLE 12.2.** List of concentrations identified in field (*) or lab from which no refits were identified.

| Structure | Grid Square | Lot |
|---|---|---|
| Temple H-17 | 18-H | 5423* |
| Temple H-17 | 11-K | 5345 |
| Temple H-17 | 14-C | 5152* |
| Temple H-17 | 4-N | 5366 |
| Temple H-17 | 12-D | 5151 |
| Temple H-17 | 5-F | 5213 |
| Temple H-17 | 6-D | 5130 |
| Temple H-17 | 6-F | 5155 |
| Temple H-17 | 5-F | 5220 |
| Temple H-17 | 3-K | 5246 |
| Temple H-17 | 5-E | 5197 |
| Temple H-17 | 7-E | 5228 |
| Temple H-17 | 7-F | 5255 |
| Temple H-17 | 7-E | 5442 |
| Temple H-17 | 6-E | 5140 |
| Temple H-17 | 18-H | 5420 |
| Temple H-17 | 18-I | 5340 |
| Temple H-17 | 3-K | 5261 |
| Temple H-17 | 11-J | 5315 |
| Temple H-17 | 3-D | 5222 |
| Temple H-17 | 7-D | 5203 |
| Temple H-17 | 8-E | 5268 |
| Temple H-17 | 12-J | 5239 |
| Temple H-17 | 3-I | 5244 |
| Temple H-17 | 5-D | 5196 |
| Temple H-17 | 12-C | 5144 |
| Temple H-17 | 4-J | 5346 |
| Temple H-17 | 4-F | 5148 |
| Hall H-15 | 5-L | 4250* |
| Hall H-15 | 12-J | 4194* |

FIGURE 12.5. *Fragments of a nonlocal censer (#14) identified from two concentrations at Temple H-17 (photos by Marilyn Masson).*

well as another effigy censer that shows a more complete example of the death god (Milbrath and Peraza Lope 2013:fig. 11.4). Like all partly reconstructed effigies from this group, the face was not refitted with the body, though a skeletal jaw and miter-like headdress with broken attachments, probably for miniature skulls, most likely belong to the same individual (figure 12.6). Refitted sherds of Effigy #1 derived primarily from two concentrations located within one 2 × 2 m grid square (11-K) on the temple's upper surface (figure 12.3). This grid square was a hotspot for smashed censers, as the same concentrations with the remains of the death god also provided refits or matched pieces for effigies #2, #3, #4, and #11 (table 12.1).

Effigies #2, #3, and #4 (from Temple H-17) were not identifiable to specific deities (figure 12.6), but were distinguished by paste, decoration, and/or distinctive headdresses. The paste of #2 was coarse, and the left and right sides

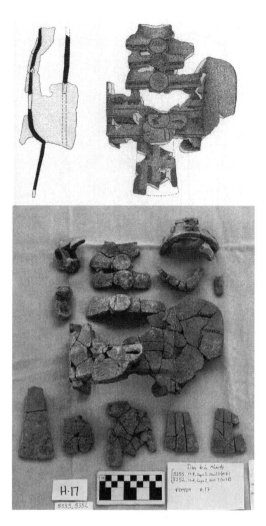

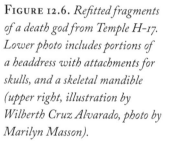

FIGURE 12.6. *Refitted fragments of a death god from Temple H-17. Lower photo includes portions of a headdress with attachments for skulls, and a skeletal mandible (upper right, illustration by Wilberth Cruz Alvarado, photo by Marilyn Masson).*

of a flaring back-rack represent the primary diagnostic fragments. Pieces of this effigy derive from two concentrations within grid square 11-K. Effigy #3 is painted in colors typical for Mayapán censers (red and blue over stucco white-wash), and its miter headdress sports a stacked jewel observed rarely on other censers at the site (e.g., Peraza Lope and Masson 2014c:fig. 6.2e). The fragments of this vessel are from a single concentration (figure 12.3, table 12.1), but the incomplete condition of this vessel reveals that more pieces are scattered elsewhere. A corner of the face revealed the straight bangs of a male individual.

In contrast, females (on examples elsewhere at the site) have hair parted in the middle that sweeps, curtain-like, on both sides, and is tucked behind the ears (e.g., Peraza Lope and Masson 2014c:466). The stacked jewel appears to be a vertical array of a tubular greenstone bead and one red and one white discoidal shell bead (Peraza Lope and Masson 2014c:439).

Effigy #4 (Temple H-17) has a pair of distinctively red-painted arms and feet, and a feathered or winged headdress with a centerpiece that may have been a proboscis (figure 12.7). This proboscis-like element, resembling that of a butterfly, is a recurring feature for Itzmal Ch'en group censers, with at least three identified (two from the temple, one from the hall, figures 12.7–12.8, 12.12). Pieces of this vessel were refitted from two concentrations within square 11-K (figure 12.3; table 12.1).

Two of the most remarkable and complete effigies (#5, #6) derive from the upper surface of Temple H-17 and represent a male and female pair (figures 12.8–12.9). These figures represent urns rather than effigy censers, lacking the back attachments found on incense-burning pedestal vessels. There are almost no other large, seated urns at Mayapán, and certainly none this complete. Effigies #5 and #6 are both in an unusual seated position on a box that resembles low thrones in Postclassic art. Pieces of Effigy #5 derive from six different concentrations in four grid squares (12-K, 12-L, 13-K, 13-L). The throne was whitewashed with stucco, over which was painted a broad horizontal band of blue, framed by two bands of red. This female effigy wore a headdress that also features a central proboscis-like element, flanked by feathers (figure 12.8). The feminine assignment to this effigy is based on the presence of slight breasts and a *quechquemitl* shawl. The male and female pair at Itzmal Ch'en recall similar pairings in contemporary murals from Tulúm that seem to reflect dynastic and/or heroic histories (Masson 2000:227–229).

The male effigy (#6) urn from Temple H-17 wears a garment on his chest, formed of at least seven horizontal braided lengths of cloth, over which vertical stripes of blue, red, and white pigment were painted (figure 12.9). He wore a long bead necklace over the mantle; beads were green (perhaps jade) and red (perhaps *Spondylus* shell). The box throne is identically painted to that of Effigy #5. A pair of oval shell ring ornaments is also pegged to the chest garment. These pendants have been identified on other censers as the oyohualli symbol (Milbrath and Peraza Lope 2013:217). This same element appears on a braided chest plate worn by an effigy censer representing the aged God N at Mayapán and is also worn by the aged opossum god in the *wayeb* ceremony on Dresden Codex 26a, as well as on effigy censers representing more youthful gods at other sites (Milbrath and Peraza Lope 2013:figs. 12.1, 12.5; Milbrath

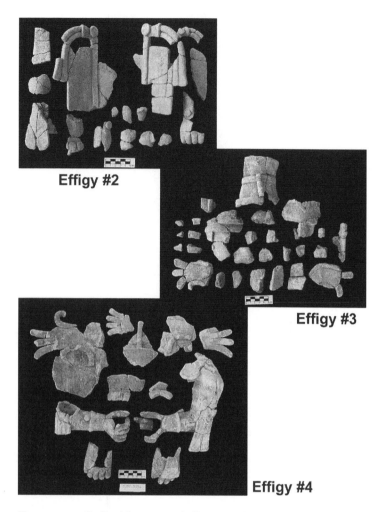

**Effigy #2**

**Effigy #3**

**Effigy #4**

FIGURE 12.7. *Refitted fragments of effigies #2, #3, and #4 from Temple H-17. A stacked jewel is present on the headdress of #3. A proboscis forms a central element of the headdress of #4 (photos by Marilyn Masson).*

and Walker 2016:199, figs. 10.4, 10.5b). In Central Mexico, it has been identified as a mussel shell ornament that may have been a symbol of female sexuality; a related concept may be the fact that pubescent girls in Contact-period Yucatán wore a shell ornament as a sign of their chastity (Tozzer 1941:106). It is interesting that this male figure wears a potential symbol of femininity, as if to co-opt female reproductive powers. Such expressions have been recognized

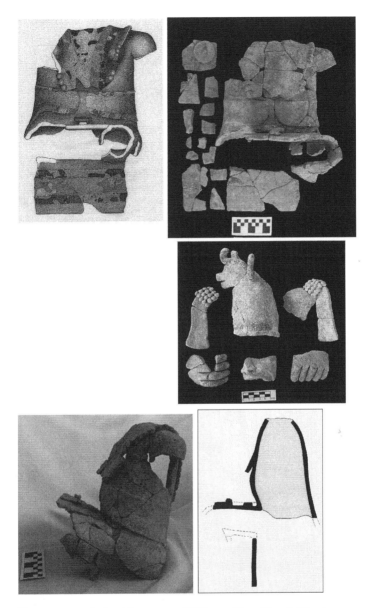

FIGURE 12.8. *Refitted fragments of Effigy #5 (from Temple H-17), a female seated on a box throne with a proboscis element in the headdress (illustrations by Wilberth Cruz Alvarado, photos by Marilyn Masson).*

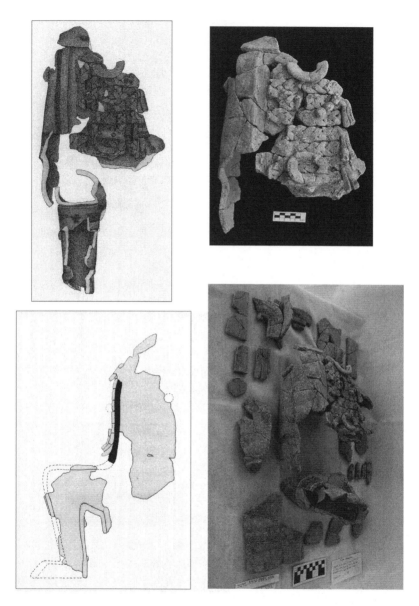

**FIGURE 12.9.** *Refitted fragments of Effigy #6 (from Temple H-17), a male seated on a box throne with* oyohualli-*like shell attachments on the frontal garment and corn foliage in the headdress (illustrations by Wilberth Cruz Alvarado, photos by Marilyn Masson).*

in the regalia of earlier Maya royal art, especially for entities impersonating the Maize God (e.g., Looper 2009; Stone 1991). Pieces of Effigy #6 derived from six different concentrations in six different grid squares (8-K, 11-J, 12-K, 12-L, 13-K, 13-L), four of which overlap with those from which Effigy #5 was refitted (figure 12.3, table 12.1).

It would be helpful to locate the faces that belong to these two examples in order to assess their age and other diagnostic attributes. Face fragments are present at many contexts of the temple (figure 12.10) but cannot be matched securely to torsos. At least one is gracile and might fit expectations for a Maize God or a female face belonging to Effigy #5 (figure 12.10e). Other themes are observed in figure 12.10's sample of faces and noses from the temple's effigies. Two share a flaring nose element (figures 12.10b and 12.10d), and several have nose rods reminiscent of Central Mexican jewelry (figures 12.10b and 12.10d). Another has an indented upper tooth row that suggest a death god (figure 12.10j), and one individual has filed, sharp teeth, a rare trait also observed in the monumental center and seen occasionally on human remains at Mayapán (figure 12.10i; Peraza Lope and Masson 2014c:fig. 7.5c). It is evident that these faces were scattered and separated from the concentrations of body and head-dress sherds. With one exception, twelve of the thirteen facial fragments in figure 12.10 were found in grid squares from which no concentrations (table 12.1) were identified. The only exception is shown in figure 12.10k, a nose fragment from grid square 11-J (Lot 5315), from which some of the male (Effigy #6) fragments were also recovered. Most of the faces and noses were single examples from different contexts; only one exception is noted in grid square 5-F (Lot 5220), on the plaza floor to the west of the temple's staircase, where three examples were located (figures 12.10e and 12.10f).

Two other effigies (#9, #13) from H-17 have fewer distinctive pieces that were recognized only from single concentrations (figure 12.11). Effigy #9 is more crudely made. One corn cob *adorno*, an arm, a headdress, and digit fragments were recovered from an area in square 11-K that was separate from concentrations that held the death god (#1) and three other unidentified entities (#2, #3, #4). Effigy #13 represents an additional presumed female entity; an arm and a portion of the quechquemitl are present. For this personage, a small number of fragments were refitted from a single concentration, also in square 11-K, from the same concentration that yielded pieces of effigies #1–#4. Her quechquemitl may be related to Mixtec and central Mexican female attire, for this type of triangular blouse is not typical of Maya costuming. Although here the blouse clearly covers the breasts, this is not always the case (Brainerd 1958:fig. 99c). The garment may have been worn for a variety of purposes

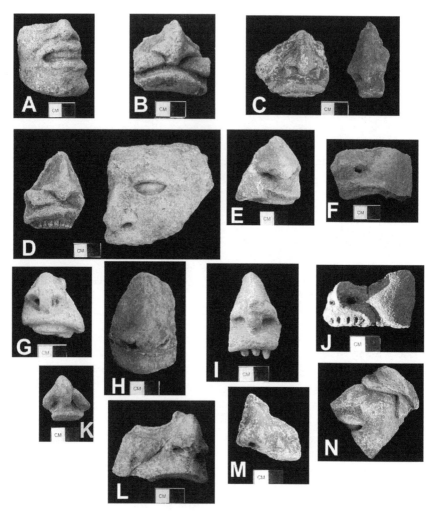

A) H-17 5236, B) H-17 5196, C) H-17 5197, D) H-17 5213,
E) H-17 5220, F) H-17 5220, G) H-17 5140, H) H-17 5155,
I) H-17 5442, J) H-17 5301, K) H-17 5315, L) H-17 5144,
M) H-17 5150, N) H-17 5366

FIGURE 12.10. *Face fragments from Temple H-17, which were not recovered in concentrations with refitted personages in table 12.1 (photos by Marilyn Masson).*

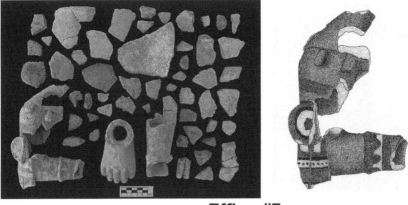

**Effigy #7**

**Effigy #9**

**Effigy #13**

FIGURE 12.11. *Refitted fragments of effigies #7 and #9 (unidentified entities from Hall H-15 and Temple H-17 respectively) and #13 (a female wearing a* quechquemitl *garment, from Temple H-17) (photos by Marilyn Masson).*

beyond the concealment of the upper torsos of females (e.g., Codex Borgia 9, 11, Codex Nuttall).

From Hall H-15, only two effigies could be matched from three concentrations (squares 5-K, 6-K, 10-K), despite the fact that more concentrations were recorded during field excavation (figure 12.4, table 12.1). A small number of fragments of Effigy #7 from Hall H-15 were refitted from three concentrations in three 2 × 2 meter grid squares (5-K, 6-K, 10-K), but additional matching pieces from this effigy were identified that could not be glued together (figure

12.11). It was not possible to identify the entity, as limb and shoulder fragments were the most diagnostic pieces present.

Hall H-15's Effigy #8 derives from the most interesting concentration recorded at this building, in square 10-K, where a well-worn greenstone chisel was found among the effigy sherds (figure 12.12; Peraza Lope and Masson 2014a:130). This deposit was near to the front of the hall's central altar. As figure 12.12 illustrates, sherds large and small represent many body and costume parts of this effigy, but most striking is the headdress miter with a third proboscis centered at the top of it and flanked by wings or feathers. This effigy had a bird head visor, of the sort that is regularly found on censers from the site. The refitted and matched pieces derive from a single concentration, from which fragments of #7 were also present (table 12.1).

Sherds from the mass grave at Itzmal Ch'en, just to the west and off-platform from Hall H-15, were more fragmented and were scattered rather than deposited in discrete concentrations. Refits were not performed from this context. Effigy #10 is represented by a female entity (with a clearly portrayed breast), but this individual is identified by a single fragment (figure 12.13). We did not assign effigy numbers to other single fragments that might represent distinct entities, but it is worth noting that a tally of death god maxillae reveals that pieces of at least seven distinct death god vessels were scattered in the mass grave (figure 12.13). However, only two of these were found close to one another (table 12.1). Six jaw fragments of ceramic effigies were also present in the mass grave that were not those of skeletal death god figures, bringing the tally of *incensarios* in this context up to thirteen.

## SUMMARY

The similarities of the discrete concentrations of effigies at the hall and temple suggest that they were part of a single, coordinated termination event. Three concentrations were present on the interior surface of the hall, and nine were found on the upper interior floor of the temple and adjacent plaza areas (Peraza Lope and Masson 2014a:130, figs. 3.11–3.12). The rough-hewn characteristics of the greenstone objects found singly in one concentration of each building is interesting. Perhaps they were inalienable possessions or were simply the only stones available for a quick ceremony under duress. Greenstones, like speleothem fragments, may have represented ensoulment devices for effigies (Lorenzen 2003:74). No concentration held the pieces of a single complete censer. The effigies had been broken prior to their deposition, their sherds mixed up, and then the fragments placed into discrete piles; others, like

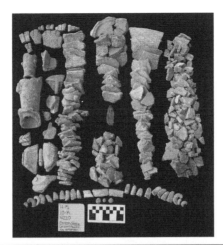

FIGURE 12.12. *Effigy #8 from Hall H-15. Top image shows sherd fragments from one concentration (Lot 4220, Square 10-K) that contained pieces of the effigy, prior to refitting. A greenstone chisel in the center of the photo was also present. Refitted pieces from Effigy #8 (from five different concentrations) are shown below, including a proboscis in the headdress (photos by Marilyn Masson).*

FIGURE 12.13. *Effigy #10, fragment of a female from the mass grave, are shown in the top image. The center row illustrates examples of death god mandibles and a maxilla from the mass grave. Face fragments from the mass grave are shown at the bottom (photos by Marilyn Masson).*

facial elements, may have been scattered. The mass grave effigy sherds were dispersed among the human bones, and unlike the hall and temple, were not placed in concentrations. The fragments of the hall, temple, and mass grave were probably from vessels portraying gods presiding over temporal cycles in Itzmal Ch'en buildings just prior to their destruction. The male and female urns may have represented other entities and purposes. Additional unexcavated buildings probably house more censer concentrations at Itzmal Ch'en, including Hall H-16, Oratory H-14, and Shrine H-13. Ann Chowning (1956) found dense concentrations of effigy censers at a plaza level sculpture/shrine, H-18a, but no photos were published of these materials in her report.

Mixed as the deposits were, refits were confined to concentrations within each building. The lack of refits between the hall and temple opens up the possibility that censer-breaking events at these locations were not strictly contemporaneous, though the similarities of these features suggest to us that they were deposited on the same occasion. Oddly, the faces of the restored effigies were not within concentrations that held the majority of matched pieces, despite the full excavation of the temple and the hall. The upper temple was partially explored by Donald Thompson (1955); perhaps the missing faces were recovered by the Carnegie project but were not published. The Carnegie project did not excavate at Hall H-15, and the scarcity of facial fragments at this structure cannot be attributed to earlier investigations. Hall H-15's faces may have been discarded in the adjacent mass grave (figure 12.13). Postdepositional collection by visitors to Mayapán after AD 1400 is unlikely responsible for missing faces, as the censers were buried beneath roof fall. Unfortunately, faces represent the most diagnostic portion of deity identities (Peraza Lope and Masson 2014c:269–429; Thompson 1957), but the death god is recognized in this assemblage by an emaciated body and skeletal jaw fragments. The temple's censer assemblage is unique in having a pair of male and female urns (#5, #6) seated on box thrones, in a manner that is exceptionally rare for the site. The bodies of these figures lack distinguishing deity markers, and they may have represented an ancestral couple. Sherds that made up the female effigy came from six concentrations, five of which overlap with concentrations from which refits for the male effigy were also recovered (table 12.1). Fragments of the male were also derived from four additional concentrations from which no female pieces were identified. The male headdress was bedecked in maize foliage, and he wears a braided cotton mantle on his chest on which are suspended shell ornaments that we suggest represent oyohualli symbols. Three proboscis elements in the headdresses of effigies #4, #5 (female), and #8 may represent butterfly imagery, a recurring insignia on Mesoamerican deities through time, including Postclassic Maya censers (Nielsen and Anderson 2004:fig. 7). One censer exhibits paste that is unlike hundreds of thousands of censer sherds was analyzed by Wilberth Cruz Alvarado and colleagues for the site (figure 12.5). It may have been imported effigy, perhaps from the east coast. These fragments came from three different concentrations at Temple H-17, all of which had pieces of other refitted censers in them (table 12.1). Chemical characterization of pastes from these examples has not yet been performed. Local and nonlocal smashed effigy censer deposits are also reported from Lamanai, Belize (Howie et al. 2014:45), but at Champotón, Campeche, effigies were locally made (Bishop et al. 2006). Beyond the distinctive characteristics of some of the Itzmal Ch'en's effigies, they share general similarities in finish, style, and decorative attributes with examples from the site center.

## DISCUSSION

From at least AD 1400 until 1458 (when the city was sacked and abandoned), the Itzmal Ch'en group was ceremonially closed. We do not know what triggered the violence leading to the mass grave or who the victims were—skeletal isotopes reveal little that distinguishes them from other humans at Mayapán (Kennett et al. 2015). If the mass grave is related to an invasion (Paris et al. 2017), perhaps the aftermath led to the ceremonious closure of places such as Itzmal Ch'en that were touched by violence. Subsequent governors did not choose to reopen the group. A higher level of sherd fragmentation in the mass grave impeded efforts to refit this sample. The possibility remains that the hall and mass grave, adjacent features, contained pieces of the same effigies. We cannot rule out that the hall and temple events preceded the violence culminating in the mass grave, but this scenario seems less likely.

Elsewhere at Mayapán, houses such as Y-45a were also ceremoniously abandoned by acts that included smashing of elaborate serving wares, effigy censers, and other vessels and subsequent covering this debris with rubble fill (Peraza Lope and Masson 2014a). Tatiana Proskouriakoff and Charles Temple (1955:305) report that the elite residents of Str. R-86 placed their censers in a cist that they reopened for this purpose upon abandonment of the group. As the whole censers did not fit into the feature, they were broken for safekeeping, according to these authors.

Analysis of the prolonged collapse of Mayapán is still in progress, but these new results touch on the importance of the interplay of archaeology and history, in the *A Forest of Kings* tradition. Prior to AMS dating, Mayapán's evidence for violence and termination rites was routinely attributed to its storied collapse due to the Xiu-Cocom war of Katun 8 Ahau in the mid-fifteenth century AD. Some of the fleeting references in the chronicles to cycles of prosperity and decline earlier in the Mayapán regime (during the fourteenth century) are given new credibility from absolute dating. The expulsion of a contingent of Xiu during Katun 1 Ahau (AD 1382–1401) correlates with this era of political upheaval (Milbrath and Peraza Lope 2003a:39, 41, table 1). These findings are complemented by emerging environmental data attesting to aggravating factors behind the political unrest of the fourteenth century and beyond (Hoggarth et al. 2017; Kennett et al. 2015; Masson and Peraza Lope 2014a). Although Mayapán was a powerful center with a complex regional economy, it suffered the problems and consequences of many regional capitals in the premodern world. Despite the evidence for a near collapse prior to AD 1400, we have emphasized that the city persevered into the fifteenth century and that this is also a story of recovery and resilience, however brief.

## ACKNOWLEDGMENTS

Research at Temple H-17 was supported in 2009 by the National Geographic Society's Committee for Research and Exploration (Grant #8598–08). Hall H-15 was excavated with a grant from the National Science Foundation (NSF-BCS-0742128). Analysis and refitting of the Itzmal Ch'en censers were supported by a (FRAP-B) grant from the College of Arts and Sciences, at the University at Albany–SUNY. We are grateful to Luis Flores for his assistance with lab refitting and to Pedro Delgado Kú and Bárbara Escamilla Ojeda for their refined work in excavating, consolidating, and reporting on the Itzmal Ch'en monumental buildings. This and other research at Mayapán have been facilitated in countless ways by codirectors of the Proyecto Económico de Mayapán: Timothy Hare, and Bradley Russell. Thanks are also due to Annabeth Headrick for providing input on Itzmal Ch'en censer iconography.

# 13

*On Copán Stela 11 and the Origins of the Ill Omen of Katun 8 Ahau*

STANLEY P. GUENTER

In the Colonial-era ethnohistorical books of Chilam Balam (Barrera Vásquez and Morley 1949; Barrera Vásquez and Rendón 1948; Edmonson 1982, 1986; Makemson 1951; Roys 1967), Katun 8 Ahau has a very bad reputation. The books of Chilam Balam of Tizimín, Maní, and Chumayel all record that disasters occurred causing the abandonment of Mayapán, Chichén Itzá, and Chanputún (Champotón) in Katun 8 Ahau dates (Roys 1962). It is true that not all of these chronicles attribute these events to Katun 8 Ahau (the chronology of these supposed historical accounts has long bedeviled Mayanists attempting to use them as sources for recovering the Postclassic history of Yucatán), but it has long been clear that by the time of the Spanish Colonial period, the Yucatec Maya saw Katun 8 Ahau as one associated with collapse, abandonment, migration, and political change. In fact, in the late seventeenth century, Spanish priests familiar with the Mayan language and Maya views of their own calendar used the coming advent of a new Katun 8 Ahau in that period to try and persuade the Itzá of Tayasal to peacefully submit to Spanish suzerainty, since it was the custom of the Itzá to abandon their city and find a new home or begin a new political situation every sequent Katun 8 Ahau (Avendaño y Loyola 1987:38–40; Roys 1962:68). While the Spanish attempt to use Maya prophecy to their own advantage failed (see G. Jones 1998), the documented attempt to do so highlights this aspect of

DOI: 10.5876/9781646420469.c013

Katun 8 Ahau, an association with societal upheaval, political change, and the abandonment of capital cities and the seeking out of new homes.

In this short chapter, I would like to examine this question about Postclassic and Colonial period Maya history by examining a couple of Classic period inscriptions from the site of Copán. The inscriptions reveal curious and interesting information about 8 Ahau that suggest possibilities for how this period of time came to hold such negative connotations for the ancient Maya and how these views may, ultimately, have been inspired by events from the Late Preclassic period. Using such a wide span of time and sites to attempt to understand deeper aspects of ancient Maya culture is something that I first read about in *A Forest of Kings*. The inscription that provides the key for this present study, namely, Stela 11 of Copán, is one that was first examined with a view to the specifics of its curious hieroglyphic inscription, in that seminal volume (Schele and Freidel 1990).

Stela 11 of Copán (figure 13.1) is actually a small column, found in two pieces that were recovered from the base of Structure 18 of the Acropolis (Baudez 1994:198; Fash 1991:177). The monument bears the image of a ruler holding a double-headed serpent bar (though the serpents are missing), wrapped around most of the column, while the remaining area on the back of the column is taken up by a hieroglyphic inscription (figure 13.1b). The image has been identified as a posthumous portrait, as not only is the figure standing atop a symbol that represents the maw of the underworld (and between bejeweled shells that also signify that same watery underworld), but also he is shown with long whiskers and the bald pate of the Maize God, out of whose forehead comes a flaming torch/axe (Baudez 1994:198; Fash 1991:177; Schele and Freidel 1990:342–343). The resemblance of this image with that of K'inich Janaab Pakal I on his famous sarcophagus lid from the Temple of the Inscriptions at Palenque has also been noted (Schele and Freidel 1990:494n82). Claude Baudez has suggested that Stela 11 was originally located inside the inner room of this temple, above a tomb looted in antiquity, but presumed to have been for Copán's last regular ruler, Yax Pasaj Chan Yopaat (Baudez 1994:198; Baudez and Dowd 1983:497). Not only is this king the subject of the other inscriptions of Temple 18, but he is also clearly the focus of Stela 11 (Schele and Freidel 1990:341–343). The funerary nature of Stela 11 is thus now well established (Fash 1991:176; Martin and Grube 2008:212; Schele and Freidel 1990:341–343).

The inscription on the back of Stela 11 (figure 13.1b) consists of eighteen hieroglyphic blocks in a single double-column of nine rows. The inscription is unusual for a number of reasons, and David Stuart has suggested that Stela

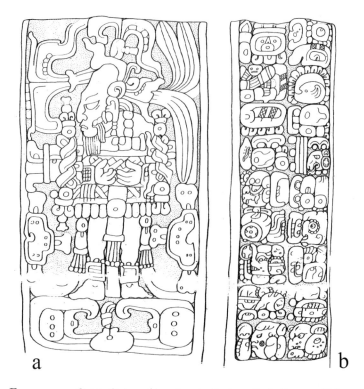

FIGURE 13.1. *Copán Stela 11 (drawings by Barbara Fash; Corpus of Maya Hieroglyphic Inscriptions, Peabody Museum, Harvard University).*

11 may be "the only Maya inscription containing a direct reference to the collapse of a local political system" (1993:346). The initial date was deciphered by Berthold Riese as 9.19.10.0.0, 8 Ahau 8 Xul (April 30, AD 820),[1] even though it is a very truncated date, given in glyphblock A1 as only *ti 8 ajaw*, "in/on 8 Ahau" (Baudez and Dowd 1983:491–493). While this date is accepted in the epigraphic community, for good historical reasons, I believe that the date is not so specific.

All scholars accept that this 8 Ahau date must correspond to a period ending. However, the lack of any *haab* date immediately following, as well as the preceding preposition *ti*, makes this date greatly resemble *katun* references from northern Yucatán. Xcalumkin Capital 1, Ek' Bahlam Capstone 1, and the Water Trough Lintel from Chichén Itzá all clarify that their dates occurred within a certain *tun* of the current katun, wherein the final part is said to have occurred "*ti X Ahau*"; this is the common form of dates in the inscriptions of Chichén Itzá, carved half a century after Copán Stela 11, but the preposition there is, with the exception of the Hacienda Water Trough lintel, *ta* instead of *ti*. Unlike these inscriptions from northern Yucatán, however, there is no preceding specific date on Copán Stela 11 that was being contextualized within the "in 8 Ahau" statement.[2] This date on Stela 11 thus refers not to a specific, date but to a period of time. The phrase that follows is being said to have occurred not *on* 8 Ahau but *within* a period 8 Ahau. In this, the phrase is most akin to the katun chronicles of the Books of Chilam Balam and, as we shall see, allows the author of this text to associate "like-in-kind" events from different 8 Ahau periods in different periods of Maya history.

The rest of the text breaks down into three verbal phrases, with the third being temporally distinct. The first phrase is very short, covering only glyphs B1–A2. The verb in B1 is spelled phonetically as **ho-mo-yi**, *homooy*. This is a mediopassive verb whose root, *hom*, has been identified by Schele and Freidel (1990:446–447n48) and by Stuart (1993:346) with a Yucatecan verb *hom(ah)*, whose glosses include *"desplomar techos, derribar edificios, cerros . . . desfondar"* (Barrera Vásquez 1980:229). Stuart (1993:346) noted that these glosses referring to the "tearing down of roofs/buildings" were particularly apt, as the subject of this verb included the word for "house." This subject, in glyphblock A2, is the famous *wite' naah* glyph,[3] of which much has been written. Schele and Freidel (1990:343) saw this originally as a glyph for the founder of Copán's Classic period dynasty, K'inich Yax K'uk' Mo'. Stuart noted that the hieroglyph included the word for "house," *naah* in Mayan, and thus likely referred to a specific building at Copán, and he suggested Temple XVI, built atop this first king of Copán's tomb (1993:345–346). In a seminal paper published a few years later, Stuart discussed the associations of this hieroglyph with the iconography of Teotihuacan (2000:492–493), and these Central Mexican connections were further elaborated in a number of further studies. The association of the *wite' naah* glyph with Teotihuacan is now generally accepted (although see the chapters in Braswell 2003c for some dissenting views), and the wite' naah structure itself has been argued to refer specifically to the Temple of the Sun at Teotihuacan (Fash et al. 2009; J. Nielsen 2003).

However, we should be cautious over interpreting all examples of the *wite'* *naah* glyph as referring to a specific structure, as the term could easily have quickly become a reference for the larger city and kingdom for which it served as a central focus of ritual and politics. A couple of examples from our own modern world help emphasize this point. Norway House is a town in central Manitoba, Canada, while College Station is a city in east-central Texas. While each of these places were originally named after specific buildings, the names quickly came to refer to the larger settlements that grew up around them. It is thus quite likely that the *wite' naah* glyph does not refer always to a specific building at Teotihuacan, but rather the larger community/city, and could even have come to characterize the entire kingdom as a whole.

These new interpretations of the *wite' naah* glyph allow for a reinterpretation of Stela 11. While this reference to the homooy of the wite' naah could be describing the destruction of an actual building, possibly the Temple of the Sun at Teotihuacan, it may refer, instead, to the collapse of the polity of Teotihuacan itself. The linguistics of the first three glyphs of this text can indeed be glossed as "in 8 Ahau Teotihuacan collapsed," a phrase certainly redolent of the katun chronicles of the Books of Chilam Balam. If so, however, we must reinterpret the date, for Teotihuacan had long since collapsed by the early ninth century. Recent reanalyses of radiocarbon and archaeomagnetic data from Teotihuacan indicate that the central part of the city was destroyed in a gigantic conflagration that can be dated to AD 550±25 (Manzanilla 2003; Soler-Arechalde et al. 2006). This is more than two centuries before the 9.19.10.0.0 period ending that, until the present study, has been the presumed Long Count for the 8 Ahau reference in glyph A1 of Copán Stela 11. However, it can be noted that another half-katun 8 Ahau date occurred precisely in the period when Teotihuacan is now known to have collapsed: 9.6.10.0.0, 8 Ahau 13 Pax, or January 25, 564. This date would be exactly thirteen katuns before the 9.19.10.0.0, 8 Ahau 8 Xul with which Stela 11 was previously associated. As we will see, there is reason to believe that both dates are being referenced on this monument and, for this reason, the preliminary date is given only as "*ti* 8 Ahau."

It should be noted that the 8 Ahau date of AD 564 is not the specific date of the event in question. Rather, the collapse is said to have occurred within that period. A katun is ruled over by its Ahau date for its full twenty years. Presumably the Ahau of a half-katun would be considered to rule over only the preceding half-katun, or approximately ten years. Thus, Copán Stela 11's reference is likely to Teotihuacan having collapsed in the half-katun period of 8 Ahau, which spanned the period between AD 554 and 564. This reference corresponds perfectly with the radiocarbon and archaeomagnetic date for the "big fire" event at Teotihuacan discussed above.

The association of events from different periods with other events that occurred in subsequent or previous iterations of those periods is absolutely characteristic of the katun chronicles of the Books of Chilam Balam (Barrera and Morley Vásquez 1949; Makemson 1951; Roys 1967). As we will see, it seems apparent that the scribe who composed this text was trying to compare the situation in Copán at the beginning of the ninth century to the collapse of Teotihuacan 13 katuns earlier, an event that also corresponded with a half-katun period of 8 Ahau. Before the scribe got to the contemporary record, however, he included a second phrase, which presents the most problems with understanding this entire text. The second phrase extends from glyphblock B2 to A5 and begins with a verbal root, **ju[lu]** *jul*, at B2. *Jul* exists as a noun "spear" as well as a transitive verbal root "to spear/pierce" in a number of Mayan languages (Barrera Vásquez 1980:242, as HUL; Pérez Martínez et al. 1996:89, as JUR). The text then continues with a couplet that mentions both flint and obsidian (Stuart 1993:344–345), apparently being the eyes of the Teotihuacan War Serpent, the Waxaklajuun Ubaah Chan. It is tempting to read this simply as "was speared, obsidian is its eye, flint is its eye, the Teotihuacan War Serpent." However, it has to be noted that in this case there would be no verbal suffixation and that the verb is clearly a root transitive; thus the passive reading is manifestly erroneous. Schele and Matthew Looper (1996:159) have suggested that the verb is actually "to arrive," but this would have been spelled in the Classic period as *hul* not *jul*, and, while this distinction did indeed break down in the Terminal Classic period (Grube 2004b:79–81), such a reading still does not explain the lack of any verbal suffixation in B2 nor would this translation make much sense.[4]

This second phrase remains "opaque," to employ the term Stuart has aptly used to describe it (1993:344). However, what we can say is that it must somehow provide a further (probably poetic) description of the fall of Teotihuacan mentioned in Phrase 1, referencing the eyes of the Teotihuacan War Serpent.

Phrase 3 of this text covers the rest of the inscription, beginning with a verb in B5 and continuing with the names of two kings of Copán, the founder of the Classic period dynasty, K'inich Yax K'uk' Mo' (glyphblocks A6–A7), and the sixteenth king, Yax Pasaj Chan Yopaat (glyphblocks B7–B9). Simon Martin and Nikolai Grube (2008:212) have said that these two kings were the "joint subjects" of this inscription, but Schele and Freidel suggested that the intended meaning was "that the people of Copán believed the dynasty of [K'inich Yax K'uk' Mo'] had ended with the death of [Yax Pasaj Chan Yopaat]" (Schele and Freidel 1990:343). In 1996 Schele and Looper glossed this final phrase of the Stela 11 text as "[Yax Pasaj Chan Yopaat] forced (or brought) out [K'inich Yax K'uk' Mo']" (Schele and Looper 1996:159). While not made explicit in their 1996 publication, the reasoning behind Schele and Looper's interpretation can readily be reconstructed. The verb in glyphblock B5 is spelled **u-lo-k'o(?)-ma**, *u lok'oom. Lok'* is a noun and verbal root found in both intransitive and transitive forms in Ch'orti', with meanings including "leaving, departure (salida), a coming up our out, escape . . . throw out, expel" (Wisdom

1950:515). The fact that the two names of the first and sixteenth king of Copán follow each other directly, with no intervening relationship glyphs, indicates that we are indeed looking at a transitive verbal phrase and that given the respective positions of their names in the phrase, Yax Pasaj Chan Yopaat did something to K'inich Yax K'uk' Mo'. It should also be noted that the verbal form in B5 bears a suffix—*oom*, which has been identified as the future marker in the hieroglyphic script (Knorosov 2001:151). Putting all of this evidence together, we can read this last phrase as saying that Yax Pasaj Chan Yopaat will remove/take away K'inich Yax K'uk' Mo', but not that he had done so already.

This future event, the removal of the founder of the dynasty by the sixteenth king, is not preceded directly by a specific date, and thus we must see this as connected to the date 8 Ahau at the beginning of the text. The text is stating that, just as Teotihuacan collapsed in the time period of the previous half-katun 8 Ahau (which ended in AD 564), so in the forthcoming half-katun 8 Ahau (ending in AD 820), Yax Pasaj Chan Yopaat will remove K'inich Yax K'uk' Mo'.

What did the Maya scribes mean to say by this? How was Yax Pasaj Chan Yopaat going to "remove" the founder of his dynasty, and why? It must be admitted up front that there is no firm evidence to conclusively answer such a question, but we can make certain observations. First, K'inich Yax K'uk' Mo' had died nearly 400 years prior to the commissioning of Stela 11, and by that time his mortal remains were deeply buried beneath the numerous buildings that over the centuries had been constructed atop his tomb. Thus, it is patently doubtful whether the scribe who designed the text of Stela 11 meant a physical removal of the old king from Copán. However, it is possible to make a case that what was being prophesied was a spiritual remover of the founder of the dynasty.

We know that the ancient city of Copán revolved around K'inich Yax K'uk' Mo', quite literally. The center of Copán is the Acropolis and the center of the Acropolis is Temple XVI (Structure 10L-16), now known to be the funerary shrine of K'inich Yax K'uk' Mo' and built atop his tomb (Stuart 2004; Taube 2004c). This king acceded, apparently at Teotihuacan, and after a journey of 153 days arrived at Copán, as related in the text carved atop Altar Q, placed in front of the staircase of Temple XVI (Stuart 1993). The central event of this inscription, both rhetorically and literally, and the one most elaborated, is not the accession but the arrival, and it is likely that this was the event that was seen as the true foundation of the kingdom of Copán. Nearly all later kings of Copán, at least those for whom we have at least a few decently preserved monuments, referred back to the founder, and no other ruler in Copán's history is so regularly referenced. Given the centrality of his mortuary temple, the tallest and most central structure in the city, it seems clear that much of the ritual life of the city in later centuries consisted of worship at this temple and probably of the founder himself. As noted by Schele and Freidel, the text of Stela 11 appears to indicate that "the people of Copán believed the dynasty of [K'inich Yax K'uk' Mo'] had ended with the death of [Yax Pasaj Chan Yopaat]" (Schele and Freidel 1990:343).

However, it is important to clarify that the future marker on the verb in B5 indicates not that the people of Copán believed that the dynasty *had died* with Yax Pasaj Chan Yopaat, but that it was *going to die*. This means that when this inscription was carved, Yax Pasaj Chan Yopaat had not yet passed away and, in fact, almost certainly commissioned this monument himself. Stela 11 is thus not a record of his death and that of his dynasty but, rather, a prophecy. Yax Pasaj Chan Yopaat thus must have commissioned this monument at some point between AD 810, his last attested date (Martin and Grube 2008:224–225), and AD 820, when the half- katun 8 Ahau would have passed. By AD 810 almost all of the Maya lowlands, other than the Upper Belize River Valley area dominated by Naranjo and Caracol, appears to have been suffering under the beginnings of the collapse period, with a devastating multiyear drought having already set (see Guenter 2014b for a detailed analysis and discussion of these points). Stela 11 would thus appear to be a prophecy of imminent and impending doom to Copán and its royal dynasty, one that is explicitly compared to the collapse of Teotihuacan in a similar 8 Ahau period, exactly thirteen katuns earlier. Most interestingly, the founder of Copán, K'inich Yax K'uk' Mo', is intimately connected to Teotihuacan and appears to have acceded at that Central Mexican city (Fash et al. 2009; Stuart 2004). In fact, his title on Stela 11 explicitly adds a *puj* glyph to his Copán Emblem Glyph (glyph-block A7), which, as shown by Stuart (2000), is a reference to Teotihuacan as "Tollan," *puj* being the Mayan word for "reeds" just as *tollan* is the Nahuatl word for the same. K'inich Yax K'uk' Mo' was thus a "Copán-Teotihuacan" lord, and his fate, at least as an object of ritual reverence and source of spiritual power for his descendants, appears to have been linked to that of the Central Mexican superpower that he served.

Accepting this interpretation of Copán Stela 11 still leaves one large question unanswered, that of the origins of this belief in the tragic nature of 8 Ahau. The chronicles of the Books of Chilam Balam are devoted to discussing katuns, not half-katuns, and we know that the Classic Maya also highlighted the commemoration of katun endings. While half katuns, and even quarter katuns, were important at some sites, they were important only at sites that both revered full katuns and expended more effort in commemorating those larger cycles. The connection that Stela 11 makes between the collapse of Teotihuacan and the later collapse of Copán is tied to half-katun 8 Ahau periods, and this presupposes the dire associations of 8 Ahau with an earlier katun 8 Ahau. Otherwise, we would expect these associations to accrue to Katun 7 Ahau, the actual katun endings that immediately followed, only ten years after, the 8 Ahau half-katun endings.

It can be noted that there is nothing inherent in 8 Ahau that would suggest such an association of ill omen with this period of time. The patron god of the number 8 is the Maize God, certainly one of the most revered deities of the Classic period (Taube 1985). In the text of the Temple of the Inscriptions at Palenque, the middle tablet discusses the ceremonies associated with two katun endings, those for 12 Ahau (9.11.0.0.0) and 10 Ahau (9.12.0.0.0). These, in turn, are associated with a celestial Maize deity and a death god respectively, and the head variants of the numbers 12 and 10 match these gods (Guenter 2007a). Thus, clearly, the ancient Maya did see an association between the number of a katun and its character, and, one would presume, the Maize deity representing Katun 8 Ahau should have imbued such a period with a good nature and character.

Accepting that the Maya were prophesying/recording destruction, abandonment, and general catastrophe for katun 8 Ahau in the Postclassic and for the half-katun 8 Ahaus associated with the onset of the Late Classic collapse, as well as for the Middle Classic collapse of Teotihuacan suggest that there may have been an earlier collapse that fell in a Katun 8 Ahau of such a great magnitude it forever after tainted this period of time with a character it would not originally have had. Prior to the dedication of Stela 11, the immediately preceding Katun 8 Ahau fell on the Long Count position of 9.13.0.0.0 (March 13, AD 692). There is no sign of a major catastrophe at this time at Copán or elsewhere in the Maya world for that matter (Martin and Grube 2008), and there were so many monuments being commissioned and temples being built in that era we can consider this one of the apogees of Classic Maya civilization. Clearly, any Katun 8 Ahau that could have inspired the ill omen of this period must have fallen earlier in time.

The closest previous Katun 8 Ahau is the one that fell on the Long Count position of 9.0.0.0.0 (December 8, AD 435). This one is not only a katun ending but also a *baktun* ending, and thus an even more important period ending than the one in AD 692. Most Classic Maya cities were not yet commissioning monuments in this era, and it is interesting to note that no stela commissioned exactly on this date has been found at Tikal or Uaxactún. However, there is one from Calakmul, and not only is there a monument dedicated on this date at Copán, Stela 63 (Fash 1991:82–83), but also this date is referenced in a number of texts commissioned by later kings and associated with the founder, K'inich Yax K'uk' Mo' (Stuart 2004). The 8 Ahau period ending of AD 435 thus also fails to qualify as a candidate for the inspiration of the bad associations of this period of time.

The next previous Katun 8 Ahau, however, is a different story. Katun 8 Ahau ended on 8.7.0.0.0, 8 Ahau 13 Zodz (September 3, AD 179), and this Katun 8 Ahau had begun immediately following the end of the previous katun, Katun 10 Ahau, which itself had ended on 8.6.0.0.0 (December 17, AD 159). It is noteworthy both that the earlier Katun 10 Ahau have been a period conceptually associated with death and that the middle of the second century AD has long been known to be the time when the Late Preclassic collapse occurred in the Maya lowlands (Hansen 2001, 2012; Hansen et al. 2008).

Another Copán monument, Stela I, may strengthen this potential association. Stela I includes a reference to the end of the 8.6.0.0.0, Katun 10 Ahau Period Ending and states that this calendar ceremony was overseen by an individual, Foliated Ajaw (Schele and Looper 1996:94). This ceremony took place at a location identified by the toponym "Chi-Metate" (Stuart 2014), which can be identified as the capital of the Preclassic Snake Kingdom (Grube 2004c; Guenter 2001). While this toponym has not yet been identified in Preclassic texts, there is good evidence that the Snake Kingdom capital in this period was El Mirador (Guenter 2009; Hansen et al. 2008). El Mirador is the largest ancient Maya site known and features the largest and tallest pyramids ever constructed in the two-millennia span of this civilization's history (Hansen 1998, 2001, 2012; Hansen et al. 2008). Its collapse must surely have inspired legends, much as that of the fall of Tollan did for the later Aztecs. It would make sense if the collapse of the Preclassic Snake Kingdom and the abandonment of its capital in a Katun 8 Ahau had inspired the ill omen that this katun would have for later Maya.

While Copán Stela I emphasizes the 10 Ahau katun ending celebrated by Foliated Ajaw at the Chi-Metate place, the text goes on to describe an event at Copán 208 days later, which I have noted must be the arrival of Foliated Ajaw in the region of Copán (Guenter 2003). Foliated Ajaw makes a good candidate for the last king of the Preclassic Snake Kingdom (Grube 2004c:129–131; Guenter 2003), and his move from the Chi-Metate place to the region of Copán would have occurred very shortly after he had celebrated the end of Katun 10 Ahau. Technically, this would have fallen in the subsequent katun, Katun 8 Ahau. If Copán Stela I was meaning to describe the abandonment of the Preclassic Snake Kingdom by its last king, this would have been an event in the era of Katun 8 Ahau.

## FINAL COMMENTS

Admittedly there are a lot of speculation and certainly uncertainty in the preceding analysis. However, I believe that this speculation is grounded in good archaeological and epigraphic evidence and provides a useful step toward understanding some of the deeper connections of ancient Maya civilization throughout its many iterations through time and space. The spark for my own interest in combining archaeological and epigraphic data in order to recover not only ancient history, but help elucidate the ancient social history and civilization of the Maya began in 1990 when reading *A Forest of Kings*. I submit this work of analysis as a tribute to Linda Schele and David A. Freidel, who first inspired me to become a Mayanist and pursue questions such as these, and to the ancient Maya, for whom the questions of connections between periods of time and the cultural and historical events they experienced so profoundly impacted the way they saw and interpreted their own culture.

## NOTES

1. All dates in the Western calendar in this chapter are given in the Julian calendar according to the 584283 correlation and are AD dates unless otherwise specified.

2. Martin and Grube have suggested that the inscription on Stela 11 is a "continuation of an inscription carved upon . . . [the] interior walls" of Structure 18 (Martin and Grube 2008:212). There are reasons to doubt this suggestion, however. Not only are there no other examples of monuments at Copan (or elsewhere) bearing the conclusion of an architectural inscription, but also the style of both the iconography on the front of Stela 11 as well as the inscription on its reverse are quite different from the style seen in the architectural carvings on Temple 18 itself. The latest date in the inscriptions of Temple 18, it should be noted, are from the year 801 (Schele and Looper 1995:158), nineteen years before the supposed 9.19.10.0.0 (AD 820) date of Stela 11. While there are similarities in subject matter between Stela 11 and the inscriptions of Temple 18, as is discussed later in this chapter, I believe these are best explained as the text of Stela 11 being a new and separate composition designed to fit into the overall themes of the already existent carvings of the location into which it was designed to rest.

3. I continue to refer to this hieroglyph as the "Wite' naah glyph," but it should be noted that a recently discovered inscription from Holmul (Estrada-Belli and Tokovinine 2016:159–161) reveals that the first part of this hieroglyph, usually shown

logographically, as on Stela 11, by a pair of crossed torches and a mirror, is not simply *wi*, as it is usually spelled when spelled phonetically, but underspelled with a final–**na** syllable. Estrada-Belli and Tokovinine suggest that this hieroglyph thus reads, "Wiinte'naah," for which they suggest a gloss of "Wood that appears in the distance" house. I am skeptical of this reading and find it more likely that the full reading of the crossed-torches-and-mirror sign is probably yet more phonetically complex and likely the whole term reads, "Wi . . . nte'naah" and that the term "Wi . . . n" is likely not Mayan at all, an alternative interpretation also suggested by Estrada-Belli and Tokovinine (159–161). I note that Cerro de la Estrella in Central Mexico, where the Aztecs conducted their New Fire ceremonies and where archaeological evidence has been found suggesting that similar ceremonies may have been conducted as much as a millennium earlier or more, was known to the Aztecs as Huizachtecatl (Helmke and Montero García 2016; Helmke and Nielsen 2014). While this toponym is said to refer to the presence of huizache grass on this mountain (Helmke and Montero García in press; Helmke and Nielsen 2014), I wonder whether this may not be a (false) folk etymology and whether Huizachtecatl may be a later reflection of whatever the original term was. In any event, I suspect the original full spelling of the "Wi . . . nte'naah" glyph includes a non-Mayan term.

4. It can be noted that the collocation **ta-ji** in glyphblock A3 could potentially be the missing verbal suffixation for the verbal root of B2. Ta-ja is a verbal suffix for a passive verb on Tikal Lintel 3 of Temple IV (at E8). However, this attempt at resolving the conundrum of Phrase 2 of Stela 11 runs into serious problems of its own. It is unclear how the verbal root in B2 could actually work with such suffixation, and it would destroy the apparent couplet between A3–B3, "obsidian is the eye of," and A4, "flint is the eye of." As should be apparent, this phrase is still far from deciphered.

# 14

*Into the Woods*

*Archaeology, Epigraphy, and Iconography in Classic Maya Studies*

Dᴀᴠɪᴅ A. Fʀᴇɪᴅᴇʟ

When we started to write *A Forest of Kings*, Linda had a hopeful vision of a unified Maya field of inquiry and interpretation bringing together archaeology, all of the analyses of materials retrieved in the course of excavation and laboratory research, all of the contexts, with epigraphy and iconography. For me, the collaboration was an exhilarating experience throughout the process of passing drafts around on disc, meeting at Linda's home, talking on the phone, a chance to see what I could bring to this unified field approach. As Wendy Ashmore points out in chapter 8, William Fash and Robert Sharer (1991) were also articulating a conjunctive approach to the field from the perspective of their work at Copán. Robert Sharer pursued the earliest buildings in the 10L-16 locality through tunneling and discovered what Linda had declared should be real and somewhere in the Acropolis: the tomb of the dynasty founder. It was not a sure thing: it was a hypothesis based on the existence of Early Classic texts that suggested the historical reality of this man. Robert Sharer, Ellen Bell, and the other archaeologists who excavated the Hunal tomb made a good case for this being the resting place of K'inich Yax K'uk' Mo' (Bell et al. 2004b). Was it a perfect case? No. But they were right for the right reasons. The field of knowledge where archaeology overlaps with history in Maya studies is destined to be a forest of questions full of promising trees, some just seedlings and others well on their way to the light. Recently, the eminent Maya

DOI: 10.5876/9781646420469.c014

ancient historian and epigrapher Simon Martin characterized tongue in cheek this overlap field as the "mammoth in the room" of our collective efforts. I was inspired to declare it the land of Snuffleupagus. Those of you who watched Sesame Street know that Snuffy was Big Bird's invisible friend. Eventually children could see him, and now, finally, adults can too. Most Maya archaeologists who work in the land of texts and images now perceive the value of collaboration in the middle ground. As Wendy Ashmore says, I started out, now some forty years ago, pretty certainly right for the wrong reasons about many things in this place of the elusive overlap; but I was, and remain, open to correction, as was Linda during her remarkable time as a mentor, teacher, and scholar. We decided never to revise the book because we saw it as a declaration of what we could know at that point in the unfolding paradigm revolution which was the decipherment. I was pleased to hear David Stuart, in commentary at the meetings resulting in this book, call it a good first draft.

As Arthur Demarest points out in his generous defense of the book and of my research strategies, many colleagues at the time regarded us as beyond the pale of scientific inquiry, me in particular as a field archaeologist. Trained in the processual archaeology of my day, I always thought in terms of hypothesis testing of ideas about the Maya past. Linda and I put the tiny print endnotes in our books to give colleagues a view of our ongoing evaluation and testing of ideas and inferences as well as attributions to the ideas of others working on the decipherment. I survived to be returned to the fold as was Linda. Even now some Mayanists such as Christophe Helmke and Jaime Awe (2016b) are referencing Linda's ideas in *A Forest of Kings* concerning ancient Maya history, in this case regarding what we now term the Kaanul regime. Obviously, what we wrote in the late 1980s has been superseded by new discoveries and advanced methods of decipherment, but our effort is for some still part of the history of the evolving exploration of that between-ground forest of questions.

The notion of soul force as something pervasive in Maya perception and conception, what Demarest terms our perspective on the "inanimate," never seemed at issue to Linda and me while writing. She as an epigrapher and iconographer could see the personification or living being of what we might call the material things of the world throughout the corpus and she wrote routinely from that vantage. Trained as I was, like Arthur Demarest, by Evon Vogt, I learned from freshman year that everything material in Zinacantán and other contemporary Maya communities was immanently or overtly charged with soul force. Linda and I explicitly addressed Vogt's contributions and insights in our second book, *Maya Cosmos*. I am happy to see Christophe Helmke and James Awe (2016a) still referencing that book, with regard to the concept of K'awiil, relevant to this theme of soul force. Because ancient Maya artifacts were subject to various forms of intentional demise as well as use and engendered creation, Demarest segues to my championing of the practice of termination rituals, a pattern first proposed in publication by James Garber (1983) and Robin Robertson (1983) in our collaborative research at Cerro Maya. I will return to my own interpretations of termination rituals shortly, but here it is important to focus on Demarest's quite remarkable description in chapter 2 of the sitewide termination ritual he perceives at Cancuén. The dramatic sacrifice of a large number of courtiers, their bodies literally "entering the water" of the sacred cisterns before the royal palace, the hasty burial of the last king in a shallow grave—these are truly extraordinary examples of the regicide thematic in the edited volume of Gyles Iannone and colleagues (2016) of the demise of Maya divine kingship in the collapse era. Demarest's accomplishments as a field archaeologist, scholar, and mentor rival those of his mentor Gordon Willey, and I am honored that he would join Wendy Ashmore and other friends and colleagues in contributing to this book.

While the idea of termination ritual has gained credence, Travis Stanton and colleagues in chapter 9, revisiting the archaeology of Yaxuná, are now doubtful of the inference that Chichén Itzá carried out such termination rituals at Structure 6F-68 in the North Acropolis of that site. Their skepticism is based on cogent new analyses of chronology that make it unlikely that Chichén Itzá warriors would have attacked Yaxuná and violently terminated the building in the scenario Linda and I framed in our book. Instead, this proposed council house may have been ritually abandoned by its own people, who may have partially removed an ancestor's remains from below the floor before leaving. An intriguing feature of the argument regarding the Yaxuná building in question is its stylistic affinities to the radial pyramid to the west at Ikil that they also describe in some detail. In a discussion of Aline Magnoni and colleague's paper on the Ikil building at the 2017 SAA meetings, I suggested that this might have been a pilgrimage center disembedded from any sizable community of the kind who might build and use such an impressive edifice. The reference to a Lady Six Sky Lord and a Lady Deer Metate in the carved texts as well as a possible god house encourages the notion of a pilgrimage place of high-elite status. In light of the affinities to the building at Yaxuná, these may have been part of a processional route. The Yaxuná causeway to Cobá may have been abandoned by the time of these buildings, but very likely its existence remained an important feature of the sacred landscape and geography of the region. The east coast would serve as a major venue of pilgrims seeking the oracle of the goddess Ix Chel in the later Postclassic period, and quite possibly it already served such pilgrimage purposes in the Classic period. Certainly the Classic Maya, and the Preclassic Maya before them, revered the east as the place of the rising sun, as a symbol of resurrection, renewal, and, as pointed out by David Stuart (2005b), the returning seasonal rains.

Karl Taube is the greatest general iconographer Mesoamerican studies has ever seen, and a good friend and colleague to both Linda and me throughout our parallel careers. His study of Chichén Itzá as a heavenly place complements his own many contemplations of this exemplary city and builds on his firm conviction that to understand religion in one region of Mesoamerica requires close study of all of them—particularly true in the case of the highlands of Mexico and the Maya region. Linda also loved the art of the northern lowlands and focused considerable attention to it in all three of the syntheses she wrote, two with me and then the last one with Peter Mathews (Schele and Mathews 1998). In chapter 10, Taube explores the concepts of butterfly warriors and souls as a distinctively highland Mexican idea brought into the Maya lowlands, and that of Flower Mountain as an idea present in the Maya lowlands from the Preclassic period, but elaborated through history there and present also in highland Mexico as well. Indeed, Taube suggests this is a widely disseminated and pervasive vision of heaven in Mesoamerica, and that is the foundation of his argument that the era of Tula and Chichén Itzá witnessed the identification of the latter as the heavenly abode of flower mountain and butterfly warrior souls, the mythical east. I find his premise—that Mesoamericans had a shared vision of their world, its sacred geography, and the gods and their stories—compelling and productive. We have known for a long time that Teotihuacan interacted with the Maya world from its Preclassic origins, and I think we have a lot more to know about this relationship leading up to the quite explicit New Order era in the lowlands initiated by Kaloomte' Sihyaj K'ahk'. Relevant to that era, the research I launched at El Perú–Waka' discovered in 2003 the base of an Early Classic stela with what epigrapher Stanley P. Guenter correctly identified as a frontal image of the Teotihuacan Butterfly War God with an owl's head in its mouth. The basal position signals the place where the portrayed individual on the stela was standing. One might see this as a Teotihuacan version of Flower Mountain. I am working on the prospect that the mountain at the site, 45 m above ambient terrain and terraced into a pyramid, was not only a Water Mountain, but also an *altepetl* in the eyes of Sihyaj K'ahk' when he established a new royal government there (Freidel 2014b).

Annabeth Headrick also addresses Chichén Itzá, in chapter 11, with particular focus on the regalia of the warriors presented there as captives. I very much like her argument that these depict high-ranked individuals from far afield, even from highland Mexico, and that is why they are decked out so sumptuously. Like Karl Taube, and indeed most students of the site, Headrick envisions a city of extraordinary cosmopolitan reach in all ways. Her careful comparison of Maya and Mexican, particularly Teotihuacano, depictions of warriors is a good basis for suggesting that military organization was different among these peoples. But collectivity is celebrated at Chichén Itzá politically as well as militarily, as Linda and I proposed in the book. While I am happy to concede that the texts of earlier stages there do not sustain the rulership of brothers we saw in them, and the now discredited use of the term *multepal* to describe it, neither do they clearly support a dynastic rulership such as found in the southern lowland kingdoms we discuss in earlier chapters of *A Forest of Kings*. Rulership at Chichén Itzá remains a work in progress in our field. As Robert Sharer once queried experts on Chichén Itzá gathered in an elegant drawing room at Dumbarton Oaks at the beginning of the millennium, close to a century of archaeological research at the site has failed to yield a single royal tomb, and why is that? My own answer is that governance at Chichén Itzá was, from beginning to end, carried out by a councilor and composed of leaders chosen and initiated with appropriate insignia, led by a first among equals and not a dynastic monarch. Such rulers were less likely to end up revered as divine in death and placed where they could continue their work from the flowery heaven. Perhaps, being Maya, they expressed their individuality more than Mexican compatriots, but the architecture and iconography of the city described by Annabeth supports such a collective view of governance much better than dynastic kingship. Indeed, I have for some time thought that dynastic kingship was a distinctively southern lowland Classic period form of governance (Freidel 2012) and that northern lowland peoples, among other Maya, selected or elected their kings into a sodality of divine people and had done so since the time of El Mirador and other great Preclassic cities (Freidel 2018). This is an idea commensurate with some proposed by William Ringle (2004) for Chichén Itzá.

Not surprisingly in light of what I have just said, I now regard the government of Mayapán to be a final regional capital of collective rule in a tradition of such rule stretching back to the Preclassic in the northern lowlands. I am relieved to see that Marilyn Masson and her collaborators in their magnificent research program at Mayapán still adhere to this working hypothesis of collective governance, even if the term multepal is no longer voiced by them. To be sure, there were great lineages and lethal rivalries there as well, and disputes could be settled with blades rather than debates and consensus as may be registered in the remarkable terminal deposit of slain victims at

Itzmal Ch'en that Masson and her colleagues describe. Certainly this must have been also the case in earlier times even where formal dynastic succession was eschewed and councils of electors prevailed. The terminal rituals at Itzmal Ch'en are the focus of this chapter, and it is clear that a majority of the contributors to the book are particularly interested in this kind of deposit, its variations, and the possibilities of contextual analyses leading to useful inferences. I will have reason to revisit this matter as I go forward, but here I can point to the meticulous attention Masson and colleagues have paid to fitting ceramic effigy fragments back together, now a broadly agree-upon practice in ascertaining the behavior responsible for the deposits. First, the deposits of human remains show little evidence that effigies were carefully broken and sprinkled in contrast to the leave taking of the Hall and Oratory. Mass graves reflecting likely sacrificial events are reported elsewhere in the Maya world going back well into the Early Classic period, and surface deposits elsewhere, such as at El Perú–Waka' discussed below, contain some human remains, but the Itzmal Ch'en deposit suggests a major political and religious event that presaged or triggered the abandonment of this important ceremonial center. That the event occurred well before the historically related abandonment of Mayapán sustains Masson and her colleagues' observation that this regional capital suffered repeated crises and upheavals in its history. Macabre memorialization of massacre and political struggle does not signal imminent collapse in all cases, and did not in this one. I am intrigued by the selective removal of the faces of effigies in the case of the Oratory and Hall, and the evident piling of broken god parts along with the sprinkling. The faces are just about the size of masks held by Classic period scribes, gods and diviners, in painted vase scenes that can possibly signal divining (Freidel et al. 2017), and the action registered in the mask holding is "to order, to arrange, to shape, to mold," which involves the arrangement of diving tokens into piles. What if the terminal deposits here, thought to be part of a single extensive ceremony, laid out a final prophecy associated with abandonment?

Stanley Guenter in his audacious and engaging chapter 13, on Copán Stela 11 and Katun 8 Ahau, suggests that King Yax Pasaj was prophesizing the end of his realm and linking that catastrophe to the demise of Teotihuacan as a great power and also to the collapse of the Preclassic state of El Mirador as also occurring on 8 Ahau dates. The development of the field has significantly transformed the possibilities of interpreting this fascinating small monument from the time Linda addressed it in our book. We regarded the Copán king as deceased, one reason being that he has the torch of K'awiil in his forehead and K'inich Janaab Pakal of Palenque has such a torch on his sarcophagus when

**FIGURE 14.1.** *Yuknoom Ch'een the Great as K'awiil on El Perú–Waka' Stela 20 (photo by Phil Hofstetter).*

he is not only deceased, but resurrecting. However, as Stanley pointed out to me some time ago, El Perú–Waka' Stela 20 depicts a ruler with a large K'awiil torch in his headdress and the one preserved text on it gives the birthday of Kaanul king Yuknoom Ch'een the Great (figure 14.1). It is therefore likely that the person portrayed on this monument is the same king, who was still quite alive at the time in AD 682. And he is quite right to suggest that the association of disaster with Katun 8 Ahaw, as seen in Postclassic and Contact–period Yucatecan prophecy is worth exploring as a reference to earlier history and prophecy. Personally I am persuaded that the Chi Altar place is El Mirador as Stan proposes and that this greatest city of the Preclassic period was the legendary place of the birth and resurrection of the Maize God for the lowland Maya, a place Christophe Helmke and Felix Kupprat (2016) call Kaanul.

Another powerful place referenced on Copán Stela 11 is Wite' Naah. Linda thought this referenced dynastic founding, but as Stanley reviews in his chapter it is now generally agreed to be a building or a kind of building, with the original one located at Teotihuacan—the Pyramid of the Sun according to Fash and his colleagues (2009). While Stanley suggests that this place might encompass all of Teotihuacan and that Stela 11 would describe the demise of that metropolis, I think that the weight of evidence suggests that it is a kind of edifice because there are very likely several buildings or building locales in the Maya world that are also referenced as *wite' naah*, including the Structure 10L-16 locality at Copán (Taube 2004c). There is another edifice or locality at El Perú–Waka' that is referenced as wite' naah on El Perú–Waka' Stela 15. The text of that monument, as analyzed by David Stuart (2000) and also by Stanley (Freidel et al. 2007) makes it likely that Kaloomte' Sihyaj K'ahk' carried out a ritual in a *wite* (?) place that is local and not in highland Mexico since this event immediately follows his arrival at El Perú–Waka'.

Olivia Navarro-Farr and her colleagues focus their attention on the main temple at El Perú–Waka', locality of the commemorative *wite' naah*, and on two remarkable women who ruled there in the sixth and seventh centuries AD. Since I have worked closely with these archaeologists I am in agreement with their arguments, though they happily expand their interpretations beyond my own in ongoing discussions. It is the case that Linda and I struggled with the complexities of Classic regional politics, especially in chapter 5 of our book, and touched on matters of sustained and contemporary concern in the forest of overlap between textual history and archaeology. I very much support the centrality of Queen Ikoom Sak Wayis of the sixth century and Queen K'abel of the seventh and early eighth centuries to both of the cult of the wite' naah at the site and to governance of the realm of Waka'. Since the wite' naah at Waka' was founded by Kaloomte' Sihyaj K'ahk' and his vassal king K'inich Bahlam I, Waka' was surely a New Order kingdom allied with Tikal and other vassals of the Teotihuacan lords Sihyaj K'ahk' and his king Spearthrower Owl. But while these men are highlighted early on, it is clear that the Moon Goddess was one of the three tutelary gods of the realm as identified by Stanley Guenter on Stela 16, the monument depicting Sihyaj K'ahk' posthumously in AD 460. The Moon Goddess is again conjured along with her fellow deities on Stela 44 in AD 564 by deceased king Chak Tok Ich'aak of El Perú–Waka'. The focus on the Moon goddess is, in my view, a harbinger of the role of powerful queens in the cult of the wite' naah at El Perú–Waka' and perhaps elsewhere in the Maya world such as Yaxchilán (Karen Bassie, personal communication, 2012).

I am particularly intrigued by Queen K'abel because she carried the *kaloomte'* title in AD 692 at the height of the city's glory. It seems almost certain that she would have acquired this title from her father and not from her younger brother when he acceded to the throne in AD 687. While we lack epigraphic proof of the matter, it seems highly likely that she, a Kaanul ajaw, was always superior to her husband, as Navarro-Farr and colleagues suggest (see chapter

5). Did she carry the kaloomte' title during Yuknoom Ch'een's reign? On El Perú–Waka' Stela 20 Yuknoom Ch'een's birthday in AD 600 is prominently celebrated, presumably by his daughter K'abel and her husband. Personal information of this kind is extremely rare on Kaanul regime texts, which make reference to kin relations at La Corona. Birth statements formally link to accession statements at Palenque on the Panel of the Cross, for example, and it seems possible that the prominence of Yuknoom Ch'een's birth here signals his accession to a higher title. The anchoring calendar date is AD 682, when he was in his eighties but four years before his death. The personage on that stela, very likely Yuknoom Ch'een himself, wears a large K'awiil torch in his headdress as pointed out to me by Stanley Guenter. While this could signal a posthumous portrait, it is the case that Yuknoom Ch'een was referred to as K'awiil by his successor Yuknoom Yich'aak K'ahk' and also by the last great Kaanul king Yuknoom Ti' (Martin 2005). If he innovated the title K'awiil for himself and authorized to be celebrated at El Perú–Waka' in AD 682 following his triumph over Tikal and all of central Petén, he may have elevated his daughter K'abel to the kaloomte' status as his direct agent over the consolidation of western Petén under Kaanul regime authority. No doubt K'abel and K'inich Bahlam II acknowledged her brother Yich'aak K'ahk' as the new Kaanul king and kaloomte' in 687 and again in 692. Christophe Helmke and Jaime Awe (2016a) suggest that K'awiil in the case at hand may have signaled "authority" as a political title distinct from its clear reference to a god, and, as Linda and I elaborated in *Maya Cosmos*, to the capacity of soul force to move through material forms such as the poetic conjuring of K'awiil conjoined with flint-shield on Lintel 25 at Yaxchilán. Actually, I think that the theonymic meanings of K'awiil are in accord with the political meanings they suggest. The clear focus of Kaanul regime patrons of the Codex Painted King List vessels (Martin 2016) on the grasping of K'awiil as a declaration of rulership, as noted by Helmke and Awe, may signal that this transformation of people into divine kings is paramount over other considerations such as lineal descent from a previous king. For Yuknoom Ch'een to declare himself the living embodiment of this authority makes perfect sense to me as an innovative imperial title, particularly in light of his documented acquisition of paramount rulership through defeat of his rival Waxaklajuun Ubaah Kan of Dzibanché and not through lineal succession from the previous king (Helmke and Awe 2016a).

I am very proud to be associated with the archaeologists represented in this book who have trained with me—such as Travis Stanton, Olivia Navarro-Farr, and Stanley Guenter—and like Michelle Rich and Keith Eppich, who in chapter 6 focus on major interments and their occupants at El Perú–Waka'.

These seventh-century tombs, one in the Early Classic frontal platform of a major pyramid on the Mirador, or Temple Acropolis, hill; and the other in a smaller temple on a small ridge to the west of it in what Keith Eppich (2017) felicitously calls the "last palace," are clearly connected as they argue through meticulous consideration of ceramics and other artifacts. In particular, the elaborately slipped black background and orange glyph drinking cups featuring heads of the god K'awiil are a distinctive court ware of Waka'. I favor the idea that the cup in Burial 39, which names Bahlam Tz'am as a ruler, is the personal "breath" cup (see Fitzsimmons 2009:28–30; Freidel and Guenter 2006; Scherer 2015:56–57) of the deceased.

Rich and Eppich leave the matter of the sex of the deceased in this royal tomb, and also in the "Last Palace" tomb, open in light of the absence of clear determination from the remains. While it is intriguing to envision a great queen on the Mirador hill, there are no queen's names on the ten inscribed vessels in the tomb while there are some four royal names that appear to reference kings. Here again we are in the forest with epigraphy and archaeology. With Eppich's remarkable ongoing research in the "Last Palace," dubbed the Chok Group for purposes of nomenclature, I am increasingly confident that the person in his tomb served as a high priest(ess) to the cult linking the Mirador hill temples to the main city temple discussed by Navarro-Farr and her colleagues in chapter 5. Whoever this person in Burial 38 was, she/he grasped "K'awiil" with this ornamented and inscribed drinking cup and poured sweet breath, an aspect of soul force, into it as did the king/queen in Burial 39 on the hill above. The interred in Burial 39 had a second drinking cup lacking glyphs, and therefore not personalized. Kaloomte' K'abel in Burial 61 in the Fire Shrine of the city had a beautiful K'awiil drinking cup with just a Primary Standard Sequence inscribed on it. So, the black background and orange glyph cup in Burial 39 was special, as was its companion in Burial 38 with its text unfortunately entirely unreadable. If I am right that these cups were personal to the two people, then the interred in Burial 39 was Bahlam Tz'am, ancestor and namesake to the last great king of Waka', King Bahlam Tz'am, successor of Kaloomte' K'abel and K'inich Bahlam II (r. <728–743 AD). The person in Burial 38 must have been an intimate companion, like the *sajal* of the Yaxchilán kings.

K'awiil became a title with Yuknoom Ch'een the Great, and Charles Golden and Andrew Scherer delve deeply into this domain of spiritually charged titles in chapter 7, on Yaxchilán's king Bird Jaguar IV and his sajal (both singular and plural) in an elegantly articulated argument for the way that Classic Maya courtiers thought about the transformation of people into rulers. This process involved the creation, through ritual actions, of the rulers as beings charged with supernatural power. Initiations, transformations, are universally featured in divine rulership and certainly are well attested in the Maya case. Golden and Scherer show how *sajal* were wrought, particularly their essential beings as manifest in face (*baah*), and how, in turn, they contributed through visual witnessing and participation in rituals, to the power of their overlords. I argued in an effort called *Ajaw as Idea and Artifact* (Freidel 1992b) that rulers were made by their people along with the buildings and insignia that they crafted for them. Golden and Scherer have taken this view a quantum leap forward, synthesizing advances made by David Stuart, Stephen Houston, and Karl Taube regarding the body and personhood in Maya thought into their vision of the relational bonds between the hierarchically arranged powerful office holders of Maya governments. I especially like their application of this vision to the category of war captives. Their notion that war captives are stripped of their regalia and hence of their persona as powerful beings, is entirely commensurate with a range of material referents, including the depicted and archaeologically attested literal defacement of captives (Mock 1998) and the wide practice of defacing and stripping stelae, also acts of war. That the Maya literally embodied people in stone portraits is consistent with the close analyses by Stuart and Houston (1994) of texts and images and with many documented archaeological contexts of destroyed and manipulated monuments.

War and its consequences are themes of Arlen and Diane Chase's bold synthesis and review, in chapter 3, of the role of Caracol's greatest kings in the struggles of Late Classic Petén. Linda and I covered this subject in our book, but through dedicating their careers to researching this key city the Chases have vastly augmented the record. At the same time, the discovery of new blocks from the glorious history King Kan II commissioned and likely set atop Caana (Helmke and Awe 2016b) has firmly placed him and his father in the center court of the great wars pitting the Kaanul regime against Tikal and its allies. The really audacious argument in this chapter is the hypothesis that King Yajaw Te' K'inich and Kan II ruled Tikal and were buried there in Tikal burials 196 and 23 respectively. Here we really are in that forest of questions where the overlap between text-based history and archaeology is contested as well as mutually tested. An easy agreement over the nature of the beast—how to envision our mammoth in the room, in this particular case—is not likely. The Chases marshal an array of arguments—from the presence of a Caracol royal epithet in Burial 195 to the large Caracol style red dot on the capstones of Burial 23, and from the evidence that the interred individuals did not grow up at Tikal to the Caracol style of ceramic offerings—to make their case. Moreover, they did not find tombs of kings in their extensive excavations of Caana, only queens. If they are right, then Caracol appropriated the dynastic succession of Tikal with kings from the twenty-second to the thirty-third successors. This in itself would be astonishing but not a major rethinking of dynasty there, for we have good reason to believe that the Tikal line of succession witnessed interlopers before the twenty-second king. Truly unsettling would be the prospect that the Caracol kings would continue to write history and raise monuments at Caracol while they ruled at Tikal and raised none there during the famous hiatus. The basic problem with their proposal is that we have clear names for the twenty-second successor, and at least one of his progeny, the twenty-third or twenty-fourth successor, and they are none of them the names of the Caracol kings. These texts are few and far between, but real, both on stone and other media such as painted ceramics. For those Caracol kings to rule by different names at two different royal capitals is beyond belief in light of known practices in the ancient history. Those practices are now quite well documented, even as the burgeoning corps of epigraphers continues to make new discoveries of many kinds and even as I content myself to challenge the consensus on matters such as dynasty versus sodality. I think Linda would be delighted with such arguments were she here to witness them, and pleased by the production of this book. I certainly am.

Acuña, Mary Jane. 2014. Royal Alliances, Ritual Behavior, and the Abandonment of the Royal Couple Building at El Perú-*Waka'*. In *Archaeology at El Perú-Waka': Performances of Ritual, Memory, and Power*, edited by O. Navarro-Farr and M. Rich, 53–65. University of Arizona Press, Tucson.

Adams, R.E.W. 1999. *Rio Azul: An Ancient Maya City*. University of Oklahoma Press, Norman.

Adams, Robert M., Jr. 1953. Some Small Ceremonial Structures at Mayapan. In *Current Reports* 9, 144–179. Carnegie Institution of Washington, Department of Archaeology, Washington, DC.

Agurcia Fasquelle, Ricardo, and Barbara W. Fash. 2005. The Evolution of Structure 10L-16, Heart of the Copán Acropolis. In *Copán: The History of an Ancient Maya Kingdom*, edited by E. W. Andrews and W. L. Fash, 201–238. School of American Research Press, Santa Fe.

Alcina Franch, José, Miguel León Portilla, and Eduardo Matos Moctezuma. 1992. *Azteca Mexica*. Lunwerg Editores, S.A., Madrid.

Alcock, Susan E. 2002. *Archaeologies of the Greek Past: Landscape, Monuments, and Memories*. Cambridge University Press, Cambridge.

Aldana, Gerardo. 2005. Agency and the "Star War" Glyph: A Historical Reassessment of Classic Maya Astrology and Warfare. *Ancient Mesoamerica* 16(2):305–320.

Ambrosino, James N. 2003. The Function of a Maya Palace at Yaxuna: A Contextual Approach. In *Maya Palaces*

DOI: 10.5876/9781646420469.c015

*and Elite Residences: An Interdisciplinary Approach*, edited by J. J. Christie, 253–273. University of Texas Press, Austin.

Ambrosino, James N. 2007. Warfare and Destruction in the Maya Lowlands: Pattern and Process Archaeological Record of Yaxuna, Yucatan, Mexico. Unpublished PhD dissertation. Department of Anthropology, Southern Methodist University, Dallas.

Ambrosino, James N., Traci Ardren, and Kam Manahan. 2001. Fortificaciones defensivos en Yaxuná, Yucatán. In *Yucatán a través de los siglos*, edited by R. Gubler and P. Martel, 49–66. Universidad Autónoma de Yucatán, Mérida.

Ambrosino, James N., Traci Ardren, and Travis W. Stanton. 2003. The History of Warfare at Yaxuná. In *Ancient Mesoamerican Warfare*, edited by M. K. Brown and T. W. Stanton, 109–123. AltaMira Press, Walnut Creek, CA.

Anderson, Patricia K. 1998. Yula, Yucatan, Mexico: Terminal Classic Maya Ceramic Chronology for the Chichen Itza Area. *Ancient Mesoamerica* 9(1):151–165.

Andrews Anthony P., and Fernando Robles Castellanos. 1985. Chichen Itza and Coba: An Itza-Maya Standoff in Early Postclassic Yucatan. In *The Lowland Maya Postclassic*, edited by A. F. Chase and P. M. Rice, 62–72. University of Texas Press, Austin.

Andrews, E. Wyllys, IV, and George E. Stuart. 1968. The Ruins of Ikil, Yucatan, Mexico. In *Middle American Research Institute, Pub. 31*, 69–80. Tulane University, New Orleans.

Andrews, E. Wyllys, V. 1988. Ceramic Units from Komchen, Yucatan, Mexico. *Cerámica de Cultura Maya* 15:51–64.

Andrews, E. Wyllys, V, and William L. Fash, eds. 2005. *Copán: The History of an Ancient Maya Kingdom*. School of American Research, Santa Fe, New Mexico.

Andrews, E. Wyllys, V, William M. Ringle, Philip J. Barnes, Alfredo Barrera Rubio, and Tomás Gallareta Negrón. 1984. Komchen: An Early Maya Community in Northwest Yucatán. In *Investigaciones recientes en el área maya: XVII Mesa Redonda, Sociedad Mexicana de Antropología, Sn. Cristóbal de Las Casas, Chiapas, 21–27 Junio 1981, Tomo I*, 73–92. Sociedad Mexicana de Antropología, Chiapas.

Aoyama, Kazuo. 2005. Classic Maya Warfare and Weapons: Spear, Dart, and Arrow Points of Aguateca and Copan. *Ancient Mesoamerica* 16(2):229–247.

Ardren, Traci. 1999. Palace Termination Rituals at Yaxuna, Yucatan, Mexico. In *Land of the Turkey and the Deer*, edited by R. Gubler, 25–36. Labyrinthos, Lancaster.

Ardren, Traci, ed. 2002. *Ancient Maya Women*. AltaMira Press, Walnut Creek, CA.

Ardren, Traci. 2011. Empowered Children in Classic Maya Sacrificial Rites. *Childhood in the Past* 4(1):133–145.

Ardren, Traci, T. Kam Manahan, Julie K. Wesp, and Alejandra Alonso. 2010. Cloth Production and Economic Intensification in the Area Surrounding Chichen Itza. *Latin American Antiquity* 21(3):274–289.

Ashmore, Wendy, ed. 1981. *Lowland Maya Settlement Patterns*. University of New Mexico Press, Albuquerque.

Ashmore, Wendy. 1991. Site-Planning Principles and Concepts of Directionality among the Ancient Maya. *Latin American Antiquity* 2(3):199–225.

Ashmore, Wendy. 2007. *Settlement Archaeology at Quirigua, Guatemala. Quiriguá Reports.* Vol. 4. Museum Monographs, 126. University of Pennsylvania Museum, Philadelphia.

Ashmore, Wendy. 2009. Biographies of Place at Quiriguá, Guatemala. In *The Archaeology of Meaningful Places*, edited by Brenda Bowser and María Nieves Zedeño, 15–31. University of Utah Press, Salt Lake City.

Ashmore, Wendy. 2013. Mobile Bodies, Empty Spaces. In *The Dead Tell Tales: Jane Buikstra and Narratives of the Past*, edited by Maria Cecilia Lozada and Barra Ó Donnabháin, 106–113. Cotsen Institute of Archaeology, Los Angeles.

Ashmore, Wendy. 2015. Contingent Acts of Remembrance: Royal Ancestors of Classic Maya Copán and Quirigua. *Ancient Mesoamerica* 26(2):213–231.

Avendaño y Loyola, Fray Andrés de. 1987. *Relation of Two Trips to Petén*. Translated by Charles P. Bowditch and Guillermo Rivera. Edited and with Notes by Frank Comparato. Labyrinthos, Culver City, CA.

Aztzin Martinez, De Luna Lucha. 2005. *Murals and the Development of Merchant Activity at Chichen Itza*. Published MA thesis. Department of Anthropology, Brigham Young University, Provo.

Bacon, Wendy. 2007. The Dwarf Motif in Classic Maya Monumental Iconography: A Spatial Analysis. Unpublished PhD dissertation. Department of Anthropology, University of Pennsylvania, Philadelphia.

Ball, Joseph W. 1974. A Teotihuacan-Style Cache from the Maya Lowlands. *Archaeology* 27(1):2–9.

Ball, Joseph W. 1993. Pottery, Potters, and Polities: Some Socioeconomic and Political Implications of Late Classic Maya Ceramic Industries. In *Lowland Maya Civilization in the Eighth Century AD*, edited by J. A. Sabloff and J. S. Henderson, 243–272. Dumbarton Oaks, Washington, DC.

Baron, Joanne P. 2013. Patrons of La Corona: Deities and Power in a Classic Maya Community. Unpublished PhD dissertation. Department of Anthropology, University of Pennsylvania, Philadelphia.

Baron, Joanne P. 2016a. *Patron Gods and Patron Lords: The Semiotics of Classic Maya Community Cults*. University of Colorado Press, Boulder.

Baron, Joanne P. 2016b. Patron Deities and Politics among the Classic Maya. In *Political Strategies in Pre-Columbian Mesoamerica*, edited by S. Kurnick and J. Baron, 121–152. University Press of Colorado, Boulder.

Barrera Vásquez, Alfredo. 1980. *Diccionario Cordemex: Maya-Español, Español-Maya*. Cordemex, Mérida, Yucatán.

Barrera Vásquez, Alfredo, and Sylvanus G. Morley. 1949. *The Maya Chronicles.* Carnegie Institution of Washington, Pub. 585, Contribution, No. 48. Carnegie Institution of Washington, Washington, DC.

Barrera Vásquez, Alfredo, and Silvia Rendón. 1948. *El Libro de los libros de Chilam Balam.* Fondo de Cultura Económica, Mexico City.

Baudez, Claude F. 1994. *Maya Sculpture of Copán: The Iconography.* University of Oklahoma Press, Norman.

Baudez, Claude F. 1999. Los templos enmascarados de Yucatán. *Arqueología Mexicana* 7(37):54–59.

Baudez, Claude F., and Anne S. Dowd. 1983. La decoración de Templo 18. In *Introducción a la arqueología de Copán, Tomo II*, 447–500, edited by C. F. Baudez, 447–500. Secretaría de Estado en el Despacho de Cultura y Turismo, Tegucigalpa.

Becker, Marshall J. 1973. Archaeological Evidence for Occupational Specialization among the Classic Period Maya at Tikal, Guatemala. *American Antiquity* 38(4):372–376.

Becker, Marshall J. 1983. Indications of Social Class Differences Based on the Archaeological Evidence for Occupational Specialization among the Classic Maya at Tikal, Guatemala. *Revista Española de Antropología Americana* 8:29–46.

Beetz, Carl P., and Linton Satterthwaite. 1981. *The Monuments and Inscriptions of Caracol, Belize.* University Museum Monograph 45. University Museum, University of Pennsylvania, Philadelphia.

Bell, Ellen E., Marcello A. Canuto, and Robert J. Sharer, eds. 2004a. *Understanding Early Classic Copan.* University of Pennsylvania Museum of Archaeology and Anthropology, Philadelphia.

Bell, Ellen E., Robert J. Sharer, Loa P. Traxler, David W. Sedat, Christine W. Carrelli, and Lynn A. Grant. 2004b. Tombs and Burials in the Early Classic Acropolis at Copan. In *Understanding Early Classic Copan*, edited by E. E. Bell, M. A. Canuto, and R. J. Sharer, 131–157. University of Pennsylvania Museum of Archaeology and Anthropology, Philadelphia.

Berlin, Heinrich. 1958. El glifo "emblema" en las inscripciones mayas. *Journal de la Société des Américanistes* 47:111–119.

Berlin, Heinrich. 1959. Glifos nominales en el sarcófago de Palenque: Un ensayo. *Humanidades* 2(1):1–8.

Berlin, Heinrich. 1977. *Signos y significados en las inscripciones maya.* Instituto Nacional del Patrimonio Cultura, Ministerio de Educación Pública, Guatemala City.

Berlo, Janet C. 1976. Platelet Headdresses among the Classic Maya: A Study in Form and Social Meaning. Unpublished manuscript in possession of the author.

Berlo, Janet C. 1983. The Warrior and the Butterfly: Central Mexican Ideologies of Sacred Warfare and Teotihuacan Iconography. In *Text and Image in*

*Pre-Columbian Art*, edited by J. C. Berlo, 179–117. BAR International Series 180, Oxford.

Berlo, Janet C. 1984. *Teotihuacan Art Abroad: A Study of Metropolitan Style and Provincial Transformation in Incensario Workshops*. BAR International Series 199, Oxford.

Beutelspacher, Carlos R. 1988. *Las mariposas entre los antiguos mexicanos*. Fondo de Cultura Económica, Mexico City.

Bey, George J., III, and William M. Ringle. 2007. From the Bottom Up: The Timing and Nature of the Tula—Chichén Itzá Exchange. In *Twin Tollans: Chichén Itzá, Tula, and the Epiclassic to Early Postclassic Mesoamerican World*, edited by J. K. Kowalski and C. Kristan-Graham, 376–427. Dumbarton Oaks Research Library and Collection, Washington, DC.

Bierhorst, John. 1985. *Cantares Mexicanos: Songs of the Aztecs*. Stanford University Press, Stanford, CA.

Bierhorst, John. 1992. *History and Mythology of the Aztecs: The Codex Chimalpopoca*. University of Arizona Press, Tucson.

Bíró, Péter. 2003. The Inscriptions on Two Lintels of Ikil and the Realm of Ek' Bahlam. Manuscript. Accessed March 18, 2013. www.mesoweb.com/features/biro /Ikil.pdf.

Bíró, Péter. 2011. Piedras Negras Panel 3: Some Thoughts on Spoken Words. *Indiana* 28:291–313.

Bishop, Ronald L., M. James Blackman, Erin L. Sears, William J. Folan, and Donald W. Forsyth. 2006. Observaciones iniciales sobre el consumo de la cerámica de Champotón. In *Los Investigadores de la Cultura Maya 14*, 137–145. Universidad Autónoma de Campeche, Campeche, Mexico.

Blackman, M. James, and Ronald L. Bishop. 2007. The Smithsonian—NIST Partnership: The Application of Instrumental Neutron Activation Analysis to Archaeology. *Archaeometry* 49(2):321–341.

Borowicz, James. 2003. Images of Power and the Power of Images: Early Classic Iconographic Programs of the Carved Monuments of Tikal. In *The Maya and Teotihuacan: Reinterpreting Early Classic Interaction*, edited by G. E. Braswell, 217–234. University of Texas Press, Austin.

Bourdieu, Pierre. 1977. *Outline of a Theory of Practice*. Cambridge University Press, Cambridge.

Brainerd, George W. 1958. *The Archaeological Ceramics of Yucatan*. Anthropological Records, vol. 19. University of California, Berkeley.

Braswell, Geoffrey E. 2003a. Introduction: Reinterpreting Early Classic Interaction. In *The Maya and Teotihuacan: Reinterpreting Early Classic Interaction*, edited by G. E. Braswell, 1–43. University of Texas Press, Austin.

Braswell, Geoffrey E. 2003b. Understanding Early Classic Interaction between Kaminaljuyu and Central Mexico. In *The Maya and Teotihuacan: Reinterpreting Early Classic Interaction*, edited by G. E. Braswell, 105–142. University of Texas Press, Austin.

Braswell, Geoffrey E., ed. 2003c. *The Maya and Teotihuacan: Reinterpreting Early Classic Interaction*. University of Texas Press, Austin.

Braswell, Geoffrey E. 2010. The Rise and Fall of Market Exchange: A Dynamic Approach to Ancient Maya Economy. In *Archaeological Approaches to Market Exchange in Ancient Societies*, edited by C. P. Garraty and B. L. Stark, 127–140. University Press of Colorado, Boulder.

Braswell, Geoffrey E. 2012. The Ancient Maya of Mexico: Reinterpreting the Past of the Northern Maya Lowlands. In *The Ancient Maya of Mexico: Reinterpreting the Past of the Northern Maya Lowlands*, edited by G. E. Braswell, 1–40. Equinox Publishing, Ltd., Bristol, CT.

Braswell, Geoffrey E., and Nancy Peniche May. 2012. In the Shadow of the Pyramid: Excavations of the Great Platform of Chichen Itza. In *The Ancient Maya of Mexico: Reinterpreting the Past of the Northern Maya Lowlands*, edited by G. E. Braswell, 229–263. Equinox Publishing, Bristol, CT.

Buikstra, Jane E., T. Douglas Price, Lori E. Wright, and James A. Burton. 2004. Tombs from the Copan Acropolis: A Life-History Approach. In *Understanding Early Classic Copan*, edited by E. E. Bell, M. A. Canuto, and R. J. Sharer, 191–212. University of Pennsylvania Museum of Archaeology and Anthropology, Philadelphia.

Buikstra, Jane, and Douglas Ubelaker, eds. 1994. *Standards for Data Collection from Human Skeletal Remains*. Arkansas Archaeological Survey Research Series no. 44. Arkansas Archaeological Survey, Fayetteville.

Buttles, Palma J., and Fred Valdez. 2016. Sociopolitical Manifestations of the Terminal Classic: Colha, Northern Belize, as a Case Study. In *Ritual, Violence, and the Fall of the Classic Maya Kings*, edited by G. Iannone, B. A. Houk, and S. A. Schwake, 187–202. University of Florida Press, Gainesville.

Cagnato, Clarissa. 2015. A Paleoethnobotanical Study of Two Classic Maya Sites, El Perú-*Waka'* and La Corona. Unpublished PhD dissertation. Department of Anthropology, Washington University, St. Louis.

Cagnato, Clarissa, Buttles, Palma J., and Fred Valdez. 2013. Análisis paleoetnobotánico de las muestras exportadas de la Temporada 2012. In *Proyecto Arqueológico El Perú-Waka': Informe No. 11, Temporada 2013*, edited by Juan Carlos Pérez Calderón, 179–191. Instituto de Antropología e Historia, Guatemala City.

Calvin, Inga E. 1994. Images of Supernaturals on Classic Period Maya Ceramics: An Examination of Way Creatures. Unpublished MA thesis, University of Colorado, Denver.

Calvin, Inga E. 1997. Where the Wayob Live: A Further Examination of Classic Maya Supernaturals. In *Maya Vase Book 5: A Corpus of Rollout Photographs of Maya Vases*, edited by B. Kerr and J. Kerr, 868–883. Kerr Associates, New York.

Canuto, Marcello A. 2004. The Rural Settlement of Copan: Changes through the Early Classic. In *Understanding Early Classic Copan*, edited by E. E. Bell, M. A. Canuto, and R. J. Sharer, 29–50. University of Pennsylvania Museum of Archaeology and Anthropology, Philadelphia.

Canuto, Marcello A., and Anthony P. Andrews. 2008. Memory, Meanings, and Historical Awareness: Post-Abandonment Behaviors among the Lowland Maya. In *Ruins of the Past: The Use and Perception of Abandoned Structures in the Maya Lowlands*, edited by T. W. Stanton and A. Magnoni, 257–273. University Press of Colorado, Boulder.

Canuto, Marcello A., and Tomás Barrientos Q. 2013. The Importance of La Corona. *La Corona Notes* 1(1):1–5.

Canuto, Marcello A., and Ellen E. Bell. 2003. Classic Maya Borders and Frontiers: Excavations at El Paraíso, Copán, Honduras, 2003 Season. Report Submitted to the Foundation for the Advancement of Mesoamerican Research, Crystal River, FL.

Carmack, Robert M. 1981. *The Quiche Mayas of Utatlán*. University of Oklahoma Press, Norman.

Carr, R. F, and J. E. Hazard. 1961. *Map of the Ruins of Tikal, El Peten, Guatemala*. Tikal Report 11. University of Pennsylvania Museum, Philadelphia.

Carrasco, Davíd, Lindsay Jones, and Scott Sessions, eds. 2000. *Mesoamerica's Classic Heritage: From Teotihuacan to the Aztecs*. University Press of Colorado, Boulder.

Carrasco Vargas, Ramón. 2000. Tumbas reales de Calakmul: Ritos funerarios y estructura de poder. *Arqueología Mexicana* 7(40):28–31.

Carrasco Vargas, Ramón, Sylviane Boucher, Paula Álvarez González, Vera Tiesler Blos, Valeria Garcia Vierna, Renata Garcia Moreno, and Javier Vázquez Negrete. 1999. A Dynastic Tomb from Campeche, Mexico: New Evidence on Jaguar Paw, a Ruler from Calakmul. *Latin American Antiquity* 10(1):47–58.

Castañeda, Francisco. 2013. Monumentos del Perú-*Waka'*: Nuevos hallazgos. In *Proyecto Arqueológico El Perú-Waka': Informe No. 11, Temporada 2013*, edited by Juan Carlos Pérez Calderón, 192–191. Instituto de Antropología e Historia, Guatemala City.

Ceballos Gallareta, Teresa, and Fernando Robles Castellanos. 2012. Las etapas más tempranas de la alfarería maya en al noroeste de la península de Yucatán. *Ancient Mesoamerica* 23(2):403–419.

Chase, Arlen F. 1991. Cycles of Time: Caracol in the Maya Realm. In *Sixth Palenque Round Table, 1986*, edited by M. Greene Robertson and V. G. Fields, 32–42. University of Oklahoma Press, Norman.

Chase, Arlen F. 1994. A Contextual Approach to the Ceramics of Caracol, Belize. In *Studies in the Archaeology of Caracol, Belize,* edited by D. Z. Chase and A. F. Chase, 157–182. Monograph 7. Pre-Columbian Art Research Institute, San Francisco.

Chase, Arlen F., and Diane Z. Chase. 1987. *Investigations at the Classic Maya City of Caracol, Belize: 1985–1987.* Pre-Columbian Art Research Institute, San Francisco.

Chase, Arlen F., and Diane Z. Chase. 1989. The Investigation of Classic Period Maya Warfare at Caracol, Belize. *Mayab* 5:5–18.

Chase, Arlen F., and Diane Z. Chase. 1994. Maya Veneration of the Dead at Caracol, Belize. In *Seventh Palenque Round Table, 1989,* edited by M. Greene Robertson and V. G. Fields, 55–62. Pre-Columbian Art Research Institute, San Francisco.

Chase, Arlen F., and Diane Z. Chase. 1996. The Organization and Composition of Classic Lowland Maya Society: The View from Caracol, Belize. In *Eighth Palenque Round Table, 1993,* edited by M. J. Macri, and J. McHargue, 213–222. Pre-Columbian Art Research Institute, San Francisco.

Chase, Arlen F., and Diane Z. Chase. 1998. Late Classic Maya Political Structure, Polity Size, and Warfare Arenas. In *Anatomía de una civilización: Aproximaciones interdisciplinarias a la Cultura Maya,* edited by A. Ciudad Ruiz, Y. Fernández Marquínez, J. M. García Campillo, M. J. Iglesias Ponce de León, A. Lacandena García-Gallo, and L. T. Sanz Castro., 11–29. Sociedad Española de Estudios Mayas, Madrid.

Chase, Arlen F., and Diane Z. Chase. 2001a. Ancient Maya Causeways and Site Organization at Caracol, Belize. *Ancient Mesoamerica* 12(2):273–281.

Chase, Arlen F., and Diane Z. Chase. 2001b. The Royal Court of Caracol, Belize: Its Palaces and People. In *Royal Courts of the Ancient Maya.* Vol. 2: *Data and Case Studies,* edited by T. Inomata and S. D. Houston, 102–137. Westview Press, Boulder.

Chase, Arlen F., and Diane Z. Chase. 2003. Minor Centers, Complexity, and Scale in Lowland Maya Settlement Archaeology. In *Perspectives on Ancient Maya Rural Complexity,* edited by G. Iannone and S. V. Connell, 108–118. Monograph 49. Cotsen Institute of Archaeology, University of California, Los Angeles.

Chase, Arlen F., and Diane Z. Chase. 2009. Symbolic Egalitarianism and Homogenized Distributions in the Archaeological Record at Caracol, Belize: Method, Theory, and Complexity. *Research Reports in Belizean Archaeology* 6:15–24.

Chase, Arlen F., Diane Z. Chase, Jaime J. Awe, John F. Weishampel, Gyles Iannone, Holley Moyes, Jason Yaeger, and M. Kathryn Brown. 2014. The Use of LiDAR in Understanding the Ancient Maya Landscape: Caracol and Western Belize. *Advances in Archaeological Practice* 2(3):147–160.

Chase, Arlen F., Diane Z. Chase, Richard Terry, Jacob M. Horlacher, and Adrian S. Z. Chase. 2015. Markets among the Ancient Maya: The Case of Caracol, Belize. *The Ancient Maya Marketplace: The Archaeology of Transient Space,* edited by E. King, 226–250. University of Arizona Press, Tucson.

Chase, Arlen F., Diane Z. Chase, John F. Weishampel, Jason B. Drake, Ramesh L. Shrestha, K. Clint Slatton, Jaime J. Awe, and William E. Carter. 2011. Airborne LiDAR, Archaeology, and the Ancient Maya Landscape at Caracol, Belize. *Journal of Archaeological Science* 38(2):387–398.

Chase, Diane Z. 1985. Ganned but Not Forgotten: Late Postclassic Archaeology and Ritual at Santa Rita Corozal. In *The Lowland Maya Postclassic*, edited by A. F. Chase and P. M. Rice, 104–125. University of Texas Press, Austin.

Chase, Diane Z. 1986. Social and Political Organization in the Land of Cacao and Honey: Correlating the Archaeology and Ethnohistory of the Postclassic Lowland Maya. In *Late Lowland Maya Civilization*, edited by J. A. Sabloff and E. W. Andrews V, 347–377. University of New Mexico Press, Albuquerque.

Chase, Diane Z. 1988. Caches and Cerswares: Meaning from Maya Pottery. In *A Pot for All Reasons: Ceramic Ecology Revisited*, edited by C. C. Kolb and L. M. Lackey, 81–104. Cerámica de Cultura Maya, Garrison Printing Company, Philadelphia.

Chase, Diane Z. 1992. Postclassic Maya Elites: Ethnohistory and Archaeology. In *Mesoamerican Elites: An Archaeological Assessment*, edited by D. Z. Chase and A. F. Chase, 118–134. University of Oklahoma Press, Norman.

Chase, Diane Z. 1994. Human Osteology, Pathology, and Demography as Represented in the Burials of Caracol, Belize. In *Studies in the Archaeology of Caracol, Belize*, edited by D. Chase and A. Chase, 123–138. Monograph 7. Pre-Columbian Art Research Institute, San Francisco.

Chase, Diane Z., and Arlen F. Chase. 1988. *A Postclassic Perspective: Excavations at the Maya Site of Santa Rita Corozal, Belize.* Pre-Columbian Art Research Institute, San Francisco.

Chase, Diane Z., and Arlen F. Chase. 1996. Maya Multiples: Individuals, Entries, and Tombs in Structure A34 of Caracol, Belize. *Latin American Antiquity* 7(1):61–79.

Chase, Diane Z., and Arlen F. Chase. 1998. The Architectural Context of Caches, Burials, and Other Ritual Activities for the Classic Period Maya (as Reflected at Caracol, Belize). In *Functions and Meaning in Classic Maya Architecture*, edited by S. D. Houston, 299–332. Dumbarton Oaks Research Library and Collection, Washington, DC.

Chase, Diane Z., and Arlen F. Chase. 2000. La guerra maya del periodo Clásico desde la perspectiva de Caracol, Belice. In *La guerra entre los antiguos mayas*, edited by S. Trejo, 53–72. Instituto Nacional de Antropología e Historia, Mexico City.

Chase, Diane Z., and Arlen F. Chase. 2001. Underlying Structure in Maya Persistence: An Archaeological Perspective. *Acta Mesoamericana* 12:37–50.

Chase, Diane Z., and Arlen F. Chase. 2002. Classic Maya Warfare and Settlement Archaeology at Caracol, Belize. *Estudios de Cultura Maya* 22:33–51.

Chase, Diane Z., and Arlen F. Chase. 2003a. Texts and Contexts in Classic Maya Warfare: A Brief Consideration of Epigraphy and Archaeology at Caracol, Belize. In *Ancient Mesoamerican Warfare*, edited by M. K. Brown and T. W. Stanton, 171–188. AltaMira Press, Walnut Creek, CA.

Chase, Diane Z., and Arlen F. Chase. 2003b. Minor Centers, Complexity, and Scale in Lowland Maya Settlement Archaeology. In *Perspectives on Ancient Maya Rural Complexity*, edited by G. Iannone and S. V. Connell, 108–118. Cotsen Institute of Archaeology, University of California, Los Angeles.

Chase, Diane Z., and Arlen F. Chase. 2004a. Archaeological Perspectives on Classic Maya Social Organization from Caracol, Belize. *Ancient Mesoamerica* 15(1):139–147.

Chase, Diane Z., and Arlen F. Chase. 2004b. Patrones de enterramiento y ciclos residenciales en Caracol, Belice. In *Culto funerario en la sociedad maya: Memoria de la Cuarta Mesa Redonda de Palenque*, edited by R. Cobos, 203–230. Instituto Nacional de Antropología e Historia, Mexico City.

Chase, Diane Z., and Arlen F. Chase. 2006. Framing the Maya Collapse: Continuity, Discontinuity, Method, and Practice in the Classic to Postclassic Southern Maya Lowlands. In *After Collapse: The Regeneration of Complex Societies*, edited by G. Schwartz and J. Nichols, 168–187. University of Arizona Press, Tucson.

Chase, Diane Z., and Arlen F. Chase. 2008. ¿Qué no nos cuentan los jeroglíficos? Arqueología e historia en Caracol, Belice. *Mayab* 20:93–108.

Chase, Diane Z., and Arlen F. Chase. 2011. Ghosts amid the Ruins: Analyzing Relationships between the Living and the Dead among the Ancient Maya at Caracol, Belize. In *Living with the Dead: Mortuary Ritual in Mesoamerica*, edited by James L. Fitzsimmons and Izumi Shimada, 78–101. University of Arizona Press, Tucson.

Chase, Diane Z., and Arlen F. Chase. 2014. Ancient Maya Markets and the Economic Integration of Caracol, Belize. *Ancient Mesoamerica* 25(1):239–250.

Chase, Diane Z., and Arlen F. Chase. 2017. Caracol, Belize and Changing Perceptions of Ancient Maya Society. *Journal of Archaeological Research* 25(1):185–249.

Chinchilla, Oswaldo M., and Stephen D. Houston. 1993. Historia política de la zona de Piedras Negras: Las inscripciones de El Cayo. In *VI Simposio de Investigaciones Arqueológicas en Guatemala*, edited by J. P. Laporte, H. Escobedo, and S. V. de Brady, 63–70. Museo Nacional de Arqueología y Etnología, Guatemala, Guatemala City.

Chowning, Ann. 1956. *A Round Temple and Its Shrine at Mayapan*. Current Reports, No. 34. Carnegie Institution of Washington, Washington, DC.

Christenson, Allen J. 2007. *Popol Vuh: The Sacred Book of the Maya: The Great Classic of Central American Spirituality, Translated from the Original Maya Text*. University of Oklahoma Press, Norman.

Cobos, Rafael. 2004. Chichén Itzá: Settlement and Hegemony during the Terminal Classic Period. In *The Terminal Classic in the Maya Lowlands: Collapse, Transition, and Transformation*, edited by A. A. Demarest, P. M. Rice, and D. S. Rice, 517–544. University Press of Colorado, Boulder.

Cobos, Rafael. 2011. Multepal or Centralized Kingship?: New Evidence on Governmental Organization at Chichén Itzá. In *Twin Tollans: Chichén Itzá, Tula, and the Epiclassic to Early Postclassic Mesoamerican World*, edited by J. K. Kowalski and C. Kristan-Graham, 248–271. Dumbarton Oaks Research Library and Collection, Washington, DC.

Coe, Michael D. 1973. *The Maya Scribe and His World*. Grolier Club, New York.

Coe, Michael D. 2005. *The Maya*. 7th ed. Thames and Hudson, New York.

Coe, William R. 1959. *Piedras Negras Archaeology: Artifacts, Caches, and Burials*. Museum Monographs. University Museum, University of Pennsylvania, Philadelphia.

Coe, William R. 1967. *Tikal: A Handbook of the Ancient Maya Ruins*. University Museum, University of Pennsylvania, Philadelphia.

Coe, William R. 1990. *Excavations in the Great Plaza, North Terrace, and North Acropolis of Tikal*. Tikal Report, No. 14. University Museum, University of Pennsylvania, Philadelphia.

Coe, William R., and John J. McGinn. 1963. Tikal: The North Acropolis and an Early Tomb. *Expedition* 5(2):24–32.

Coggins, Clemency C. 1975. Painting and Drawing Styles at Tikal: An Historical and Iconographic Approach. Unpublished PhD dissertation. Department of Fine Arts, Harvard University, Cambridge, Massachusetts.

Coggins, Clemency C. 1979. Teotihuacan at Tikal in the Early Classic Period. *Actes XLII Congres Internacional des Américanistes* 3:251–269.

Coggins, Clemency C. 1984. The Cenote of Sacrifice Catalogue. In *Cenote of Sacrifice: Maya Treasures from the Sacred Well at Chichén Itzá*, edited by C. C. Coggins and O. C. Shane III, 22–29. University of Texas Press, Austin.

Coggins, Clemency C., and Orin C. Shane, III. 1984. *Cenote of Sacrifice: Maya Treasures from the Sacred Well at Chichen Itza*. University of Texas Press, Austin.

Couch, N. C. Christopher. 1988. *Pre-Columbian Art from the Ernest Erickson Collection*. American Museum of Natural History, New York.

Cowgill, George L. 1988. Onward and Upward with Collapse. In *The Collapse of Ancient States and Civilizations*, edited by N. Yoffee and G. Cowgill, 244–276. University of Arizona Press, Tucson.

Cruz Alvarado, Wilberth A. 2012. Las esculturas de roca caliza en Itzmal Ch'en. In *Los Fundamentos Económicos de Mayapán, Temporadas 2008–2009, Informe Final para el Consejo de Arqueología*, edited by M. A. Masson, C. Peraza Lope, T. S. Hare, and B. W. Russell, 1311–1358. University at Albany–SUNY, Centro INAH–Yucatán, Albany, NY, and Mérida, Mexico.

Cruz Alvarado, Wilberth A., Carlos Peraza Lope, Luis Flores Cobá, and Marilyn A. Masson. 2012. Análisis de la cerámica: Temporadas 2008–2009. In *Los Fundamentos económicos de Mayapán, temporadas 2008–2009, Informe Final para el Consejo de Arqueología*, edited by M. A. Masson, C. Peraza Lope, T. S. Hare, and B. W. Russell, 1119–1162. University at Albany–SUNY, Centro INAH–Yucatán, Albany, NY, and Mérida, Mexico.

Culbert, T. Patrick. 1991. Polities in the Northeast Petén, Guatemala. In *Classic Maya Political History: Hieroglyphic and Archaeological Evidence*, edited by T. P. Culbert, 128–146. Cambridge University Press, Cambridge.

Culbert, T. Patrick, ed. 1991. *Classic Maya Political History: Hieroglyphic and Archaeological Evidence*. Cambridge University Press, Cambridge.

Culbert, T. Patrick. 1993. *The Ceramics of Tikal: Vessels from the Burials, Caches, and Problematical Deposits*. Tikal Report, No. 25, Part A. University of Pennsylvania, University Museum, Philadelphia.

Cyphers, Ann, and Kenneth G. Hirth. 2000. Ceramics of Western Morelos: The Cañada through Gobernador Phases at Xochicalco. In *The Xochicalco Mapping Project: Archaeological Research at Xochicalco*. Vol. 2, edited by K. G. Hirth, 102–135. University of Utah Press, Salt Lake City.

Dahlin, Bruce H., Daniel Bair, Tim Beach, Matthew Moriarty, and Richard Terry. 2010. The Dirt on Food: Ancient Feasts and Markets among the Lowland Maya. In *Pre-Columbian Foodways: Interdisciplinary Approaches to Food, Culture, and Markets in Mesoamerica*, edited by J. E. Staller and M. Carrasco, 191–232. Springer-Verlag, New York.

Dahlin, Bruce H., Christopher T. Jensen, Richard E. Terry, David Wright, and Timothy Beach. 2007. In Search of an Ancient Maya Market. *Latin American Antiquity* 18(4):363–384.

Davenport, Bryce, and Charles W. Golden. 2016. Landscapes, Lordships, and Sovreignty in Mesoamerica. In *Political Strategies in Precolumbian Mesoamerica*, edited by S. Kurnick and J. Baron, 181–216. University Press of Colorado, Boulder.

de Landa, Diego. 1941. *Relaciones de las cosas de Yucatan*. Translated by Alfred Tozzer. Papers of the Peabody Museum of Archaeology and Ethnology 18. Harvard University Press, Cambridge.

de la Fuente, Beatriz, Silvia Trejo, and Nelly Gutiérrez Solana. 1988. *Escultura en piedra de Tula*. Universidad Nacional Autónoma de México, Mexico City.

Delgado Kú, Miguel Ángel. 2009. La pintura mural de Mayapán, Yucatán: Una interpretación iconográfica. Unpublished Licenciatura thesis. Facultad de Ciencias Antropológicas, Universidad Autónoma de Yucatán, Mérida.

Delgado Kú, Pedro C. 2004. Estudio de la arquitectura pública del núcleo principal de Mayapán, Yucatán. Unpublished Licenciatura thesis. Facultad de Ciencias Antropológicas, Universidad Autónoma de Yucatán, Mérida.

Delgado Kú, Pedro C., Bárbara del C. Escamilla Ojeda, and Carlos Peraza Lope. 2012a. Itzmal Ch'en Sala Hipóstila H-15. In *Los fundamentos económicos de Mayapán, temporada 2008, Informe Final para el Consejo de Arqueología*, edited by M. A. Masson, C. Peraza Lope, T. S. Hare, and B. W. Russell, 423–538. University at Albany–SUNY, Centro INAH–Yucatán, Albany, NY, and Mérida, Mexico.

Delgado Kú, Pedro C., Bárbara del C. Escamilla Ojeda, and Carlos Peraza Lope. 2012b. Templo Itzmal Ch'en H-17 y Altar H-17a. In *Los fundamentos económicos de Mayapán, temporadas 2008–2009, Informe Final para el Consejo de Arqueología*, edited by M. A. Masson, C. Peraza Lope, T. S. Hare, and B. W. Russell, 257–422. University at Albany–SUNY, Centro INAH-Yucatán, Albany, NY, and Mérida, Mexico.

Delgado Kú, Pedro C., Carlos Peraza Lope, Marilyn A. Masson, Bárbara Escamilla Ojeda, Wilberth Cruz Alvarado, Bradley W. Russell, and Douglas J. Kennett. 2020. The Architecture and Sculptures of a Colonnaded Hall and Temple at the Itzmal Ch'en Group, Mayapán. In *Settlement, Economy, and Society at Mayapán, Yucatan, Mexico*, edited by M. A. Masson, T. S. Hare, C. Peraza Lope, and B. W. Russell. Center for Comparative Archaeology, University of Pittsburgh, Pittsburg, PA.

Demarest, Arthur A., and Federico Fahsen. 2003. Nuevos datos e interpretaciones de los reinos occidentales del Clásico Tardío: Hacia una visión sintética de la historia Pasión/Usumacinta. In *XVI Simposio de Investigaciones Arqueológicas en Guatemala 2002*, edited by J. P. Laporte, B. Arroyo, H. Escobedo, and H. Mejía, 160–176. Museo Nacional de Arqueología y Etnología, Guatemala City.

Demarest, Arthur A., and Antonia E. Foias. 1993. Mesoamerican Horizons and the Cultural Transformations of Maya Civilization. In *Latin American Horizons*, edited by D. S Rice, 147–191. Dumbarton Oaks Research Library and Collection, Washington, DC.

Demarest, Arthur A., Matt O'Mansky, Claudia Woolley, Dirk Van Tuerenhart, Takeshi Inomata, Joel Palka, and Héctor Escobedo. 1997. Classic Maya Defensive Systems and Warfare in the Petexbatun Region. *Ancient Mesoamerica* 8(2):229–253.

Demarest, Arthur A., Claudia Quintanilla, and José Samuel Suasnávar. 2016. The Collapses in the West and the Violent Ritual Termination of the Classic Maya Capital Center of Cancuen: Causes and Consequence. In *Ritual, Violence, and the Fall of the Classic Maya Kings*, edited by G. Iannone, B. A. Houk, and S. A. Schwake, 159–186. University of Florida Press, Gainesville.

Dixon, Boyd. 1992. Prehistoric Political Variability on the Southeast Mesoamerican Periphery. *Ancient Mesoamerica* 3(1):11–25.

Doyle, James. 2015. Sacrifice, Fealty, and a Sculptor's Signature on a Maya Relief. In *Now at the Met*. http://www.metmuseum.org/blogs/now-at-the-met/2015 /sculptors-signature.

Duncan, William N., and Charles A. Hofling. 2011. Why the Head? Cranial Modification as Protection and Ensoulment among the Maya. *Ancient Mesoamerica* 22(1):199–210.

Dunning, Nicholas P. 1992. *Lords of the Hills: Ancient Maya Settlement in the Puuc Region, Yucatan, Mexico*. Monographs in World Prehistory, No. 15. Prehistory Press, Madison, WI.

du Solier, Wilfrido. 1943. A Reconnaissance on Isla de Sacrificios, Veracruz, Mexico. *Notes on Middle American Archaeology and Ethnology* 1(14):63–80.

Eberl, Markus. 2005. *Muerte, entierro y ascensión: Ritos funerarios entre los antiguos mayas*. Ediciones de la Universidad Autónoma de Yucatán, Mérida.

Edmonson, Munro S. 1982. *The Ancient Future of the Itza: The Book of Chilam Balam of Tizimin*. University of Texas Press, Austin.

Edmonson, Munro S. 1986. *Heaven Born Merida and Its Destiny: The Book of Chilam Balam of Chumayel*. University of Texas Press, Austin.

Englehardt, Joshua. 2013. Structuration of the Conjuncture: Agency in Classic Maya Iconography and Texts. In *Agency in Ancient Writing*, edited by J. Englehardt, 185–207. University Press of Colorado, Boulder.

Eppich, E. Keith. 2007. Death and Veneration at El Perú-Waka': Structure M14–15 as Ancestor Shrine. *The PARI Journal* 8(1):1–16.

Eppich, E. Keith. 2009a. Operation 1 Memo. Unpublished manuscript in possession of the authors.

Eppich, E. Keith. 2009b. Feast and Sacrifice at El Perú-Waka': The N14–2 Deposit as Dedication. *The PARI Journal* 10(2):1–19.

Eppich, E. Keith. 2010. Tracking the Late to Terminal Classic Transition at El Perú-Waka': A Ceramic Perspective. Paper Presented at the 75th Annual Meeting of the Society for American Archaeology, St. Louis.

Eppich, E. Keith. 2011. Lineage and State at El Perú-Waka': Ceramic and Architectural Perspectives on the Classic Maya Social Dynamic. Unpublished PhD dissertation. Department of Anthropology, Southern Methodist University, Dallas.

Eppich, E. Keith. 2012. Burial 61 Preliminary Ceramics Analysis. Unpublished manuscript in possession of the authors.

Eppich, E. Keith. 2015. The Decline and Fall of the Classic Maya City. In *Archaeology for the People, Joukowsky Institute Perspectives*, edited by J. Cherry and F. Rojas Silva, 81–94. Oxbow Books, Oxford.

Eppich, E. Keith. 2017. The Last Palace: Stones, Bones and Feasts. Recent Excavations at El Peru-Waka'. Paper presented at the 8th Annual Conference on Mesoamerica, Tulane University, New Orleans.

Escobedo, Héctor L., and David A. Freidel. 2004. La primera temporada del Proyecto Arqueológico El Perú-Waka'. In *Proyecto Arqueológico El Perú-Waka' Informe No. 1, Temporada 2003*, edited by H. L. Escobedo and D. A. Freidel, 1–6. Instituto de Antropología e Historia, Guatemala City.

Estrada-Belli, Francisco, and Alexandre Tokovinine 2016. A King's Apotheosis: Iconography, Text, and Politics from a Classic Maya Temple at Holmul. *Latin American Antiquity* 27(2):149–168.

Estrada-Belli, Francisco, Alexandre Tokovinine, Jennifer M. Foley, Heather Hurst, Gene A. Ware, David Stuart, and Nikolai Grube. 2009. A Maya Palace at Holmul, Peten, Guatemala and the Teotihuacan "Entrada": Evidence from Murals 7 and 9. *Latin American Antiquity* 20(1):228–259.

Fash, William L., Jr. 1991. *Scribes, Warriors, and Kings: The City of Copan and the Ancient Maya*. Thames and Hudson, London.

Fash, William L., Jr., and Barbara W. Fash. 2000. Teotihuacan and the Maya: A Classic Heritage. In *Mesoamerica's Classic Heritage: From Teotihuacan to the* Aztecs, edited by D. Carrasco, L. Jones, and S. Sessions, 433–463. University Press of Colorado, Boulder.

Fash, William L., and Robert J. Sharer. 1991. Sociopolitical Developments and Methodological Issues at Copan, Honduras: A Conjunctive Approach. *Latin American Antiquity* 2(2):166–187.

Fash, William L., Alexandre Tokovinine, and Barbara W. Fash. 2009. The House of New Fire at Teotihuacan and Its Legacy in Mesoamerica. In *Art of Urbanism: How Mesoamerican Kingdoms Represented Themselves in Architecture and Imagery*, edited by W. L. Fash and L. López Luján, 201–229. Dumbarton Oaks Research Library and Collection, Washington, DC.

Fedick, Scott L., ed. 1996. *The Managed Mosaic: Ancient Maya Agriculture and Resource Use*. University of Utah Press, Salt Lake City.

Feeley-Harnik, Gillian. 1978. Divine Kingship and the Meaning of History among the Sakalava of Madagascar. *Man* 13(3):402–417.

Feeley-Harnik, Gillian. 1985. Issues in Divine Kingship. *Annual Review of Anthropology* 14:273–313.

Fentress, James, and Chris Wickham. 1992. *Social Memory*. Blackwell, Oxford.

Finamore, Daniel, and Stephen D. Houston, eds. 2010. *Fiery Pool: The Maya and the Mythic Sea*. Yale University Press, New Haven, CT.

Fitzsimmons, James L. 2009. *Death and the Classic Maya Kings*. University of Texas Press, Austin.

Foias, Antonia. 1987. The Influence of Teotihuacan in the Maya Culture during the Middle Classic: A Reconsideration of the Ceramic Evidence from Kaminaljuyu, Uaxactun, and Copan. Unpublished BA honors thesis. Department of Anthropology, Harvard University, Cambridge, MA.

Foias, Antonia. 2000. Entre la política y economía: Resultados preliminares de las primeras dos temporadas del Proyecto Arqueológico Motul de San José. In *XII Simposio de Investigaciones Arqueológicas en Guatemala*, edited by J. P. Laporte, H. L. Escobedo, A. C. de Suasnavar, and B. Arroyo, 943–973. Museo Nacional de Arqueología y Etnología, Guatemala City.

Foias, Antonia. 2004. The Past and Future of Maya Ceramic Studies. In *Continuities and Changes in Maya Archaeology: Perspectives at the Millennium*, edited by C. W. Golden and G. Borgstede, 141–174. Routledge, London.

Folan, William J. 1992. Calakmul, Campeche: A Centralized Urban Administrative Center in the Northern Petén. *World Archaeology* 24(1):158–168.

Folan, William J., Joyce Marcus, Sophie Pincemin, María del Rosario Domínguez Carrasco, Laraine Fletcher, and Abel Morales López. 1995. Calakmul: New Data from an Ancient Maya Capital in Campeche, Mexico. *Latin American Antiquity* 6(4):310–334.

Fowler, C. 2004. *The Archaeology of Personhood: An Anthropological Approach*. Routledge, London.

Franco C., José Luis. 1959. Representaciones de la mariposa en Mesoamérica. *El México Antiguo* 9:195–244.

Frazer, James. 1905. *Lectures on the Early History of Kingship*. Macmillan, London.

Freidel, David A. 1986. Maya Warfare: An Example of Peer Polity Interaction. In *Peer Polity Interaction and Socio-Political Change*, edited by C. Renfrew and J. F. Cherry, 93–108. Cambridge University Press, London.

Freidel, David A. 1992a. Children of First Father's Skull: Terminal Classic Warfare in the Northern Maya Lowlands. In *Mesoamerican Elites: An Archaeological Assessment*, edited by D. Z. Chase and A. F. Chase, 99–117. University of Oklahoma Press, Norman.

Freidel, David A. 1992b. The Trees of Life: Ahau as Idea and Artifact in Classic Maya Civilization. In *Ideology and Pre-Columbian Civilizations*, edited by A. A. Demarest and G. W. Conrad, 115–133. School of American Research Press, Santa Fe.

Freidel, David A. 2007. War and Statecraft in the Northern Maya Lowlands: Yaxuna and Chichén Itzá. In *Twin Tollans: Chichén Itzá, Tula, and the Epiclassic and Early Postclassic Mesoamerican World*, edited by J. K. Kowalski and C. Kristen-Graham, 345–375. Dumbarton Oaks, Washington, DC.

Freidel, David A. 2012. Maya and the Idea of Empire: A View from the Field. Gordon R. Willey Lecture, Peabody Museum of Archaeology and Ethnology at Harvard University. https://www.peabody.harvard.edu/node/764.

Freidel, David A. 2014a. The Origins and Development of Lowland Maya Civilization. In *The Cambridge World Prehistory*. Vol. 2: *East Asia and the Americas*, edited by Colin Renfrew and Paul Bahn, 1043–1057. Cambridge University Press, New York.

Freidel, David A. 2014b. La montaña sagrada de Waka', paisaje e historia. In *Proyecto Regional Arqueológico El Perú-Waka' Informe No. 12, Temporada 2014*, edited by J. C. Pérez, G. Pérez and D. A. Freidel, 9–17. Report submitted to the Instituto de Antropología e Historia, Guatemala City.

Freidel, David A. 2018. Maya and the Idea of Empire. In *Pathways to Complexity: A View from the Maya Lowlands*, edited by M. K. Brown and G. J. Bey III, 363–386. University Press of Florida, Gainesville.

Freidel, David A., Héctor L. Escobedo, and Stanley P. Guenter. 2007. A Crossroads of Conquerors: Waka' and Gordon Willey's "Rehearsal for the Collapse" Hypothesis. In *Gordon R. Willey and American Archaeology: Contemporary Perspectives*, edited by J. A. Sabloff and W. L. Fash, 187–208. University of Oklahoma Press, Norman.

Freidel, David A., and Stanley Guenter. 2003. Bearers of War and Creation. *Archaeology Magazine Archive*. www.archaeology.org/online/features/siteq2/.

Freidel, David A., and Stanley Guenter. 2006. Soul Bundle Caches, Tombs, and Cenotaphs: Creating the Places of Resurrection and Accession in Maya Kingship. In *Sacred Bindings of the Cosmos: Ritual Acts of Bundling and Wrapping in Mesoamerica*, edited by J. Guernsey and F. K. Reilly, 59–79. Ancient America Special Publications Number 1. Boundary End Archaeology Research Center, Barnardsville, NC.

Freidel, David A, Marilyn A. Masson, and Michelle E. Rich. 2017. Imagining a Complex Maya Political Economy: Counting Tokens and Currencies in Image, Text, and the Archaeological Record. *Cambridge Archaeological Journal* 27(1):29–54.

Freidel, David A., Olivia Navarro-Farr, and Michelle Rich. 2013. Teotihuacan-Lowland Maya Interaction: The Wite' Naah Fire Shrines at El Perú-Waka'. Paper presented at the 78th Annual Meeting of the Society for American Archaeology, Honolulu.

Freidel, David, Griselda Pérez, Olivia Navarro-Farr, Juan Carlos Pérez, and Michelle Rich. 2017. Descubrimiento de las estelas 43, 44, y 45 de El Perú, Petén, Guatemala: Nuevos datos iconográficos en la historia del reino de *Waka'*. *Anuario de la Dirección General del Patrimonio Cultural y Natural* 3(16):7–36.

Freidel, David A., and Jeremy A. Sabloff. 1984. *Cozumel: Late Maya Settlement Patterns*. Academic Press, New York.

Freidel, David A., Linda Schele, and Joy Parker. 1993. *Maya Cosmos: Three Thousand Years on the Shaman's Path*. William Morrow, New York.

Garber, James F. 1983. Patterns of Jade Consumption and Disposal at Cerros, Northern Belize. *American Antiquity* 48(4):800–807.

Garber, James F. 1986. The Artifacts. In *Archaeology at Cerros, Belize, Central America*. Vol. 1: *An Interim Report*, edited by D. A. Freidel and R. A. Robertson, 117–126. Southern Methodist University Press, Dallas.

Garibay Kintana, Ángel María. 1979. *Teogonía e historia de los mexicanos: Tres opúsculos del siglo XVI*. Edition prepared by Ángel María Garibay K. 3rd ed. Editorial Porrúa, México, D.F.

Geller, Pamela L. 2006. Altering Identities: Body Modification and the Pre-Columbian Maya. In *Social Archaeology of Funerary Remains*, edited by R. Gowland and C. Knüsel, 279–291. Oxbow Books, Oxford.

Geller, Pamela L. 2011. Getting a Head Start in Life: Pre-Columbian Maya Cranial Modification from Infancy to Ancestorhood. In *The Bioarchaeology of the Human Head*, edited by M. Bonogofsky, 241–261. University Press of Florida, Gainesville.

Gendrop, Paul. 1983. *Los estilos Río Bec, Chenes y Puuc en la arquitectura maya*. Universidad Nacional Autónoma de México, D.F.

Golden, Charles W. 2003. The Politics of Warfare in the Usumacinta Basin: La Pasadita and the Realm of Bird Jaguar. In *Ancient Mesoamerican Warfare*, edited by M. K. Brown and T. W. Stanton, 31–48. AltaMira Press, Walnut Creek, CA.

Golden, Charles W. 2010. Frayed at the Edges: Collective Memory and History on the Borders of Classic Maya Polities. *Ancient Mesoamerica* 21:373–384.

Golden, Charles W., and Bryce Davenport. 2013. The Promise and Problem of Modeling Viewsheds in the Western Maya Lowlands. In *Mapping Archaeological Landscapes from Space*, edited by D. C. Comer and M. J. Harrower, 145–158. Springer, New York.

Golden, Charles W., and Andrew Scherer. 2013. Territory, Trust, Growth, and Collapse in Classic Period Maya Kingdoms. *Current Anthropology* 54(4):397–435.

Golden, Charles, Andrew K. Scherer, A. Rene Muñoz, and Zachary Hruby. 2012. Polities, Boundaries, and Trade in the Classic Period Usumacinta River Basin. *Mexicon* XXXIV (1):11–19.

Golden, Charles, Andrew K. Scherer, A. René Muñoz, and Rosaura Vásquez. 2008. Piedras Negras and Yaxchilan: Divergent Political Trajectories in Adjacent Maya Polities. *Latin American Antiquity* 19(2):249–274.

Gómez, Yajaira. 2012. Los grupos cerámicos Xanabá y Chuburná: estudio de una tradición cerámica prehispánica de Yaxuná, Yucatán. Licenciatura thesis. Department of Anthropology, Universidad de las Américas Puebla, Cholula, Mexico.

González de la Mata, María Rocío, Francisco Pérez Ruíz, and José Osorio León. 2006. Vida más allá de Cumtún: El Sacbé No. 3 de Chichén Itzá. In *Los Investigadores de la Cultura Maya 14*, 419–429. Universidad Autónoma de Campeche, Campeche, Mexico.

Gordon, George B. 1902. *The Hieroglyphic Stairway: Ruins of Copan*. Memoirs of the Peabody Museum of American Archaeology and Ethnology, Harvard University 1(6). Harvard University, Cambridge, MA.

Gossen, Gary H. 1974. *Chamulas in the World of the Sun: Time and Space in a Maya Oral Tradition*. Harvard University Press, Cambridge, MA.

Graff, Donald H. 1997. Dating a Section of the Madrid Codex: Astronomical and Iconographic Evidence, In *Papers on the Madrid Codex*, edited by V. R. Bricker and G. Vail, 147–167. Publication 64. Middle American Research Institute, Tulane University, New Orleans.

Graham, Ian. 1971. *The Art of Maya Hieroglyphic Writing*. Peabody Museum of Archaeology and Ethnology, Harvard University, Cambridge, MA.

Graham, Ian. 1978. *Corpus of Maya Hieroglyphic Inscriptions: Naranjo, Chunhitz, Xunantunich*. Peabody Museum of Archaeology and Ethnology. Vol. 2. Pt. 2. Harvard University, Cambridge, MA.

Graham, Ian. 1980. *Corpus of Maya Hieroglyphic Inscriptions: Ixkun, Ucanal, Ixtutz, and Naranjo*. Peabody Museum of Archaeology and Ethnology. Vol. 2. Pt. 3. Harvard University, Cambridge, MA.

Graham, Ian. 1988. Homeless Hieroglyphs. *Antiquity* 62 (234):122–126.

Graham, Ian. 1996. *Corpus of Maya Hieroglyphic Inscriptions: Seibal*. Peabody Museum of Archaeology and Ethnology 7(1). Harvard University, Cambridge, MA.

Graña-Behrens, Daniel. 2006. Emblem Glyphs and Political Organization in Northwestern Yucatan in the Classic Period (AD 300–1000). *Ancient Mesoamerica* 17(2):105–123.

Graña-Behrens, Daniel, Christian Prager, and Elisabeth Wagner. 1999. The Hieroglyphic Inscription of the "High Priest's Grave" at Chichén Itzá, Yucatán, Mexico. *Mexicon* 21(3):61–66.

Greene Robertson, Merle, Robert L. Rands. and John A. Graham. 1972. *Maya Sculpture from the Southern Lowlands, the Highlands and Pacific Piedmont: Guatemala, Mexico, Honduras*. Lederer, Street, and Zeus, Berkeley.

Groark, Kevin P. 2009. Discourses of the Soul: The Negotiation of Personal Agency in Tzotzil Maya Dream Narrative. *American Ethnologist* 36(4):705–721.

Groark, Kevin P. 2010. Willful Souls: Dreaming and the Dialectics of Self-Experience among the Tzotzil Maya of Highland Chiapas, Mexico. In *Toward an Anthropology of the Will*, edited by K. M. Murphy and C. J. Throop, 101–215. Stanford University Press, Stanford, CA.

Gronemeyer, Sven. 2004. A Preliminary Ruling Sequence of Cobá, Quintana Roo. Wayeb Note No. 14. Accessed January 21, 2015. www.wayeb.org/notes/wayeb _notes004.pdf.

Grube, Nikolai. 1992. Classic Maya Dance: Evidence from Hieroglyphs and Iconography. *Ancient Mesoamerica* 3(2):201–218.

Grube, Nikolai. 1994. Epigraphic Research at Caracol, Belize. In *Studies in the Archaeology of Caracol, Belize*, edited by D. Z. Chase and A. F. Chase, 83–122. Monograph 7. Pre-Columbian Art Research Institute, San Francisco.

Grube, Nikolai. 2003. Hieroglyphic Inscriptions from Northwestern Yucatan: An Update of Recent Research. In *Escondido en la selva: Arqueología en el norte de Yucatán*, edited by Hanns J. Prem, 339–370. Colección Obra Diversa, Instituto Nacional de Antropología e Historia and Universität Bonn, Mexico City, and Bonn, Germany.

Grube, Nikolai. 2004a. "Akan: The God of Drinking, Disease, and Death." In *Continuity and Change: Maya Religious Practices in Temporal Perspective*, edited by D. G. Behrens, N. Grube, C. M. Praeger, K. Sachse, S. Teufel, and E. Wagner, 59–76. Acta Mesoamericana, Vol. 14. Verlag Anton Saurwein, Markt Schwaben, Germany.

Grube, Nikolai. 2004b. The Orthographic Distinction between Velar and Glottal Spirants in Maya Hieroglyphic Writing. In *The Linguistics of Maya Writing*, edited by S. Wichmann, 61–81. University of Utah Press, Salt Lake City.

Grube, Nikolai. 2004c. El origen de la dinastía Kaan. In *Los cautivos de Dzibanché*, edited by Enrique Nalda, 117–131. Instituto de Antropología e Historia, Mexico City.

Grube, Nikolai, Kai Delvendahl, Nicolaus Seefeld, and Beniamino Volta. 2012. Under the Rule of the Snake Kings: Uxul in the 7th and 8th Centuries. *Estudios de Cultura Maya* 40:11–49.

Grube, Nikolai, and Ruth J. Krochok. 2007. Reading between the Lines: Hieroglyphic Texts from Chichén Itzá and Its Neighbors. In *Twin Tollans: Chichén Itzá, Tula, and the Epiclassic to Early Postclassic Mesoamerican World*, edited by J. K. Kowalski and C. Kristan-Graham, 205–249. Dumbarton Oaks Research Library and Collection. Harvard University Press, Washington, DC.

Grube, Nikolai, and Simon Martin. 2001. The Dynastic History of the Maya. In *Maya: Divine Kings of the Rainforest*, edited by N. Grube, 149–171. Köneman, Cologne, Germany.

Grube, Nikolai, and Werner Nahm. 1994. A Census of Xibalba: A Complete Inventory of Way Characters on Maya Ceramics. In *The Maya Vase Book: A Corpus Rollout of Maya Vases*. Vol. 4, edited by B. Kerr and J. Kerr, 688–715. Kerr Associates, New York.

Guenter, Stanley P. 2001. Foliated Ajaw and the Fall of El Mirador. Paper presented at the 6th Annual European Maya Conference, Hamburg, Germany.

Guenter, Stanley P. 2003. El Mirador and Teotihuacan: The Cultural Foundations of Classic Maya Civilization. Paper presented at the 2003 Symposium of the Pre-Columbian Society of Washington, DC.

Guenter, Stanley P. 2005. Informe preliminar de la epigrafía de El Perú. In *Proyecto Arqueológico El Perú-Waka': Informe No. 2, Temporada 2004*, edited by H. L. Escobedo and D. A. Freidel, 363–399. Report presented to the Instituto de Antropología e Historia, Guatemala City.

Guenter, Stanley P. 2007a. The Tomb of K'inich Janaab Pakal: The Temple of the Inscriptions at Palenque. *Mesoweb*. Accessed January 2017. www.mesoweb.com /articles/guenter/TI.pdf.

Guenter, Stanley P. 2007b. On the Emblem Glyph of El Peru. *PARI Journal* 8(2):20–23.

Guenter, Stanley P. 2009. Kingdom in the Shadows: The Snake Kingdom in the Early Classic (3rd–4th Centuries AD). Paper presented at the 2009 Maya Meetings and Symposium, University of Texas, Austin.

Guenter, Stanley P. 2014a. The Queen of Cobá: A Reanalysis of the Macanxoc Stelae. In *The Archaeology of Yucatán: New Directions and Data*, edited by T. W. Stanton, 395–421. BAR International Series. Archaeopress, Oxford.

Guenter, Stanley P. 2014b. The Classic Maya Collapse: Chronology and Causation. Unpublished PhD dissertation. Department of Anthropology, Southern Methodist University, Dallas.

Guenter, Stanley P. 2014c The Epigraphy of El Perú-Waka'. In *Archaeology at El Perú-Waka': Ancient Maya Performances of Ritual, Memory, and Power*, edited by O. Navarro-Farr and M. Rich, 147–166. University of Arizona Press, Tucson.

Guiteras-Holmes, Calixta. 1961. *Perils of the Soul: The World View of a Tzotzil Indian.* Free Press of Glencoe, New York.

Gunn, Joel D., William J. Folan, Christian Isendahl, María del Rosario Domínguez Carrasco, Betty B. Faust, and Beniamino Volta. 2014. Calakmul: Agent Risk and Sustainability in the Western Maya Lowlands. In *The Resilience and Vulnerability of Ancient Landscapes: Transforming Maya Archaeology through IHOPE*, edited by A. F. Chase and V. L. Scarborough, 101–123. Archaeological Papers of the American Anthropological Association 24. American Anthropological Association, Washington, DC.

Gunn, Joel D., John E. Foss, William J. Folan, and María del Rosario Domínguez Carrasco. 2002. Bajo Sediments and the Hydraulic System of Calakmul, Campeche, Mexico. *Ancient Mesoamerica* 13(2):297–315.

Hagerdal, Hans. 2008. White and Dark Stranger Kings: Kupang in the Early Colonial Era. *Recherche en Sciences Humaines sur l'Asie du sud-Est* 12:137–161.

Halperin, Christina T. 2017. Ancient Cosmopolitanism: Feminism and the Re-Thinking of Maya Inter-Regional Interactions during the Late Classic to Postclassic Periods (ca. 600–1521 CE). *Journal of Social Archaeology* 17(3):349–375.

Halperin, Christina T., and Antonia E. Foias. 2010. Pottery Politics: Late Classic Maya Palace Production at Motul de San José, Petén, Guatemala. *Journal of Anthropological Archaeology* 29(3):392–411.

Hansen, Richard. 1998. Continuity and Disjunction: The Pre-Classic Antecedents of Classic Maya Architecture. In *Function and Meaning in Classic Maya Architecture*, edited by S. D. Houston, 49–122. Dumbarton Oaks Research Library and Collection, Washington, DC.

Hansen, Richard. 2001. The First Cities: The Beginnings of Urbanization and State Formation in the Maya Lowlands. In *Maya: Divine Kings of the Rain Forest*, edited by N. Grube, 50–65. Konemann Verlag, Königswinter, Germany.

Hansen, Richard. 2008. *Mirador Basin 2008: A Report on the 2008 Field Season*. Report on file at the Foundation for Anthropological Research and Environmental Studies, Boise State University, Idaho.

Hansen, Richard. 2012. The Beginning of the End: Conspicuous Consumption and Environmental Impact of the Preclassic Lowland Maya. In *An Archaeological Legacy: Essays in Honor of Ray T. Matheny*, edited by D. G. Matheny, J. C. Janetski, and G. Nielen, 241–285. Brigham Young University, Provo.

Hansen, Richard D., and Stanley P. Guenter. 2005. Early Social Complexity and Kingship in the Mirador Basin. In *Lords of Creation: The Origins of Sacred Maya Kingship*, edited by V. M. Fields and D. Reents-Budet, 60–61. Los Angeles County Museum of Art in association with Scalia Publishers, Los Angeles.

Hansen, Richard D., Wayne K. Howell, and Stanley P. Guenter. 2008. Forgotten Structures, Haunted Houses, and Occupied Hearts: Ancient Perspectives and Contemporary Interpretations of Abandoned Sites and Buildings in the Mirador Basin, Guatemala. In *Ruins of the Past: The Use and Perception of Abandoned Structures in the Maya Lowlands*, edited by T. W. Stanton and A. Magnoni, 25–64. University Press of Colorado, Boulder.

Hare, Timothy S., Marilyn A. Masson, and Carlos Peraza Lope. 2014. The Urban Cityscape. In *Kukulcan's Realm: Urban Life at Ancient Mayapán*, by M. Masson and C. Peraza Lope, 149–192. University Press of Colorado, Boulder.

Harrison-Buck, Eleanor. 2016. Killing the "Kings of Stone": The Defacement of Classic Maya Monuments. In *Ritual, Violence, and the Fall of Classic Maya Kings*, edited by G. Iannone, B. Houk, and S. Schwake, 61–88. University Press of Florida, Gainesville.

Hassig, Ross. 1992. *War and Society in Ancient Mesoamerica*. University of California Press, Berkeley.

Haviland, William A. 1977. Dynastic Genealogies from Tikal, Guatemala: Implications for Descent and Political Organization. *American Antiquity* 42(1):61–67.

Haviland, William A. 1992. From Double Bird to Ah Cacao: Dynastic Troubles and the Cycle of Katuns at Tikal, Guatemala. In *New Theories of the Ancient Maya*, edited by E. Danien and R. J. Sharer, 71–80. University of Pennsylvania Museum, Philadelphia.

Headrick, Annabeth. 1996. The Teotihuacan Trinity: UnMASKing the Political Structure. Unpublished PhD dissertation, Department of Art History, University of Texas, Austin.

Headrick, Annabeth. 2001. Merging Myth and Politics: The Three Temple Complex at Teotihuacan. In *Landscape and Power in Ancient Mesoamerica*, edited by R. Koontz, K. Reese-Taylor, and A. Headrick, 169–195. Westview Press, Boulder.

Headrick, Annabeth. 2007. *The Teotihuacan Trinity: The Sociopolitical Structure of an Ancient Mesoamerican City*. University of Texas Press, Austin.

Headrick, Annabeth. 2015. In Search of the New Bling: The Economic Role of the Chichen Itza's Military. Paper presented at the 55th Congreso Internacional de Americanistas, San Salvador, El Salvador.

Headrick, Annabeth. 2018. The Osario of Chichen Itza: Where Warriors Danced in Paradise. In *Landscapes of the Itza: Archaeology and Art History at Chichen Itza and Neighboring Sites*, edited by L. Wren, C. Kristan-Graham, T. Nygard, and K. Spencer, 198–225. University of Florida Press, Gainesville.

Headrick, Annabeth, and John W. Hoopes. 2018. Foreign Encounters: Warfare, Trade, and Status at Chichen Itza. Manuscript on file, School of Art and Art History, University of Denver, Denver Colorado, and University of Kansas, Department of Anthropology, Lawrence, Kansas.

Helmke, Christophe, and Jaime J. Awe. 2016a. Death Becomes Her: An Analysis of Panel 3, Xunantunich, Belize. *PARI Journal* 16(4):1–14.

Helmke, Christophe, and Jaime J. Awe. 2016b. Sharper than a Serpent's Tomb: A Tale of the Snake-Head Dynasty as Recounted on Xunantunich Panel 4. *The PARI Journal* 17(2):1–22.

Helmke, Christophe, and Harri Kettunen. 2012. Riflessioni sulla Decifrazione della Scrittura Maya. Paper presented at the XXXIV Convegno Internazionale de Americanistica. Dipartimento di Paleografia e Medievistica, Complesso di San Giovanni in Monte, Universita di Bologna, Bologna.

Helmke, Christophe, and Felix A. Kupprat. 2016. Where Snakes Abound: Supernatural Places of Origin and Founding Myths in the Titles of Classic Maya Kings. In *Places of Power and Memory in Mesoamerica's Past and Present: How Toponyms,*

Landscapes and Boundaries Shape History and Remembrance, edited by D. Graña-Behrens, 33–83. Indiana Series. Gebrüder Mann Verlag, Berlin.

Helmke, Christophe, and Ismael Arturo Montero García. 2016. Caves and New Fire Ceremonies in the Central Mexican Highlands: The Case of the Cerro de la Estrella, Iztapalapa, Mexico. *Contributions in New World Archaeology* 10:55–100.

Helmke, Christophe, and Jesper Nielsen. 2009. Hidden Identity and Power in Ancient Mesoamerica: Supernatural Alter Egos as Personified Diseases. *Acta Americana* 17(2):49–98.

Henley, David. 2004. Conflict, Justice, and the Stranger King: Indigenous Roots of Colonial Rule in Indonesia and Elsewhere. *Modern Asian Studies* 38(1):85–144.

Heusch, Luc de. 1997. The Symbolic Mechanisms of Sacred Kingship: Rediscovering Frazer. *Journal of the Royal Anthropological Institute* 3(2):213–232.

Hill, Jane H. 1992. The Flower World of Old Uto-Aztecan. *Journal of Anthropological Research* 48(2):117–144.

Hocart, Arthur Maurice. 1927. *Kingship*. Oxford University Press, London.

Hoggarth, Julia A., Matthew Restall, James W. Wood, and Douglas J. Kennett. 2017. Drought and Its Demographic Effects in the Maya Lowlands. *Current Anthropology* 58(1):82–113.

Holland, William R. 1961. El tonalismo y el nagualismo entre los Tzotziles. *Estudios de Cultura Maya* 1:176–181.

Houston, Stephen D. 1991. Appendix: Caracol Altar 21. In *Sixth Palenque Round Table, 1986*, edited by M. Greene Robertson and V. M. Fields, 38–41. University of Oklahoma Press, Norman.

Houston, Stephen D. 1993. *Hieroglyphs and History at Dos Pilas: Dynastic Politics of the Classic Maya*. University of Texas Press, Austin.

Houston, Stephen D. 1996. Symbolic Sweatbaths of the Maya: Architectural Meaning in the Cross Group at Palenque, Mexico. *Latin American Antiquity* 7(2):132–151.

Houston, Stephen D. 2001. Decorous Bodies and Disordered Passions: Representations of Emotion Among the Classic Maya. *World Archaeology* 33(2):260–219.

Houston, Stephen D. 2006. Impersonation, Dance, and the Problem of Spectacle among the Classic Maya. In *Archaeology of Performance: Theaters of Power, Community, and Politics*, edited by T. Inomata and L.S. Coben. AltaMira Press, Oxford.

Houston, Stephen D. 2009. A Splendid Predicament: Young Men in Classic Maya Society. *Cambridge Archaeological Journal* 19(2):149–178.

Houston, Stephen D., Charles W. Golden, A. René Muñoz, and Andrew Scherer. 2006. A Yaxchilan-Style Lintel Possibly from the Area of Retalteco, Petén, Guatemala. *Research Reports on Ancient Maya Writing* 61:1–10.

Houston, Stephen D., and Peter Mathews. 1985. *The Dynastic Sequence of Dos Pilas*. PARI Monograph 1. PARI, San Francisco.

Houston, Stephen D., Sarah Newman, Edwin Román, and Thomas G. Garrison. 2015. *Temple of the Night Sun: A Royal Tomb at El Diablo*. Precolumbia Mesoweb Press, San Francisco.

Houston, Stephen D., and Andrew K. Scherer. 2010. La ofrenda máxima: El sacrificio humano en la parte central del área maya. In *Nuevas perspectivas sobre el sacrificio humano entre los mexicas*, edited by L. López Luján and G. Olivier, 167–191. Instituto Nacional de Antropología e Historia, Mexico City.

Houston, Stephen D., and David Stuart. 1989. *The Way Glyph: Evidence for "Co-Essences" among the Classic Maya*. Research Reports on Ancient Maya Writing 30. Center for Maya Research, Washington, DC.

Houston, Stephen D., and David Stuart. 1996. Of Gods, Glyphs, and Kings: Divinity and Rulership among the Classic Maya. *Antiquity* 70(268):289–312.

Houston, Stephen D., and David Stuart. 1998. The Ancient Maya Self: Personhood and Portraiture in the Classic Period. *RES* 33:72–101.

Houston, Stephen D., and David Stuart. 2001. Peopling the Classic Maya Court. In *Royal Courts of the Ancient Maya*. Volume 1: *Theory, Comparison, and Synthesis*, edited by T. Inomata and S. D. Houston, 54–83. Westview Press, Boulder.

Houston, Stephen D., David Stuart, and Karl A. Taube. 2006. *The Memory of Bones: Body, Being, and Experience among the Classic Maya*. University of Texas Press, Austin.

Houston, Stephen D., and Karl Taube. 2000. An Archaeology of the Senses: Perception and Cultural Expression in Ancient Mesoamerica. *Cambridge Archaeological Journal* 10(2):261–294.

Howie, Linda, James Aimers, and Elizabeth Graham. 2014. 50 Left Feet: The Manufacture and Meaning of Effigy Censers from Lamanai, Belize. In *Craft and Science: International Perspectives on Archaeological Ceramics*, edited by M. Martinón-Torres, 39–51. Bloomsbury Qatar Foundation, Doha, Qatar.

Hull, Kerry Michael. 2003. Verbal Art and Performance in Ch'orti' and Maya Hieroglyphic Writing. Unpublished PhD disseration, Department of Anthropology, University of Texas, Austin.

Iannone, Gyles, Brett Houk, and Sonja A. Schwake, eds. 2016. *Ritual, Violence and the Fall of the Classic Maya Kings*. University Press of Florida, Gainesville.

Inomata, Takeshi. 2003. War, Destruction, and Abandonment: The Fall of the Classic Maya Center of Aguateca, Guatemala. In *The Archaeology of Settlement Abandonment in Middle America*, edited by T. Inomata and R. A. Webb, 43–60. University of Utah Press, Salt Lake City.

Inomata, Takeshi. 2006. Politics and Theatricality in Mayan Society. In *Archaeology of Performance: Theaters of Power, Community, and Politics*, edited by T. Inomata and L. S. Cohen, 187–221. AltaMira Press, Lanham, MD.

Inomata, Takeshi, and Laura Stiver. 1998. Floor Assemblages from Burned Structures at Aguateca, Guatemala: A Study of Classic Maya Households. *Journal of Field Archaeology* 25(4):431–452.

Jackson, Sarah E. 2013. *Politics of the Maya Court: Hierarchy and Change in the Late Classic Period*. University of Oklahoma Press, Norman, Oklahoma.

Jackson, Sarah E., and David Stuart. 2001. Aj K'uhun Title: Deciphering a Classic Maya Term of Rank. *Ancient Mesoamerica* 12(2):217–228.

Jaramillo Arango, Antonio. 2016. Bitácora de un colgante Darién en el "Cenote Sagrado" de Chichén Itzá: In *Cuevas y cenotes mayas: Una mirada multidisciplinaria*, edited by Roberto Romero Sandoval, 173–195. Universidad Nacional Autónoma de México, Mexico City.

Johnson, Scott A. J. 2012. Late and Terminal Classic Power Shifts in Yucatan: The View from Popola. Unpublished PhD dissertation, Department of Anthropology, Tulane University, New Orleans.

Johnstone, Dave. 2001. The Ceramics of Yaxuna. Unpublished PhD dissertation, Department of Anthropology, Southern Methodist University, Dallas.

Jones, Christopher. 1977. Inauguration Dates of Three Late Classic Rulers of Tikal, Guatemala. *American Antiquity* 42(1):28–60.

Jones, Christopher. 1991. Cycles of Growth at Tikal. In *Classic Maya Political History*, edited by T. P. Culbert, 102–127. Cambridge University Press, Cambridge.

Jones, Christopher, and Miguel Orrego C. 1987. Corosal Stela 1 and Tikal Miscellaneous Stone 167: Two New Monuments from the Tikal Vicinity, Guatemala. *Mexicon* 9(6):129–133.

Jones, Christopher, and Linton Satterthwaite. 1982. *The Monuments and Inscriptions of Tikal: The Carved Monuments*. Tikal Report 33, Part A. University Museum, University of Pennsylvania, Philadelphia.

Jones, Grant D. 1998. *The Conquest of the Last Maya Kingdom*. Stanford University Press, Stanford, CA.

Josserand, J. Kathryn. 2007. The Missing Heir at Yaxchilan: Literary Analysis of a Maya Historical Puzzle. *Latin American Antiquity* 18(3):295–312.

Joyce, Rosemary A. 2011. Recognizing Religion in Mesoamerican Archaeology. In *The Oxford Handbook of the Archaeology of Ritual and Religion*, edited by T. Insoll, 541–555. Oxford University Press, Oxford.

Joyce, Rosemary A., and Julia A. Hendon. 2000. Heterarchy, History, and Material Reality: 'Communities' in Late Classic Honduras. In *The Archaeology of Communities: A New World Perspective*, edited by Marcello-Andrea Canuto and Jason Yaeger, 143–159. Routledge, London.

Just, Bryan R. 2005. Modifications of Ancient Maya Sculpture. *RES: Anthropology and Aesthetics* 48:69–82.

Kamal, Omar S., Gene A. Ware, Stephen D Houston, Douglas M. Chabries, Richard W. Christiansen, James Brady, and Ian Graham. 1999. Multispectral Image Processing for Detail Reconstruction and Enhancement of Maya Murals from La Pasadita, Guatemala. *Journal of Archaeological Science* 26(11):1391–1397.

Kathirithamby-Wells, Jeyamalar. 2009. "Strangers" and "Stranger-Kings": The Sayyid in Eighteenth-Century Maritime Southeast Asia. *Journal of Southeast Asian Studies* 40(3):567–591.

Keller, Kathryn C., and Plácido Luciano G. 1997. *Diccionario Chontal de Tabasco.* Instituto Lingüístico de Verano, Tucson, AZ.

Kelley, David H. 1962. Glyphic Evidence for a Dynastic Sequence at Quiriguá, Guatemala. *American Antiquity* 27(3):323–335.

Kelley, David H. 1965. The Birth of the Gods at Palenque. *Estudios de Cultura Maya* 5:93–134.

Kelley, David H. 1968. Kakupacal and the Itzas. *Estudios de Cultura Maya* 7:255–268.

Kelley, David H. 1976. *Deciphering the Maya Script.* Austin, University of Texas Press.

Kennett, Douglas J., Marilyn A. Masson, Stanley Serafin, Brendan J. Culleton, and Carlos Peraza Lope. 2015. War and Food Production at the Postclassic Maya City of Mayapán. In *The Archaeology of Food and Warfare: Food Insecurity in Prehistory*, edited by A. M. VanDerwarker and G. D. Wilson, 161–192. Springer, New York.

Kidder, Alfred V., Jesse D. Jennings, and Edwin M. Shook. 1946. *Excavations at Kaminaljuyu, Guatemala.* Carnegie Institution of Washington, Pub. 561, Washington, DC.

King, Eleanor M., ed. 2015. *The Ancient Maya Marketplace: The Archaeology of Transient Space.* University of Arizona Press, Tucson.

Klein, Cecelia. 1987. The Ideology of Sacrifice at the Templo Mayor. In *The Aztec Templo Mayor*, edited by E. H. Boone, 293–370. Dumbarton Oaks Research Library and Collection, Washington, DC.

Kluckhohn, Clyde. 1940. The Conceptual Structure in Middle American Archaeology. In *The Maya and Their Neighbors*, edited by C. L. Hay, R. L. Linton, S. K. Lothrop, H. L. Shapiro, and G. C. Valliant, 41–51. D. Appleton-Century, New York.

Knorosov, Yuri. 2001. New Data on the Maya Written Language. In *The Decipherment of Ancient Maya Writing*, edited by Stephen Houston, Oswaldo Chinchilla Mazariegos, and David Stuart, 144–152. University of Oklahoma Press, Norman.

Kristan-Graham, Cynthia. 1989. Art, Rulership, and the Mesoamerican Body Politic at Tula and Chichen Itza. Unpublished PhD dissertation, Department of Art History, University of California, Los Angeles.

Kristan-Graham, Cynthia. 1999. The Architecture of the Tula Body Politic. In *Mesoamerican Architecture as a Cultural Symbol*, edited by J. K. Kowalski, 162–175. Oxford University Press, New York.

Kristan-Graham, Cynthia. 2011. Structuring Identity at Tula: The Design and Symbolism of Colonnaded Halls and Sunken Spaces. In *Twin Tollans: Chichén Itzá, Tula, and the Epiclassic to Early Postclassic Mesoamerican World*, edited by Jeff K. Kowalski and Cynthia Kristan-Graham, 428–467. Dumbarton Oaks Research Library and Collection, Washington, DC.

Krochock, Ruth. 1988. The Hieroglyphic Inscriptions and iconography of the Temple of the Four Lintels and Related Monuments, Chichén Itzá, Yucatán, México. Unpublished MA thesis, Department of Art History, University of Texas, Austin.

Laporte, Juan Pedro. 2003. Architectural Aspects of Interaction between Tikal and Teotihuacan during the Early Classic Period. In *The Maya and Teotihuacan: Reinterpreting Early Classic Interaction*, edited by G. E. Braswell, 249–271. University of Texas Press, Austin.

Laporte, Juan Pedro, and Vilma Fialko C. 1990. New Perspectives on Old Problems: Dynastic References for the Early Classic at Tikal. In *Vision and Revision in Maya Studies*, edited by F. S. Clancy and P. D. Harrison, 33–66. University of New Mexico Press, Albuquerque.

Laporte, Juan Pedro, and Vilma Fialko C. 1995. Un reencuentro con Mundo Perdido, Tikal, Guatemala. *Ancient Mesoamerica* 6:41–94.

LeBlanc, Steven A., and Katherine E. Register. 2003. *Constant Battles: The Myth of the Peaceful, Noble Savage*. St. Martin's Press, New York.

LeCount, Lisa J. 1999. Polychrome Pottery and Political Strategies in Late and Terminal Classic Lowland Maya Society. *Latin American Antiquity* 10(3):239–258.

LeCount, Lisa J. 2001. Like Water for Chocolate: Feasting and Political Ritual among the Late Classic Maya at Xunantunich, Belize. *American Anthropologist* 103(4):935–953.

LeCount, Lisa J., and Jason Yaeger, eds. 2010. *Classic Maya Provincial Politics: Xunantunich and Its Hinterlands*. University of Arizona Press, Tucson.

Lee, David F. 2005. WK-06: Excavaciones en la Estructura L11–38, en el Complejo Palaciego Noroeste. In *Proyecto Arqueológico El Perú-Waka': Informe No. 2, Temporada 2004*, edited by H. L. Escobedo and D. A. Freidel, 111–42. Report submitted to the Instituto de Antropología e Historia, Guatemala City.

Lee, David F. 2012. Deciphering Indications of Social Memory in an Ancient Maya City Analysis of the Special Deposits from the Palace Complex at El Perú-Waka', Petén Guatemala. Unpublished PhD dissertation, Department of Anthropology, Southern Methodist University, Dallas.

León Portilla, Miguel. 1963 *Aztec Thought and Culture*. University of Oklahoma Press, Norman.

Lincoln, Charles E. 1986. The Chronology of Chichen Itza: A Review of the Literature. In *Late Lowland Maya Civilization*, edited by J. A. Sabloff and E. W. Andrews, 141–196. University of New Mexico Press, Albuquerque.

Lincoln, Charles E. 1990. Ethnicity and Social Organization at Chichen Itza, Yucatan, Mexico. Unpublished PhD dissertation, Department of Anthropology, Harvard University, Cambridge.

Looper, Matthew G. 1999. New Perspectives on the Late Classic Political History of Quirigua, Guatemala. *Ancient Mesoamerica* 10(2):263–280.

Looper, Matthew G. 2003. *Lightning Warrior: Maya Art and Kingship at Quirigua.* Linda Schele Series in Maya and Pre-Columbian Studies. University of Texas Press, Austin.

Looper, Matthew G. 2009. *To Be Like Gods: Dance in Ancient Maya Civilization.* University of Texas Press, Austin.

Looper, Matthew G., and Yuriy Polyukhovych. 2016. *A Familial Relationship between Nobles of El Peru (Waka') and El Zotz (Pa'chan) as Recorded on a Polychrome Vessel.* Glyph Dwellers, Report 47. Online report accessed X. Accessed February 12, 2015. http://myweb.csuchico.edu/~mlooper/glyphdwellers/pdf/R47.pdf.

López Luján, Leonardo. 2003. The Aztecs' Search for the Past. In *Aztecs*, edited by Eduardo Matos Moctezuma and Felipe Solís Olguín, 22–29. Thames and Hudson, London.

López Luján, Leonardo, and Alfredo López Austin. 2009. The Mexica in Tula and Tula in Mexico-Tenochtitlan. In *The Art of Urbanism: How Mesoamerican Kingdoms Represented Themselves in Architecture and Imagery*, edited by W. L. Fash and L. López Luján, 384–422. Dumbarton Oaks, Washington, DC.

López Luján, Leonardo, and Saburo Sugiyama. 2017. The Ritual Deposits in the Moon Pyramid at Teotihuacan. In *Teotihuacan: City of Water, City of Fire*, edited by M. Robb, 82–89. Fine Arts Museums of San Francisco and University of California Press, San Francisco and Oakland.

Lorenzen, Karl J. 2003. Miniature Masonry Shrines of the Yucatan Peninsula: Ancestor Deification in Late Postclassic Maya Ritual and Religion. Unpublished PhD dissertation, Department of Anthropology, University of California, Riverside.

Loten, H. Stanley. 2007. *Additions and Alterations: A Commentary on the Architecture of the North Acropolis, Tikal, Guatemala. Tikal Report 34, Part A.* University Museum Monograph 128. University of Pennsylvania Museum of Archaeology and Anthropology, Philadelphia.

Lothrop, Samuel K. 1952. *Metals from the Cenote of Sacrifice, Chichen Itza, Yucatan.* Memoirs of the Peabody Museum of Archaeology and Ethnology, Harvard University, Vol. 10, No. 2. Harvard University, Cambridge.

Loughmiller-Cardinal, Jennifer, and Clarissa Cagnato. 2016. Análisis del contenido de las vasijas del Entierro 61. In *Proyecto Arqueológico El Perú-Waka': Informe No. 13, Temporada 2015*, edited by J. C. Pérez Calderón, 219–249. Instituto de Antropología e Historia, Guatemala, City.

Love, Bruce. 1994. *The Paris Codex: Handbook for a Maya Priest.* University of Texas Press, Austin.

Loya González, Tatiana, and Travis W. Stanton. 2013. The Impact of Politics on Material Culture: Evaluating the Yaxuná-Cobá Sacbé. *Ancient Mesoamerica* 24(1):25–42.

Loya González, Tatiana, and Travis W. Stanton. 2014. Petrographic Analysis of Arena Red Ceramics at Yaxuná, Yucatán. In *The Archaeology of Yucatán: New Directions and Data*, edited by T. W. Stanton, 337–362. BAR International Series. Archaeopress, Oxford.

Lynch, Kevin. 1960. *The Image of the City.* Harvard University Press, Cambridge. MA.

Magnoni, Aline, Scott A. Johnson, and Travis W. Stanton. 2014. En la sombra de Chichén Itzá: Evaluando la iconografía de la región sureña de Chichén Itzá durante el Clásico Terminal. In *The Archaeology of Yucatán: New Directions and Data*, edited by T. W. Stanton, 297–314. BAR International Series. Archaeopress, Oxford.

Makemson, Maud Worcester. 1951. *The Book of the Jaguar Priest: A Translation of the Book of Chilam Balam of Tizimin.* Henry Schuman, New York.

Maler, Teobert. 1908. *Explorations in the Department of Peten, Guatemala and Adjacent Region: Topoxte, Yaxha, Benque Viejo, Naranjo.* Peabody Museum of American Archaeology and Ethnology, Harvard University, Cambridge, MA.

Manahan, T. Kam, and Marcello A. Canuto. 2009. Bracketing the Copan Dynasty: Late Preclassic and Early Postclassic Settlements at Copan, Honduras. *Latin American Antiquity* 20(3):553–580.

Manzanilla, Linda. 2003. Teopancazo: Un conjunto residencial teotihuacano. *Arqueología Mexicana* XI(64):50–53.

Marcus, Joyce. 1976. *Emblem and State in the Classic Maya Lowlands: An Epigraphic Approach to Terrestrial Organization.* Dumbarton Oaks, Washington, DC.

Marcus, Joyce. 1994. A Zapotec Inauguration in Comparative Perspective. In *Caciques and Their People*, edited by J. Marcus and J. F. Zeitlin, 245–274. Anthropological Paper 89. Museum of Anthropology University of Michigan, Ann Arbor.

Marcus, Joyce. 2000. Cinco mitos sobre la guerra maya. In *La guerra entre los antiguos mayas*, edited by S. Trejo, 225–247. Instituto Nacional de Antropología e Historia, Mexico City.

Marcus, Joyce. 2001. Breaking the Glass Ceiling: The Strategies of Royal Women in Ancient States. In *Gender in Pre-Hispanic America*, edited by C. Klein, 305–340. Dumbarton Oaks Research Library and Collection, Washington, DC.

Marcus, Joyce. 2003. The Maya and Teotihuacan. In *The Maya and Teotihuacan: Reinterpreting Early Classic Interaction*, edited by G. E. Braswell, 337–356. University of Texas Press, Austin.

Marcus, Joyce. 2004a. Calakmul y su papel en el origen del estado maya. In *Los investigadores de la cultura maya* 12. Vol. 1:14–31. Universidad Autónoma de Campeche, Campeche, Mexico.

Marcus, Joyce. 2004b. Primary and Secondary State Formation in Southern Mesoamerica. In *Understanding Early Classic Copan*, edited by E. E. Bell, M. A. Canuto, and R. J. Sharer, 357–373. University of Pennsylvania Museum of Archaeology and Anthropology, Philadelphia.

Marcus, Joyce. 2006. Identifying Elites and Their Strategies. In *Intermediate Elites in Pre-Columbian States and Empires*, edited by C. M. Elson and R. A. Covey, 212–246. University of Arizona Press, Tucson.

Marengo, Nelda. 2013. Análisis funcional de cerámica en un basurero de una acrópolis triádica en Yaxuná, Yucatán. Licenciatura thesis, Department of Anthropology, Universidad de las Américas Puebla, Cholula, Mexico.

Marken, Damien B. 2011. City and State: Urbanism, Rural Settlement, and Polity in the Classic Maya Lowlands. Unpublished PhD dissertation, Department of Anthropology, Southern Methodist University, Dallas.

Marken, Damien B. 2015. Conceptualizing the Spatial Dimensions of Classic Maya States: Polity and Urbanism at El Peru-Waka', Peten. In *Classic Maya Polities of the Southern Lowlands: Integration, Interaction, Dissolution,* edited by D. B. Marken and J. L. Fitzsimmons, 123–166. University Press of Colorado, Boulder.

Marquina, Ignacio. 1951. *Arquitectura prehispánica.* Instituto Nacional de Antropología e Historia, Mexico City.

Martin, Simon. 1993. Site Q: The Case for a Classic Maya Super-Polity. Manuscript accessed online. http://www.mesoweb.com/articles/martin/SiteQ.html.

Martin, Simon. 1997. The Painted King List: A Commentary on Codex-Style Dynastic Vases. In *The Maya Vase Book: A Corpus of Rollout Photographs of Maya Vases.* Vol. 5, edited by B. Kerr and J, Kerr, 846–867. Kerr and Associates, New York.

Martin, Simon. 2000. At the Periphery: The Movement, Modification, and Re-Use of Early Monuments in the Environs of Tikal. In *The Sacred and the Profane: Architecture and Identity in the Maya Lowlands*, edited by P. R. Colas, K. Delvendahl, M. Kuhnert, and A. Schubart, 51–61. Acta Mesoamericana 10. Verlag Anton Saurwein, Möckmühl, Germany.

Martin, Simon. 2003. In Line of the Founder: A View of Dynastic Politics at Tikal. In *Tikal: Dynasties, Foreigners, and Affairs of State*, edited by J. A. Sabloff, 3–45. School of American Research Press, Santa Fe.

Martin, Simon. 2004. A Broken Sky: The Ancient Name of Yaxchilan as Pa'Chan. *PARI Journal* 5(1):1–7.

Martin, Simon. 2005. Of Snakes and Bats: Shifting Identities at Calakmul. *PARI Journal* 6(2):5–13.

Martin, Simon. 2008a. A Caracol Emblem Glyph at Tikal. In *Artifacts, Emblems and Toponyms, Tikal, Uncategorized*, edited by D. Stuart. Blog. Accessed October 1, 2016. https://decipherment.wordpress.com/category/tikal/page/2/.

Martin, Simon. 2008b. Wives and Daughters on the Dallas Altar. Manuscript. Mesoweb, accessed online. www.mesoweb.com/articles/martin/Wives&Daughters.pdf.

Martin, Simon. 2015. The Old Man of the Maya Universe: Unified Aspects to Ancient Maya Religion. In *Maya Archaeology 3*, edited by C. W. Golden, S. D. Houston, and J. Skidmore, 196–228. Precolumbia Mesoweb Press, San Francisco.

Martin, Simon, and Dmitri Beliaev. 2017. K'ahk' Ti' Ch'ich': A New Snake King from the Early Classic Period. *PARI Journal* 17(3):1–7.

Martin, Simon, and Nikolai Grube. 1995. Maya Superstates. *Archaeology* 48(6):41–46.

Martin, Simon, and Nikolai Grube. 2000. *Chronicle of the Maya Kings and Queens: Deciphering the Dynasties of the Ancient Maya*. Thames and Hudson, New York.

Martin, Simon, and Nikolai Grube. 2008. *Chronicle of the Maya Kings and Queens: Deciphering the Dynasties of the Ancient Maya*. 2nd ed. Thames and Hudson, New York.

Masson, Marilyn A. 1999. Postclassic Maya Communities at Progresso Lagoon and Laguna Seca, Northern Belize. *Journal of Field Archaeology* 25(3):285–306.

Masson, Marilyn A. 2000. *In the Realm of Nachan Kan: Postclassic Maya Archaeology at Laguna de On, Belize*. University of Colorado Press, Boulder.

Masson, Marilyn A., Timothy S. Hare, Carlos Peraza Lope, Bárbara C. Escamilla Ojeda, Elizabeth Paris, Betsy Kohut, Bradley W. Russell, and Wilberth Cruz Alvarado. 2016. Household Craft Production in the Prehispanic Urban Setting of Mayapán, Yucatan, Mexico. *Journal of Archaeological Research*. 24(3):1–46.

Masson, Marilyn A., and Carlos Peraza Lope. 2007. Kukulkan/Quetzalcoatl, Death God, and Creation Mythology of Burial Shaft Temples at Mayapán. *Mexicon* 24 (3):77–85.

Masson, Marilyn A., and Carlos Peraza Lope. 2013. The Distribution and Diversity of Faunal Exploitation at Mayapan: From Temple to Houselot. In *The Archaeology of Mesoamerican Animals*, edited by C. M. Götz and K. F. Emery, 233–280. Archaeobiology Series. Lockwood Press, Atlanta.

Masson, Marilyn A., and Carlos Peraza Lope. 2014a. Militarism, Misery, and Collapse. In *Kukulcan's Realm: Urban Life at Ancient Mayapán*, by M. Masson and C. Peraza Lope, 521–540. University Press of Colorado, Boulder.

Masson, Marilyn A., and Carlos Peraza Lope. 2014b. Archaeological Investigations of an Ancient Urban Place. In *Kukulcan's Realm: Urban Life at Ancient Mayapán*, by M. Masson and C. Peraza Lope, 38–75. University Press of Colorado, Boulder.

Masson, Marilyn A., and Carlos Peraza Lope. 2014c. The Economic Foundations. In *Kukulcan's Realm: Urban Life at Ancient Mayapán*, by Marilyn Masson and Carlos Peraza Lope, 269–424. University Press of Colorado, Boulder.

Mastache, Alba Guadalupe, Robert Cobean, and Dan Healan. 2002. *Ancient Tollan: Tula and the Toltec Heartland*. University of Colorado Press, Boulder.

Mastache, Alba Guadalupe, Dan M. Healan, and Robert H. Cobean. 2009. Four Hundred Years of Settlement and Cultural Continuity in Epiclassic and Early Postclassic Tula. In *The Art of Urbanism: How Mesoamerican Kingdoms Represented Themselves in Architecture and Imagery*, edited by W. L. Fash and L. López Luján, 290–328. Dumbarton Oaks, Washington, DC.

Mathews, Peter. 1988. The Sculpture of Yaxchilán. Unpublished PhD dissertation, Department of Anthropology, Yale University, New Haven, CT.

Mathews, Peter. 1997. *La escultura de Yaxchilán*. Colección Científica del Instituto Nacional de Antropología e Historia 368. Instituto Nacional de Antropología e Historia, Mexico City.

Mathews, Peter, and Linda Schele. 1974. Lords of Palenque: The Glyphic Evidence. In *Primera Mesa Redonda de Palenque*. Pt. 1, edited by M. Greene Robertson, 63–75. Robert Louis Stevenson School, Pebble Beach.

Matsumoto, Mallory. 2013. Reflection as Transformation: Mirror-Image Structure on Maya Monumental Texts as a Visual Metaphor for Ritual Participation. *Estudios de Cultura Maya* 41(41):93–128.

May Ciau, Rossana B. 2000. Análisis de las torres este y oeste de la Estructura 8 de Labná, Yucatán. Unpublished Licenciatura thesis, Facultad de Ciencias Antropológicas, Universidad Autónoma de Yucatán, Mérida.

Mayer, Karl H. 1995. *Maya Monuments: Sculptures of Unknown Provenance, Supplement 4*. Academic Publishers, Graz, Austria.

McAnany, Patricia A. 1995. *Living with the Ancestors*. University of Texas Press, Austin.

McGee, R. Jon. 1998. The Lacandon Incense Burner Renewal Ceremony. In *The Sowing and the Dawning: Termination, Dedication, and Transformation in the Archaeological and Ethnographic Record of Mesoamerica*, edited by S. B. Mock, 41–46. University of New Mexico Press, Albuquerque.

Melgar Tísoc, Emiliano Ricardo, and Chloé Andrieu. 2016. Informe del análisis tecnológico de objetos de jadeíta de El Perú-Waka'. In *Proyecto Arqueológico El*

*Perú-Waka': Informe No. 13, Temporada 2015*, edited by Juan Carlos Pérez Calderón, 265–280. Instituto de Antropología e Historia, Guatemala, City.

Mendieta, Gerónimo. 1980. *Historia eclesiástica indiana*. Editorial Porrúa, Mexico City.

Milbrath, Susan, and Carlos Peraza Lope. 2003a. Revisiting Mayapan: Mexico's Last Maya Capital. *Ancient Mesoamerica* 14(1):1–46.

Milbrath, Susan, and Carlos Peraza Lope. 2003b. Mayapán's Scribe: A Link with Classic Maya Artists. *Mexicon* 25:120–123.

Milbrath, Susan, and Carlos Peraza Lope. 2013. Mayapán's Effigy Censers: Iconography and Archaeological Context. In *Ancient Maya Pottery: Classification, Analysis, and Interpretation*, edited by J. J. Aimers, 203–228. University Press of Florida, Gainesville.

Milbrath, Susan, and Debra S. Walker. 2016. Regional Expressions of the Postclassic Effigy Censer System in the Chetumal Bay Area. In *Perspectives on the Ancient Maya of Chetumal Bay*, edited by D. S. Walker, 185–213. University Press of Florida, Gainesville.

Miller, Arthur G. 1977. "Captains of the Itza": Unpublished Mural Evidence from Chichen Itza. In *Social Process in Maya Prehistory*, edited by N. Hammond, 197–225. Academic Press, London.

Millon, Clara. 1973. Painting, Writing, and Polity at Teotihuacan, Mexico. *American Antiquity* 38(3):294–314.

Miller, Mary Ellen, and Marcos Samayoa. 1998. Where Maize May Grow: Jade, Chacmools, and the Maize God. *RES* 33 (Spring):54–72.

Millon, René. 1988. The Last Years of Teotihuacan Dominance. In *The Collapse of Ancient States and Civilizations*, edited by N. Yoffee and G. L. Cowgill, 102–164. University of Arizona Press, Tucson.

Mills, Barbara, and William H. Walker, eds. 2008. *Memory Work: Archaeologies of Material Practices*. School of Advanced Research Press, Santa Fe.

Mock, Shirley B. 1998. Prelude. In *The Sowing and the Dawning: Termination, Dedication, and Transformation in the Archaeological and Ethnographic Record of Mesoamerica*, edited by S. B. Mock, 3–18. University of New Mexico Press, Albuquerque.

Mock, Shirley B., ed. 1998. *The Sowing and the Dawning: Termination, Dedication, and Transformation in the Archaeological and Ethnographic Record of Mesoamerica*. University of New Mexico Press, Albuquerque.

Moholy-Nagy, Hattula. 2003. The Hiatus at Tikal, Guatemala. *Ancient Mesoamerica* 14(1):77–83.

Moholy-Nagy, Hattula. 2008. *The Artifacts of Tikal: Ornamental and Ceremonial Artifacts and Unworked Material*. Tikal Report 27A. University of Pennsylvania Museum of Archaeology and Anthropology, Philadelphia.

Moholy-Nagy, Hattula. 2016. Set in Stone: Hiatuses and Dynastic Politics at Tikal, Guatemala. *Ancient Mesoamerica* 27(2):255–266.

Monaghan, John D. 1998. The Person, Destiny, and the Construction of Difference in Mesoamerica. *RES* 33:137–146.

Morehart, Christopher T., and Shanti Morell-Hart. 2015. Beyond the Ecofact: Toward a Social Paleoethnobotany in Mesoamerica. *Journal of Archaeological Method and Theory* 22(2): 483–511.

Morley, Sylvanus G., and George W. Brainerd. 1983. *The Ancient Maya.* 4th ed., revised by R. J. Sharer. Stanford University Press, Stanford, CA.

Morris, Earl H., Jean Charlot, and Ann A. Morris. 1931. *The Temple of the Warriors at Chichen Itza, Yucatan.* Carnegie Institution of Washington, Pub 406. Carnegie Institution of Washington, Washington, DC.

Navarro-Farr, Olivia. 2005. WK-01: Excavaciones en la Estructura M13–1, segunda temporada. In *Proyecto Arqueológico El Perú-Waka': Informe No. 2, Temporada 2004*, edited by H. L. Escobedo and D. A. Freidel, 05–36. Instituto de Antropología e Historia, Guatemala City.

Navarro-Farr, Olivia. 2009. Ritual, Process, and Continuity in the Late to Terminal Classic Transition: Investigations at Structure M13–1 in the Ancient Maya Site of El Perú-Waka', Petén, Guatemala. Unpublished PhD dissertation, Department of Anthropology, Southern Methodist University, Dallas.

Navarro-Farr, Olivia C., Griselda Pérez Robles, and Damaris Menéndez Bolaños. 2013. WK-01: Excavaciones en la Estructura M13–1. In *Proyecto Arqueológico El Perú-Waka': Informe No. 10, Temporada 2012*, edited by J. C. Pérez Calderón, 12–100. Instituto de Antropología e Historia, Guatemala City.

Navarro-Farr, Olivia C., Griselda Pérez Robles, Juan Carlos Pérez, and Damaris Menéndez Bolaños. 2016. Investigaciones en El Perú-Waka', Guatemala. *Arqueología Mexicana* 137:32–37.

Navarro-Farr, Olivia C., and Michelle Rich, eds. 2014. *Archaeology at El Perú-Waka': Performances of Ritual, Memory, and Power.* University of Arizona Press, Tucson.

Nicholson, H. B., and Eloise Quiñones Keber. 1983. *Art of Aztec Mexico: Treasures of Tenochtitlan.* National Gallery of Art, Washington, DC.

Nielsen, Jesper. 2003. Art of the Empire: Teotihuacan Iconography and Style in Early Classic Maya Society (AD 380–500). Unpublished PhD dissertation, Department of American Indian Languages and Cultures, Institute of History of Religions, University of Copenhagen, Copenhagen.

Nielsen, Jesper, and Christophe Helmke. 2008. Spearthrower Owl Hill: A Toponym at Atetelco, Teotihuacan. *Latin American Antiquity* 19(4):459–474.

Nielsen, Jesper, and Bente Juhl Andersen. 2004. Collecting in Corozal: Late Postclassic Maya Effigy Censers from Belize in the Danish National Museum (1860–1865). *Mayab* 17:84–98.

Nielson, Axel E., and William H. Walker, eds. 2014. *Warfare in Cultural Context: Practice, Agency, and the Archaeology of Violence*. University of Arizona Press, Tucson.

Novelo Rincón, Gustavo A. 2012. La arquitectura del grupo Puuc de Yaxuná. Unpublished Licenciatura thesis, Facultad de Ciencias Antropológicas, Universidad Autónoma de Yucatán, Mérida.

Otterbein, Keith F. 1973. The Anthropology of War. In *Handbook of Social and Cultural Anthropology*, edited by J. Honigmann, 923–958. Rand McNally and Company, Chicago.

Otterbein, Keith F. 2009. *The Anthropology of Wa.*, Waveland Press, Long Grove, IL.

Pagliaro, Jonathan B., James F. Garber, and Travis W. Stanton. 2003. Evaluating the Archaeological Signatures of Maya Ritual and Conflict. In *Ancient Mesoamerican Warfare*, edited by M. K. Brown and T. W. Stanton, 75–89. AltaMira Press, Walnut Creek.

Palka, Joel W. 2003. Social Status and Differential Processes of Abandonment at the Classic Maya Center of Dos Pilas, Peten, Guatemala. In *The Archaeology of Settlement Abandonment in Middle America*, edited by T. Inomata and R. A. Webb, 121–133. University of Utah Press, Salt Lake City.

Paris, Elizabeth H., and Carlos Peraza Lope. 2013. Breaking the Mold: The Socioeconomic Significance of Metal Artifacts at Mayapan. In *Archaeometallurgy in Mesoamerica: Current Approaches and New Perspectives*, edited by A. N. Shugar and S. E. Simmons, 161–201. University Press of Colorado, Boulder.

Paris, Elizabeth H., and Bradley W. Russell. 2012. Zona de entierros Itzmal Ch'en. In *Proyecto Los Fundamentos del Poder Económico de Mayapán, Temporada 2008: Informe Final para el Consejo Nacional de Arqueología de México*, edited by M. A. Masson, C. Peraza Lope, T. S. Hare, and B. W. Russell 71–236. Department of Anthropology, University at Albany–SUNY, Albany.

Paris, Elizabeth H., Stanley Serafin, Marilyn A. Masson, Carlos Peraza Lope, Cuauhtémoc Vidal Guzmán, and Bradley W. Russell. 2017. Violence, Desecration, and Urban Collapse at the Postclassic Maya Capital of Mayapán. *Journal of Anthropological Archaeology* 48:63–86.

Parmington, Alexander. 2003. Classic Maya Status and the Subsidiary "Office" of Sajal: A Comparative Study of Status as Represented in Costume and Composition in the Iconography of Monuments. *Mexicon* 25(2):46–53.

Patterson, Erin. 2013. Análisis preliminar de restos óseos humanos: Temporada 2012. In *Proyecto Arqueológico El Perú-Waka': Informe No. 10, Temporada 2012*, edited by

Juan Carlos Pérez Calderón, 92–105. Instituto de Antropología e Historia, Guatemala City.

Peraza Lope, Carlos A. 1999. Mayapán: Ciudad-capital del Posclásico. *Arqueología* 7(37):48–53.

Peraza Lope, Carlos, Pedro Delgado Kú, and Bárbara Escamilla Ojeda. 2002. *Trabajos de mantenimiento y conservación arquitectónica en Mayapán, Yucatán, Informe de la Tercera Temporada 1998, Tomo I.* Unpublished report presented to the Consejo de Arqueología del Instituto Nacional de Antropología e Historia. Centro INAH–Yucatán, Mérida.

Peraza Lope, Carlos, and Marilyn A. Masson. 2014a. An Outlying Temple, Hall, and Elite Residence. In *Kukulcan's Realm: Urban Life at Ancient Mayapán*, by M. Masson and C. Peraza Lope, 105–148. University Press of Colorado, Boulder.

Peraza Lope, Carlos, and Marilyn A. Masson. 2014b. Politics and Monumental Legacies. In *Kukulcan's Realm: Urban Life at Ancient Mayapán*, by M. Masson and C. Peraza Lope, 39–104. University Press of Colorado, Boulder.

Peraza Lope, Carlos, and Marilyn A. Masson. 2014c. Religious Practice. In *Kukulcan's Realm: Urban Life at Ancient Mayapán*, by M. Masson and C. Peraza Lope, 427–520. University Press of Colorado, Boulder.

Peraza Lope, Carlos, Marilyn A. Masson, and Wilberth Cruz Alvarado. n.d. Imágenes de los dioses: artesanos e incensarios efigie del Postclásico en Mayapán. In *II Mesa Redonda del Mayab: Lla ciencia y las artes entre los mayas*, edited by A. Barrera Rubio. Solar Servicios Editoriales, Mérida Unpublished manuscript.

Peraza Lope, Carlos, Marilyn A. Masson, Timothy S. Hare, and Pedro C. Delgado Kú. 2006. The Chronology of Mayapán: New Radiocarbon Evidence. *Ancient Mesoamerica* 17:153–175.

Pérez de Heredia Puente, Eduardo J. 2012. The Yabnal-Motul Ceramic Complex of the Late Classic Period at Chichen Itza. *Ancient Mesoamerica* 23(2):379–402.

Pérez Martínez, Vitalino, Federico García, Felipe Martínez, and Jeremias López. 1996. *Diccionario del idioma ch'orti'.* Proyecto Lingüístico Francisco Marroquín, La Antigua, Guatemala City.

Pérez Robles, Griselda, and Olivia Navarro-Farr. 2013. WK01: excavaciones en M13-1 y el descubrimiento de la Estela 44. In *Proyecto Arqueológico El Perú-Waka': Informe No. 11, Temporada 2013*, edited by J. C. Pérez Calderón, 3–26. Instituto de Antropología e Historia, Guatemala City.

Piehl, Jennifer. 2008. Análisis preliminar de los restos humanos de contextos mortuorios y rituales en Waka' y Chakah. In *Proyecto Arqueológico El Perú-Waka': Informe No.7, Temporada 2009*, edited by H. L. Escobedo, J. C. Meléndez, and D. A. Freidel, 173–206. Report submitted to the Instituto de Antropología e Historia, Guatemala City.

Piehl, Jennifer. 2009. Análisis de estroncio en muestras de fauna y restos óseos humanos: Informe de los materiales exportados en marzo 2008. Internal Project Memorandum, Waka' Archaeological Research Project, in possession of the authors.

Pitarch, Pedro. 2011. *The Jaguar and the Priest: An Ethnography of Tzeltal Souls*. University of Texas Press, Austin.

Plank, Shannon E. 2004. *Maya Dwellings in Hieroglyphs and Archaeology: An Integrative Approach to Ancient Architectural and Spatial Cognition*. BAR International Series 1324. Archaeopress, Oxford.

Polian, Gilles. 2015 Diccionario multidialectal del tseltal: Tseltal-Español. Accessed February 17, 2020. https://tseltaltokal.org/wp-content/uploads/2018/09/Polian_Diccionario-multidialectal-del-tseltal-enero2015-2.pdf.

Pollock, H.E.D. 1936. *The Casa Redonda at Chichen Itza, Yucatan*. Carnegie Institution of Washington, Pub. 559, 129–154, Washington, DC.

Prager, Christian, and Elisabeth Wagner. 2013. A Possible Hieroglyphic Reference to Yax K'uk' Mo at Caracol, Belize. *Mexicon* 35(2):31–32.

Price, T. Douglas, James H. Burton, Peter D. Fullager, Lori E. Wright, Jane E. Buikstra, and Vera Tiesler. 2008. Strontium Isotopes and the Study of Human Mobility in Ancient Mesoamerica. *Latin American Antiquity* 19(2):167–180.

Price, T. Douglas, James A. Burton, Robert J. Sharer, Jane E. Buikstra, Lori E. Wright, Loa P. Traxler, and Katherine A. Miller. 2010. Kings and Commoners at Copán: Isotopic Evidence for Origins and Movement in the Classic Maya Period. *Journal of Anthropological Archaeology* 29(1):15–32.

Price, T. Douglas, James H. Burton, Lori E. Wright, Christine D. White, and Fred Longstaffe. 2007. Victims of Sacrifice: Isotopic Evidence for Place of Origin. In *New Perspectives on Human Sacrifice and Ritual Body Treatments in Ancient Maya Society*, edited by V. Tiesler and A. Cucina, 263–292. Springer-Verlag, New York.

Price, T. Douglas, Seiichi Nakamura, Shintaro Suzuki, James H. Burton, and Vera Tiesler. 2014. New Isotope Data on Maya Mobility and Enclaves at Classic Copan, Honduras. *Journal of Anthropological Archaeology* 36(1):32–47.

Price, T. Douglas, Travis W. Stanton, and Andrea Cucina. 2018. Isotopes, Dental Morphology, and Human Provenience at the Maya Site of Yaxuna, Yucatan, Mexico: Mobility, Interaction, and Ethnicity. In *Bioarchaeology of Pre-Columbian Mesoamerica: An Interdisciplinary Approach*, edited by C. Willermet and A. Cucina, 70–98. University of Florida Press, Gainesville.

Proskouriakoff, Tatiana. 1960. Historical Implications of a Pattern of Dates at Piedras Negras, Guatemala. *American Antiquity* 25(4):454–475.

Proskouriakoff, Tatiana. 1962. Civic and Religious Structures of Mayapan. In *Mayapan, Yucatan, Mexico*, edited by H.E.D. Pollock, R. L. Roys, T. Proskouriakoff, and A. L. Smith, 87–140. Carnegie Institution of Washington Pub. 619. Carnegie Institution of Washington, Washington, DC.

Proskouriakoff, Tatiana. 1963. Historical Data in the Inscriptions of Yaxchilan, Part I. *Estudios de Cultura Maya* 3:149–167.

Proskouriakoff, Tatiana. 1964. Historical Data in the Inscriptions of Yaxchilan, Part II. *Estudios de Cultura Maya* 4:177–201.

Proskouriakoff, Tatiana. 1968. The Jog and Jaguar Signs in Maya Writing. *American Antiquity* 33(2):247–251.

Proskouriakoff, Tatiana. 1993. *Maya History*. University of Texas Press, Austin.

Proskouriakoff, Tatiana, and Charles R. Temple. 1955. A Residential Quadrangle: Structures R-85 to R-90. In *Current Reports* 29:289–362. Carnegie Institution of Washington, Washington, DC.

Pugh, Timothy W. 2001. Flood Reptiles, Serpent Temples, and the Quadripartite Universe: The Imago Mundi of Late Postclassic Mayapan. *Ancient Mesoamerica* 12:247–258.

Pugh, Timothy W. 2002. Remembering Mayapan: Peten Kowoj Architecture as Social Metaphor and Power. In *The Dynamics of Power*, edited by M. O'Donovan, 301–323. Center for Archaeological Investigations, Carbondale, IL.

Pugh, Timothy W., and Leslie G. Cecil. 2012. The Contact Period of Central Petén, Guatemala in Color. *RES: Anthropology and Aesthetics* 61/62:315–329.

Pugh, Timothy W., and Prudence M. Rice. 2009. Kowoj Ritual Performance and Societal Representations at Zacpetén. In *The Kowoj: Identity, Migrations, and Geopolitics in Late Postclassic Petén, Guatemala*, edited by P. M. Rice and D. S. Rice, 141–191. University Press of Colorado, Boulder.

Puleston, Dennis E. 1974. Intersite Areas in the Vicinity of Tikal and Uaxactun. In *Mesoamerican Archaeology*, edited by N. Hammond, 303–311. University of Texas Press, Austin.

Rathje, William L. 2002. The Nouveau Elite Potlatch: One Scenario for the Monumental Rise of Early Civilizations. In *Ancient Maya Political Economies*, edited by M. A. Masson and D. A. Freidel, 31–40. AltaMira Press, Walnut Creek.

Reents-Budet, Dorie. 1994. *Painting the Maya Universe: Royal Ceramics of the Classic Period*. Duke University Press, Durham, NC.

Reents-Budet, Dorie, Ronald L. Bishop, Jennifer T. Taschek, and Joseph W. Ball. 2000. Out of the Palace Dumps. *Ancient Mesoamerica* 11(1):99–121.

Reese-Taylor, Kathryn, Peter Mathews, Julia Guernsey, and Marlene Fritzler. 2009. Warrior Queens among the Classic Maya. In *Blood and Beauty: Organized Violence in the Art and Archaeology of Mesoamerica and Central America*, edited by H. O. Orr and R. Koontz, 39–72. Ideas, Debates, and Perspectives 4. Cotsen Institute of Archaeology Press, Los Angeles.

Renfrew, Colin, and John F. Cherry, eds. 1986. *Peer Polity Interaction and Socio-Political Change.* Cambridge University Press, Cambridge.

Rice, Prudence M. 1999. Rethinking Classic Lowland Maya Pottery Censers. *Ancient Mesoamerica* 10(1):25–50.

Rice, Prudence M. 2004. *Maya Political Science: Time, Astronomy, and the Cosmos.* University of Texas Press, Austin.

Rice, Prudence M. 2009. Incense Burners and Other Ritual Ceramics. In *The Kowoj: Identity, Migration and Geopolitics in Late Postclassic Peten, Guatemala,* edited by Prudence M. Rice and Don S. Rice, 276–315. University Press of Colorado, Boulder.

Riese, Berthold. 1984. Kriegsberichte der klassichen Maya. *Baessler-Archiv, Beiträge zur Völkerkunde* 30(2):255–321.

Ringle, William M. 2004. On the Political Organization of Chichen Itza. *Ancient Mesoamerica* 15(2):167–218.

Ringle, William M., and George J. Bey III. 2001. Post-Classic and Terminal Classic Courts of the Northern Maya Lowlands. In *Royal Courts of the Ancient Maya, Volume Two: Data and Case Studies,* edited by T. Inomata and S. D. Houston, 266–307. Westview Press, Boulder.

Robertson, Robin A. 1983. Functional Analysis and Social Process in Ceramics: The Pottery from Cerros, Belize. In *Civilization in the Ancient Americas: Essays in Honor of Gordon R. Willey,* edited by R. M. Leventhal and A. L. Kolata, 105–142. University of New Mexico Press. Albuquerque.

Robles Castellanos, Fernando. 1990. *La secuencia cerámica de la región de Cobá, Quintana Roo.* Instituto Nacional de Antropología e Historia, Mexico City.

Robles Salmerón, Amparo, Travis W. Stanton, and Aline Magnoni. 2011. Investigaciones preliminares en el sitio de Ikil, Yucatán. In *Los Investigadores de la Cultura Maya 19,* 123–140. Universidad Autónoma de Campeche, Campeche, Mexico.

Romero Blanco, Karina. 2002. Museo Arqueológico de Cancún. *Arqueología Mexicana* 9(54):50–51.

Roys, Ralph L. 1933. *The Book of Chilam Balam of Chumayel.* Carnegie Institution of Washington, Pub. 438. Carnegie Institution of Washington, Washington, DC.

Roys, Ralph L. 1943. *The Indian Background of Colonial Yucatan.* Carnegie Institution of Washington, Pub. 548. Carnegie Institution of Washington, Washington, DC.

Roys, Ralph L. 1962. Literary Sources for the History of Mayapán. In *Mayapan, Yucatan, Mexico,* edited by H.E.D. Pollock, Ralph L. Roys, Tatiana Proskouriakoff, and A. L. Smith, 2–86. Carnegie Institution of Washington, Pub. 619. Carnegie Institution of Washington, Washington, DC.

Roys, Ralph L. 1967. *The Book of Chilam Balam of Chumayel.* University of Oklahoma Press, Norman.

Ruppert, Karl. 1935. *The Caracol at Chichen Itza*. Carnegie Institution of Washington, Pub. 454. Carnegie Institution of Washington, Washington, DC.

Ruppert, Karl. 1952. *Chichen Itza: Architectural Notes and Plans*. Carnegie Institution of Washington, Pub. 593. Carnegie Institution of Washington, Washington, DC.

Russell, Bradley W. 2000. Pottery Censer Form, Function, and Symbolism in the Postclassic Lowlands. Unpublished MA thesis, Department of Anthropology, State University of New York, Albany.

Russell, Bradley W. 2007. Colonnaded Hall Group Discovered outside Mayapan City Walls. *Mexicon* 29(4):93–94.

Russell, Bradley W. 2013. Fortress Mayapan: Key Defensive Features of a Postclassic Maya Fortification. *Ancient Mesoamerica* 24(2):275–294.

Sabloff, Jeremy A. 1983. Classic Maya Settlement Pattern Studies: Past Problems, Future Prospects. In *Prehistoric Settlement Pattern Studies: Retrospect and Prospect*, edited by E. Z. Vogt and R. M. Leventhal, 413–422. Peabody Museum, Harvard University and University of New Mexico Press, Cambridge, MA, and Albuquerque.

Sabloff, Jeremy A. 1986. Interaction among Classic Maya Polities: A Preliminary Examination. In *Peer Polity Interaction and Socio-Political Change*, edited by Colin Renfrew and J. F. Cherry, 109–116. Cambridge University Press, Cambridge.

Sabloff, Jeremy A. 1990. *The New Archaeology and the Ancient Maya*. Scientific American Library. W. H. Freeman, San Francisco.

Sabloff, Jeremy A. 2004. Looking Backward and Looking Forward: How Maya Studies of Yesterday Shape Today. In *Continuities and Changes in Maya Archaeology: Perspectives at the Millennium*, edited by C. W. Golden and G. Borgstede, 13–20. Routledge, New York.

Sabloff, Jeremy A. 2015. On the History of Archaeological Research in Mesoamerica, with Particular Reference to Pre-Columbian Maya Civilization. In *Globalized Antiquity: Uses and Perceptions of the Past in South Asia, Mesoamerica, and Europe*, edited by U. Schurer, D. M. Segesser, and T. Spath, 219–229. Reimer, Berlin.

Sabloff, Jeremy A., and Wendy Ashmore. 2001. An Aspect of Archaeology's Recent Past and Its Relevance in the New Millennium. In *Archaeology in the New Millennium*, edited by G. Feinman and T. D. Price, 11–32. Kluwer Academic/Plenum, New York.

Sahagún, Bernadino de. 1950–1982. *General History of the Things of New Spain: Florentine Codex*. Translated by Arthur J. O. Anderson and Charles E. Dibble, 13 vols. University of Utah Press, Salt Lake City.

Sahlins, Marshall D. 1981. The Stranger-King or Dumezil among the Fijans. *Journal of Pacific History* 16(3):107–132.

Sahlins, Marshall D. 2008. The Stranger-King or, Elementary Forms of the Politicas of Life. *Indonesia and the Malay World* 36(105):177–199.

Sampeck, Kathryn E. 2007. Late Postclassic to Colonial Landscapes and Political Economy of the Izalcos Region, El Salvador. Unpublished PhD dissertation, Department of Anthropology, Tulane University, New Orleans.

Sanders, William T. 1960. *Prehistoric Ceramics and Settlement Patterns in Quintana Roo, Mexico*. Contributions to American Anthropology and History, No. 60, Carnegie Institution of Washington, Pub. 606. Carnegie Institution of Washington, Washington, DC.

Sanders, William T., and Joseph W. Michels, eds. 1977. *Teotihuacan and Kaminaljuyu: A Study in Prehistoric Culture Contact*. Pennsylvania State University Press Monograph Series on Kaminaljuyu, State College.

Satterthwaite, Linton. 1958. *The Problem of Abnormal Stela Placements at Tikal and Elsewhere*. Tikal Report No. 3. University Museum Press, Philadelphia.

Saturno, William A., Karl A. Taube, and David Stuart. 2005. *The Murals of San Bartolo, El Peten, Guatemala: Part 1, North Wall*. Ancient America 7. Center for Ancient American Studies, Barnardsville, NC.

Saville, Marshall H. 1925. *The Wood-Carver's Art in Ancient Mexico*. Contributions 9. Museum of the American Indian, Heye Foundation, New York.

Schele, Linda. 1992. The Founders of Lineages at Copan and Other Maya Sites. *Ancient Mesoamerica* 3(1):135–144.

Schele, Linda, and David A. Freidel. 1990. *A Forest of Kings: The Untold Story of the Ancient Maya*. Quill, New York.

Schele, Linda, and Matthew Looper. 1996. Part 2: The Inscriptions of Quirigua and Copan. In *Notebook for the XXth Maya Hieroglyphic Forum, March 9–10, 1996*. Department of Art and Art History, the College of Fine Arts, and the Institute of the Latin American Studies. University of Texas, Austin.

Schele, Linda, and Peter Mathews. 1998. *The Code of Kings: The Language of Seven Sacred Maya Temples and Tombs*. Scribner, New York.

Schele, Linda, and Mary E. Miller. 1986. *Blood of Kings: Dynasty and Ritual in Maya Art*. George Barziller, New York.

Scherer, Andrew K. 2015. *Mortuary Landscapes of the Ancient Maya: Rituals of Body and Soul*. University of Texas, Austin.

Scherer, Andrew K. 2018. Head Shaping and Tooth Modification among the Classic Maya of the Usumacinta River Kingdoms. In *Social Skins of the Head: Body Beliefs and Ritual in Ancient Mesoamerica and the Andes*, edited by V. Tiesler, 59–80. University of New Mexico Press, Albuquerque.

Scherer, Andrew K., and Charles W. Golden. 2009. Tecolote, Guatemala: Archaeological Evidence for a Fortified Late Classic Maya Political Border. *Journal of Field
Archaeology* 34(3):285–304.

Scherer, Andrew K., and Charles W. Golden. 2012. *Revisiting Maler's Usumacinta:
Recent Archaeological Investigation in Chiapas, Mexico.* Precolumbia Mesoweb
Monographs 1. Precolumbia Mesoweb Press, San Francisco.

Scherer, Andrew K., and Charles W. Golden. 2014. War in the West: History,
Landscape, and Classic Maya Conflict. In *Embattled Bodies, Embattled Places: War
in Pre-Columbian Mesoamerica and the Andes*, edited by A. K. Scherer and J. W.
Verano, 57–92. Dumbarton Oaks, Washington, DC.

Scherer, Andrew K., Charles W. Golden, Ana Lucía Arroyave, and Griselda Pérez
Robles. 2014. Danse Macabre: Death, Community, and Kingdom at El Kinel,
Guatemala. In *The Bioarchaeology of Space and Place: Ideology, Power, and Meaning
in Maya Mortuary Contexts*, edited by G. Wrobel, 193–224. Springer, New York.

Schmidt, Peter. 1998. Contacts with Central Mexico and the Transition to the
Postclassic: Chichen Itza in Central Yucatan. In *Maya*, edited by P. Schmidt, M.
de la Garza, and E. Nalda, 427–449. Rizzoli International Publications, New York.

Schmidt, Peter. 2003. Proyecto Chichén Itzá: Informe de actividades julio de 1999 a
diciembre de 2002. Report submitted to the Instituto Nacional de Antropología e
Historia, Mexico City.

Schmidt, Peter. 2007. Birds, Ceramics, and Cacao: New Excavations at Chichén Itzá,
Yucatan. In *Twin Tollans: Chichén Itzá, Tula, and the Epiclassic to Early Postclas-
sic Mesoamerican World*, edited by J. K. Kowalski and C. Kristan-Graham, 151–203.
Dumbarton Oaks, Washington, DC.

Schmidt, Peter J., Péter Biró, and Eduardo Pérez de Heredia. 2018. El Temple de los
Búhos de Chichén Itzá y su emplazamiento cronológico: Una nueva propuesta.
*Estudios de Cultura Maya* 52:11–49.

Schmidt, Peter, David Stuart, and Bruce Love. 2008. Inscriptions and Iconography of
Castillo Viejo, Chichen Itza. *PARI Journal* 11(2):1–17.

Schortman, Edward M., and Wendy Ashmore. 2012. History, Networks, and the
Quest for Power: Ancient Political Competition in the Lower Motagua Valley,
Guatemala. *Journal of the Royal Anthropological Institute* 18(1):1–21.

Schortman, Edward, and Seiichi Nakamura. 1991. A Crisis of Identity: Late Classic
Competition and Interaction on the Southeast Maya Periphery. *Latin American
Antiquity* 2(4):311–336.

Schortman, Edward M., and Patricia A. Urban. 1994. Living on the Edge: Core-
Periphery Relations in Ancient Southeastern Mesoamerica. *Current Anthropology*
35(4):401–430.

Schortman, Edward M., Patricia A. Urban, Wendy A. Ashmore, and Julie C. Benyo. 1986. Interregional Interaction in the SE Maya Periphery: The Santa Barbara Archaeological Project 1983–1984 Seasons. *Journal of Field Archaeology* 13:259–272.

Seler, Eduard E. 1902–1923. *Gesammelte Abhandlungen zur Amerikanischen Sprach und Alterthumskunde.* Ascher and Co., Berlin.

Seler, Eduard E. 1916. *Die Quetzalcoatl-Fassaden Yukatekischer Bauten.* Der Königl, Akademie der Wissenschaften, Berlin.

Seler, Eduard E. 1963. *Comentarios al Códice Borgia.* 2 vols. accompanying facsimile. Trans. M. Fenk. Fonda de Cultura Económica, México, D.F.

Serafin, Stanley. 2010. Bioarchaeological Investigation of Violence at Mayapan. Unpublished PhD dissertation, Department of Anthropology, Tulane University, New Orleans.

Serafin, Stanley, and Carlos Peraza Lope. 2007. Human Sacrificial Rites among the Maya of Mayapan: A Bioarchaeological Perspective. In *New Perspectives on Human Sacrifice and Ritual Body Treatments in Ancient Maya Society*, edited by V. Tiesler and A. Cucina, 232–250. Springer, New York.

Sharer, Robert J. 1978. Archaeology and History at Quirigua, Guatemala. *Journal of Field Archaeology* 5(1):51–70.

Sharer, Robert J. 1999. Archaeology and History in the Royal Acropolis, Copán, Honduras. *Expedition* 41(2):8–15.

Sharer, Robert J. 2002. Early Classic Dynastic Origins in the Southeastern Maya Lowlands. In *Incidents of Archaeology in Central America and Yucatan: Essays in Honor of Edwin M. Shook*, edited by M. Love, M. Poponoe de Hatch, and H. Escobedo, 459–476. University Press of America, Lanham, MD.

Sharer, Robert J. 2003. Founding Events and Teotihuacan Connections at Copán, Honduras. In *The Maya and Teotihuacan: Reinterpreting Early Classic Interaction*, edited by G. E. Braswell, 143–165. University of Texas Press, Austin.

Sharer, Robert J. 2004. External Interaction at Early Classic Copan. In *Understanding Early Classic Copan*, edited by E. E. Bell, M. A. Canuto, and R. J. Sharer, 299–317. University of Pennsylvania Museum of Archaeology and Anthropology, Philadelphia.

Sharer, Robert J., William L. Fash, David W. Sedat, Loa P. Traxler, and Richard Williamson. 1999. Continuities and Contrasts in Early Classic Architecture of Central Copan. In *Mesoamerican Architecture as a Cultural Symbol*, edited by J. K. Kowalski, 220–249. Oxford University Press, New York.

Sharer, Robert J., David W. Sedat, Loa P. Traxler, Julia C. Miller, and Ellen E. Bell. 2005. Early Classic Royal Power in Copan: The Origins and Development of the Acropolis (ca. AD 250–600). In *Copán: The History of an Ancient Maya Kingdom*, edited by E. W. Andrews V and W. L. Fash, 139–200. School of American Research Press, Santa Fe.

Sharer, Robert J., and Loa P. Traxler. 2006. *The Ancient Maya*. 6th ed. Stanford University Press, Stanford, CA.

Sharer, Robert J., and Loa P. Traxler. 2009. Copán and Quirigua: Shifting Destinies in the Southeastern Lowlands. Paper presented at the 14th European Maya Conference, Kraków.

Shatto, Rahilla Corinne Abbas. 1998. *Maritime Trade and Seafaring of the Precolumbian Maya*. Unpublished MA thesis, Department of Anthropology, Texas A&M University, College Station.

Shaw, Justine M. 1998. The Community Settlement Patterns and Community Architecture of Yaxuna from AD 600–1400. Unpublished PhD thesis, Department of Anthropology, Southern Methodist University, Dallas.

Shaw, Justine M. 2001. Maya Sacbeob: Form and Function. *Ancient Mesoamerica* 12(2):261–272.

Shaw, Justine M., and Dave Johnstone. 2001. The Late Classic of Yaxuna, Yucatan, Mexico. *Mexicon* 23(1):10–14.

Shaw, Justine M., and Dave Johnstone. 2006. Classic Politics in the Northern Maya Lowlands. In *Lifeways in the Northern Maya Lowlands: New Approaches to Archaeology in the Yucatán Peninsula*, edited by J. P. Mathews and B. A. Morrison, 142–154. University of Arizona Press, Tucson.

Shook, Edwin M. 1954. A Round Temple at Mayapán. In *Current Reports 16*, 15–26. Carnegie Institution of Washington, Washington, DC.

Shook, Edwin M., and William N. Irving. 1955. Colonnaded Buildings at Mayapán. *Current Reports 22*, 127–224. Carnegie Institute of Washington, Department of Archaeology, Washington, DC.

Slocum, Marianna C., Florence L. Gerdel, and Manuel Cruz Aguilar. 1999. *Diccionario tzeltal de Bachajón, Chiapas*. Instituto Lingüístico de Verano, México, D.F.

Smith, A. Ledyard. 1962. Residential and Associated Structures at Mayapan. In *Mayapan, Yucatan, Mexico*, edited by H.E.D. Pollock, R. L. Roys, T. Proskouriakoff, and A. L. Smith, 165–320. Carnegie Institution of Washington, Pub. 335. Carnegie Institution of Washington, Washington, DC.

Smith, Robert E. 1971. *The Pottery of Mayapan*. Papers of the Peabody Museum of Archaeology and Ethnology. Vol. 66. Harvard University, Cambridge, MA.

Smyth, Michael P., José Ligorred Perramon, David Ortegón Zapata, and Pat Farrell. 1998. An Early Classic Center in the Puuc Region: New Data from Chac II, Yucatán, Mexico. *Ancient Mesoamerica* 9(2):233–257.

Soler-Arechalde, A. M., F. Sánchez, M. Rodriguez, C. Caballero-Miranda, A. Goguitchaishvili, J. Urrutia-Fucugauchi, L. Manzanilla, and D. H. Tarling. 2006.

Archaeomagnetic Investigation of Oriented Pre-Columbian Lime-Plasters from Teotihuacan, Mesoamerica. *Earth Planets Space* 58(10):1433–1439.

Solís, Felipe, ed. 2009. *Teotihuacan: Cité des Dieux.* Musée du quai Branley, Paris.

Sosa, John R., and Dorie J. Reents. 1980. Glyphic Evidence for Classic Maya Militarism. *Belizean Studies* 8(3):2–11.

Stanton, Travis W., M. Kathryn Brown, and Jonathan B. Pagliaro. 2008. Garbage of the Gods? Squatters, Refuse Disposal, and Termination Rituals among the Ancient Maya. *Latin American Antiquity* 19(3):227–247.

Stanton, Travis W., and David A. Freidel. 2005. Placing the Centre, Centering the Place: The Influence of Formative Sacbeob in Classic Site Design at Yaxuná, Yucatán. *Cambridge Archaeological Journal* 15(2):225–249.

Stanton, Travis W., David A. Freidel, Charles K. Suhler, Traci Ardren, James N. Ambrosino, Justine M. Shaw, and Sharon Bennett. 2010. *Excavations at Yaxuná, 1986–1996: Results of the Selz Foundation Yaxuná Project.* BAR International Series 2056. Archaeopress, Oxford.

Stanton, Travis W., and Tomás Gallareta Negrón. 2001. Warfare, Ceramic Economy, and the Itzá: A Reconsideration of the Itzá Polity in Ancient Yucatán. *Ancient Mesoamerica* 12(2):229–246.

Stanton, Travis W., and Aline Magnoni. 2008. Places of Remembrance: The Use and Perception of Abandoned Structures in the Maya Lowlands. In *Ruins of the Past: The Use and Perception of Abandoned Structures in the Maya Lowlands,* edited by T. W. Stanton and A. Magnoni, 1–24. University Press of Colorado, Boulder.

Stanton, Travis W., and Aline Magnoni. 2016. Proyecto de Interacción Política del Centro de Yucatán: Séptima Temporada de Campo. Technical report submitted to the Consejo de Arqueología del Instituto Nacional de Antropología e Historia, Mexico City.

Stanton, Travis W., and Nelda I. Marengo Camacho. 2014. Una cueva colapsada en la Acrópolis Norte de Yaxuná. In *The Archaeology of Yucatán: New Directions and Data,* edited by T. W. Stanton, 363–375. BAR International Series. Archaeopress, Oxford.

Stone, Andrea J. 1989. Disconnection, Foreign Insignia, and Political Expansion: Teotihuacan and the Warrior Stelae of Piedras Negras. In *Mesoamerica after the Decline of Teotihuacan,* AD 700–900, edited by R. A. Diehl and J. C. Berlo, 153–172. Dumbarton Oaks Research Library and Collection, Washington, DC.

Stone, Andrea J. 1991. *Aspects of Impersonation in Classic Maya Art. In Sixth Palenque Round Table, 1986,* edited by M. Greene Robertson and V. Fields. University of Oklahoma Press, Norman.

Stone, Andrea J., Dorie Reents, and Robert Coffman. 1985. Genealogical Documentation of the Middle Classic Dynasty of Caracol, El Cayo, Belize. In *Fourth*

*Palenque Round Table 1980*, edited by M. Robertson and E. Benson, 267–275. Pre-Columbian Art Research Institute, San Francisco.

Stone, Andrea, and Marc Zender. 2011. *Reading Maya Art: A Hieroglyphic Guide to Ancient Maya Painting and Sculpture*. Thames and Hudson, London.

Storey, Rebecca. 2005. Health and Lifestyle (before and after Death) among the Copán Elite. In *Copán: The History of an Ancient Maya Kingdom*, edited by E. W. Andrews V and W. L. Fash, 315–343. School of American Research. Santa Fe, New Mexico.

Stuart, David. 1985. The Inscriptions on Four Shell Plaques from Piedras Negras, Guatemala. In *Fourth Palenque Round Table, 1980*, edited by M. Greene Robertson and E. P. Benson, 175–183. The Pre-Columbian Art Research Institute, San Francisco.

Stuart, David. 1987. *Ten Phonetic Syllables*. Research Reports on Ancient Maya Writing 14. Center for Maya Research, Washington, DC.

Stuart, David. 1993. Historical Inscriptions and the Maya Collapse. In *Lowland Maya Civilization in the Eighth Century* AD, edited by J. A. Sabloff and J. S. Henderson, 321–354. Dumbarton Oaks, Washington, DC.

Stuart, David. 1996. Kings of Stone: A Consideration of Stelae in Maya Ritual and Representation, *RES* 29/30:149–171.

Stuart, David. 1998. "The Fire Enters His House": Architecture and Ritual in Classic Maya Texts. In *Function and Meaning in Classic Maya Architecture*, edited by S. D. Houston, 373–425. Dumbarton Oaks Research Library and Collection, Washington, DC.

Stuart, David. 2000. "The Arrival of Strangers": Teotihuacan and Tollan in Classic Maya History. In *Mesoamerica's Classic Heritage: From Teotihuacan to the* Aztecs, edited by D. Carrasco, L. Jones, and S. Sessions, 465–513. University Press of Colorado, Boulder.

Stuart, David. 2004. The Beginnings of the Copan Dynasty: A Review of the Hieroglyphic and Historical Evidence. In *Understanding Early Classic Copan*, edited by E. E. Bell, M. A. Canuto, and R. J. Sharer, 215–247. University of Pennsylvania Museum of Archaeology and Anthropology, Philadelphia.

Stuart, David. 2005a. Glyphs on Pots: Decoding Classic Maya Ceramics. Part II: Selected Topics. In *Sourcebook for the 29th Maya Hieroglyphic Forum, March 11–16, 2005*, 115–165. Department of Art and Art History, University of Texas, Austin.

Stuart, David. 2005b. *The Inscriptions from Temple XIX at Palenque*. The Pre-Columbian Art Research Institute, San Francisco, CA.

Stuart, David. 2006. The Palenque Mythology. In *Sourcebook for the 30th Maya Meetings, March 14–19, 2006*, 85–194. The Mesoamerica Center, Department of Art and Art History, University of Texas, Austin.

Stuart, David. 2007. The Origin of Copan's Founder. Maya Decipherment: Ideas on Ancient Maya Writing and Iconography, blog entry June 25, 2007. Blog. September 22, 2015. https://decipherment.wordpress.com/2007/06/25/the-origin-of-copans-founder/.

Stuart, David. 2008. Unusual Signs 1: A Possible Co syllable. http://decipherment.wordpress.com/2008/09/13/unusual-signs-1-a-possible-co-syllable/.

Stuart, David. 2008. A Childhood Ritual on The Hauberg Stela. In *Maya Decipherment: Ideas on Ancient Maya Writing and Iconography*. https://decipherment.wordpress.com/2008/03/27/a-childhood-ritual-on-the-hauberg-stela/.

Stuart, David. 2010a. Shining Stones: Observations on the Ritual Meaning of Early Maya Stelae. In *The Place of Stone Monuments: Context, Use, and Meaning in Mesoamerica's Preclassic Tradition*, edited by J. Guernsey, J. E. Clark, and B. Arroyo, 283–297. Dumbarton Oaks, Washington, DC.

Stuart, David. 2010b. Notes on Accession Dates in the Inscriptions of Coba. www.mesoweb.com/stuart/notes/Coba.pdf.

Stuart, David. 2011. *The Order of Days: The Maya World and the Truth about 2012*. Harmony Books, New York.

Stuart, David. 2012a. Maya Spooks. In *Maya Decipherment: A Weblog on the Ancient Maya Script*. https://decipherment.wordpress.com/2012/10/26/maya-spooks/.

Stuart, David. 2012b. The Name of Paper: The Mythology of Crowning and Royal Nomenclature on Palenque's Palace Tablet. In *Maya Archaeology 2*, edited by C. W. Golden, S. D. Houston, and J. Skidmore, 116–142. Precolumbia Mesoweb Press, San Francisco.

Stuart, David. 2014. A Possible Sign for Metate. *Maya Decipherment* https://decipherment.wordpress.com/2014/02/04/a-possible-sign-for-metate/.

Stuart, David, and Stephen D. Houston. 1994. *Classic Maya Place Names*, Studies in Pre-Columbian Art and Archaeology 33. Dumbarton Oaks, Washington, DC.

Stuart, David, Stephen D. Houston, and John Roberts. 1999. *Notebook for the XXIII Maya Hieroglyphic Forum at Texas, March 1999, Part II*, transcribed and edited by Phil Wanyerka. Maya Workshop Foundation, University of Texas, Austin.

Stuart, David, and Linda Schele. 1986. Yax-K'uk'-Mo', the Founder of the Lineage of Copán. *Copán Note 6*. Instituto Hondureño de Antropología e Historia and the Copán Acropolis Archaeological Project, Austin, TX.

Sugiyama, Nawa. 2014. Animals and Sacred Mountains: How Ritualized Performances Materialized State-Ideologies at Teotihuacan, Mexico. Unpublished PhD dissertation, Department of Anthropology, Harvard University, Cambridge, MA.

Sugiyama, Nawa. 2017. Pumas Eating Human Hearts? Animal Sacrifice and Captivity at the Moon Pyramid. In *Teotihuacan: City of Water, City of Fire*, edited by M.

Robb, 90–93. Fine Arts Museums of San Francisco and University of California Press, San Francisco.

Sugiyama, Saburo. 1989. Burials Dedicated to the Old Temple of Quetzalcoatl at Teotihuacan. *American Antiquity* 54(1):85–106.

Sugiyama, Saburo. 1992. Rulership, Warfare, and Human Sacrifice at the Ciudadela: An Iconographic Study of Feathered Serpent Representations. In *Art, Ideology, and the City of Teotihuacan*, edited by J. C. Berlo, 205–230. Dumbarton Oaks Research Library and Collection, Washington, DC.

Sugiyama, Saburo. 2005. *Human Sacrifice, Militarism, and Rulership: Materialization of State Ideology at the Feathered Serpent Pyramid, Teotihuacan*. Cambridge University Press, Cambridge.

Sugiyama, Saburo. 2017. The Feathered Serpent Pyramid at Teotihuacan: Monumentality and Sacrificial Burials. In *Teotihuacan: City of Water, City of Fire*, edited by M. Robb, 56–61. Fine Arts Museums of San Francisco and University of California Press, San Francisco.

Sugiyama, Saburo, Rubén Cabrera Castro, and Leonardo López Luján. 2004. The Moon Pyramid Burials. In *Voyage to the Center of the Moon Pyramid: Recent Discoveries in Teotihuacan*, edited by S. Sugiyama, 20–30. Arizona State University, Tempe.

Sugiyama, Saburo, and Leonardo López Luján. 2007. Dedicatory Burial/Offering Complexes at the Moon Pyramid, Teotihuacan. *Ancient Mesoamerica* 18(1):127–146.

Suhler, Charles K. 1996. Excavations at the North Acropolis, Yaxuna, Yucatan, Mexico. Unpublished PhD dissertation, Department of Anthropology, Southern Methodist University, Dallas.

Suhler, Charles, Traci Ardren, and David Johnstone. 1998. The Chronology of Yaxuna: Evidence from Excavation and Ceramics. *Ancient Mesoamerica* 9(1):167–182.

Suhler, Charles K., and David A. Freidel. 1998. Life and Death in a Maya War Zone. *Archaeology* 51(3):28–34.

Swensen, Edward. 2015. The Archaeology of Ritual. *Annual Review of Anthropology* 44:329–345.

Tate, Carolyn E. 1992. *Yaxchilan: The Design of a Maya Ceremonial City*. University of Texas Press, Austin.

Taube, Karl A. 1985. The Classic Maya Maize God: A Reappraisal. In *Fifth Palenque Round Table, 1983*, edited by M. Greene Robertson and V. M. Fields, 171–181. The Pre-Columbian Art Research Institute, San Francisco.

Taube, Karl A. 1992a. *The Major Gods of Ancient Yucatan*. Dumbarton Oaks Research Library and Collection, Washington, DC.

Taube, Karl A. 1992b. The Temple of Quetzalcoatl and the Cult of Sacred War at Teotihuacan. *RES* 21:53–87.

Taube, Karl A. 1994. The Iconography of Toltec Period Chichen Itza. In *Hidden among the Hills: Maya Archaeology of the Northwest Yucatan Peninsula*, edited by H. J. Prem, 197–211. Acta Mesoamericana 7. Verlag Von Fleming, Möckmühl.

Taube, Karl A. 2000. The Turquoise Hearth: Fire, Self-Sacrifice, and the Central Mexican Cult of War. In *Mesoamerica's Classic Heritage: From Teotihuacan to the Aztecs*, edited by D. Carrasco, L. Jones, and S. Sessions, 269–340. University Press of Colorado, Boulder.

Taube, Karl A. 2001. The Breath of Life: The Symbolism of Wind in Mesoamerica and the American Southwest. In *The Road to Aztlan: Art From a Mythic Homeland*, edited by V. M. Fields and V. Zamudio-Taylor, 102–123. Los Angeles County Museum of Art, Los Angeles.

Taube, Karl A. 2003a. Ancient and Contemporary Maya Conceptions about Field and Forest. In *The Lowland Maya Area: Three Millennia at the Human-Wildland Interface*, edited by A. Gómez-Pompa, M. F. Allen, S. L. Fedick, and J. J. Jiménez-Osornio, 461–492. Food Products Press, New York.

Taube, Karl A. 2003b. Tetitla and the Maya Presence at Teotihuacan. In *The Maya and Teotihuacan: Reinterpreting Early Classic Interaction*, edited by G. E. Braswell, 273–314. University of Texas Press, Austin.

Taube, Karl A. 2004a. Aztec Religion: Creation, Sacrifice, and Renewal. In *The Aztec Empire*, edited by Felipe Solís, 168–177. Guggenheim Museum, New York.

Taube, Karl A. 2004b. "Flower Mountain: Concepts of Life, Beauty, and Paradise among the Classic Maya." *RES: Anthropology and Aesthetics* 45:69–98.

Taube, Karl A. 2004c. Structure 10L-16 and Its Early Classic Antecedents: Fire and the Evocation and the Resurrection of K'inich Yax K'uk' Mo'. In *Understanding Early Classic Copan*, edited by E. E. Bell, M. A. Canuto, and R. J. Sharer, 265–295. University of Pennsylvania Museum of Archaeology and Anthropology, Philadelphia.

Taube, Karl A. 2005. Representaciones del paraíso en el arte cerámico del Clásico Temprano de Escuintla, Guatemala. In *Iconografía y escritura teotihuacana en la costa sur de Guatemala y Chiapas*, edited by Oswaldo Chinchilla and Barbara Arroyo, *U tz'ib*, Serie Reportes 1(5):33–54. Asociación Tikal, Guatemala City.

Taube, Karl A. 2006. Climbing Flower Mountain: Concepts of Resurrection and the Afterlife at Teotihuacan. In *Arqueología e historia del centro de México*, edited by L. López Luján, D. Carrasco, and L. Cué, 153–170. Instituto Nacional de Antropología e Historia, Mexico City.

Taube, Karl A. 2009a. The Maya Maize God and the Mythic Origins of Dance. In *The Maya and Their Sacred Narratives: Text and Context of Maya Mythologies*, edited by G. Le Fort, R. Gardiol, S. Matteo, and C. Helmke, 41–52. Verlag Anton Saurwein, Markt Schwaben, Germany.

Taube, Karl A. 2009b. The Womb of the World: The *Cuauhxicalli* and Other Offering Bowls of Ancient and Contemporary Mesoamerica. In *Maya Archaeology 1*, edited by C. Golden, S. Houston, and J. Skidmore, 86–106. Precolumbia Mesoweb Press, San Francisco.

Taube, Karl A. 2010a. At Dawn's Edge: Tulúm, Santa Rita, and Floral Symbolism in the International Style of Late Postclassic Mesoamerica. In *Astronomers, Scribes, and Priests: Intellectual Interchange between the Northern Maya Lowlands and Highland Mexico in the Late Postclassic Period*, edited by G. Vail and C. Hernández, 145–191. Dumbarton Oaks, Washington, DC.

Taube, Karl A. 2010b. Gateways to Another World: The Symbolism of Flowers in Mesoamerica and the American Southwest. In *The Land Brightened with Flowers: The Hopi Iconography Project*, edited by K. Hays-Gilpin and P. Schaafsma, 73–120. Museum of Northern Arizona Bulletin 67, Museum of Northern Arizona, Flagstaff.

Taube, Karl A. 2011. Teotihuacan and the Development of Writing in Early Classic Central Mexico. In *Their Way of Writing: Scripts, Signs, and Pictographies in Pre-Columbian America*, edited by E. H. Boone and G. Urton, 77–109. Dumbarton Oaks, Washington, DC.

Taube, Karl A. 2012. The Symbolism of Turquoise in Postclassic Mexico. In *Turquoise in Mexico and North America: Science, Conservation, Culture and Collections*, edited by J.C.H. King, M. Carocci, C. Cartwright, C. McEwan, and R. Stacy, 117–134. British Museum, London.

Taube, Karl A. 2013. The Classic Maya Temple: Centrality, Cosmology and Sacred Geography in Ancient Mesoamerica. In *Heaven on Earth: Temples, Ritual and Cosmic Symbolism in the Ancient World*, edited by D. Ragavan, 89–125. Oriental Institute, University of Chicago, Chicago.

Taube, Karl A. 2015. The Huastec Sun God: Portrayals of Solar Imagery, Sacrifice, and War in Postclassic Huastec Iconography. In *The Huasteca: Cultural History and Regional Exchange*, edited by K. A. Faust and K. N. Richter, 98–127. University of Oklahoma Press, Norman.

Taube, Karl A. 2017 Aquellos del este: Representaciones de dioses y hombres mayas en las pinturas realistas de Tetitla, Teotihuacan. In *Las pinturas realistas de Tetitla, Teotihuacan: Estudios a través las acuarelas de Agustín Villagra Caleti*, edited by L. Staines Cicero and C. Helmke, 71–99. Universidad Nacional Autónoma de México, Mexico City.

Taube, Karl A. 2018. Orígines y simbolismo de la diedad de Viento en Mesoamérica. *Arqueología Mexicana* 152:34–39.

Taube, Karl, David Stuart, William A. Saturno, and Heather Hurst. 2010. *The Murals of San Bartolo, El Petén, Guatemala.* Part 2: *The West Wall.* Ancient America 10. Center for Ancient American Studies, Barnardsville, NC.

Taube, Rhonda, and Karl Taube. 2009. The Beautiful, the Bad, and the Ugly: Aesthetics and Morality in Maya Figurines. In *Mesoamerican Figurines: Small Scale Indices Large Scale Phenomena*, edited by C. Halperin, K. Faust, R. Taube, and A. Giguet, 236–58. University Press of Florida, Gainesville.

Taylor, Walter W. 1948. *A Study of Archaeology.* Memoirs of the American Anthropological Association 69. Anthropological Association, Menasha, WI.

Tedlock, Dennis. 1985. *Popul Vuh: The Mayan Book of the Dawn of Life.* Simon and Schuster, New York.

Tedlock, Dennis. 2003. *Rabinal Achi: A Mayan Drama of War and Sacrifice.* Oxford University Press, Oxford.

Teufel, Stefanie. 2008. Marriage Diplomacy: Women at the Royal Court. In *Maya: Divine Kings of the Rain Forest*, edited by N. Grube, 172–173. Könemann, Cologne, Germany.

Thompson, Donald E. 1955. An Altar and Platform at Mayapán. In *Current Reports 28*, 281–288. Carnegie Institution of Washington, Washington, DC.

Thompson, J. Eric S. 1954. *The Rise and Fall of Maya Civilization.* University of Oklahoma Press, Norman.

Thompson, J. Eric S. 1957. *Deities Portrayed on Censers at Mayapan.* Current Reports 40. Carnegie Institution of Washington, Washington, DC.

Thompson, J. Eric S. 1962. *A Catalog of Maya Hieroglyphs.* University of Oklahoma Press, Norman.

Tiesler, Vera. 2011. Becoming Maya: Infancy and Upbringing through the Lens of Pre-Hispanic Head Shaping. *Childhood in the Past* 4(1):117–132.

Tiesler, Vera. 2013. *The Bioarchaeology of Artificial Cranial Modification: New Approaches to Head-Shaping and Its Meanings in Pre-Columbian Mesoamerica and Beyond.* Springer Press, New York.

Tiesler, Vera, Andrea Cucina, Travis W. Stanton, and David A. Freidel. 2017. *Before Kukulkán: Maya Life, Death, and Identity at Classic Period Yaxuná, Yucatan, Mexico.* University of Arizona Press, Tucson.

Tokovinine, Alexandre. 2005. The Dynastic Struggle and the Biography of a Sajal: I was with *That* King. In *Wars and Conflicts in Prehispanic Mesoamerica and Andes*, edited by P. Eeckhout and G. LeFort, 37–49. BAR International Series 1385. Archaeopress, Oxford.

Tokovinine, Alexandre. 2007. Of Snake Kings and Cannibals: A Fresh Look at the Naranjo Hieroglyphic Stairway. *PARI Journal* 7(4):15–22.

Toscano Hernández, Lourdes, and David Ortegón Zapata. 2003. Yaxuná: Un centro de acopio del tributo itzá. In *Los Investigadores de la Cultura Maya 11*, 438–445. Universidad Autónoma de Campeche, Campeche, Mexico.

Tozzer, Alfred M. 1941. *Landa's Relación de las cosas de Yucatán*. Papers of the Peabody Museum of American Archaeology and Ethnology, Paper 18. Harvard University, Cambridge.

Tozzer, Alfred M. 1957. *Chichen Itza and Its Cenote of Sacrifice*. Memoirs of the Peabody Museum of Archaeology and Ethnology, Vols. 11 and 12. Harvard University, Cambridge.

Traxler, Loa P. 2001. The Royal Court of Early Classic Copan. In *Royal Courts of the Ancient Maya*, Vol. 2: *Data and Case Studies*, edited by T. Inomata and S. D. Houston, 46–73. Westview Press, Boulder.

Traxler, Loa P. 2003. At Court in Copan: Palace Groups of the Early Classic. In *Maya Palaces and Elite Residences: An Interdisciplinary Approach*, edited by J. J. Christie, 46–68. University of Texas Press, Austin.

Traxler, Loa P. 2004. Redesigning Copan: Early Architecture of the Polity Center. In *Understanding Early Classic Copan*, edited by E. E. Bell, M. A. Canuto, and R. J. Sharer, 53–64. University of Pennsylvania Museum of Archaeology and Anthropology, Philadelphia.

Trombold, Charles D., ed. 1991. *Ancient Road Networks and Settlement Hierarchies in The New World*. Cambridge University Press, Cambridge.

Urban, Patricia A., and Edward M. Schortman, eds. 1986. *The Southeast Maya Periphery*. University of Texas Press, Austin.

Urban, Patricia A., and Edward M. Schortman. 1988. The Southeast Zone Viewed from the East: Lower Motagua-Naco Valleys. In *The Southeast Classic Maya Zone*, edited by E. Hill Boone and G. R. Willey, 223–267. Dumbarton Oaks, Washington, DC.

Urban, Patricia A., Edward M. Schortman, and Marne Ausec. 2002. Power without Bounds? Middle Preclassic Political Developments in the Naco Valley, Honduras. *Latin American Antiquity* 13(2):131–152.

Valdés, Juan Antonio, and Federico Fahsen. 1995. The Reigning Dynasty of Uaxactun During the Early Classic: The Rulers and the Ruled. *Ancient Mesoamerica* 6(2):197–219.

Vallejo Cáliz, Daniel, and T. Kam Manahan. 2014. Procesos de abandono de una estructura doméstica en Xuenkal durante el Clásico Tardío-Terminal. In *The Archaeology of Yucatán: New Directions and Data*, edited by T. W. Stanton, 257–279. BAR International Series. Archaeopress, Oxford.

Van Dyke, Ruth M., and Susan E. Alcock, eds. 2003. *Archaeologies of Memory*. Blackwell Publishing, Oxford.

Van Oss, Sarah Elizabeth. 2016. The Queen's Serpent: An Examination of the Serpent Vessel from Burial 61 from El Perú-Waka'. Unpublished BA thesis. College of Wooster, Wooster, OH.

Varela Torrecilla, Carmen. 1998. *El Clásico Medio en el noroccidente de Yucatán*. Paris Monographs in American Archaeology, No. 2, BAR International Series 739. BAR, Oxford.

Varela Torrecilla, Carmen, and Geoffrey E. Braswell. 2003. Teotihuacan and Oxkintok: New Perspectives from Yucatán. In *The Maya and Teotihuacan: Reinterpreting Early Classic Interaction*, edited by G. E. Braswell, 249–271. University of Texas Press, Austin.

Vargas de la Peña, Leticia, and Víctor Castillo Borges. 2001. La pintura mural prehispánica en Ek'balam, Yucatán. In *La pintura mural prehispánica en México: Area maya*, edited by B. de la Fuente, 403–418. Universidad Nacional Autónoma de México, Mexico City.

Velázquez Morlet, Adriana. 1995. Cosmogonía y vida cotidiana en Kohunlich. *Arqueología Mexicana* 3(11):32–36.

Vidal Guzmán, Cuauhtémoc. 2011. Violence at Mayapan: The Taphonomy of Battered and Burned Remains from Itzmal Ch'en. Unpublished paper on file, Department of Anthropology, University at Albany–SUNY, Albany.

Villa Rojas, Alfonso. 1945. *The Maya of East Central Quintana Roo*. Carnegie Institution of Washington, Pub. 559. Washington, DC.

Vogt, Evon Z. 1969. *Zinacantan: A Maya Community in the Highlands of Chiapas*. Harvard University Press, Cambridge. MA.

Vogt, Evon Z. 1970. Human Souls and Animal Spirits in Zinacantan. In *Échanges et communications: Mélanges offerts à Claude Lévi-Strauss à l'occasion de son 60ème anniversaire*, edited by J. Pouillon and P. Maranda, 1148–1167. The Hague, Mouton.

Vogt, Evon Z., and David Stuart. 2005. Some Notes on Ritual Caves among the Ancient and Modern Maya. In *In the Maw of the Earth Monster: Mesoamerican Ritual Cave Use*, edited by J. E. Brady and K. M. Prufer, 155–185. University of Texas Press, Austin.

von Winning, Hasso. 1948. The Teotihuacan Owl-and-Weapon Symbol and Its Association with "Serpent Head X" at Kaminaljuyu. *American Antiquity* 14(2):129–132.

von Winning, Hasso. 1987. *La iconografía de Teotihuacan: Los dioses y los signos*. Universidad Nacional Autónoma de México, Mexico City.

Walker, Debra S. 1990. Cerros Revisited: Ceramic Indicators of Terminal Classic and Postclassic Settlement and Pilgrimage in Northern Belize. Unpublished PhD dissertation, Department of Anthropology, Southern Methodist University, Dallas.

Wanyerka, Phil. 1996. A Fresh Look at a Maya Masterpiece. *Cleveland Studies in the History of Art* 1:72–97.

Webster, David A. 1976. *Defensive Earthworks at Becan, Campeche, Mexico: Implications for Maya Warfare*. Middle American Research Institute, Pub. 41. Tulane University, New Orleans.

Webster, David A. 2000. The Not So Peaceful Civilization: A Review of Maya War. *Journal of World Prehistory* 14(1):65–119.

Webster, David A. 2005. Political Ecology, Political Economy, and the Culture History of Resource Management at Copán. In *Copán: The History of an Ancient Maya Kingdom*, edited by E. W. Andrews V and W. L. Fash, 33–72. School of American Research. Santa Fe, New Mexico.

Weeks, John M., ed. 2012. *The Carnegie Maya: The Carnegie Institution of Washington Maya Research Program, 1913–1957*. University Press of Colorado, Boulder.

Weiner, Annette B. 1992. *Inalienable Possessions: The Paradox of Keeping while Giving*. University of California Press, Berkeley.

Welch, W.B.M. 1988. *An Analysis of Classic Lowland Maya Burials*. BAR International Series 409. BAR, Oxford.

Werness, Maline Diane. 2003. Pabellon Molded-Carved Ceramics: A Consideration in Light of the Terminal Classic Collapse of Classic Maya Civilization. Unpublished master's thesis, Department of Anthropology, University of Texas, Austin.

Willey, Gordon R. 1956. The Structure of Ancient Maya Society: Evidence from the Southern Lowlands. *American Anthropologist* 58(5):777–782.

Willey, Gordon R., William R. Bullard, Jr., John B. Glass, and James C. Gifford. 1965. *Prehistoric Maya Settlements in the Belize Valley*. Papers of the Peabody Museum of Archaeology and Ethnology, vol. 54. Harvard University, Cambridge, MA.

Willey, Gordon R., William R. Coe, and Robert J. Sharer. 1976. Un proyecto para el desarrollo de investigación y preservación arqueológica en Copán (Honduras) y vecindad, 1976–1981. *Yaxkin* 1(2):10–29.

Willey, Gordon R., Richard M. Leventhal, Arthur A. Demarest, and William L. Fash. 1994. *Ceramics and Artifacts from Excavations in the Copan Residential Zone*. Papers of the Peabody Museum 80. Peabody Museum of Archaeology and Ethnology, Harvard University, Cambridge, MA.

Winters, Howard D. 1955. Excavation of a Colonnaded Hall at Mayapán. In *Current Reports 31*, 381–396. Carnegie Institute of Washington, Washington, DC.

Wisdom, Charles. 1950. *Materials on the Chorti Languages*. Microfilm Collection of Manuscripts on Middle American Cultural Anthropology, No. 28. Chicago. Transliterated and computerized by Brian Stross. Unpublished manuscript.

Woodfill, Brent, and Chloé Andreu. 2012. Tikal's Early Classic Domination of the Great Western Trade Route: Ceramic, Lithic, and Iconographic Evidence. *Ancient Mesoamerica* 23(2):189–209.

Wright, Lori E. 2005. Identifying Immigrants to Tikal, Guatemala: Defining Local Variability in Strontium Isotope Ratios of Human Tooth Enamel. *Journal of Archaeological Science* 32(4):555–566.

Wright, Lori E. 2012. Immigration to Tikal, Guatemala: Evidence from Stable Strontium and Oxygen Isotopes. *Journal of Anthropological Archaeology* 31(3):334–352.

Zender, Marc U. 2004. A Study of Classic Maya Priesthood. Unpublished PhD dissertation, Department of Archaeology, University of Calgary, Calgary.

WENDY ASHMORE, Distinguished Professor Emeritus, Department of Anthropology, University of California, Riverside

M. KATHRYN BROWN, Lutcher Brown Endowed Associate Professor, Department of Anthropology, University of Texas, San Antonio

ARLEN F. CHASE, Professor, Department of Anthropology, Pomona College, Claremont, CA

DIANE Z. CHASE, Vice President for Academic Innovation, Student Success, and Strategic Initiatives, Claremont Graduate University, CA

WILBERTH CRUZ ALVARADO, Archaeologist, Instituto Nacional de Antropología e Historia, Centro-INAH Yucatán, Mexico

ARTHUR A. DEMAREST, Ingram Professor, Department of Anthropology, Vanderbilt University, Nashville

KEITH EPPICH, Professor, Department of History and Anthropology, Tyler Junior College–The College of East Texas, and the Proyecto Arqueología Waka', Guatemala

DAVID A. FREIDEL, Professor, Department of Anthropology, Washington University of St. Louis

MARÍA ROCIO GONZÁLEZ DE LA MATA, Investigator, Instituto Nacional de Antropología e Historia, Centro-INAH Yucatán, Mexico

CHARLES W. GOLDEN, Associate Professor, Department of Anthropology, Brandeis University, Waltham, MA

STANLEY P. GUENTER, American Foreign Academic Research, Foundation for Archaeological Research and Environmental Studies, Rupert, Idaho

ANNABETH HEADRICK, Associate Professor, School of Art and Art History, University of Denver

ALINE MAGNONI, Cultural Heritage and Archaeology in the Maya Area

JOYCE MARCUS, Robert L. Carneiro Distinguished Professor of Social Evolution, Museum of Anthropological Archaeology, University of Michigan, Ann Arbor

MARILYN A. MASSON, Professor, Department of Anthropology, State University of New York, Albany

DAMARIS MENÉNDEZ, Investigator for the Proyecto Arqueológico Waka', Guatemala, and Universidad de San Carlos de Guatemala and Universidade de Trás-os-Montes e Alto Douro, Portugal

SUSAN MILBRATH, Curator Emeritus, Department of Natural History, Florida Museum, University of Florida, Gainesville

OLIVIA C. NAVARRO-FARR, Associate Professor, Department of Sociology and Anthropology and Program in Archaeology, the College of Wooster, Wooster, OH, and Investigator and Co-Director of the Proyecto Arqueológico Waka', Guatemala

JOSÉ OSORIO LEÓN, Archaeologist, Project Director, Instituto Nacional de Antropología e Historia, Centro-INAH Yucatán, Mexico

CARLOS PERAZA LOPE, Archaeologist, Project Director, Instituto Nacional de Antropología e Historia, Centro-INAH Yucatán, Mexico

JUAN CARLOS PÉREZ CALDERÓN, Investigator and Co-Director of the Proyecto Arqueológico Waka', Guatemala, and Universidad de San Carlos de Guatemala and Universidad Cooperación Internacional de Costa Rica

GRISELDA PÉREZ ROBLES, Investigator and Director of Conservation for the Proyecto Arqueológico Waka', Guatemala, and Universidad de San Carlos de Guatemala

FRANCISCO PÉREZ RUÍZ, Investigator, Instituto Nacional de Antropología e Historia, Centro-INAH Yucatán, Mexico

MICHELLE RICH, The Ellen and Harry S. Parker III Assistant Curator of the Arts of the Americas at the Dallas Museum of Art and the Proyecto Arqueológico Waka'

JEREMY A. SABLOFF, External Professor Emeritus, Santa Fe Institute, and Christopher H. Browne Distinguished Professor of Anthropology, Emeritus, University of Pennsylvania, Philadelphia

ANDREW K. SCHERER, Associate Professor, Department of Anthropology, Brown University, Providence, RI

TRAVIS W. STANTON, Professor, Department of Anthropology, University of California, Riverside

KARL A. TAUBE, Distinguished Professor, Department of Anthropology, University of California, Riverside

axis mundi, at Copán, *130*
aztaxelli, 198
Aztecs, 7, 155, 172; Atlantean sculptures, *182*; butterfly imagery, 166–*67*, 168

baah, 109, 112, 114, 117, 121
Bahlam Tz'am, 86, 257
bak'etal (flesh bodies), 112, 117, 123
ballcourts, at Yaxuná, 143
ballgame, iconography, 39
Batres Red, 142
battle murals, at Chichén Itzá, 155
Batz Ek', Lady, 28, 33
Becán, War Serpent imagery, *165*, 166
Bejucal, 56
Belize Valley, 35
bioarchaeological studies, 70, Copán, 129; Waka', 81
Bird Jaguar IV. *See* Yaxuun Bahlam IV
birds, and paradise, *183*. *See also* duckbilled deities
bloodletting, 89, 114–15
Blue Creek, 17
bodies: and personhood, 109–11, 113; shaping of, 114–15, 117; and spiritual co-essences, 111–12
Bonampak, 116, 117, 122
Books of Chilam Balam, 8; events in, 236, 239, 240–41, 243–44
borders, boundaries: Yaxchilán, 121–22; Yaxuná, 137–38
bundled burials, at Tikal, 39
Burial 23 (Tikal), 35, *37*, 38, 39, 41, 44, 45, 258
Burial 24 (Tikal), *38*, 39, 41, 45, 46
Burial 38 (Waka'), 90, 257; ceramics in, 100, 101, 103; context of, 93–*94*; mortuary assemblage in, 96–97, 104–5; ritual reentering of, 98–99
Burial 39 (Waka'), 90, 93–94, 99, 104, 105; ceramics in, 100–103, 257; context, *95*–96; mortuary assemblage in, 97–98
Burial 61 (Waka'), excavation and identity of, 78–82, 86, 257
Burial 85 (Tikal), 54–55
Burial 116 (Tikal), 44
Burial 193 (Tikal), 37
Burial 195 (Tikal), 35, *36*, 37, 39–40, 41, 46, 158
burials, 15, 46, 47, 63, 151, 197; alliance markers in, 103–4; Caracol, 28–29; El Perú-Waka',

71, 78–82, 93–98; isotopic data from, 34, 38–39; Mayapán mass, 205, 207, 208, 212(table), 230, *232*, 233, 234, 252–53; ritual reentering of, 84–85, 98–100; in Tikal North Acropolis, 35–40, 41, 44, 45, 66, 258–59
butterflies, 251; Central Mexican imagery, 156–57, 185; Early Postclassic symbolism of, 164–72, 184; on Mayapán effigy censers, 233–34

Caana, 45
cacao, imagery of, 184–85
Cacaxtla, 157, *165*, 178
caches, 12, 25, 26, 201(n4)
Cahal Pichik, 26
Calakmul, 68, 70, 71, 92, 190, 245; and Holmul, 60, 65; royal burials in, 79, 80–81
Campamento Fine Orange, 15
Campeche, 59
Cancuén, 4, 250; late occupation at, 14–15; termination rituals at, 15–16, 17
*Cantares mexicanos*, 172
captive-taking, captives, 50, 122, 132, 198, 258; at Chichén Itzá, 195–96, 251–52; sacrifices of, 193, 197–98; sajal as, 123, 124
Caracol, 5, 17, 48, 123, 259; burials at, 28–29; causeway system, 26–27; dynastic events, 33–34; epigraphic dates, 29–33(table); and Naranjo, 41–46; residential groups at, 24–26; star-war events, 27–28, 34, 70; and Tikal North Acropolis burials, 35–40; warfare, 22–24
Caracol (Chichén Itzá), 149
Casa Colorada (Chichén Itzá), 189
Casa de los Caracoles (Chichén Itzá), Ehecatl images at, 181, 183
Castillo (Chichén Itzá), 150, 164, 202(n6)
Castillo Viejo (Chichén Itzá), 168, 183–84
Cauac Monster, 158, 159
causeway systems (sacbeob), 188; Caracol, 26–27; and sacred landscapes, 250–51; Yucatán, 138, 140–42, 146
caves, 158, 209
Cehpech ceramics, 141
Cehpech phase, at Chichén Itzá, 148–49
Ceh'Yax, 145
Ceiba, 27
Ceibal, 17–18, 178, 180

Cenote Sagrado (Cenote of Sacrifice). *See* Sacred Cenote

censers, 213; termination rituals, 7, 205, 207, 208–12. *See also* effigy censers

centipede, as El Perú-Waka' emblem, 90

Central Acropolis (Naranjo), 43

Central lowlands, warfare in, 21–22

Central Mexican highlands, 185; butterfly imagery of, 156–57; floral paradise, 155–56; military strategies, 191–92; symbolism from, 53–64, 65, 66. *See also* Teotihuacan; Tula

Central Petén, 17

ceramics, 58, 70, 112, 180, 188; with butterfly images, 170–72; Caracol iconography on, *40, 41,* 258–59; chronological revisions, 14, 138–42; in El Perú-Waka' burials, 100–103, 257; Puuc confederation and, 136–37; at Quiriguá, 132, *133*; reclining figures on, *177,* 178; in Waka' adosada, 79–80; Yaxuná, 139–40(table), 141–42, 150, 151

ceremonial deposits, 72, 201(n4); at Chichén Itzá, 197–99, 203(n18)

Cerro Maya, 250

Cerros, as pilgrimage site, 209

Chablekal Fine Gray, 14

Cha Chaac ceremonies, 207

Chac II, 143

Chahk masks, 159

Chak Mool site (Santa Rosa), butterfly imagery, 169–70, 185

Chak Nik Ye'Xook, 64

Chak Took (Tok) Ich'aak Wak Ahau (Great Fiery Claw), 83, 84, 255

Chamelecón Valley, 134

Chan Chich, 17

Chanputún, 236

chemical analyses, in Waka' Burial 61, 81

Chenes, 158; architectural styles, 159–63

Ch'en Mul, effigy of, 217

Chi Altar, 254

Chicanel phase, 54

Chichén Itzá, 6, 7, 51, 136, 137, 138, 146, 150, 152, 154–55, 157, *165,* 187, 192, *201,* 202(nn6, 7), 203(n18), 209, 236, 250; afterlife imagery, 184–85; butterfly imagery, 164, 168, *170,* 172, 251; carved lintels, 188–89; Chahk masks, 158–59; Ehecatl images in, 181–83; flowery paradise imagery in, *160,* 183–84; flying figures, 175–76, 178; high-rank captives

at, 197–98, 251–52; iconography, 180–81; incorporation at, 195–96; Katun dates, 238–39; Teotihuacan imagery at, 189–90, *191, 193–95*; warrior-merchants at, 198–200; Yabnal Complex, 148–49

Chicozapote, 116

childhood, children, body shaping in, 114, 115

Chi-Metate, 245

Chok Group (El Perú-Waka'), 96, 257

ch'ok ajaw, 119

ch'ok sajal, 109

Chontal, 117

chronologies: Cancuén, 14–15; Yaxuná ceramic, 138–42

Chuburná Group, 141, 142

Chumayel, 236

cinnabar, in Waka' Burial 61, 81

circular monument, at El Perú-Waka', 73, 75

City of the Centipede. *See* El Perú-Waka'

Classic period, 4, 5, 6, 67, 82, 104, 109, 158, 237, 251; body and co-essences, 111–12; dynastic events, 33–34; statecraft, 89–90

Cobá, 6, 7, 140, 142, 145, 152, 250; Puuc confederation, 136, 137–38

Cocom lineage, 7–8, 64–66, 209, 235

Codex Borbonicus, butterfly images, 166, *167,* 172

Codex Borgia, 166, 178, 180, 181, 184; music origins in, 173, *174,* 175

Codex Dresden, *160, 161*

Codex Madrid, 158

Codex Vindobonensis, 180

co-essences, spiritual, 111–12

Colha, 17

collapse, 18, 21; of El Mirador, 245, 253; of Teotihuacan, 240, 241, 243, 255

colonialism, 46

Colonial period, 8

Comayagua Valley, 134

commemoration dates, Tikal, 35–36

conflict, 4, 136, 151. *See also* violence; warfare

Copán, 5, 6, 17, 34, 65, 71, 89, 90, 126, 132, 133, 134, 158, *177,* 178, 190; Acropolis, *131,* 242–43, 248; 8 Ahau date at, 238–39, 245; Stela I inscriptions, 245–46; Stela II inscriptions, 8, *237–38,* 239, 240–42, 253–55; stranger-kings at, 60–64; tunneling programs, 128–29

*Copán: The History of an Ancient Maya Kingdom* (Andrews and Fash), 130